D1310751

The Gardener's Guide to

PERENNIALS

The Gardener's Guide to

PERENNIALS

GRAHAM RICE

Mitchell Beazley

First published in 1996 by Mitchell Beazley,
an imprint of Reed International Books Ltd,
Michelin House, 81 Fulham Road, London
SW3 6RB and Auckland, Melbourne,
Singapore and Toronto

Plant Directory: Richard Bird
Publisher: Jane Aspden
Executive Art Editor: Mark Richardson
Project Editor: Selina Higgins
Designers: Geoff Borin, Louise Griffiths
Editors: Paul Barnett, Penelope Cream,
    Diane Pengelly
Assistant Editors: Kirsty Brackenridge,
    Claire Musters
Production Controller: Heather O'Connell
Picture Research: Maria Gibbs
Commissioned Artwork: Fiona Bell Currie
Indexer: Hilary Bird

Front jacket: *Paeonia* 'Bowl of Beauty' by
    Andrew Lawson
Back jacket: Red Gables, Worcestershire,
    England by Clive Nichols

Title page: *Corydalis flexuosa* (left),
Buphthalmum salicifolium (centre), *Primula
denticulata* (right)

ISBN 1 85732 537 0

A CIP catalogue record for this book is
available from the British Library

Produced by Mandarin Offset Ltd,
Hong Kong

Printed in China

CONTENTS

FOREWORD

This book portrays the vital contribution that perennials make to our gardens, describes the very best of perennial plants, and reveals how easy they are to grow.

Covering every aspect in detail, *The Gardener's Guide to Perennials* begins with a comprehensive section on growing perennials. After an assessment of the various ways of acquiring plants, it spells out the important practical steps you can take to ensure that perennials give their best in the garden. Soil preparation and planting methods, the various cultural techniques that help perennials to thrive, propagation methods, and controlling pests and diseases are all explained in a clear and logical way. Step-by-step illustrations guide you through the details of each technique.

This practical information is followed by inspirational advice on how to use perennials in the garden to the best effect. Perennials are adaptable plants that can be used in a great many ways, and this section is full of ideas for every type of garden and situation. The many different styles that are discussed range from the organized chaos of the cottage garden to more formal herbaceous borders and from modern mixed borders to easy-maintenance island beds. Wildflower plantings and growing perennials in containers are also covered. A broad range of attractive and imaginative planting designs are beautifully illustrated and reveal the many ways in which perennials can be used successfully in the garden.

Finally there is a comprehensive alphabetical listing of the best perennials available today. Each plant is concisely and clearly introduced with an outline of its general characteristics, and this is followed by a selection of the best forms, chosen for their quality, availability, and ability to stand the test of time. Their special features are described, and any individual cultivation requirements are pointed out. A glossary, an explanation of hardiness zones, and a guide to where to buy perennials complete the book.

Right: This border of autumn-blooming perennials, including solidago, helenium, asters in many colours, and *Sedum* 'Autumn Joy' ('Herbstfreude'), is backed by an old brick wall to provide shelter from autumn winds and support for climbers.

6

WHAT ARE PERENNIALS?

To the gardener, perennials are long-lived plants that have no permanent woody growth above the ground and are suitable for cultivating in a garden setting. This horticultural sense of the word excludes trees and shrubs as they have woody growth above the ground. Similarly, it discounts many other plants a botanist would call perennials; weeds are a good example.

Perennials differ from annuals in that the latter usually die as soon as they have produced seed, and perennials will go on living. The lifespan varies greatly from species to species. Some, like pinks and lupins, can be quite short-lived, lasting two to five years; others, like bergenias and peonies, may last 15–20 years or more. The lifespan of plants of the same type also varies widely depending on many factors, including the condition of the soil in which they are planted and the care taken to protect them from pests and diseases. In practical terms, the life of a perennial ends when it becomes starved or overcrowded, or outgrows its position.

The life-cycle starts in early spring, with new leafy growth. In spring and summer the plants display leaves and flowers. There are a few varieties that flower for six months; other varieties for less than six weeks. The top-growth of the majority of perennials dies down in the autumn, although some have green leaves over the winter which die away in the spring as new leaves emerge.

Delphinium spires contrast well with bushy perennials that also hide the bare delphinium stems.

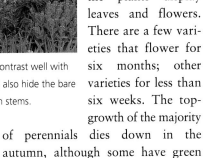

Left: These informal perennial borders, seen in mid-summer, tumble onto the grass path and lead the eye to the sundial and white gate set against the background wooded area. The display was carefully planted with variations in colour and height to create a harmonious effect.

TYPES OF PERENNIAL

Over the centuries perennials have become known by a variety of names. *Herbaceous perennials*, the oldest term, originally referred to plants whose growth dies down completely in winter, but now it is used more generally. The term *border perennials* refers to the traditional positioning of these plants in the border. *Hardy perennials* refers to perennials with the ability to withstand cold winters, while *tender perennials* describes those unlikely to survive cold winters. 'Hardiness' and 'tenderness' are both relative terms: for specific information relating to a plant's ability to survive at a certain temperature, check its zone indicator (pp.228–231). The term *hardy plants* is also quite common, but today the most common term is simply 'perennials'.

PERENNIALS IN THE WILD

Perennials are found all over the world in a wide variety of natural habitats, but most of those covered in this book grow naturally in cool- or warm-temperate areas. Some are found in open situations where there is little shade except, perhaps, from their taller neighbours. These open places may be sunny meadows, river valleys, alpine pastures, dry prairies,

The range of perennials

Perennials vary enormously in size and growth habit. The range of mature perennial plants shown here reveals their diversity.

1 *Traditional delphinium hybrids develop from a tight crown and produce bold leaves followed by tall spires of flowers.*

2 *Many euphorbias have upright, semi-woody, over-wintering stems carrying cylindrical heads of yellowish flowers.*

3 *Garden pinks are woody at the base with low, bushy growth of blue-grey leaves and single or double flowers on floppy stems.*

4 *Bugle produces leafy runners that creep over the soil, rooting as they go. The short spikes of flowers stand up vertically.*

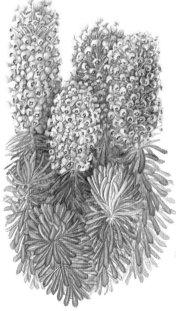

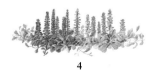

1

2

3

4

mountainsides or seashores. Other perennials thrive in shaded situations, for example in woods and copses, along hedgerows, in deep gullies or on relatively sunless hillsides. Perennials also vary in their moisture requirements: some grow in dry, inhospitable habitats while others flourish beside streams or in bogs. Their growth habits in these diverse habitats are varied. In a woodland clearing, a single species may become dominant to the exclusion of most others, while in moist meadows, a rich tapestry of species may develop.

PERENNIALS IN THE GARDEN

The fact that perennials grow in such a wide array of natural habitats ensures that there is a variety for almost every situation in the garden. And because these garden perennials are derived from such a huge range of wild species, the diversity of their size, vigour, habit of growth, flowering season and colour makes it possible to choose exactly the right plant for any seasonal planting and any colour scheme. Perennials are also both tolerant and adaptable, often thriving in garden situations noticeably different from those in which they grow naturally. For these

5 Autumn anemones have vigorously spreading roots, foliage gathered towards the base, and tall, airy heads of flowers.

9 The fat, fleshy roots of agapanthus produce long, slender foliage and rounded heads of flowers on stiff, upright stems.

8 The upright stems of coreopsis carry finely cut foliage with neat daisy-like flowers. The roots spread steadily.

6 Many hardy geraniums grow out from a central root-stock to form a low, bushy dome or a spreading carpet of flowers.

7 Primrose leaves emerge in early spring as a neat rosette; the flowers are carried singly or in loose clusters.

5   6   7   8   9

reasons and because they are among the easiest plants to grow, perennials have gained great popularity, and are often the most important constituent of a successful garden.

Traditionally, perennials were used in two main ways. In large gardens they stood on their own in borders, called herbaceous borders, in which bold groups of brightly coloured plants created an impressive effect. In more humble surroundings, perennials were often mixed with bulbs, annuals and even fruit bushes in the more informal displays characteristic of the cottage garden. Today we are open-minded in our approach to growing perennials. We mix them with bulbs, hardy annuals, bedding plants, easy alpines, climbers and shrubs. Each can complement the other so that, together, they provide an attractive and diverse range of colour and form throughout the year.

This mixed planting shows today's most popular approach to growing perennials in the border.

NAMING PERENNIALS

Perennials, like other garden plants, are named by botanists, professional horticulturalists and also gardeners. Botanists usually give plants their Latin (botanical or taxonomic) names, based on specimens found growing in their natural habitat. Internationally agreed rules govern how this must be done. The variety or, more correctly, cultivar names of garden plants are given by both professional and amateur gardeners, and here, too, international rules apply.

Plant names are a form of shorthand, a neat and concise way of referring to a plant. The botanists' plant names, following a system originated by the 18th-century botanist Linnaeus, are made up of multiple parts. For example, *Campanula persicifolia* 'Telham Beauty'. The first name, *Campanula*, refers to the plant's genus, a range of broadly similar plants with basic shared features. The next part of the name, *persicifolia*, indicates the plant's species, a much smaller group of more closely related campanulas. The two names together make up the botanical name. A cultivar name like 'Telham Beauty' denotes a distinctive form of a species, cultivated for one or two particular features, usually qualities valued in gardens, like flower colour.

RENAMING

Problems arise when sophisticated botanical research reveals fundamental differences between plants which, for hundreds of years, were considered very closely related. Then a new name must be devised. For example, the genus *Chrysanthemum*: species originally thought a part of this genus have now been allocated a new one, *Dendranthema*; others have been renamed *Leucanthemella*; the few that remain part of the *Chrysanthemum* genus are all annuals, not perennials.

Another problem is that the same plant might have been discovered in more than one country by different botanists, who each gave it their preferred name. When the plants were eventually studied closely, or grown side by side, they may have been found to be identical. Only one name would be selected for official use.

A different kind of difficulty can arise when a cultivar that should be propagated by division to ensure that all the offspring are the same, is raised from seed. In this case the seedlings may well differ both from the parent and from each other, but they may still be passed around with the same name.

In all these cases, botanists look at individual problems in the light of the international rules and make their decisions accordingly. The most significant of these rules is that the name that should be used is the first name that was given to a particular plant, provided it has been published in a book, journal or catalogue with an adequate description.

COMMON NAMES

There are many opportunities for botanical names to create confusion, but using only common names would cause even more problems. In England the plant known as the bluebell is a woodland bulb, *Hyacinthoides non-scriptus*; in Scotland the bluebell is a small perennial, *Campanula rotundifolia*; while in the Pacific Northwest of the United States the name 'bluebell' is sometimes used for *Mertensia longifolia*. Three entirely different plants are known by the same name; botanical names suddenly seem far more dependable.

The bluebell in England, *Hyacinthoides non-scriptus*.

The bluebell in Scotland, *Campanula rotundifolia*.

The bluebell in the Pacific Northwest, *Mertensia longifolia*.

GROWING PERENNIALS

There are perennials to suit every garden, whatever the situation and climate. Perennials are among the most accommodating of plants. As long as their basic needs are met they will usually repay a little care with a great deal of pleasure.

Given the opportunity, perennials can reward you for many years, but they are most likely to thrive when you start with strong, healthy plants. A weak or diseased plant will very probably languish, although patient nurturing may sometimes rescue it.

Choosing plants to suit both the soils and the situations into which they are to be planted is very important. There is no doubt that it is always a gamble simply to buy a plant that appears attractive and plant it where there happens to be an available space. Instead, first assess the site to determine its suitability for different perennials; then

Shrubs make a colourful background for perennials in this cottage garden.

make improvements to help ensure that the plants grow well once they are planted. A plant in the wrong place will never thrive.

Planting in the right manner and at the right time gives the perennials a healthy start. Careful attention in the first few weeks after planting ensures they acclimatize well. But over the years they need regular attention. Weeds must not be allowed to smother them, and perennials also need to be watered, fed, deadheaded, staked and, from time to time, revitalized.

As with all plants, perennials can be vulnerable to attack from pests and diseases, and these must be prevented as far as possible or dealt with promptly when they appear. Some troubles affect a wide range of garden plants; others are more specific. But, if left to multiply, the pests will weaken your plants, and may kill them altogether.

Left: This informal double border with its slightly meandering path features a wide range of perennials augmented with a few shrubs and annuals to add variety.

ACQUIRING PLANTS

Taking a serious interest in perennials is closely linked to the enjoyment of acquiring plants, which may be bought from mail-order catalogues or local garden centres, or given to you by friends and neighbours. Often, as interest grows and tastes develop, gardeners become more exacting in their requirements and look to specialist nurseries and seed companies for unusual plants that are not generally available.

PLANTS FROM NEIGHBOURS

Taking cuttings from the gardens of friends and neighbours not only encourages the spread of good plants but also preserves them. An advantage of exchanging plants with neighbours, particularly for newcomers to gardening, is that, if the plant is already thriving in the garden next door, it will probably thrive in yours. However, exchanging plants is not entirely without problems. For example, few plants respond well to being transplanted in full flower. So whether you are giving or receiving a plant, wait until its best propagation time (see Plant Directory, pp.142-227).

PEST AND DISEASE CONTROL
A more serious problem concerns pests and diseases. No garden is entirely pest-free, but that is no reason to import your neighbour's pests to add to your own. Keep a close watch on all new acquisitions, for, even when no problems are visible, insect eggs or fungus spores may be present. Use a broad-spectrum pest and disease spray on the plants, and then be prepared to spray for any specific problems that might arise.
Soil-borne problems Some problems can be more insidious. Root-feeding insect pests such as vine weevil may be hidden in the soil, and spraying the plant's foliage will not kill them.

For those plants that are especially susceptible to these pests, wash the soil from the roots when you return home. Epimediums, primulas and heucheras are particularly vulnerable to attack from vine weevil. There is also a lesser but still noteworthy danger of introducing soil-borne problems into your garden. Fungal diseases of vegetables or trees may be in your neighbour's soil and could start an infection in your own. Pests such as eelworms, which attack fruit bushes, may be in the soil around the roots of a columbine plant transplanted from a friend's fruit garden.

SEED CATALOGUES

Perennial seeds are available from shops, garden centres and nurseries, but often the choice of varieties is poor. Mail-order seed catalogues offer the widest range of varieties and represent extremely good value, as a large number of plants can be raised for the price of a single plant from the garden centre or nursery.

ADVANTAGES OF SEED
Economy is the main reason for raising perennials from seed; when planting a new garden, this can be an especially important factor. But there are other advantages. Some species are available from seed companies in mixed colours, so that a range can be raised from a single packet. Seed

provides an economical way of filling beds and borders in a new garden. Then, as the garden fills up, you can discard those plants which have colours you find less attractive, while allowing those you prefer to spread. Many of the more recent perennial introductions into seed catalogues are specially bred for vigorous growth, and often flower prolifically in their first year after sowing. They can thus serve as bedding plants in their first year and then carry on to give you many more years of pleasure. Some new introductions may be available only as seed in the first few years before nurseries take them up. Some uncommon species which are very hard to find on sale as plants may be found in seed catalogues. And, of course, you can buy from a seed catalogue by mail, obviating the need for long journeys to nurseries.

PERENNIALS TO GROW FROM SEED
In general, the varieties that feature in the seed catalogues that will most likely be successful are those specifically intended to be raised from seed.

Coreopsis 'Early Sunrise' flowers well in its first year after sowing; it continues to bloom every year but on taller stems.

These varieties are often the most vigorous, most prolific and the most tolerant of less-than-perfect conditions. Examples include *Achillea* 'Summer Pastels', *Campanula carpatica* 'Clips', *Coreopsis* 'Early Sunrise', *Delphinium* 'Southern Noblemen', *Echinacea* 'White Swan', *Gaillardia* 'Kobold', *Geum* 'Lady Stratheden' and 'Mrs Bradshaw', *Kniphofia* 'Border Ballet', *Lobelia* 'Compliment Scarlet', *Lupinus* 'Gallery', *Salvia* × *sylvestris* 'Blue Queen' ('Blaukönigin'), *Salvia* × *sylvestris* 'Rose Queen' and *Sidalcea* 'Party Girl'.

Unusual species, not listed in nursery catalogues, are also worth trying. Special consideration should also be given to those plants that have received an award – this is often mentioned in the catalogue.

PROBLEMS WITH MAIL-ORDER

There are drawbacks, though, to buying seed by mail. The seed of some plants, like hellebores and primulas, has a very short life, so by the time it is sent out in the normal winter mail-order season, it may already have deteriorated. The chances of raising a good crop of seedlings will then be slim. Other plants, like peonies, are difficult for home gardeners to germinate successfully, so these too should be avoided. Even when these plants are listed in a catalogue, it is generally best not to buy them until you have had some experience of raising plants from seed.

Another problem affects a much wider range of plants: when seed is collected from the very best perennials – the named varieties that are usually propagated by division – the offspring are rarely as good as the parent. The unpredictability of seed collected from these plants means that seed companies cannot state

Sown in spring, *Achillea* 'Summer Pastels' flowers prolifically in summer, choose the best colours from the mixture which can then be propagated by division.

exactly what their seed will produce, so they tend not to list it at all. Thus, for the very finest forms of *Delphinium*, *Helleborus*, *Phlox*, *Aster* and *Monarda*, it pays to buy plants. In general, avoid varieties that require special facilities which you do not have (for example a greenhouse) and those that are usually raised by division, and so will not come true from seed.

ORDERING BY POST

When ordering seed from mail-order catalogues, follow some simple rules to help the process flow smoothly.

Send off for catalogues as soon as they are advertised, and place your order as soon as possible after the catalogue arrives. The newest and best varieties may sell out quickly. Keep a photocopy of your order in case of problems later.

Check the figure given for the number of seeds in each packet before deciding how many packets you need. The seed content may vary enormously from one variety to another: you may find you need two packets of some varieties to raise the number of plants you require, while a single packet of another may contain enough seed to share with friends.

If your order arrives incomplete, without explanation, or if the seed has not arrived within the period stated in the catalogue, contact the company promptly, sending them a copy of your order.

If the seed arrives before the correct time for sowing, do not leave it in the greenhouse or the garden shed until sowing time; it is best stored cool and dry. The most effective way to store seed is in a screw-topped jar placed in the bottom of the refrigerator. Adding a few crystals of silica gel to the jar, to absorb excess moisture, helps keep the seed fresh.

GARDEN CENTRES

The first port of call for the majority of gardeners buying plants is the local garden centre. This has the great advantage of convenience and, sometimes, good prices. But unfortunately the range of perennials available in garden centres is usually restricted to well-established and well-known varieties, together with ones that are easy to propagate and that are therefore relatively inexpensive.

A high proportion of perennials on sale in garden centres are seed-raised plants, so it may be difficult to find the best named varieties of, for example, lupins, delphiniums or hellebores. Unpredictable seed-raised mixtures are the sole choice in many garden centres. This is ideal if you are looking for large quantities of plants and are happy with varieties of average quality, but in some cases the only advantage is the price.

Fortunately, an increasing number of larger garden centres have areas devoted to special plants. The better-quality varieties will often be found here, but these may also be more expensive or a little more difficult to grow than other perennials. They are often accompanied by unusually detailed explanatory labels to help you choose them and grow them well.

SPECIALIST PLANT CENTRES

In recent years things have moved a stage further with the development of plant centres. Here the balance has shifted: there are no patio sets, barbecues or jam, no spades, sprays or watering cans. The plants take precedence; apart from seed, and perhaps books and refreshments, these centres concentrate on them. The result is a far wider range of varieties, and it is often the selection of perennials that benefits the most.

CHOOSING GARDEN CENTRE PERENNIALS

Perennials are not ideally suited to the garden centre mode of selling. Unlike shrubs, small perennials may attempt to reach the same height in the small pots in which they are so often sold that they would in the garden. As a result, the perennials become starved and top-heavy, and may blow over and look tatty by flowering time. Fortunately there is a developing trend towards growing them in larger pots.

The best approach is to purchase perennials as strong, young plants in spring or autumn and to plant them at once, before they fill their pots with tightly packed roots. Such plants are often nicely presented in neat pots, sometimes topped with gravel and often with a helpful colour label. Choose those plants with the most growing points, as this is a sign of a potential rapid increase in size. Sometimes these plants will be in flower, but selecting a strong and bushy plant

Seed-raised mixtures, like these Russell hybrid lupins, can be spectacular; but an individual plant from the garden centre may prove to be any of these colours unless you buy it in flower.

that is likely to grow vigorously in the future is more important than taking home a plant in flower. Plants that have been in their pots too long will have lost their lower leaves, have only a few small flowers struggling to open, and generally look bedraggled.

Plants that are in good-sized pots and have been well cared for can look very impressive, especially if they are displayed in a sheltered area where they are not battered by wind. You can then see clearly how they grow and how they will look in the garden. Sometimes these more established plants can be unexpectedly good buys, for, although they are more expensive at first, you may be able to split them into two pieces for planting, giving you two plants for the price of one.

Before you buy, inspect all plants closely for pests and diseases, especially aphids, and examine the pots in case some of the stems have died off at soil level. Check that the roots, which may have grown through the drainage holes in the base of the pots, are not too well entrenched in the gravel or sand on which the plants are standing.

SPECIAL PROMOTIONS

There are two other ways in which perennials are sold in garden centres: as special promotions and as seed. Some new introductions are given lavish presentation, with display boards, coloured pots and labels and a great deal of publicity. Such lavish campaigns are usually reserved for particularly good new varieties, although they may not be quite as good as the publicity leads us to believe. They are usually sold in larger than average pots and at premium prices, far higher than for other high-quality perennials.

Specialist nurseries will advise on which rock plants are tough enough for perennial borders. These blue and white *Campanula carpatica* flowers are ideal.

Garden centres also sell seed, but the range of perennials on offer is usually very restricted. A few rows on the seed racks are sometimes reserved for perennials, but a far wider choice is available in the mail-order seed catalogues (see p.16).

SPECIALIST NURSERIES

In many parts of the country there are nurseries, often small family businesses, that specialize in perennial plants. Unlike garden and plant centres, which buy their stock from wholesale nurseries, these small specialist nurseries propagate most of their plants themselves and grow them on until they are ready for sale. The result is that they have a far more intimate knowledge of the plants they grow, and usually stock a much wider range of varieties than other outlets. Being specialists, they also have a deeper understanding of perennial plants in general. The standard of advice available in garden centres may be improving, but the staff at a specialist nursery will know about a far wider range of perennials and how to grow them successfully.

KNOWING A GOOD SPECIALIST

The success of a specialist nursery depends on two things: the choice of varieties they grow and how well they grow their plants for sale. Specialists who know all about their plants are in a good position to select the best varieties. They often raise new varieties themselves and, being in personal contact with their customers, have a network of contacts who may bring them new plants to introduce. As these specialist nurseries tend to grow most or all of their plants themselves, they can also ensure their quality. They may stagger propagation so that different batches of the same variety are at their best at different times of the season, and, if they sell out of a particular variety, they should know when the next batch will be ready.

Another advantage of using specialist nurseries is that many of them

When building up a collection of a specific plant, such as these autumn asters, visiting a nursery with a good display garden will make choosing less difficult.

have display gardens where mature specimens of the varieties on sale can be viewed in a realistic garden situation. You can see at first-hand the features and faults of the plants.

The best specialist nurseries are very good indeed. Being a regular customer and getting to know the people who run the nursery will enhance your enjoyment of growing and buying the plants.

Other specialists are less good, but you can often tell the good from the bad at first glance. Weeds are a bad sign. The problem with a weedy nursery is that, even if the varieties are well chosen, you will almost certainly be buying weeds or weed seeds along with the plants. And you may well buy other problems as well, for weeds not only harbour pests and diseases which attack perennials but are a sign of a careless attitude that probably affects other aspects of the nursery.

There are further factors to consider. Are the staff helpful? Does the catalogue have good descriptions and advice? Is the nursery organized logically? Are the sales beds laid out clearly? Are the plants well labelled?

VISITING SPECIALIST NURSERIES
When considering visiting a specialist nursery, send for its catalogue first. This will not only give the opening hours but will also provide directions and most probably a map; many specialist nurseries are situated in rural areas of the country and may prove difficult to find. Often these nurseries will allow you to order plants to collect when you visit. Note that a large number have additional varieties (in small numbers) not listed in the catalogue: you might want to make these your focus on arriving.

Observe the same precautions when choosing plants as at a garden

or plant centre. For example, do not always pick those in flower – bushy habit and the potential for flower are more important. Check for pests, diseases and weeds, and avoid plants whose roots have grown through the drainage holes.

One problem which can arise when visiting specialist nurseries derives from the sheer number of varieties on offer; those new to growing perennials may find it difficult to choose. Always ask for advice: explain what you like, and describe the situation and soil in your garden, and you will usually benefit from suggestions as to which varieties to try. You may also pick up some tips on how best to grow them. Establishing a good relationship with a specialist nursery will ensure you take home the right plants with the right advice and, if anything should go wrong, will increase the chances of difficulties being resolved amicably.

MAIL-ORDER

For many gardeners, especially those living in rural areas, buying plants by mail-order is the only way to obtain any but the most commonplace varieties. Postal and courier services give access to a huge range of plants from nurseries all over the country. There are two ways of using them. One way is to request catalogues from the nurseries themselves and order plants direct from them; the other is to respond to advertisements for plants in newspapers and magazines.

NURSERIES AND CATALOGUES
Mail-order nurseries advertise themselves in gardening magazines and specialist journals, or may be mentioned in articles. But they vary in the quality of the plants they supply and

the care with which the plants are packed, so a recommendation from a friend is valuable. If you are interested in specific types of plant, specialist journals and society bulletins will often carry appropriate advertisements. Many are small operations run by one or two people, so try to save them a great deal of unnecessary work and speed up the service by finding out what they charge for their catalogue and sending the right amount. Requests which are not accompanied by the required payment may be ignored.

Catalogues can vary enormously. Some are fully illustrated in colour, although it is often the case that, the more colourful the catalogue and the more lavish the descriptions, the fewer varieties it contains. At the other extreme, some mail-order catalogues are little more than a list of plant names; to get the best from these more spartan publications you need to have a good reference book to hand when planning your order.

Each mail-order nursery has its own way of trading, so it is vital to read the advice to customers in the catalogue before sending off your order. Some nurseries send plants only at certain seasons or will post only

certain plants from their collections and not others; some have a minimum order charge or suggest you pay in particular ways; some have codes to indicate plants that will not be available until late in the season. Ignoring these points can lead to confusion and frustration for both you and the nursery. Once you have made out your order, photocopy it before you send it off, and mark on your calendar the date by which the catalogue indicates your plants should arrive.

ORDERING FROM AN ADVERTISEMENT

When you order from an advertisement in a magazine, you usually fill in a coupon and send it off with your money. These advertisements are often for collections of plants, and rarely list a large number of individual varieties from which to choose. Read the small print, taking special note of the size of plants you will receive and relate this to their cost. Again, keep a copy of your order and mark the last delivery date on the calendar. Complain promptly if you don't receive your plants by then.

WHEN PLANTS ARRIVE

As soon as your plants are delivered, unpack them and check what has been sent against both your original order and the packing list that may have come with the parcel. If you are away around the time the plants are due to arrive, ask a neighbour to look after them for you. If you find the wrong plants have been sent, you are dissatisfied with the quality of the plants, or if they have been damaged in transit, try to photograph the plants; if possible, use a camera that prints the date in the corner of the picture. Complain promptly to the nursery concerned, sending a copy of

your order and the photograph. Most nurseries will quickly respond with a fresh consignment or a refund.

Problems may arise some time after your plants arrive. You may have ordered a white iris which, when it flowers, turns out to be blue. Again, photograph the plant and complain. In the UK, case law suggests that, not only should a wrongly named plant be replaced, compensation should be given according to the number of seasons lost in its development. So, a year after you were sent one wrongly named plant, three plants of the correct variety might be the appropriate recompense.

After unpacking, stand any plants still in their pots in a cold frame to settle down for a few days before planting. Bare-rooted plants and those knocked out of their pots need planting more quickly. Any plants that have suffered in transit may need a period of recuperation, and can be potted and grown on in a cold frame or cold greenhouse until they are ready to go outside. Plants sometimes come with flimsy temporary labels, so write permanent ones as soon as possible. Check them for pests and diseases (and even weeds) and spray them if necessary.

Try to order pot-grown autumn anemones, as they dislike disturbance.

It is better to buy new hostas rather than lift and divide mature and well-established specimens.

SITE AND SOIL

Conditions vary from one garden to another and even from one border to another. Although perennials are not fussy plants, they do grow better in some places than in others. It is thus important to assess the situation and the soil before planting them, in order to ensure that the right varieties are planted in the right place. In smaller gardens, where planting options are limited, you may have to opt for the least unsuitable site and then improve the situation (see below). In large gardens, you may want to consider a number of good sites before opting for the one that best suits the particular plant.

PLANTING SITES FOR PERENNIALS

Once a site has been selected, any factors that pose problems for perennials must be considered. Areas of sun and shade and features like walls, fences and trees cannot usually be changed, so you must adapt your plans to take these into account.

SUN OR SHADE
Although perennials will thrive in varying degrees of shade, most do best in plenty of light. In a sunny and completely open situation, the soil needs plenty of extra organic matter to increase its capacity for retaining water; this enables plants to cope with the drying effects of the light, warmth and wind. In a very exposed spot, choose short, self-supporting varieties that are relatively resistant to damage from the wind.

ASPECT
A south-facing site is often very hot. This suits perennial plants that come from Mediterranean climates but increases the danger of the soil drying out, so less tolerant plants may suffer from drought. East-facing sites are good for tough perennials that flower in mid-summer, although plants may be scorched by cold winds unless shelter is provided. Wind combined with frost can be devastating. The plants may also be damaged when frost is followed by a quick early-morning thaw; soft, new shoots and early flowers are especially vulnerable.

On north-facing sites, use tough, late-emerging plants. Cold in winter and warming only slowly in spring, these sites subject plants to long periods of frozen ground that not all can tolerate. Although shade-loving plants may do well in winter and spring, in summer, when the sun is high, they may be scorched. West-facing sites warm up slowly in the spring, but they are valuable for autumn perennials as plants remain undamaged by frost until late in the year.

Planting sites
Conditions vary in different parts of even the smallest garden. Although perennials are not fussy, they grow better if they are sited according to the conditions they prefer.

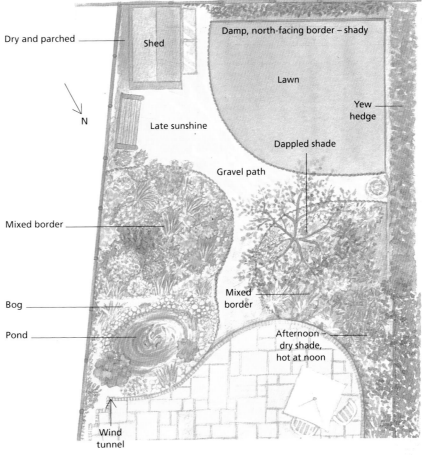

Left: An open, sunny site will suit the widest range of flowering and foliage perennials.

Scale: 1:100

PERENNIALS UNDER TREES

Planting under established trees requires thoughtful consideration. Trees vary in the nature of the shade that they cast: the dappled shade cast by high-branched deciduous trees for part of the year is attractive to many plants, while the dense, permanent shade created by an evergreen tree is very inhospitable. Evergreen trees present further problems in that they keep rain off the soil all year round, causing drought conditions, and the fallen needles of some conifers create acidic soils that are low in nutrients and suit few perennials. Removing low branches and thinning the crown can help a little, but it is more realistic to accept the fact that few perennials will succeed under evergreen trees. If the deciduous trees in

Planting around roots

The dry, rooty soil under trees presents difficult conditions in which to grow perennials. These can be improved by using logs to raise the level, then adding organic matter to create the right conditions for a wide variety of woodland plants.

your garden are planted very close together, increase the available light by felling poor specimens and by sensitively removing the lower branches or thinning the crowns of the stronger trees. These jobs are best left to a skilled tree surgeon, who will take care not to destroy the overall character of the trees.

Planting around roots The roots of trees are often shallow and intrusive. Finding a space among them in which to plant perennials may be a problem, and, if you do establish a planting, competition for both water and nutrients will follow. The simplest way to reduce root competition under trees is to create raised beds containing moisture-retentive soil. Most of the tree roots that are actively taking moisture and nutrients from the soil are positioned at the edge of the root system, which is usually under the tips of the branches, so position raised beds near the trunk. Use lengths of log to raise the level of the bed by 15–23cm (6–9in), and get the plants off to a strong start by mixing fresh soil with plenty of leaf mould

or garden compost. Before filling the bed with soil, loosen as much of the underlying earth as is practicable.

DRAINAGE

Drainage is a site characteristic that is not easy to assess. If water lies on the surface in winter and especially if it does so in summer the soil is not draining properly. This may be the result of a heavy clay soil, which naturally holds a great deal of water, or it may be the result of poor soil structure inhibiting water from draining easily. Heavy clay soils can be made more suitable for growing a wider range of perennials by the addition of organic matter. Poor soil structure is often the result of compaction; deep digging, to loosen the soil, will greatly improve the situation.

WALLS AND FENCES

If the border is positioned in front of a wall or fence, the wind may cause particular difficulties as it swirls past the solid barrier, creating eddies among the plants; a hedge will filter the wind and prevent this problem.

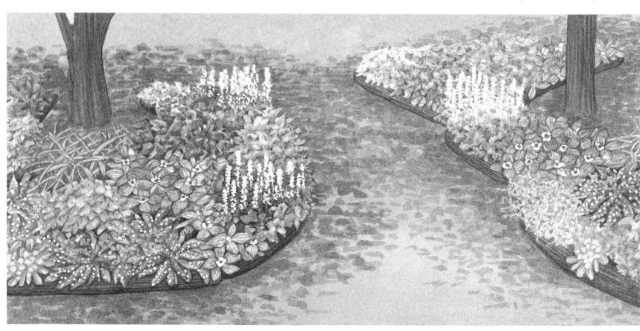

Walls versus hedges

A wall makes a solid barrier and creates turbulence, which may damage plants on both sides in stormy weather.

A hedge filters the wind and creates gentler conditions.

Plants growing in front of walls and fences may also need support to prevent them leaning towards the light and to counteract swirling air currents. Plant perennials at least 45cm (1½ft) from a wall and 30cm (1ft) from a wooden fence to avoid problems arising from poor soil, drought or excess moisture. If climbers are trained against a wall or fence, the competition from their roots for moisture and nutrients should be considered before you introduce other plants to the border.

HEDGES

Hedges provide a verdant natural background to a border but they do pose particular problems. First, a hedge develops an extensive but shallow root system, so space must be left between the hedge and the plants to reduce root competition. Also, access to the hedge is necessary for clipping. Allow a strip about 90cm (3ft) wide between the hedge and the perennials. In a small border, a space 45cm (1½ft) wide will suffice.

WEEDS

Weeds are always a problem, both in the early stages of establishing a new planting of perennials and when revitalizing a neglected site. There are two types of weeds: annuals and perennials. Annual weeds are relatively easy to deal with, but perennial weeds are more troublesome.

Annual weeds Annual weeds are prolific but are generally soft in texture. Although they flower and seed quickly, they are relatively easy to pull or dig out, or to hoe off, because they have no substantial underground roots. Remove annual weeds when preparing the soil, then leave it fallow for several weeks to allow more annual weeds to germinate. Once you have eradicated the second growth of weeds, plant your perennials. Finally, apply a sterile mulch such as bark chips around the plants to prevent further annual weeds appearing.

Perennial weeds Perennial weeds tend to have roots that are deep and spreading and, although the top-growth may be pulled or hoed off,

shoots inevitably spring again from the roots. Competition from perennial weeds for space, light, moisture and nutrients can be a significant problem, so it is essential they are eliminated before planting. As you prepare the soil, you must take painstaking care to remove the entire roots of perennial weeds, because many of the most harmful ones will grow from small and apparently insignificant pieces. If an area intended for perennials is severely infested, use chemical or other methods of control before working on the soil itself.

SOIL FOR PERENNIALS

Good soil is fundamental to the growing of good perennials. But it is heartening to know that, whatever the state of the soil when you start, it can usually be improved sufficiently. When assessing your soil for the first time, start by digging a hole about 45cm (1½ft) square. Take out 23cm (9in) of soil about the depth of the blade on the digging spade and pile it on one side, then continue down for a further 23cm (9in), this time piling the soil on the other side. Examining the soil and the hole from which it has come can tell you a great deal.

In a few cases you will find it impossible to dig a hole this deep. If the spade hits chalk or other rock only a few centimetres below the surface, you must resign yourself to having a problem which can be only partially solved. The soil may not be so shallow across the entire garden. Use a crowbar to go over the whole area at 2m (6ft) intervals, driving it into the soil to locate areas with deeper soil, which can then be marked out as areas for beds; in this way the garden will design itself. If the whole garden is made up of a thin layer of soil over solid rock, however, the only solution is to build raised beds to increase the depth of soil.

If the hole proves very difficult to dig, this may be because the soil is compacted. This condition could have been created by the use of heavy equipment during building work or by regular traffic across the same part of the garden, or through regular digging or rotary tilling over many years. In such cases deep digging is the only answer to the problem. Known also as double-digging, this involves loosening the soil to two spades' depth, or 45cm (1½ft). Although hard work, this not only improves root penetration and drainage but also facilitates the addition of organic matter.

ASSESSING THE SOIL

If the soil is sufficiently deep to allow the excavation of a hole, take note of how the colour and consistency of the soil change from top to bottom. If the soil remains dark and crumbly from the surface to the base of the hole, it is potentially very fertile. Usually, however, the deeper you go the less dark and crumbly the soil becomes. The greater the depth of dark topsoil, and the darker it is, the better.

Inspecting the soil below about 23cm (9in) usually reveals its fundamental characteristic; in fact, at this depth it is often obvious. Pure sand or gravel may appear, indicating a dry, fast-draining soil but one that is usually easy to work. If you find red, yellow or grey clay, the drainage will be less good and the soil will dry out less quickly after heavy rain, but has the advantage that it will also retain moisture for longer in dry weather. To confirm this, take some slightly damp soil and rub it between your thumb and forefinger. If it smears smoothly it contains a great deal of clay; if it feels gritty and rough it contains grains of sand or grit. The extent to which it crumbles in your fingers is also a clue. If it sticks in a lump or falls into fine grains it is more likely to require improvement than if it crumbles into granules.

IMPROVING THE SOIL

Organic matter is the most valuable soil improver, as it has the surprising capacity to improve both clay and sandy soils. It helps break up clay soils from solid lumps into crumbly granules that will allow water to drain through, yet it also helps bind sandy soils together, so that rain and

Loamy soil: naturally rich and fertile and good for many plants.

Alkaline soil: dry, hungry, and limy, but some plants love it.

plant foods drain through it less quickly. Organic matter needs constant renewal. Even if the soil is found to be rich, dark in colour and crumbly to a good depth and needs relatively little to bring it up to an acceptable standard, periodic additions of organic matter will be needed to maintain a high level of fertility.

ORGANIC MATTER FOR SOIL IMPROVEMENT

Many types of organic matter are available for soil improvement. Garden compost is often the most accessible; you can make it yourself in the garden from weeds, trimmings and other vegetable kitchen waste.

Heavy clay: sticky and difficult to work, best improved with organic matter.

Stony soil: well drained, needs regular enriching with fertilizer.

Unfortunately, unless it is made well, it often contains weed seeds. Animal manure is excellent but must be well rotted before use. Peat should be avoided, not only because it is a diminishing natural resource but because it contains almost no plant foods. Many of the so-called peat substitutes are, however, excellent. These are made from a variety of composted materials including wood and paper waste, bark, spent mushroom compost, coir (coconut fibre) and straw; they are weed-free, last well in the soil and contain valuable plant foods which are usually released slowly. Other, less familiar, forms of organic matter are sometimes available locally. Any is usually better than none, but some materials may be unusually limy or have an imbalance of plant foods.

LIME

Some aspects of soil fertility are not immediately apparent. The amount of lime in the soil (its alkalinity) is less crucial for perennials than it is for many shrubs, but some, such as lupins, are particular, preferring lime-free soil. Clues can be picked up from looking at the plants growing in neighbouring gardens. If hydrangeas are blue, the soil is likely to be acid; if they tend to be pink, the soil is more likely to be alkaline. If azaleas and rhododendrons are widespread and grow well, the soil will be acid; if they are seen only in tubs or raised beds, the local soil is probably limy.

A more accurate measure can be made using a simple kit available at most garden centres. While not infallible, soil-test kits give a fairly good indication of the acidity or alkalinity of the soil; information on how to interpret the results is usually supplied with the kit. Soil acidity is

The pH scale

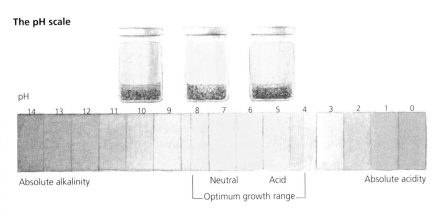

Test kits can assess the alkalinity or acidity of the soil and show the result on a coloured chart. A pH of 6.5 is suitable for the widest range of perennials.

measured on what is known as the pH scale. Most garden soils are in the band between pH5 and pH8. All you need to know is that pH7 is neutral; figures below indicate an increasingly acid soil; higher figures indicate increasing levels of lime. The best level for most perennials is about pH6.5.

The test kit will give information on how much lime to apply to reduce soil acidity. This varies according to the soil type. On an average soil, one application of garden lime at 190g per sq metre (6oz per sq yard) will reduce the level of acidity from pH5.5 to the ideal pH6.5. Wearing gloves, apply the lime on a still day; rake it in and do not plant or sow seeds for at least a month. One important general rule is that it is easy to make soil more alkaline simply by adding lime, but much harder to make soil more acid. Few perennials are like rhododendrons, insistent on an acid soil. Those like lupins that prefer lime-free conditions will grow on neutral soil.

PLANT FOODS

It is also helpful to know how much nutrient there is in the soil. A look at the plants already growing can be a help. Roses or shrubs with dead and twiggy growth, small leaves and a sparse show of small flowers may indicate a starved soil. Neglected borders showing patches of bare soil in mid-summer may also point to a shortage of plant nutrients. Weeds that flower when tall and lush often indicate rich soil, but if they rush into flower when just a few centimetres high the soil may be low in nutrients. The presence of stinging nettles is a good indicator of fertile soil being wasted on weeds.

Kits are available to test for the main plant nutrients: nitrogen, phosphorus and potassium. Although less accurate and more expensive than the lime-test kits, these may be worth using in a small garden.

The levels of plant foods in the soil are usually increased by the addition of organic matter, but fertilizer will often be necessary as well. Fertilizers may be organic or inorganic in origin, but both are effective, so the choice is yours. If a soil test reveals a significant shortage of any one material, the kit will advise on how to deal with it. But perennials are not usually fussy, and a balanced general fertilizer, such as Growmore, applied in the spring in accordance with the manufacturer's instructions, will usually work well.

PLANTING

Planting is the most exciting of the many tasks associated with growing perennials, full of promise and anticipation. Of course, often perennials will grow despite being planted thoughtlessly or at the wrong time of year. But, when planted properly, they will respond with speedy growth, a profusion of flowers or foliage in their first season and an inclination to increase well.

PREPARING FOR PLANTING

It is easiest to prepare thoroughly for planting when you are putting in a whole new bed or border rather than just a few plants. The main aim should be to bring the soil into the best possible condition for the plants. In practice, this means reducing compaction, breaking up the soil to create a more friable texture, improving its drainage, increasing its organic content and ensuring there are adequate nutrients for the plants. These goals are best achieved by digging the soil, which also provides an opportunity to eliminate perennial weeds.

PREPARING WHOLE BORDERS BY DIGGING

The soil and therefore the plants will be best served by double-digging to a depth of approximately 45cm (1½ft). This gives you a chance to incorporate plenty of organic matter into the soil, which is valuable to plants even when the soil is already in good shape. Perennials vary in the depth to which their roots will go in search of moisture and plant foods, and in the extent to which they appreciate rich conditions. In general, however, thorough preparation is invaluable.

Left: By dealing with all of the border at the same time, the preparation can be extremely thorough. All the varieties will benefit and develop well together.

On sandy soils the best time to dig is in the spring, but on clay soils it should be timed for when the soil is neither so dry that a spade will hardly penetrate nor so wet that it sticks to your boots in clods. Heavy soil should preferably be dug in the autumn, as the frost helps break up the clods. The act of digging, combined with frost action, helps break up the soil and improve the drainage.

When digging, large stones should be removed, but smaller stones and pebbles may improve drainage on heavy soils and should be left. Weeds, though, should not be left, and the roots of perennial weeds must be removed and burnt. The roots of many perennial weeds run very deep, and a few produce shoots that emerge at the surface having grown from depths of 45cm (1½ft) or more, so it pays to remove every piece.

Preparing for planting in enriched soil

1 *Fork over the soil, taking care to remove the roots of perennial weeds.*

2 *Rake off stones and other debris, and leave a reasonably level finish.*

3 *Tread the soil well to remove air pockets and prevent uneven settling.*

4 *Scatter fertilizer evenly, rake it in lightly, and the border is ready to plant.*

29

ORGANIC MATTER

The type of organic matter used is worth considering. The traditional technique was to use coarse, bulky materials such as farmyard manure and, after forking over the lower 23cm (9in) of soil during digging, to place the manure in a 7.5cm (3in) layer before covering it with the top-soil. This approach was well suited to the days of large-scale borders, when both manure and labour were in plentiful supply. In today's gardens it is preferable to use a finer, more crumbly material. This may be manure or compost that has rotted down very thoroughly, or it may be one of the many bulky materials developed from wood or paper waste. Either way, the material's fine texture allows it to be worked evenly through the full depth of soil using a garden fork, so that its benefits can be enjoyed by plant roots at all depths.

Once digging is finished, level the soil off and tread the area to remove air pockets. Then rake it roughly and, if possible, leave the area for a few weeks to allow weed seeds to germinate and any remaining pieces of weed root to sprout. These weeds can then be hoed or sprayed off before perennials are planted. As planting time approaches, final preparations can be made. Rake the soil surface again, correct any bumps and hollows, remove the last of the weeds, then give a dressing of a balanced general fertilizer and rake it in. The bed is now ready to plant. germinate

PLANTING SMALL POCKETS

The same principles apply to planting two or three plants into a small part of an existing border, although the presence of nearby plants necessarily imposes some restrictions. For a small planting space the process can

be simplified, as there is little point in extending it over many months. The quick way is to remove the existing plants or weeds, fork over the site to a depth of about 23cm (9in) mixing in some organic matter. Tread down, and then rake in fertilizer. Clearly this method does not allow the addition of organic matter to the lower level of the soil, but it does minimize disturbance to neighbouring plants.

It still pays to excavate all the soil to a depth of about 23cm (9in) if possible, then pile the soil on a sheet of polythene spread out nearby. Next, remove a little of the soil from the base of the hole; otherwise, when organic matter is added, the final level will be higher than that of the neighbouring soil. Fork over the base of the hole and mix in the organic matter. Then replace the topsoil, fork in more organic matter and tread the area. Dress it with fertilizer, and rake. Planting can then begin at once.

PLANTING SEASON

Most perennials have a great urge to grow but, whether your new plants come in pots or have been dug from the open ground at the nursery, a few basic points on timing apply. Never plant into soil that is frozen, or is likely to be frozen soon after planting; avoid waterlogged soil. Planting into dry soil in summer is another mistake, as is planting when icy winds are forecast or just before you go away for a long holiday.

CONTAINER-GROWN PLANTS

Now that most perennials are grown and sold in containers, they can, in theory at least, be planted at almost any time of year. It is often tempting to buy them in spring or summer, when they are in full flower, for at

Plant out lupins from pots in spring. Those dug from open ground may not transplant well.

that time you can see exactly what you are buying. They will usually survive at this time of year, but planting in summer is not good practice. Most perennials make fresh roots in early spring or autumn, and these are the best times to plant. Indeed, most perennials grown in pots are best planted in early spring. This allows new root growth to take hold quickly in the garden soil, lets the plant take advantage of natural seasonal moisture as it grows, and ensures that, by the time water stress threatens in summer, the roots are established in the garden soil. Another consideration is that, if you buy plants in early spring, the nursery rather than you will have taken responsibility for them during the winter.

The only plants unsuitable for spring planting are those, like hellebores, that start to make their growth

Tanacetum 'Brenda' is best planted in the spring rather than in the autumn, as it dislikes winter wetness when newly planted.

in winter or even in autumn, and flower in late winter or early spring; these are best planted in the autumn. Spring planting is especially necessary for autumn flowering plants like asters, which are often still in flower at a time when other perennials are being planted and which make strong root growth in spring. In warmer climates it is sensible to plant those varieties that are a little frost-tender in spring, so they can become well established by winter and the arrival of frosty weather. Planting in autumn is more appropriate for plants that are dug from the open ground, as they can establish new roots without suffering the increasing spring temperatures, which cause too much moisture to evaporate from the new leaves. Autumn is less suitable for planting container-grown specimens as the plant sits in its ball of water-

retentive compost during the season when it is most likely to remain sodden anyway, and this can cause the roots to rot. Perennials best planted in spring include *Aster*, *Catananche*, and *Gaillardia*; *Kniphofia*, *Lobelia*, and *Monarda*; *Penstemon*, *Scabiosa*, *Schizostylis* and *Tanacetum*.

PLANTS DUG FROM THE OPEN GROUND

Perennials dug from the ground before being despatched from the nursery must be considered differently. Keep in mind that the plants should be out of the soil for as short a time as possible. Nurseries may send out bare-rooted plants at any time from early autumn until well into spring. They try to lift plants when their soil is in the right condition which may be when your soil, in another part of the country, is frozen.

If bare-rooted plants arrive during the autumn months, they can often be planted out straight away. If they come in the winter, when the soil may be frozen or waterlogged, pot them up as soon they arrive and then keep them in a cold frame or a cold greenhouse until the spring. The little extra warmth provided by the protection will encourage the roots to grow, so that when you put the plants outside they settle in quickly.

Sometimes less well-organized nurseries send out plants dug from the open quite late in spring, when they have started growing. Apart from complaining about this, you need to give the plants special care. You can plant them at once, perhaps with the protection of shade netting, and water carefully. Alternatively, pot them up and keep them in a shaded frame until they are established, then plant them out later.

One or two plants, bearded irises in particular, are dug from the ground and sent out in late spring or summer, just after flowering. This sounds strange, but these irises make strong root growth at this stage and so establish themselves quickly.

PLANTS FROM YOUR OWN GARDEN

When lifting and replanting are being done in your own garden, you can choose the timing of the operation to suit the circumstances. It is true that perennials replanted within a few minutes of being lifted stand a far better chance of settling down quickly than those that are lifted and left for some time. Taking the opportunity to retain as much soil on the roots as possible always increases the chances of success. If necessary, you can lift and replant some perennials like asters, hardy chrysanthemums, hellebores and even lupins in full flower, but doing this successfully depends on watering them thoroughly first, retaining a great deal of soil on the roots, replanting and watering them in quickly, and providing protection from strong sun and fierce winds. Except in emergencies, it is not recommended.

PLANTING TECHNIQUES

Choose a day for planting when the soil is moist but not wet and, if possible, when there is little wind and no sun; a calm, bright but overcast day, with drizzle forecast for later, is ideal. This is especially important for a large-scale planting because, if conditions are wrong, many young plants could be lost; for a single plant, it is less crucial. Water plants in pots with a liquid tomato feed the night before planting, and at the same time water clumps of perennials in the garden that are to be moved to the border. The ready access to plant foods will ensure that growth into new soil can begin unhindered.

PLANTING MIX

Even if the whole border has been carefully prepared in advance, individual plants still appreciate good treatment. The best policy is to use a planting mix, either bought or made up at home. Bagged planting mixes from the garden centre usually comprise an organic base such as peat or bark plus a slow-release plant food. The most serviceable home-made mix comprises used potting compost, which can be stored in plastic sacks. Any used compost from pot plants that have died, the previous year's hanging baskets, growing bags and so on should be saved for use in a planting mix. If this old compost is mostly

Planting individual plants

1 *Using a trowel, dig a hole that is big enough for the root ball of the plant.*

2 *Grip the plant between your fingers, and loosen the pot with a tap from the trowel.*

3 *Set the plant in the hole at the right depth, then refill with soil and firm gently.*

4 *Water in thoroughly, adding some liquid fertilizer to give the plant a good start.*

peat- or coir-based, the addition of a little grit is a help. Then combine a 9-litre (2-gallon) bucketful with 60g (2oz) of a balanced general fertilizer to make the final planting mix.

PLANTING INDIVIDUAL PLANTS

Planting perennials from large pots, or those that have come in big clumps from another part of the garden, demands the use of a spade. Dig a hole to a depth of 23cm (9in) and

clearly wider than the pot or the clump's root ball, then fork some planting mix into the base of the hole. It is very difficult to be precise about how much mix to add: it depends on the condition of the soil. As a guide, when planting a mature hosta into average soil, which demands a hole 45cm (1½ft) across, you should use a whole bucket of planting mix. Add more planting mix to the soil taken from the hole before refilling.

Planting depths

Perennials with deep dormant buds, such as polygonatums, should be planted deeply to imitate the way they naturally grow.

Many plants, such as this hosta, should be set either at about soil level or just above if they are to be mulched after planting.

Perennials that like a dry crown, such as Sisyrinchium striatum *and irises, are planted with the crown just above soil level.*

Much smaller plants from pots require different treatment. If the ground has already been well prepared, no extra work may be required but, as a counsel of perfection, a 5cm (2in) layer of planting mix should be spread and forked in over the area where the plants are to go. Then put the plants in with a trowel.

Planting depths The level at which plants are set is important. Some perennials will rot at the crown if planted too deeply, but none should be planted too shallowly. If the intention is to mulch the bed after planting to conserve moisture and suppress weeds, the plant should be set so that the top of the root ball is at soil level. In most cases, apply about 5cm (2in) of mulch between the plants; do not cover the crowns. If a mulch is not to be applied, the plants can go slightly deeper and the root ball can be covered with a little soil from the bed. This same rule applies to clumps of plants dug from the garden, but small divisions are less tolerant. Plant them at the same level as they were growing previously, if they are not to be mulched; if they are to be, plant them

at a slightly more shallow level. Having much less in the way of food reserves in their roots, they are less tolerant of a deep mulch. Set the plant at the right depth and filter improved soil in around the roots, firming this with your fingers so that it is uniformly compacted. Using your foot to firm perennials, which is sometimes recommended, results in overcompaction of the soil, especially if the soil is heavy.

WATERING AND MULCHING

After the planting, all debris should be cleared away from the site and the soil should be raked over to remove footmarks and leave a neat finish; then the plants must be watered in.

When a whole new bed has been planted, a sprinkler can be used; this has the advantage for the plant roots of ensuring that all the soil is at the same level of moisture. It has the disadvantage, however, of not allowing the new plants to be fed at the same time as being watered. When one or a few perennials have been planted, they can be watered in with liquid tomato feed from a watering can. It

is especially important to make regular checks on perennials planted in summer in full growth, as it is difficult to tell how much the roots have dried out until the leaves collapse and the damage is done; lack of rain over a short period and one scorching afternoon may quite easily kill the entire new planting.

Once you have planted either a whole bed or a single plant, a mulch will help to keep the roots moist and prevent the germination of weed seeds. Many materials are available for mulching, but garden compost should be last on the list. Unless it is unusually well made, it will undoubtedly contain weed seeds, which will then germinate and engulf the new plantings. Lawn mowings also make a bad mulch as they too often contain grass seeds which will germinate in your borders. Use your planting mix as a mulch for small plantings or, for larger areas, any weed-free, bulky mulch such as bagged mulching mixtures from the garden centre. Always spread mulch after watering or rain so that the mulch retains the maximum amount of moisture.

PLANTING BEDS AND BORDERS

Planting a new bed or border can be daunting as well as exciting. A systematic approach is the key to increasing the pleasure and reducing the stress on both gardener and plants.

ASSEMBLING THE PLANTS

Once the soil has been prepared, the plants can be brought to the site. Lay out a sheet of polythene and assemble all those plants which are in pots. Group plants of the same variety together, with their labels still in view. It is sound practice to feed all plants in pots the day before planting with a weak liquid fertilizer. If plants are to be lifted from other parts of the garden or from neighbours' gardens, this can be done next. To protect the roots from damage or drying out and to help move the plants easily to the planting site, each variety can be placed in a plastic carrier bag.

Organizing border planting

1 *Gather all the plants together on a plastic sheet in roughly the spots they will have in the new border. Mark out the groups if it helps you visualize the end result.*

2 *Plant the bare-root plants and those at the back of the border first, then put in the pot-grown plants. Water the plants when they are in their final positions.*

ORGANIZING THE PLANTS

The next stage is to group the different varieties together in the pattern in which they will finally be planted. If you are working from a plan, it can be helpful to begin by organizing the different varieties on your polythene sheet in the same pattern as they will be planted in the bed – only without spacing them out. Then, if you decide to make some adjustments to your plan, you can do so before the plants are moved to the border. If you are adopting a less structured approach, it can still be useful to organize the plants on your polythene sheet before transferring them to the bed. This avoids too many tiresome trips to move plants from one end of the bed to the other, and perhaps back again, whenever you change your mind.

SETTING OUT THE PLANTS

Once you have settled on exactly how the planting is to be organized, you can move the plants onto the border itself. Many gardeners find it helpful to mark out the extent of each group on the border before moving the plants, especially if working from a plan. You can make lines on the border soil using dry sand to demarcate the area set aside for each variety. Alternatively use the point of a stick.

The individual plants can now be moved onto the border. First, place the plants of each variety together in the area in which they are to be planted; do not space them out straight away, as you may still decide to swap them around. When you are satisfied that all the varieties are where they should be, space out those in pots to fill their allotted areas. Depending on the varieties and their size and vigour, you may have just a single plant of some varieties and more of others. When planting a group of one variety, space the plants out evenly but not in regular shapes, like squares or circles, as this can look regimented. Spacing between individual plants depends on their vigour and height (see the Plant Directory).

When the plants in pots have been set out, remove the transplanted or bare-rooted plants from their bags and set these out in the same way, splitting them up as necessary (see p.65). Plant the ones that are not in pots first to ensure their roots have the minimum possible time to dry out. Put their labels in place immediately, and remove the bags from the scene. Next, deal with the plants in pots: label them and collect and stack the pots as you go. When all the plants are planted, water them in (see p.46) and use a hoe or rake to tidy up the soil. Finally, it is a good idea to amend your original paper plan to take account of any changes made during the planting process.

MIXED AND MATURE PLANTINGS

Planting a completely new border presents one sort of challenge, but planting new perennials into an established border requires a different approach. Individual pockets must be prepared separately (see p.32). Planting into a traditional border, in which the different varieties are grown in their own clumps, presents few difficulties. Other perennials rarely resent the disturbance when soil is being prepared alongside them, especially if their own soil is enriched in the process and the space where the new plants are to go is clearly defined. It can sometimes be helpful to lift and replant neighbouring perennials at the same time in order to ensure that they look good together.

PLANTING PERENNIALS AMONG BULBS

Growing perennials among bulbs can be very effective. There are two techniques that you can use in order to minimize damage to the bulbs.

One way is to plant the perennials while the bulbs are in growth. Then it will be clear exactly where the bulbs are growing, and the perennials can simply be planted between them. You cannot always plant at the ideal spacing, and it will certainly be impossible to prepare the soil as thoroughly as usual, but at least the bulbs will be spared. The other approach is to wait until the foliage of the bulbs is dying down. This technique is especially useful if the bulbs are so densely planted that it is impossible to plant among them when they are in flower or if the soil is in need of improvement. Spring bulbs, such as daffodils, die down in late spring and early summer; summer bulbs such as galtonias die down in late summer and

autumn. As the leaves die down, but before they have disappeared altogether, the positions of the bulbs will be clear, and this is also a good time to move them. Dig up the bulbs and place them on one side, then prepare the soil. Now plant the perennials and finally replant the bulbs between the perennials. (You must plant the perennials first as otherwise the bulbs may be speared as you make the planting holes for the perennials.)

PLANTING PERENNIALS AMONG SHRUBS

Planting perennials among shrubs may present more problems. The roots of roses, for example, will often throw up suckers when damaged, and magnolias tend to languish if their roots are disturbed. Rather than vigorous digging out of the soil, careful work with a border fork or even a hand fork will reveal where the main shrub roots are and how they can best be avoided.

Planting perennials among bulbs

1 *As the bulb foliage dies down, decide where the perennials are to go and transplant any bulbs that are in the way.*

2 *Choose small perennials and plant with a trowel; the remains of the foliage will indicate the presence of bulbs.*

Where roots are encountered, the tougher, non-suckering shrubs will not object to one or two being carefully removed. Cut them away with secateurs; never chop them through with the spade as this leaves rough edges and divisions which are more likely to rot. Roses present more of a problem, and their roots should not be cut unless absolutely necessary. Rather than disturb them, it is usually better to prepare less deeply and to mulch and feed well after planting.

One thing that can help where perennials are being planted into existing borders is using small plants. Perennials from small pots are preferable to those from larger pots, as they need smaller planting holes and so the preparation creates less disturbance. An alternative is to use rooted splits taken from the edges of existing plants in your own garden, or you can split perennials in large pots into two or three pieces before planting them. When using small plants, which must face competition from exisiting shrub roots, pay particular attention to watering and feeding.

PLANTING SEQUENCE FOR NEW MIXED BORDERS

When planting a completely new mixed border with shrubs, climbers and bulbs as well as perennials, the basic preparation should be the same as for a herbaceous border (see p.34). First, plant wall shrubs and climbers on any fence or wall at the back, tying them in with wires. Then put in any posts or wigwams as support for other climbers, which are next to be planted, followed by the evergreen and deciduous shrubs. Single specimen perennials should be planted next, followed by groups of perennials and any tougher alpines as frontal plants, with the bulbs going in last.

WILDFLOWER PLANTINGS

Gardeners are becoming increasingly interested in creating wildflower gardens. The enthusiasm for this type of garden is growing due to a number of reasons, partly because they are extremely beautiful but also because they attract so many birds and insects, many of which are beneficial.

Plantings of native wildflowers, especially wildflower meadows, require a very different approach to that used for growing garden varieties in beds and borders. In particular, if the soil is prepared lavishly in the way already described for other perennials, grasses and weeds can soon take over, smother the choicer flowers and eventually kill them. For wildflowers the opposite approach from usual is needed: the aim is to create conditions of low fertility in order to prevent the invasion of these coarser unwanted plants. The other main problem is weeds. Whether they spread by perennial roots, like some of the coarse grasses, or by seed, like the undesirable annuals, they are a danger.

SITE AND SOIL

Rather than choosing a site to suit the plants you wish to grow, it is often more appropriate to choose the plants to suit the site you have available: use woodland plants for shade and meadow plants for sunny places. The ideal site has soil that is somewhat impoverished, as, in rich soils, vigorous weeds may swamp the more restrained wildflowers.

Converting existing borders The soil in borders where cultivated perennials or other plants have previously been grown is likely to be too rich for wildflowers. To remedy this, remove the topsoil (use it to improve the soil

Reducing soil fertility

To prepare for wildflowers, remove the lawn or topsoil to reduce the soil's fertility.

in another part of the garden) and replace it with poorer soil. Alternatively, you can sow a succession of green manure crops, such as mustard, winter-grazing rye, lucerne (alfalfa) or winter tares, but, instead of digging them in when they are mature, remove them and dig them into the soil elsewhere. This results in a steady reduction of soil fertility. Then dig or fork over the site and leave it fallow for one growing season to assess the weed situation. Hoeing the soil may be sufficient to remove annual weeds, although in some cases a total weedkiller is valuable to guarantee the destruction of all weeds. Gardeners who prefer not to use weedkiller can cover the area with an old carpet or thick black polythene for a year to smother weeds as they come through. **Converting lawns** A lawn that has rarely or never been fed and that has been regularly mown, with the clippings removed, has the potential to be turned into a wildflower meadow. Even a change of mowing and feeding regime can start the conversion of

Removing weeds

1 *Cover the area with old carpet or black polythene to smother perennial weeds.*

2 *The weed roots will exhaust themselves searching for light.*

SOWING AND PLANTING

Plants of some wildflowers are not easy to find in nurseries, and it is often more practicable to raise them from seed. While it is possible and sometimes quite useful to raise them in pots, you may have more success sowing them where they are to flower. Mixtures of perennial wildflowers are available from seed companies, formulated to suit different soil-types and situations; these often contain annuals to provide colour in the first season and to create cover, which prevents the invasion of weeds.

Making new plantings Before sowing, dig the soil, then tread and rake it to create a fine seed bed. Check the seed packet for advice on the amount of seed required for a given area. It is most convenient to sow in rows because the rows of seedlings will stand out clearly when the seed first germinates and any weeds growing between the rows can be easily distinguished and removed. As the plants develop, the row pattern will disappear. In most areas, spring is

a well tended lawn into a wildflower meadow. The absence of feeding and the removal of clippings create a steady reduction of the fertility and, at the same time, finer grasses disappear and broad-leaved plants move in. Often, ceasing to mow allows a delightful tapestry of flowers to appear from plants that have been

there for some time, their flowers cut off by regular mowing. Low-fertility lawns can be converted into wildflower plantings in one of three ways. Seed can be sown into the grass; wildflowers can be established by planting young plants; or the top 5cm (2in) of lawn can be removed entirely and the soil dug and treated as a new site.

Sowing wildflowers

1 *Make a drill with the edge of a hand trowel in friable soil.*

2 *Sow the seeds thinly, gently tapping them out of the packet.*

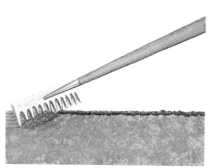

3 *Cover the seeds carefully with soil using a rake, and tap down gently.*

Wild poppies and daisies blend with garden violas and lychnis in a lively planting.

Planting into lawns requires more care, mainly because the roots of the new plants will face competition for moisture and nutrients from the roots of the existing lawn grasses and other plants. Relatively small plants are often most successful. Use a bulb planter to remove a cylinder of soil, fill the hole with used potting compost to give the young plants a good start, then plant the seedlings. They may need occasional watering during their first summer.

WILDFLOWERS IN CONVENTIONAL BORDERS

Wildflowers can also be grown in more organized beds and borders in exactly the same way as cultivated varieties. They can either be grown among garden varieties or be given a border of their own. The richness of the soil often causes them to grow far taller than in their natural habitats, so they may need staking in borders (though not in meadows). They may also spread far more vigorously and seed themselves all too freely.

usually the best time to sow although, in areas with mild winters, autumn sowing is successful.

Lawns Seed can be sown directly in lawns, although because of the competition from the existing plants this can be an unpredictable method. Cut the grass short, then rake the lawn to remove thatch and moss. Make seed drills 15–23cm (6–9in) apart using the corner of a metal hoe or the tip of a trowel or similar sharp tool. This can be quite hard work, as the soil under lawns is often compacted. Now sow the seed thinly in the drills and lightly cover it with sand. As the seedlings mature, the rows will at first be obvious, but the random distribution of the many species in the mixture will ensure that the pattern disappears.

Planting young plants Wildflower plantings can be created by raising the plants in pots and planting them out in the prepared soil or lawn. Young plants are also available at some garden centres, by mail-order or from specialist wildflower nurseries. Starting with plants rather than seed

allows plantings to establish more quickly. If the soil has been prepared, planting young plants in clumps rather than sowing seed gives you another season in which to deal with any weed problems by hoeing and spot treatment before the coverage of wildflowers becomes too dense.

Planting wildflowers in a lawn

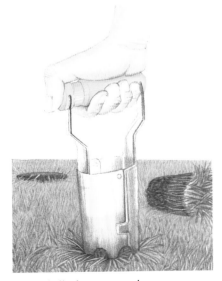

1 *Use a bulb planter to neatly remove a cylinder of grass and soil.*

2 *Set the young plant in the hole, and refill with used potting soil.*

CONTAINER PLANTINGS

Growing perennials in containers successfully depends on choosing the right plant and the right container for the individual situation, then using the most appropriate compost and drainage materials. It is important to say at the outset that many perennials are unsuitable for growing in containers. Some, like hellebores, have such a deep root system that they do not adapt well to restricted root space. Others, like delphiniums, look entirely out of scale and out of place. Still others have a restricted season of interest: although they are attractive for a few weeks, thereafter their container is best moved out of sight – a tedious task. The best perennials to grow in containers:

• are modest in size, so are naturally the right scale for most containers;
• have a long flowering season;
• have attractive foliage for many months, or are evergreen;
• have both good foliage and good flowers, and thus maximum appeal;
• have the character to make specimen plants;
• benefit from close inspection of their flowers.

Perennials for containers include *Acanthus*, *Ajuga*, *Epimedium*, ferns, hardy geraniums (both the low and trailing types), *Heuchera*, *Hosta*, *Lamium*, *Primula*, *Pulmonaria* and variegated grasses.

CONTAINERS

Containers made of natural materials are generally more attractive than those made of synthetic materials, and usually look better in the garden. Matching the size of the container to the size of the plant is crucial: putting a small plant in a large container is not only wasteful but, since the compost may stay too wet, it may cause the roots to rot. A large plant in a small pot will need constant watering, and with insufficient root room will never develop naturally and will probably keep blowing over. It is a mistake to put even the smallest perennials, such as primroses, in pots smaller than 12.5cm (5in) in diameter; at the other extreme, some of the more vigorous hostas, like 'Krossa Regal', will eventually need a pot 45cm (1½ft) or more across to look and grow their best.

Frost-resistant earthenware flowerpots are often the most suitable containers for perennials, along with stone or terracotta urns and containers cast in a stone and concrete mix. Wooden tubs, too, are very attractive, and are quite inexpensive if made at home. Deep wooden boxes, at least 23cm (9in) wide and deep, are good for smaller plants.

COMPOST

Always start with good, fresh potting compost; never use old compost or soil from the garden. A compost containing some loam is preferable, and for many perennials John Innes Potting Compost Number 3 is ideal. For plants that appreciate moisture, 25 per cent additional peat or coir potting compost can be mixed in, while for those preferring unusually good drainage 25 per cent extra grit or perlite can be added.

Before filling the container with compost, you must add drainage material. Any large drainage holes are best covered with fine plastic mesh (for example small squares of greenhouse shading) to keep out insects. Then, to help excess moisture drain away quickly, a layer of gravel at least 2.5cm (1in) deep – it need be no more than 5cm (2in) deep in even the

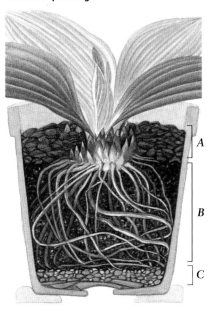

A maturing specimen hosta grown in a container with its extensive root system and expanding crown of shoots: A Mulch, B Roots in potting soil, C Drainage Material.

largest pots. To prevent the compost from filtering into the gravel and clogging it, the gravel should be covered with a layer of water-permeable fabric. This fabric allows moisture and possibly some roots through, but prevents the compost filtering downwards and blocking the drainage; it also makes an additional barrier to worms and woodlice.

PLANTING STYLES

There are two methods of planting containers. They can be planted to make individual features, with a single carefully chosen plant as an attractive specimen; the same effect can be created by planting three plants of the same variety in a neat triangle, so that they grow together and look like one plant. This is often the most effective way of planting pots up to about 30cm (1ft) in diameter. Alternatively, larger pots and long boxes can be planted with a carefully chosen selection of perennials. In this case consideration must be given to the eventual location of the container. If it is to be viewed from all sides, a symmetrical arrangement may be most successful, with the tallest plant in the centre surrounded by lower, bushier plants, and perhaps sprawling ones around the edge. If it is to be backed by a wall or fence or placed in a corner site, you would be better to place the tallest plant near the back. Whichever style is adopted, choose the varieties carefully, for plants in containers always come in for close scrutiny.

PLANTING CONTAINERS

Before planting a large container, move it to its final site; it may be unmanoeuvrable afterwards. At this point, containers that are to stand on the ground should be propped up on low blocks about 2.5cm (1in) high, to allow unimpeded drainage. Now assemble all the drainage materials, compost and plants. Cover the drainage hole, add and cover the gravel, and start to add the compost; firming it gently as you go. Then, if a single specimen is to be planted, set it in place in its pot in the centre of the container to check its level.

If possible, leave a 2.5cm (1in) space between the top of the compost and the top of the container. Once the plant is sitting in place at the right level, it can be removed from its pot and set back in the container; add more compost, gently firming it, until the required level is reached. Finally, the whole surface of the compost should be covered with mulch. The space between the compost and the top of the container can be filled entirely with washed medium or coarse gravel, or very coarse bark to reduce evaporation, prevent the compost being splashed out during watering, and enhance the appearance of the container. When planting a mixed container, fix the position of the plant in the largest pot first, then add more compost and the smaller plants until planting is complete.

Planting a mixed container

1 *Set the container in its final position; prop it on blocks to help drainage.*

2 *Place drainage material in the base of the container, cover and start to fill with soil.*

3 *Put the plants in place as the container is filled, firming the soil around them.*

4 *Finish off with a mulch of coarse bark or gravel, and water thoroughly.*

WATERING AND FEEDING

After planting, the container should be watered using a weak liquid feed until liquid drips from the base. As the roots fill the compost, containers need watering regularly, particularly in warmer months when they need water sometimes as often as every day. Although the compost will contain some plant foods, after the first few weeks it pays to water every week in the growing season with a liquid tomato feed to encourage robustness and steady growth.

Right: Place the tallest plant in the centre if the arrangement is to be viewed from all sides.

CARE AND CULTIVATION

Perennials are not demanding plants, but regular care encourages them to give their best for as long as possible, to increase well and to resist the attacks of pests and diseases. Much of the care required is routine watering, weeding and the removal of dead flowers, but the more occasional tasks such as feeding, mulching and staking are no less vital. The periodic need for replanting is crucial: while some perennials survive for decades without division, others need replanting every other year.

MULCHING

Mulching is the spreading on the soil surface of a layer of grit, gravel or, more often, organic matter. This treatment not only replicates the natural cycle in many plant habitats, where a dense covering of fallen leaves or dead stems accumulates every autumn, it also suppresses weeds, provides plant foods, retains moisture in the soil and offers a simple and attractive background to the plants. Grit and gravel mulches are not often used – usually only on beds prepared for good drainage, in drought gardens and in Mediterranean plantings. Grit helps water drain away from the crowns of plants, which may be susceptible to rotting in wet winters.

ORGANIC MULCHES
Most mulches are organic, and here the most important characteristic is that they should be free of weeds. The time and effort spent removing weeds from the soil, then mulching to keep it that way, are completely wasted if the mulch itself is full of weed roots or, more likely, weed seeds. An organic mulch is less permanent than a gravel mulch, but as it rots down, the organic material releases nutrients beneficial to plants.

Garden compost Most types of garden compost contain weed seeds unless they have been made to a very high standard. During the rotting process the compost needs to heat up to at least 49°C (120°F) and preferably more to kill weed seeds. To achieve this, use a wooden box as a container and build the heap in layers, using an activator and ensuring a good supply of air and moisture. Unless you can be sure your compost is of the highest quality, it is usually better to dig it into the soil than to use it as a mulch.

Manure Raw, lumpy manure is sometimes used as a mulch, but it does not cover the soil sufficiently to be effective and may also burn plant roots. Animal manure must be well rotted before use on the garden; it can take over a year to rot down to a suitably crumbly texture. It usually has the benefit of being free of weed seeds.

Peat In some ways peat is an excellent mulch; its texture is good, it is usually completely weed-free, and it can be bought in handy polythene sacks. It contains almost no plant nutrients, however, and using peat on the garden depletes a limited natural resource unnecessarily. It is preferable to use the bagged mulches now available at most garden centres.

Bagged mulches Many peat substitutes have been developed, and these

Compost bin

A compost bin constructed of treated wood will last well and keep the compost at a high temperature to help kill weeds.

make ideal mulches. They contain a balanced mix of nutrients and are weed-free and of good texture, being made from a variety of ingredients including coir, bark, wood waste, paper waste, straw and spent mushroom compost. They are usually ready-composted and mixed.

Manure mulch

Bark Coarse bark partially composted to darken its colour and help create a better nutrient balance, is an attractive and popular mulch. Bark lasts a great deal longer than peat or bagged mulches before rotting; unfortunately, it provides almost no plant foods. Some gardeners also use a mixture of fresh bark and wood chips which, although pale, is effective.

Leaves Commonly used, leaves can be applied in the autumn either whole or partially composted. Worms pull them into the soil, which gradually improves in texture.

Other materials In different parts of the country other bulky organic materials, like brewery waste or the waste from local farm crops, may be available. These materials are always worth investigating and are often good value. Some gardeners spread grass clippings on their borders but, while these may suppress weeds growing in the border soil, they usually contain so much grass seed that the border is soon carpeted in green. Shredded garden prunings are becoming more popular and can be applied directly to borders or composted first. They rot and disappear more quickly than bark or wood chips.

TIMING

A mulch should be applied only to damp soil that is free of weeds. Initially it should be applied immediately after planting has been carried out, to a depth of at least 2.5cm (1in); a depth of 5cm (2in) is often more effective in terms of water conservation and weed prevention, but will smother small plants. An established herbaceous border should be mulched in the autumn, after the border has been tidied up for the winter, but, if it contains a high proportion of late-flowering plants, tidying and mulching can be left until the spring.

Timing a mulch for mixed borders that also contain autumn and spring bulbs is more difficult. The trick is to get it onto the border when there is little in flower or likely to be damaged, so the best time is immediately after the autumn bulbs fade but before the spring bulbs start to grow.

Apply the mulch in late autumn or early winter in colder areas, or during the winter months in more temperate climates. If possible, try to renew the mulch regularly. Annual mulching is valuable on poor soil, but mulching every other year is usually adequate for most gardens.

FEEDING

In nature, dead plant stems and leaves fall around the plants, rot, and are taken back into the soil to provide food for the plants in succeeding years. In our gardens we cut down the top-growth in the autumn and remove it, so we must replace the nutrients lost in that process. Most perennials are neither demanding nor unusually fussy about feeding. The process starts with thorough preparation of the soil before planting, so the soil already contains good reserves of nutrients to which roots will have access as the plants develop. In succeeding years, regular additions of plant foods, either as bulky organic matter or as fertilizers, are essential to keep plants healthy.

PLANTING TIME

Adding bulky organic material to the soil at planting time not only improves the structure of the soil but also provides a reservoir of plant foods which are steadily released over the years as the organic matter decomposes. A general fertilizer, too, is usually applied shortly before planting to ensure the plants have access to nutrients in the shorter term (see p.32). Applying a liquid feed immediately before or after planting gives the plants a flying start.

REGULAR FEEDING

An annual mulch of organic matter can provide the majority of nutrients that perennials require. Unfortunately, materials vary in the amount of plant foods they contain. Some, like bark and peat, are relatively low in nutrients; manure and many bagged mulches are richer, but even then the precise balance of nutrients in manure can vary from batch to batch

Bark mulch

Leaves used as mulch

and in bagged products from brand to brand. Many gardeners rely solely on regular annual mulching to provide the nutrients their plants require. In most gardens, however, additional annual feeding using a dry organic or inorganic fertilizer is beneficial.

Fertilizer and mulch The frequency with which fertilizer is required depends on the regularity of mulching and the material used.

• If materials poor in plant foods, like peat or coarse bark, are used as mulch, annual application of fertilizer is advisable.

• If good mulching materials are in short supply, a mulch can be applied every other year, with a dry feed at full strength in alternate years.

• If mulching materials are not available at all, fertilizer is best applied every year.

• Even if beds and borders are mulched regularly, an occasional application of fertilizer helps redress any imbalances created by the continual use of one type of mulch. This is especially true in the early years of

a new planting, when fertility can be built up by applying fertilizer immediately after the border has been tidied, then applying a mulch.

Timing In general, fertilizer is best applied in late winter or early spring, just as plants are starting to grow. If it is applied in autumn, the winter rains may wash some of the nutrients away through the soil while the plants are dormant and unable to absorb them. It is not always possible to follow the best practice, however. Also, changing tastes have led to the use of more plants like hellebores and bergenias, which grow during the winter, so spring application is less crucial; and, where beds are carpeted with early-spring bulbs, it is often more convenient to apply fertilizer in winter or autumn.

Materials Perennials do not demand special fertilizer. A well-balanced general fertilizer containing the three main plant foods nitrogen, phosphorus and potassium is ideal. Such feeds come in a variety of strengths, so follow the manufacturer's instructions

on rates of application. Try to choose a brand that includes minor or trace elements, like manganese and zinc, in its formulation, especially if you are unable to mulch regularly. Perennials rarely show signs of being deficient in these minor nutrients, but their availability does help keep the plants healthy. Organic and inorganic materials are equally effective; if you prefer to garden without artificial fertilizers, plenty of effective organic dry feeds are available.

Technique First check the rate of application on the fertilizer pack; this is usually given in grams per square metre or ounces per square yard. Note and follow any safety warnings. Although fertilizers are among the least dangerous of garden chemicals, they can irritate or dry your skin, so it is wise to wear disposable plastic gloves when handling them.

Take a comfortable handful of fertilizer and weigh it. Check the weight against the application rate and adjust the handful accordingly; your aim is to grasp a handful of fertilizer

Applying fertilizer

1 *To help apply fertilizer evenly use bamboo canes to mark out sections.*

2 *Spread the fertilizer evenly holding your hand 30–60cm (1–2ft) above the soil.*

3 *Rake the fertilizer into the soil's surface to keep it from drifting away in the wind.*

containing approximately the amount required for a square metre or yard.

To ensure that the fertilizer is distributed at the correct rate, tie four bamboo canes, about 1.2m (4ft) long, into a square, with each side a metre (yard) long. Lay this on the soil in one corner of the bed and spread the fertilizer on this area. Then move the square along and repeat the process. Continue until the bed is completed. You may find that you can soon visualize a square metre or yard fairly accurately, and dispense with the bamboo square.

Apply fertilizer on a still, dry day. Move your hand from side to side, releasing the fertilizer about 30–60cm (1–2ft) above the soil. Aim to spread almost all of each handful in one pass, retaining a little to cover any bare patches. Some perennials will be in leaf; if so, try to spread it beneath their leaves. After spreading the fertilizer, it pays to rake or hoe it in lightly to prevent the wind blowing it away. If rain does not fall within a week of a spring application, watering in will help to activate the fertilizer promptly.

SPOT FEEDING

Occasionally the poor growth of a particular plant may tempt you to consider giving it a boost. This is best done with a liquid seaweed or a tomato feed, which encourages robust growth rather than soft sappy shoots and also provides trace elements.

WATERING

As water becomes an increasingly scarce natural resource in many areas during long hot summers, gardeners must think more carefully about how to keep their perennials supplied with moisture during the growing season.

MOISTURE-RETENTIVE SOIL

Organic matter retains water: one of the main reasons for adding generous amounts of it while preparing for planting is to increase the moisture-holding capacity of the soil. This ensures that, during dry spells, the soil contains reserves of water that help keep the plants growing well. The level of organic matter in the soil drops as it decomposes over the years, however, and so it needs regular replenishing. This is one of the main reasons for regular mulching. Although the organic matter is applied to the surface, earthworms soon draw it down into the soil and cultivation eventually results in it being mixed into the lower levels.

A substantial layer of mulch has the advantage of helping prevent the soil from losing moisture directly from its bare surface through evaporation. Thorough preparation of planting sites when perennials are replaced or replanted also helps keep the soil rich in moisture-retentive humus.

WIND AND SHELTER

Strong winds can greatly increase evaporation of moisture from both plant leaves and the surface of the soil, so shelter can be helpful in preventing water loss. This can be provided by fences; even a hedge can be worthwhile, as the benefit of the shelter it provides greatly outweighs the fact that its own roots take moisture from the soil. Many traditional herbaceous borders are backed by an evergreen hedge, and some are also fronted by a low box hedge. The shelter these hedges provide is as valuable as their decorative role, providing a background to offset the flowers.

WHEN TO WATER

Newly planted perennials appreciate a good soak to ensure that their roots do not dry out and to encourage new roots to grow into the garden soil. But once they are established, be cautious about watering. Watering at the first sign of a dry spell encourages the roots to remain in the surface layer of

In shady, moisture-retentive situations choose plants that enjoy the conditions like these primulas, ferns, meconopsis and hostas.

the soil rather than to grow more deeply in search of water reserves. The time may come, however, when watering is necessary. Look out for these signs of water shortage:

• Growth slows almost to a stop.
• Leaves and flower heads wilt.
• Lower leaves shrivel.
• Leaves lose their gloss.
• Newly opened flowers seem unusually small.
• The plants in the border look collectively limp.

Ideally, watering should be carried out before these symptoms are seen. Experience will teach you a sensitivity to the state of your plants.

The time of day at which watering is done is important if the water is to be used efficiently. Water on calm days, so that wind does not distort the area of coverage or hasten evaporation. Always water in the evening so the moisture has time to penetrate the soil before the heat of the morning sun increases evaporation.

HOW TO WATER

Watering individual plants with a watering can is usually futile except when especially sensitive varieties like candelabra primulas, for example, grow among more tolerant plants; even then, many canfuls may be needed to help the plants, for it is essential that plants be watered thoroughly. If the moisture soaks only a few centimetres into the soil, the roots will grow up towards it and so be more vulnerable to drought in the future. Only the use of a hose can properly ensure that sufficient quantities are applied.

There are four main ways of applying water with a hose: a seep-hose, a sprinkler, a soaker hose and a drip-irrigation system.

Sprinkler systems Sprinklers come in various designs, all intended to apply an even covering of water without constant attention. All waste a lot of water in evaporation during hot weather. In addition, the oscillating

units can cause compaction due to the large droplet size. The most common types are:

• Simple static units that water a small circular area with a constant fine spray. Although inexpensive, these are difficult to adjust and may create puddles by constantly watering the same small area.
• Adjustable rotating pulse-jet sprinklers that cover a circular area and generally apply the water more evenly than other units. They are often the most expensive, but both the area of coverage and the fineness of the spray can usually be adjusted.
• Adjustable oscillating units that cover a more or less rectangular area, which can be varied to suit the shape of the border. While more expensive, they do not puddle the soil and are also the most effective type to use when water pressure is low.

It is essential when using any of these sprinklers that you apply plenty of water. It is not possible to be specific about how long a sprinkler should be left watering one area because the rate of application depends on the nature of the individual unit, how the sprinkler is set, the water pressure and the nature of the soil. But the water must penetrate deeply, preferably deeper than the roots of most of the plants – a depth of at least 60cm (2ft). Excavating a hole the day after watering will give some indication of how far the water has penetrated. Finally, always make sure that the sprinkler is adjusted to water exactly the right area: when watering a large area, move the sprinkler so there is no overlap with areas you have already watered; when placing the sprinkler in the border rather than at its edge, raise it on an old box so that it is above the level of the surrounding plants.

Many shade- or moisture-loving plants, such as these primulas and meconopsis, thrive in open, sunny locations if the soil is kept sufficiently damp.

Types of sprinkler

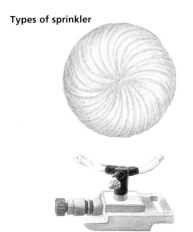

Simple rotating sprinklers are inexpensive. They water a circular area but are uneven in their distribution of water.

Pulse-jet sprinklers are expensive. They water a circular area or part of a circle, are very adjustable, and water evenly.

Oscillating sprinklers vary in price. They water a rectangular area, are partially adjustable, and water fairly evenly.

Soaker hose Available in different lengths, these hoses have a double row of small holes on one side. When connected to a water supply they give a fine spray of water on either side. Being flexible, they can be snaked through the border, bending to pass around plants. If placed with the holes facing up they water a wide strip, but a lot of water is lost through evaporation in the air. When they are placed with the holes downward, all the water goes into the soil, soaking down to the roots in an inverted-V pattern.

Seep-hose In recent years another useful way of applying water has become available: perforated hose is manufactured with a large number of tiny holes through which water seeps. It is laid on the soil or even buried under a mulch; water oozes from the hose directly into the soil. The great advantage of this system is that very little water is lost through evaporation, so the amount of water required is reduced, but there are also disadvantages. In limy areas the pores of the seep-hose can become clogged with lime deposits, reducing the amount of water that penetrates to the soil. Furthermore, it can be difficult to assess just how thoroughly the soil has been watered. A seep-hose is perhaps most useful for watering rows of young plants or cut flowers, because it can be laid directly along the row to ensure that the water reaches the roots.

Drip-irrigation system It is possible to water plants individually rather than soak the soil. Using a supply-line along the centre of the bed, small 'spaghetti-tube' pipes can be run to each plant. A small emitter on the end of each pipe prevents the water washing holes in the soil. Where winters are mild and severe freezing unlikely, these can be left in place year-round, hidden beneath the mulch. If winters are more severe, remove or empty them before freeze-up. This system can also be used for containers.

CHOOSING THE RIGHT PLANTS
One way of reducing the demand for water in areas where droughts are common or there are frequent restrictions on garden watering is to make use of drought-resistant plants. These plants usually grow naturally in Mediterranean regions or other areas with hot, dry summers, and so are best able to thrive in such conditions in the garden. Some drought-resistant perennial plants include *Armeria, Dianthus, Diascia, Elymus magellanicus, Erodium, Euphorbia characias, Festuca, Helianthemum, Iris unguicularis* and *Phlox douglasii* varieties.

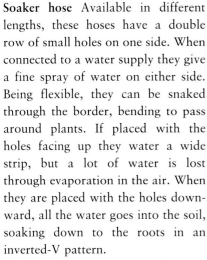

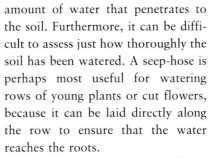

In damp or well-watered gardens, a drought-loving plant, such as this *Euphorbia characias* subsp. *wulfenii,* can be grown in a container and thus kept in the drier soil it prefers.

WEEDING

Keeping perennial borders weed-free demands thorough preparation and constant vigilance. The seeds of some weeds, like poppies and nightshades, can remain viable in the soil for decades, so the old saying that 'one year's seeding brings seven years' weeding' is more than true.

PREPARATION

Planting a new border which has not been cleared of perennial weeds is asking for trouble. Part of the point of digging the soil thoroughly before planting is to remove the roots of perennial weeds. Unfortunately some weeds, such as couch grass, will regenerate from a piece of root less than half a centimetre (quarter of an inch) long if a bud is present, so it is important to try to remove every piece during digging. Inevitably some small pieces of root will be missed, but waiting a few months between digging and planting allows these pieces to sprout, and then they can be removed individually.

When adding organic matter to the soil, it is important not to add more weeds at the same time. The roots of perennial weeds should never be added to the compost heap in the first place, but ensuring that compost is made properly, so it heats up well and kills the weed seeds, is a preventative measure.

Another way of dealing with perennial weeds is to kill them all using a systemic (translocated) weed-killer before the ground is dug. This technique is especially useful when you are creating a bed in an area that has not previously been cultivated. Apply a broad-spectrum systemic weedkiller to the whole area in late spring or early summer, or at any time when weeds are growing strongly. After a few weeks you can clear away the dead material and dig the bed. When difficult weeds like bindweed are present, you may need a second application to kill any regrowth. An alternative total weed treatment is to cover the area with an opaque material to smother the weeds. Old carpet is often recommended for this and is very successful; heavy-duty black polythene also works well. The covering must be left in place for at least a year to ensure that weeds are killed; this demands some advance planning.

GROUND-COVER PLANTS

Once a bed is prepared and free of perennial weeds, planting can begin. If you wish to minimize the time spent weeding, consider planting perennials that are particularly good at smothering weeds. Many hardy perennials have such dense growth that weeds find it difficult to penetrate. Hostas, for example, have foliage which is so broad and dense that weeds stand little chance of establishing themselves underneath, and many hardy geraniums make mounds of crowded shoots that have the same effect. It is important to remember, however, that no ground-cover plants can smother weeds well if planted into already weedy ground. Weed-smothering perennials include *Alchemilla*, *Astrantia*, and *Bergenia*, *Geranium*, *Heuchera*, *Hosta*, *Lamium*, *Nepeta*, *Rheum* and *Symphytum*.

WEEDING TECHNIQUES

However careful the preparation, weeds are bound to grow. Weed seeds that have been lying dormant in the soil will germinate; the wind will blow them in; or they may even arrive on plants bought from a nursery or garden centre.

Hand weeding Many gardeners find removing weeds by hand a satisfying experience. It is not only an effective way of dealing with weeds, as long as there are not too many of them, but also provides an opportunity to look at the plants at close quarters. Annual weeds, such as groundsel and chickweed, are easy to pull out: the soil can be knocked off their roots and they can be added to the compost heap. Always remove these weeds before they have a chance to seed. Keep a separate bag or bucket for perennial weeds, and when these are encountered a little more excavation may be needed to ensure that all the root is removed; such weeds should be burned. One of the advantages of hand weeding is that, when seedlings of garden plants are discovered, they can be left in place or moved to a suitable situation. Other methods of control fail to discriminate between flowers and weeds.

Mulching The application of a layer of weed-free mulch is one of the most effective ways of preventing

Hand weeding

Use a hand fork to help remove weeds, then shake the soil off the roots.

the growth of weeds Although any weed-free organic matter will make a reasonably effective weed-suppressing mulch, the most useful materials are those sufficiently dense to prevent germination of weed seeds already in the soil, yet sufficiently coarse to provide a poor seed bed for weeds blown in on the wind. Bark chips and coco shell are good examples. The soil should be cleared of weeds before the mulch is applied, as established weeds may have the strength to grow through the mulch and then spread.

Hoeing When no mulch is applied, hoeing can be a useful method of weed control, especially in the early months after planting. Hoeing is not advisable when a mulch has been applied, as it disturbs the mulch and reduces its effectiveness. Hoeing between the plants on a warm day when the surface of the soil is dry slices off the weeds, and they usually shrivel in the sun. It is important, however, that you take care to remove perennial weeds individually, as these will almost always regrow from their roots.

Take particular care when hoeing through a border not to damage the stems of your perennials. A hoe can easily slice through a flowering stem if used carelessly. As the perennials in the border begin to grow strongly, their foliage fills the space between the clumps. It then becomes increasingly difficult to use a hoe without damaging plants, until eventually it becomes impossible. Other methods, especially, for instance, hand weeding and mulching, must be used instead.

• **Weedkillers** Weedkillers can be invaluable aids, but it is vital to use them carefully and thoughtfully. There are two main groups: total weedkillers, which kill all plants whether weeds or precious perennials and selective weedkillers, which kill some plants and not others. Total weedkillers themselves come in two types: systemic weedkillers, which travel through the sap to all parts of the plant, and contact weedkillers, which simply kill the leaves and stems they touch.

• Systemic total weedkillers kill foliage, stems and roots of annual and, more usefully, difficult perennial weeds. They are used to kill weeds in areas where there are no garden plants, particularly if you are starting to prepare the ground for a new planting. They can also be used on perennial weeds in mature borders if applied carefully and selectively with a hand sprayer or brush. Some weeds may need two treatments.

• Contact total weedkillers affect any green tissue they touch, killing annual weeds, which have no perennial roots, but only the top-growth of perennial weeds. They have limited use in perennial plantings.

• Systemic selective weedkillers have limited use in perennial borders, being used mostly for killing broad-leaved weeds in lawns. In general, weedkillers are of most value in the early stages of preparing a border and as a spot treatment to kill individual perennial weeds found growing in mature borders.

• **Guidelines for using weedkillers**

• Always read the instructions on the pack and follow them carefully.

• Never increase the concentration at which you apply weedkiller: it will not necessarily work better.

• Unless using the appropriate selective weedkiller, always ensure that none falls on your perennials.

• Use a spot treatment, using a hand sprayer or brush, whenever possible.

• If spraying, always choose a cool dry windless day.

Weeds and their roots

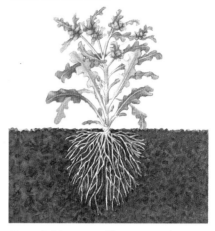

Groundsel has many fibrous roots that carry a lot of soil; shake them well.

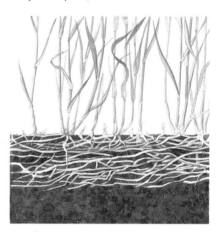

Couch grass roots make a dense mass; almost every small piece will grow.

Dandelions have a stout taproot that shoots again if the top is broken off.

STAKING

When plants growing in the wild fall over, it usually makes little difference to their general health. But, in the garden you want your plants to look their best, and supporting perennials is an important part of their care. The tendency to flop is increased by the fact that, in rich garden soils, plants tend to grow taller than they do in the wild; moreover, varieties bred for their large or double flowers are also naturally less self-supporting.

MATERIALS

Brushwood Traditionally, twiggy branches from deciduous trees and shrubs were used to support perennials. They had the advantage of looking natural and not spoiling the look of the border; also, local forests provided an annual supply that could be cut each winter. In some areas, brushwood is still available, often from local conservation organizations, and some gardeners with plenty of space plant hazel specifically to supply plant supports. If you choose to do this, cut the twigs to a little less than the eventual height of the plant to be supported. Then, when the plant is still less than a quarter of its final height, push the twigs into place in a ring around the edge of the clump; large clumps also benefit from a few pieces being placed within the clump. When pushed in firmly, the tops of the brushwood should be about three-quarters of the eventual height of the plant. To complete the operation, loop string from one brushwood stem to the next to give extra strength. Brushwood will often last for a second year; at the end of the season, when the perennials are cut down, remove the brushwood, cut off the base of the stem that has been in the soil, and store the rest in a dry shed for the following year.

Canes and string In gardens where brushwood is not available, bamboo canes and string make a practical alternative. Choose canes a little less than the eventual height of the plant. Spacing them evenly around the clump about 38–45cm (15–18in) apart, push them in by about a quarter of their depth. Place a rubber eye-protector on the top of each cane. Next, run the string all the way round, looping it around each cane and then taking it across the centre of the clump from cane to cane. The result will be a ring of canes and string around the clump, with a crossing pattern of strings over the clump itself. This arrangement ensures both the edge and the centre of the clump are supported. One lower piece of string can be put in place first, with another higher up as the plants grow. At the end of the season the canes can be rubbed down and stored in a dry place for the following year; they will usually last at least two or three years.

Peonies and lupins need support or they will blow over in the wind or collapse under the weight of rain. The simplest system is to use canes and string.

Metal supports Ever since the 19th century steel hoops or mesh frames have been manufactured specifically for use in gardens in order to support plants, and these are the easiest of all supports to use. They come in three forms. One consists of two uprights with a loop fixed between them and is best used to prevent naturally floppy plants from falling forward too far. Another form is a wire mesh mounted on four legs that you place over the clump early in the season; the plant grows through the mesh as the season progresses. A third type consists of a series of interconnecting stakes and cross-pieces.

All of these forms of support have the advantages of being quick to fit over the plants, needing no special preparation, and lasting for many years if well cleaned at the end of the growing season. But they are less versatile than brushwood or canes, and more expensive.

Other plants The most natural supports, especially for climbers, are other plants. Perennial climbers like *Lathyrus latifolius* can be planted under stout shrubs like elders and

Staking methods

Brushwood: Place the cane in the soil so that it is close to the plant, but not so close that it damages the bulb or roots. A wire hoop can be fixed around the stem and adjusted for height.

Canes and string: Push bamboo canes firmly into the soil around the plant, and twist string between them to form a cat's cradle. If the plant is a large one, use some additional canes in the middle of the clump for extra support.

Metal supports: Place the supports around the outside of the plant to make a continuous support that follows the outline of the clump. Simply link the hook of one support into the loop of the next.

Tying individually: Plants with tall spires of flowers can be tied to individual canes with soft garden twine. Make a figure eight between the stem and the cane to prevent chafing, then tie the knot behind the cane.

they will grow up through the branches, which support them. Smaller climbers, such as herbaceous clematis and *Codonopsis clematidea*, can be trained effectively through dwarf shrubs like potentillas.

TIMING

The most important rule is always to stake plants before they need it. Nothing looks worse than a plant that has collapsed and is then tied up to its supports afterwards. A plant that has grown through its supports will eventually look so natural that it appears unsupported; this is the ideal. Staking early is crucial, but means that the stakes themselves will dominate the border for some time, until hidden by the plants. Because plants grow at different rates, it is impossible to be specific about exactly when to stake, and a balance must be struck between putting supports in place (a) early enough to be really effective and (b) not so early that the stakes are obtrusive for too long.

TECHNIQUE

Most plants that grow into increasing clumps do not need to have their stems supported individually – the clump as a whole can be supported. Some plants, *Crambe cordifolia*, for example, appreciate a single tall cane to support each stem. In windy situations delphiniums, too, can be staked in this way. The drawback with staking individual stems is not only the time it takes and the cost of the canes but the fact that, even when the plants are in full flower, the canes may show. Another disadvantage is that tall, top-heavy flower stems can snap at the point where they are tied to the cane. In general, it is preferable to provide support for a whole clump rather than for individual stems.

DEADHEADING

There are three reasons why the removal of dead flowers from perennials is a good thing. First, many perennials will continue to produce more flowers if the old ones are removed regularly. If dying flowers are left on the plant, a great deal of its energy goes into the development of seedpods, which usually add nothing to its attractiveness. If the dead flowers are removed, however, this energy is usually diverted into producing more flowers; in some perennials, while deadheading may not result in more flowers, it will encourage a mass of fresh new foliage. The second reason for deadheading is simply tidiness. Gardeners vary in their attitude to this: some hardly notice a few dead heads, others pounce with the secateurs as soon as petals drop in their eagerness to keep borders looking neat. The final reason for deadheading is that many plants produce so much seed that their seedlings can be a nuisance. Foxgloves, alchemillas and lamiums, for example, can become weeds if their seedheads are not removed.

In some plants such as ornamental grasses it is often more important to leave the dead seedheads on the plants for their attractive decorative effect in the autumn and winter months than to cut them for the sake of tidiness.

DEADHEADING DIFFERENT PERENNIALS

Perennials can be divided into two main groups. Those like phlox, salvia and anthemis, which produce leaves on the lower part of their stems and flowers at the top, should have the dead flower heads cut off just above the leaves. On the other hand, plants like hardy geraniums, pulmonarias and hellebores, which carry flowers on relatively bare stems with the leaves growing separately from the

Deadheading plants, such as this anthemis, as the petals drop not only improves the look of the plant but also encourages further flowering.

Deadheading

Flowers on individual stems are snipped off above foliage or a branch.

When flowers come in spikes, the whole spike can be cut off above the basal leaves.

Plants with a few large flowers can be deadheaded individually as each fades.

base, should have the old flower heads cut out at ground level.

Perennials vary so much, however, that it is worth considering a few groups separately:

• Delphiniums, which produce their flowers in spikes, should have the whole spike cut out low down, but above most of the foliage, when the last flowers fade. Cutting the spike out at ground level will encourage a second flowering, but this may be at the expense of good flowers the following year.

• Some plants, like hardy geraniums, doronicums, astrantias and alchemillas, can be cut right to the ground after the main flush of flower and will then produce lush new foliage, which may be followed by more flowers. Ensure that the plants are kept moist immediately after they are cut back.

• Hardy chrysanthemums and other plants that produce a long succession of flowers from the same flower head should have the individual flowers snipped out as they fade, then the whole flower head cut off when all the flowers are over.

• Oriental poppies produce single flowers on bare stems and should have the stems cut out at ground level as soon as the petals drop. Their leaves die away soon after, at which time they too can be cleared away.

• Plants with large numbers of very small flowers, like gypsophilas, are impossible to deadhead individually. Some gardeners simply leave them untouched; others clip them over.

RETAINING SEEDHEADS

Although it is generally wise to cut off dead flowers, some plants are so attractive in seed that the seedheads are best left in place. For example, the seedheads of many grasses can remain a feature until well into the winter; the fluffy heads of pulsatillas and herbaceous clematis are very pretty; and the berries of *Iris foetidissima* are its most colourful feature. Another time for being cautious about deadheading is when you

would like a plant to spread by seed or when you wish to collect seed from plants to give away or to raise seedlings yourself. In this case, a few seedheads can be left in place.

REPLANTING

After growing in the same place for some years, many perennials begin to deteriorate. Growth becomes less vigorous, stems shorter, foliage less luxuriant and flowering less prolific.

WHY REPLANT?

Perennials deteriorate partly because their roots exhaust the supplies of plant foods in the soil. Another reason is that, as the plants spread outwards, their centre becomes starved, leaving a ring of relatively healthy growth surrounding a weak centre. This creates an uneven clump. As this growth takes place, the overall size of the clump increases so that it becomes too large for its position. Plants that have a strongly spreading habit, such as Oriental poppies and *Campanula takesimana*, may begin to invade their neighbours. The solution to all these problems is to dig up the whole clump, improve the soil and replant healthy pieces in the required area. Although generous mulching and feeding may keep a plant healthy when it would otherwise languish, they only hasten the day when the plant outgrows its space and needs replanting in a smaller group.

Lifting and replanting

1 *Dig up long-established plants with a fork, retaining as much root as possible.*

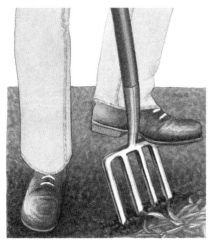

3 *Replant the chosen pieces in soil which has been improved with organic matter.*

WHAT TO REPLANT

Plants that both grow quickly and are hungry feeders need replanting most frequently. Some perennials should be divided every other year, while those which naturally form tight, dense clumps can be left to develop into substantial specimens.

Plants needing frequent replanting include *Anthemis*, *Aster*, *Bellis*, *Campanula* (particularly *C. glomerata*, *C. takesimana* and 'Elizabeth'). Also

2 *From the resulting shoots choose healthy growth from the edge of the clump.*

4 *The newly replanted area showing seven evenly spaced leafy shoots.*

Doronicum, *Iris*, *Lobelia*, *Monarda*, *Tanacetum* and *Viola*.

Plants best left to form mature clumps, and not be split, include *Bergenia*, *Clematis*, and *Eremurus*, *Euphorbia characias*, *Foeniculum*, *Helleborus*, *Hosta*, *Kniphofia*, *Paeonia* and *Rheum*.

TIMING AND TECHNIQUE

The rules for the timing of replanting are much the same as those for planting (see p.30): some plants prefer to be lifted and replanted in the spring while others prefer the autumn.

The technique is not difficult. First, dig up the whole clump and lay the plants on a polythene sheet nearby, covered with polythene or damp sacking to protect them while you work on the soil. Then fork the soil over or dig it in the same way as when preparing for planting new plants (see p.29). The dug-up plants should then be examined and, using the traditional two-forks technique (see p.66), be broken up into manageable pieces. Any dead, weak or unproductive growth, especially from the centre of the clump, should be discarded, while the strongest pieces from the edge should be retained.

The treatment of the remaining plant material varies enormously, since different plants grow in a variety ways. (See the section on propagation by division pp.65–67.) If you simply want to replant an existing clump into its original space rather than expand its area, you can split off pieces with a number of strong shoots using the two-forks technique, bare hands and secateurs, and then replant.

Right: Mature clumps, such as these, will deteriorate unless the plants are lifted, divided, and replanted regularly.

PESTS AND DISEASES

However well you look after your perennials, they may still suffer from pests and diseases. You can, though, take steps to prevent these attacks. If pests and diseases do strike, choosing the appropriate method of control and going about it in the right way can greatly reduce the damage.

PRINCIPLES OF PEST AND DISEASE CONTROL

It is useful to understand the general principles of pest and disease control; in particular, some knowledge of how to prevent trouble arising will ensure that far fewer plants are attacked in the first place.

PREVENTION
The first principle to keep in mind is that a healthy plant is less likely to suffer from pests or diseases than a sickly one, and will also prove more resilient if it should be attacked. Follow these rules as a first step in preventing perennials from being attacked by pests and diseases:

• Always grow plants in the type of soil they prefer. For example, a plant needing good drainage will be more likely to suffer from root rot if grown in damp soil.
• Always grow plants in the amount of light they prefer. For example, a sun-loving plant may be more likely to suffer from rot if it is grown in full shade.
• Ensure plants are given the feeding and watering that they require and remember that plants vary in their requirements: treat each specimen as an individual.
• When they are available, choose varieties resistant to problems that have been troublesome in the past.

Another important way to prevent pest and disease attack is to reduce the possibility of infection:

• Keep the garden weed-free. Weeds can be reservoirs of infection, and insects and fungal diseases may spread from weeds to reinfect border plants after you think you've just solved all your problems.
• Do not leave garden debris lying in piles in odd corners of the garden: compost it.
• Inspect all new plants carefully to ensure that fresh pest and disease problems are not introduced from neighbours or nurseries.
• Be aware of problems suffered by neighbours, and be prepared to take preventative action.
• Recognize how the weather may affect your plants. For example, in long, hot, dry spells powdery mildew and red spider mite are more likely to be troublesome.

CONTROLLING PESTS AND DISEASES
However thoroughly you try to prevent problems, plants will still be attacked. The most important way to ensure that they suffer as little as possible is to be watchful. Dealing with the very first signs of a problem, before it has had time to cause too much damage, will ensure your plants remain as healthy as possible. As soon as you notice worrying symptoms, identify the problem, then treat it promptly.

Once plants have been attacked there are three practical ways of controlling pests and diseases: cultural methods, which involve practical techniques like simply picking off caterpillars; biological methods, which include introducing a predatory insect to kill pests (although there are more applications for this in the greenhouse than in the perennial border); and chemical-control methods, which use chemical pesticides and fungicides.

Cultural control This includes many of the techniques already described for ensuring plants thrive, but there are a number of other valuable procedures:
• Examine the leaves of susceptible plants for the egg clusters of caterpillars, and then squash them before they hatch.
• Pick the caterpillars off plants whose leaves are being eaten.
• Fork over the soil between plants in order to expose soil-living pests to predatory birds.
• Pick off leaves affected by leaf miners, which burrow under the skin of the leaf.
• Collect slugs and snails by torchlight on damp evenings when they are most easily visible.
• Erect fences or put up netting to prevent attack from large animals, such as rabbits or birds.
• Try scaring devices, like silhouettes of cats or birds of prey: these can be useful in some situations.

Biological control These techniques involve using a creature that does not harm plants to control another that does. These beneficial creatures are either parasites or predators, and even simple measures like encouraging garden birds can often have a noticeable effect on the caterpillar and aphid population.
• Provide nestboxes, birdtables, shelter and winter food to encourage garden birds.
• Use one of the biological controls available for slugs, there are two

basic types: one which you can buy, works by disrupting their breeding; the other on sale is actually a parasite that penetrates the slug body and infects them with disease.

• Encourage beneficial insects by growing their food plants. For example, hoverflies, which help in the control of aphids, appreciate fennel and annual convolvulus.

• Choose from a number of forms of biological control available for controlling red spider mite, whitefly and other pests in the greenhouse during propagation.

• If mice are a problem, keep a cat.

Chemical control Various chemicals are available to control pests and diseases. Some of these are derived from natural substances while others are synthetic. Even the natural, organic chemicals can be dangerous if used incorrectly or at the wrong dosage. In general, use chemical controls only as a last resort, when the build-up of the pest has reached unacceptable levels. Be sure the chemical you intend to use is the right one for the problem; as an obvious example, insecticides are no use against a fungal attack.

USING CHEMICALS SAFELY

• Always read the instructions on the pack and follow them precisely.

• Always wear any protective clothing recommended. Wear gloves when handling concentrate.

• Never mix a stronger concentration than stipulated: you may damage the plant and still not solve the problem.

• Wherever possible use granular formulations rather than concentrated liquids; try to choose pre-measured chemicals or those supplied with a measuring device.

• Never mix different chemicals together unless the pack instructions specifically suggest it.

• Never inhale the vapour while spraying and keep as much skin as possible covered.

• Store chemicals in a locked cupboard. Keep pets and children away from the area when spraying.

• Always spray in calm conditions, preferably on an overcast day. If you must spray open flowers, try to do so in the evening to prevent the chemical affecting bees.

• Try to cover the whole plant with spray, including the upper- and under-side of the leaves.

Selinum wallichianum attracts many insects that are useful in the garden.

THE ORGANIC APPROACH

Many gardeners now feel that using garden chemicals to control pests and diseases is unnecessary, and that these problems can be dealt with effectively without using products that might harm pets and wildlife. For many gardeners, the organic approach works very well, although it is often true that gardening without chemicals is more time-consuming than simply resorting to a spray. The use of organic methods can be divided into six parts:

• Choosing resistant varieties.
• Good growing techniques.
• Encouraging natural predators.
• Cultural control.
• Biological control.
• Using safe sprays.

CHOOSING RESISTANT VARIETIES

Unfortunately, although many types of food crops, like vegetables and fruits, have been developed to be resistant to important pests and diseases, few hardy perennial cultivars have been specially developed with this in mind. This is partly because it can be a long, time-consuming and expensive enterprise to develop such plants and partly because the same disease can vary very slightly from one part of the country to another, so a variety resistant in one area may be attacked in another. One approach that can help is to plant varieties that local gardeners find are able to resist infection successfully, even if they are not generally described as resistant. Another, of course, is to seek out those varieties which have been found to have general resistance. For example, while purple delphiniums like 'Bruce' and 'Chelsea Star' are usually very susceptible to mildew, others,

such as the blue 'Loch Leven' and the deep pink 'Rosemary Brock' are among the most resistant. The Star Series of monardas, like the pink 'Pisces' and purple 'Scorpio', are generally resistant to mildew. While most varieties of *Phlox paniculata* are unfortunately susceptible to mildew, all the various forms of *Phlox maculata* are resistant.

GOOD GROWING TECHNIQUES

All the ideas discussed under Prevention (see p.56) are doubly important when avoiding the use of garden chemicals. If the plants are growing well and are robust they are less likely to be attacked by disease and will be more able to survive the infection should they be so.

ENCOURAGING NATURAL PREDATORS

A large number of creatures that live in the garden can be a great help in controlling pests. Sometimes predators and pests will set up an uneasy balance naturally, with just enough pests around to keep the predators fed, but not so many as to cause much

damage. But the pests often multiply too quickly for their enemies to deal with, so gardeners must intervene by setting out to attract beneficial creatures. Here are some stratagems:

• Plant annual plants like annual convolvulus, poached-egg plant (*Limnanthes*) and buckwheat (*Fagopyrum* spp.) among perennials. These attract hoverflies, whose larvae are useful in the garden because they eat aphids in large numbers. Perennials like purple-leafed fennel and *Selinum tenuifolium* likewise attract hoverflies.

• Leave a stack of sticks in a corner of the garden where hedgehogs can hibernate, as they eat a great many slugs and snails.

• Set out a shallow dish of water and some flat rocks to attract toads, which eat slugs.

• During the winter months, hang up nuts near perennial borders so that blue tits might be attracted. The birds will eat overwintering insect eggs, aphids and larvae on the plants while waiting their turn at the nuts.

• Leave logs in any out-of-the-way corners so as to provide cover for carnivorous beetles.

The poached-egg plant (*Limnanthes douglasii*) attracts hoverflies, whose larvae are useful in the garden because they eat large numbers of aphids.

CULTURAL CONTROL

Cultural methods, like picking off caterpillars and collecting slugs by hand, can be effective ways of controlling pests, but it is important to check plants frequently to be sure of catching and dealing with infestations before they cause too much damage. This can be time-consuming, and a few days' bad weather or a weekend away can result in problems building up. (See also p.56.)

BIOLOGICAL CONTROL

Most biological controls have the enormous advantage of affecting only the target pest, leaving beneficial insects or other wildlife unscathed. Unfortunately, most work best in the greenhouse or conservatory; but four are useful out of doors:

• The eelworm that carries the bacterium to control vine weevil and some other soil-dwelling pests.
• The predator that controls red spider mite.
• The eelworm that infects slugs with a deadly bacterium.
• The bacterium that kills caterpillars; perennials are attacked by a wide range of caterpillars, large and small, but all can be controlled by spraying plants with this bacterial preparation. (See also p.56.)

USING SAFE SPRAYS

Many organic gardeners are happy to use natural pesticides; indeed, most associations of organic gardeners approve a certain number. It must be remembered, however, that a substance of natural origin will not necessarily be harmless to people or wildlife. For example, the plant extract rotenone, although a natural material and an effective treatment for a wide range of pests, is dangerous to fish. The safest sprays are the soap extracts used as insecticides, but they have the disadvantage of being indiscriminate in their action, harming a wide range of insects.

PESTS COMMON TO PERENNIALS

Pest problems are caused by insects and other small creatures eating the plants themselves, sucking their sap, or creating problems indirectly, for example by undermining roots or spreading disease.

actual size: 6mm (¼in)

ANTS

Ants excavate the soil from among the roots of perennials. They also 'farm' aphids that provide secretions on which ants feed by carrying the aphids to new shoots, where the aphids eat and proceed to multiply.

Damage: Plants grow poorly and collapse in hot weather due to drought caused by removal of soil from roots.

Prevention: Vigilance and prompt control to reduce the spread of ants.

Ensure that containers are stood on blocks to deter infestation.

Control: Pouring boiling water into nests is sometimes recommended but rarely affords complete extermination. Powders and baits are effective, but it is important to continue treatment until all activity has ceased. You can lift precious plants that have become severely affected, wash all soil off their roots, cut down the shoots, pot the plants and grow on for replanting.

actual size: 3mm (⅛in)

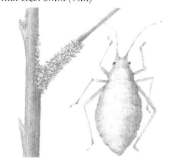

APHIDS

Aphids cause damage by sucking sap from their hosts. Some types attack a wide variety of plants; others are more selective. Aphids also transmit viral diseases.

Damage: Stunted growth and deformed shoots, leaves, buds and sometimes flowers. Groups of insects congregate together, especially under leaves and on shoot tips.

Prevention: Encourage garden predators like ladybirds, hoverflies and lacewings. Avoid using broad-spectrum pesticides, which kill these beneficial predators as well as aphids.

Control: Spray with insecticidal soap or with an aphid-specific insecticide. Be sure to spray the buds, the undersides of the leaves and the shoot tips with insecticide as this is where the insects congregate.

actual size:
10mm (½in)

CAPSIDS

The tiny pale green grubs and the larger green adults attack a wide range of perennials, particularly early in the season. They suck sap and are often concentrated in the unfurling shoot tips.

Damage: Small, rather ragged holes, often edged in yellow, are found in the new leaves around the shoot tips, often becoming larger as the leaves begin to expand.

Prevention: Prompt attention at the first signs of attack.

Control: Pinch out shoot tips or spray with a systemic insecticide; contact insecticides do not always reach the grubs inside the shoot tips.

actual size:
2cm (¾in)

CHAFER GRUBS

These soft, white, brown-headed C-shaped grubs eventually develop into beetles. They attack roots, causing plants to wilt or grow poorly.

Damage: Grubs eat through roots and also eat bulbs and tubers. They are especially troublesome when lawn or grassland is dug up for flowerbeds.

Prevention: Regular cultivation exposes them to birds.

Control: Use a soil insecticide when planting. Little can be done when established plants are attacked.

actual size:
5cm (2in)

CRANE FLY LARVAE

These soft, fat grey-brown grubs are the larvae of the cranefly, or daddy-longlegs, and are most troublesome when new flowerbeds are made in a lawn or meadow; they may also cause problems in beds near rough grass.

Damage: Plants appear weak and may collapse completely or partially because of the grubs feeding on the roots below the soil.

Prevention: Repeated cultivation before planting exposes the grubs to predatory birds.

Control: Soil insecticides and some slug killers also control cranefly larvae.

actual size: 5cm (2in)

CUTWORMS

These fat grey or brown grubs eventually hatch into moths.

Damage: Stems are eaten through at ground level. Cutworms most often seen on young plants and seedlings.

Prevention: Cultivate the soil in winter to expose the grubs to feeding birds.

Control: Use a soil insecticide when planting young plants or sowing seed.

actual size:
1.5–2cm
(⁶⁄₁₀–¼in)

EARWIGS

These small, brown, mobile insects have noticeable pincers at the rear.

Damage: Flowers with fleshy petals, especially double chrysanthemums and dahlias, are eaten.

Prevention: Keep the garden tidy and promptly remove any debris.

Control: Trap the insects in pieces of orange peel laid on the soil, in rolls of corrugated paper, or in inverted flowerpots stuffed with straw. Alternatively, spray with a systemic insecticide in the evening.

actual size: 1mm
(0.004in)

EELWORMS

These microscopic worm-like creatures feed on stems or leaves. Different species attack different plants.

Damage: Causes distortion of the foliage in phlox; browning of lower leaves in penstemon.

Prevention: Buy healthy stock. Propagate phlox by root cuttings and penstemon only by shoot tips.

Control: Apart from destroying infected plants, there is no control.

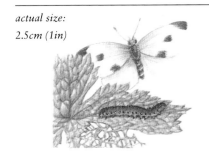

actual size:
2.5cm (1in)

LEAF CATERPILLARS

The caterpillars of a wide variety of butterflies and moths can attack perennials. They come in many sizes and colours. Some feed only on specific plants, but others are less fussy.
Damage: Leaves, flowers, buds and perhaps stems are eaten, sometimes from the edge, or less discriminately.
Prevention: Squash the clusters of eggs if you find them on the undersides of leaves, and encourage insect-eating birds like blue tits.
Control: Pick off caterpillars by hand; spray with a parasitic bacterium or with an appropriate insecticide.

LEAF MINERS

When tiny white dots appear on leaves it is a sign that an adult fly has already laid its eggs.
Damage: Eggs hatch into small grubs which tunnel just under the leaf surface, leaving blisters or a maze of tunnels. In several species the larvae make large brown, hollow, blisters, which are known as blotch mines. Leaf miners will attack most plants but chrysanthemums and aquilegias are especially prone to attack. Damage is not normally critical.
Prevention: Control weeds in the daisy family, like sowthistle and groundsel, which may host this pest.
Control: Pick off affected leaves. Chemical control is difficult; inspect susceptible plants regularly and spray with a systemic insecticide at the first sign of any tiny white dots appearing.

actual size: 4.5cm (1¾in)

MILLIPEDES

These slim, slow-moving, usually black grubs coil up when disturbed. Do not confuse them with the very active, usually reddish centipedes, which are useful carnivores.
Damage: Seedlings and the fleshy parts of plants are eaten.
Prevention: Clear away garden debris. Look in dark hiding places.
Control: Soil insecticide can be forked into the soil when planting.

actual size:
9cm (3¼in)

SLUGS AND SNAILS

These familiar creatures, which come in all shapes and sizes, can cause an enormous amount of damage. It is said that snails are more common on limy soils and slugs more troublesome on acid soils, but many gardens suffer from too many of both.
Damage: Seedlings, new shoots and any soft and succulent growths, including flowers, are eaten, as are roots and fruits.
Prevention: Keep the garden tidy; clear away long grass and other cover which provides damp spots where slugs and snails can hide themselves during the day.
Control: Many types available, from orange skins or traps baited with beer laid on the soil to biological controls.

actual size:
0.5–1mm
(0.002–0.004in)

SPIDER MITES

An almost invisible pest that can be very destructive in hot, dry seasons through sucking sap and disfiguring plants with webs.
Damage: Fine, pale mottling of leaves, followed by the development of grey webs. Spider mites particularly attack crocosmias, penstemons and especially primroses, which may be killed. Usually more troublesome in glasshouses and conservatories.
Prevention: Do not plant susceptible varieties in hot, dry conditions.
Control: Control is very difficult. Some insecticides are partially effective.

actual size:
6mm (¼in)

SPITTLEBUGS, OR FROGHOPPERS

These small green bugs suck sap and surround themselves with white, protective foam known as cuckoo spit which can be found on many plants in late spring to early summer. Eventually they become an insect resembling a tiny green frog.

Damage: Attacks a wide range of perennials but usually more unsightly than damaging. May cause distortion and some wilting.
Prevention: None.
Control: Wash off with a jet of water from a hose, or pick off by hand. Alternatively, spray with a systemic insecticide if the attack is severe.

actual size:
8mm (⅓₁₀in)

VINE WEEVIL

This has become an increasingly troublesome pest because the chemical controls previously used by nurserymen have been taken off the market. Fortunately, a substitute has now been introduced.

Damage: Adult weevils eat foliage, characteristically by taking semi-circular notches out of the leaf edges. The orange-headed white grubs feed on roots and tubers, especially damaging primulas, cyclamens, heucheras and tiarellas. They are more often seen in the greenhouse, but increasingly are found outside.

Prevention: Wash the soil off susceptible plants and re-pot in new compost.
Control: Some insecticides will control adults. Use biological control: there is a parasitic eelworm that seeks out and penetrates the vine weevil larvae.

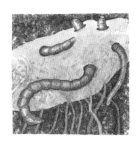

actual size:
2.5cm (1in)

WIREWORMS

These slim, creamy grubs eventually develop into click beetles, and are especially common in new flowerbeds made in grass and lawns.

Damage: Holes are eaten in fleshy roots, bulbs and tubers, usually weakening the plant rather than killing it.
Prevention: Dig over a number of times before planting so that predators are given an opportunity to eat them. Regular hoeing on established borders will reduce numbers. Control weeds, on which they may also feed.
Control: Protect individual plants by forking in a soil insecticide when planting or by forking it in lightly around established plants.

DISEASES COMMON TO PERENNIALS

Diseases are caused by mainly fungal organisms. The likelihood of disease is increased by extremes of weather and by poor or inappropriate conditions.

DAMPING OFF

This problem is caused by soil-living fungi, the presence of which can be detected only by the damage they do. It occurs when seedlings are grown in wet, compacted compost and when seed is sown too thickly.

Damage: Seedlings collapse as the result of fungus attack, usually at the soil surface. Perennials raised in a propagator or warm greenhouse are the most likely to suffer.
Prevention: Always use clean pots or trays together with fresh, bagged seed compost; never use garden soil. Do not overfirm the seed compost; sow seeds thinly; water with tap water and not water from a water barrel. Handle seedlings gently when pricking out.
Control: Water the compost with a liquid copper fungicide after sowing and when seedlings have emerged.

GREY MOULD, OR BOTRYTIS

This widespread problem is less troublesome in the perennial border than it is in the greenhouse. The fungus is especially virulent in cool, damp conditions but some plants may suffer even in high summer if conditions are damp and humid.

Damage: Especially dangerous to fully double flowers with soft or succulent petals; dahlias and chrysanthemums are particularly susceptible. Sometimes the infection is confined to spotting, but it may attack old flowers as the petals collapse, then spread through the flower stem.

Prevention: Regular deadheading of susceptible plants is crucial. Remove flowers which have been damaged by bad weather or frost.

Control: Spray the plant with a systemic fungicide.

LEAF SPOT

This problem is caused by a number of different fungi and bacteria, each of which attacks only one type of plant. It is usually most troublesome in warm, wet weather.

Damage: Dark blotches or spots disfigure the foliage of a wide range of perennials. In some cases there is little serious damage, but severe infections can be fatal.

Prevention: Picking off the infected foliage to restrict the spread of the disease is the only real prevention.

Control: Systemic fungicides are sometimes effective.

MILDEW

Powdery mildew is especially troublesome in hot, dry weather, on shade-loving plants growing in full sun and in locations with poor air circulation. Pulmonarias, aquilegias, and asters, are among many affected.

Damage: Fungus attacks foliage, buds, flowers and stems, covering them with a white coating. Leaves may then turn yellow and the whole plant may die.

Prevention: Plant susceptible varieties in the conditions they prefer. Divide them frequently to keep clumps small.

Control: Remove worst affected plants. Spray with a systemic insecticide.

ROOT ROT

Many perennials are subject to root rot caused by a variety of fungi, and this is often the cause of seemingly inexplicable collapse.

Damage: Soil-borne fungi attack roots causing reduced growth and leaf yellowing at first, then poor flowering and sometimes, eventually, sudden collapse.

Prevention: Keep plants growing well in conditions they enjoy. Some forms of root-rotting fungi can lie dormant in the soil for years, so never replace an affected plant with another of the same type.

Control: No chemical treatment is yet available to control this disease.

VIRUSES

These microscopic organisms can cause severe damage. Destructive strains are increasingly common.

Damage: Viruses can cause a wide range of symptoms, including stunted growth, distorted flowers, foliage and stems, pale or yellow streaking and mottling in many different forms.

Prevention: Sterilize secateurs or knife when taking cuttings of susceptible plants, as the virus is spread in sap. Control aphids, which are the main carriers of viral diseases.

Control: At an early stage, dig up and burn any infected plants.

PROPAGATION

For many gardeners, propagation is the most exciting of the practical tasks associated with perennials, but it can also create doubts and uncertainties. Fortunately, hardy perennials are among the easiest of all plants to propagate, and most can be increased using basic techniques without the need for too much special equipment. There are two main types of propagation: by division or cuttings, and by seed. Propagating perennials by division, by stem cuttings or by root cuttings results in the new plants being exact replicas of their parent; plants raised from seed may be identical to both the parent plant and to each other, but conversely they may vary significantly.

DIVISION

Division is the most basic and most valuable of all methods of propagating hardy perennials. No special equipment is required, success is all but guaranteed, and the method is suitable for the vast majority of perennial plants. Many perennials also benefit from being dug up, split into small pieces and replanted every few years, even if there is no requirement to increase stock (see p.54). The increased vigour that results from fresh divisions often means that the plants are more productive.

SEASON
Perennials are best divided either in spring or in autumn. (Many can also be split in the winter, but more losses are likely at that time of year.) The majority of varieties will divide well in either season, but there are other factors to consider.

Where the soil is unusually heavy and in areas of high rainfall, spring is usually the best season. If you divide and replant in autumn, the new divisions must spend three or four months in cold, wet soil before it is warm enough for them to grow, and

this can lead to losses. In very dry soils and in areas of unusually low spring rainfall, new divisions may be slow to establish themselves without adequate moisture; in these circumstances dividing in autumn is best.

A few plants have distinct seasonal preferences. Bearded irises, for example, are usually best divided in summer, soon after flowering, as this is the season at which a burst of root growth takes place. New roots can

then grow into the soil at once, and this allows the plants to settle down quickly. Hellebores are best divided in late summer or early in autumn, just before their main burst of root growth, while primroses are best split in late spring or early summer, after flowering. Peonies are also best divided at this season to give them time to make new roots before winter.

Rather more plants prefer to be divided in spring, and they fall into two groups. First there are those that naturally flower very late in the year and so may well be at their best in the autumn, when other plants are ready for division. Second there are those that are unhappy spending the wet winter months without a well established root system.

Plants to divide in spring include *Agapanthus, Alstroemeria, Anthemis, Aster, Chelone, Delphinium, Dendranthema, Gaillardia, Helenium, Helianthus, Imperata, Kniphofia,*

Left: For a varied and colourful display fill your border with home-grown perennials.

Some perennials, such as these asters and sedums, are best divided in spring, as they are often still in full flower in the autumn.

Lobelia, Morina, Sedum, Tanacetum, Tricyrtis and *Viola*. A few plants, while not difficult to divide, make better specimens in the garden if they are left in place to mature. Plants best left undisturbed for some years include *Bergenia, Clematis, Cortaderia, Helleborus, Hosta, Miscanthus* and *Paeonia*.

TECHNIQUE

Dealing with the whole plant Use the two-forks system. Take a digging fork and dig up the whole clump with as much root as possible. Borrow another, similar fork from a neighbour and insert the two forks vertically, back to back, through the middle of the clump. Some effort may be required to penetrate plants with tight root systems. Now press the handles of the forks together. This results in the tines forcing the two halves of the plant apart. Working the handles backwards and forwards should eventually split the plant into two pieces. The process can be repeated on each half, and the resultant pieces can either be pulled apart by hand or cut up with secateurs.

Strong, vigorous pieces, usually from the edge of the clump, are the best choice for propagation. Each piece should have one or two strong buds or emerging shoots and a good portion of young root system attached. Trim the chosen pieces with secateurs to remove any dead foliage, old or dead roots, and ragged cuts. The size of the pieces selected depends, to some extent, on whether they are to be replanted in the open or potted up and kept in a frame or cold greenhouse. If the aim is simply to extend a clump in the border or make a second clump elsewhere in the garden, the pieces chosen can each have three or four shoots or buds and an established root system, although the majority of roots should be relatively young. Try to use material from the edge of the clump. These pieces can be planted into the open ground at once, as described on page 31. If a large number of new plants are required, perhaps to provide stock for a plant sale, smaller divisions can be used; it may be necessary to cut the best growth into small pieces, each with a single, good shoot

and a section of root. It is advisable to wash the soil off any pieces which are to be potted to prevent the soil in the pot from being contaminated with pests or worms. These portions will establish well in 9cm or 12.5cm (3½in or 5in) pots of proprietary potting compost, as long as they are protected from hot sun and drying winds, for example in a greenhouse or frame for the first few weeks.

Weak plants and plants you wish to increase quickly from a young original plant can be propagated in the same way. Very small pieces, which may struggle to survive when replanted directly into the garden, often establish themselves well in pots if given a little protection. In some cases it may be necessary to use old growth from the centre of the clump. While this may be tough or weak, when potted up and protected it often recovers sufficiently to make a good young plant.

Dealing with part of the plant Sometimes, if only a small number of new plants are required, it is not necessary to dig up a whole plant in order to propagate from it, and the

Propagation by division

1 Insert the tines of two forks close together, back to back, in the centre of a clump of perennials.

2 Push the handles together, then work them back and forth to split the crown and tease the roots apart.

3 To provide further divisions, use pruning shears to cut the resulting clumps into smaller pieces, then discard the oldest.

majority of the clump can be left in place. In the case of kniphofias, for example, shoots with roots can be detached from the side of the clump and potted up. Propagating material can be removed from hostas by using a spade to cut out a wedge-shaped section, rather like cutting a slice of cake. The pieces removed are washed and pulled apart, then the individual shoots are potted up; the hole in the main clump is then filled with old potting compost. Shoots with roots can easily be cut from the edge of clumps of some plants, like asters. There is a danger, however, in repeatedly removing propagating material from the edge of a clump. The old original growth in the centre becomes increasingly weak and eventually you may find that, although you have propagated many new plants, the original dies.

STEM CUTTINGS

Raising perennials from cuttings may not be the first method that springs to mind, but it has the great advantage that you can propagate a perennial without having to disturb it by digging it up. A little more equipment is required than for division but, like division, taking cuttings ensures that all the new plants raised will be exactly like their parent.

EQUIPMENT
Cuttings need protection from the harshness of the natural environment to encourage rooting, and this is best provided by a thermostatically controlled propagator. Its clear cover admits light while at the same time creating a humid environment that prevents the cuttings collapsing and dying in the weeks before roots are formed. Its heating element speeds up

Equipment for cuttings

Cuttings often root most quickly in a heated propagator but they should be misted regularly with a sprayer to keep them moist.

Cuttings of many perennials can be rooted under a plastic bag on a windowsill or in the greenhouse.

the rooting process, so that roots are formed before the cuttings rot.

Ideally the propagator should be situated in a greenhouse for extra protection from wind and cold. A sunny windowsill is also an option, although the fact that the cuttings will be lit from just one direction means they may become stretched and weak. In both situations, shading may be required to protect cuttings from bright sunshine, which can cause overheating and scorch foliage.

At a simpler level, it is possible to root some perennials in an unheated propagator; this is more useful in the house, where the environment is naturally warmer. If sited on a windowsill, it can easily be turned to ensure the cuttings are exposed to light on all sides. Perennials can also be rooted indoors or in a heated greenhouse in individual 9cm (3½in) pots, each covered with a clear polythene bag. This method is often successful with the tougher varieties.

SEASON AND TECHNIQUE
Cuttings of hardy perennials are almost always taken in the spring, often the early spring, although a few

can be taken later in the season. The best growth to use for cuttings is the newest spring shoots, soon after they emerge at the base of the plant. Sever each shoot from the plant as near to the base as possible; an artists' scalpel or craft knife is often more effective for cutting away shoots cleanly than a garden knife or secateurs. The size of cuttings required varies from species to species: 5–7.5cm (2–3in) is the usual length, but a slightly shorter cutting is sometimes required for plants which are naturally dwarf.

A few plants, like delphiniums and dahlias, tend to develop a hollow stem as their shoots lengthen. Cuttings with hollow stems rarely root well, so you should use only the shortest, earliest shoots, which still have solid stems. Plants from which cuttings are to be taken should be protected from slugs. When the shoots have grown sufficiently, sever them cleanly and place them immediately in a polythene bag with a label.

Now take the cuttings indoors and trim them at the base, just below a leaf joint. On cuttings of this sort, the leaf joints may well be quite difficult to see, as their leaves are sometimes

Taking cuttings of hardy chrysanthemums

1 *Remove strong young shoots from the base of the plant in spring.*

2 *Trim each cutting just below a leaf joint and trim off any lower leaves.*

3 *Dip the base of each cutting in rooting powder, then insert in a moist compost.*

greatly reduced in size at the base of the stems. Cuttings that have normal leaves at the base should have these nipped off to discourage rotting. Then dip the base of each cutting in rooting powder and insert the cuttings to about half their length in pots of moist compost.

A proprietary rooting or seed compost should be used, never garden soil, although it is often advisable to add extra grit or perlite, at a proportion of anything up to 50 per cent depending on the drainage capacity of the original compost. Relatively small 9cm (3½in) pots are adequate. If there are more cuttings of one variety than will fill a single pot, use two pots rather than a larger one or a seed tray to minimize the risk of any rot spreading between cuttings.

Insert cuttings using a dibber or pencil to make a hole in the compost the same depth as the distance between the base of the cutting and the lowest remaining leaf. Then place each cutting in one of the holes and, when the pot is full, tap it sharply on the table or bench to settle the compost. Do not firm the compost with your fingers. On average, six to ten cuttings will go into a 9cm (3½in) pot, depending on their size. After a thorough watering, place the pots in a propagator; if this has a thermostat, set it to 21°C (70°F). Alternatively, you can stand each pot in a polythene bag and close the top above the tips of the cuttings with a wire tie.

During the period before rooting it is essential to keep the compost moist and the atmosphere around the cuttings humid. Cuttings rooted in an unheated propagator or polythene bag often need little watering until rooting has begun, but they may still require regular spraying with a hand mister containing warm water to keep the air around them damp. Cuttings in a heated propagator will dry out more quickly and will require watering as well as misting.

AFTER ROOTING
Cuttings vary in the time they take to root: while some may root in a week, others may take much longer. Rooting is usually indicated by the shoots' tips beginning to grow, root tips emerging from the drainage holes in the pot, and a slight resistance when the cutting is gently pulled. When the cuttings have developed roots 1–2.5cm (½–1in) long, depending on the size and vigour of the plant, they should be moved into individual pots containing proprietary potting compost. It is advisable not to let the cuttings stay in their original pots for too long after rooting, as this will retard their growth. They should be given protection immediately after potting – in an unheated propagator, for example – and then as they grow they should be moved into increasingly unprotected conditions, or hardened off, before planting out.

OTHER WAYS WITH CUTTINGS
Some perennials can be rooted later in the season, using the same general technique. It is often more convenient to use slightly longer cuttings. While tip cuttings give the best results, it is sometimes also possible to root lower portions of the stems. This technique is especially valuable when you acquire a new variety and wish to make as many offspring as possible in the shortest time. Sometimes it is even possible to root the stems of cut flowers. Penstemons, *Phlox maculata*, variegated forms of *Phlox paniculata*, chrysanthemums, dianthus, achilleas and veronicas can all be propagated from longer stems in this way.

ROOT CUTTINGS

There are a few perennials which are not easy to divide or which cannot be raised from stem or tip cuttings, but which will produce viable shoots from short pieces of root. This tendency is familiar from the more pernicious perennial weeds, but it can be an advantage in the propagation of some perennials, enabling the gardener to propagate large numbers of plants that would otherwise be slow or difficult to increase. It is possible to raise large quantities of certain varieties in a shorter time than is possible by the usual methods. It is not, however, suitable for variegated varieties, as plants grown from root cuttings usually produce green leaves.

TIMING, EQUIPMENT AND TECHNIQUE

Take root cuttings during the late winter or early spring, before the plant naturally starts into growth. A thermostatically controlled propagator is very useful for this technique; if you don't have one, use a cold frame to provide protection until the vulnerable roots have established shoots. The precise techniques vary slightly according to the nature of the plant.

Plants with fat roots Plants like Oriental poppies (*Papaver orientale*) and *Echinops* have fat, fleshy roots. Here the technique is to dig up the plant in late winter and wash off the soil so that healthy roots can easily be identified. Roots about the thickness of a pencil are the most suitable and they should be undamaged and disease-free. Cut off a length of root with sharp secateurs, then immediately cut it into 5cm (2in) lengths. Make a horizontal cut at the end of each piece nearest to the crown of the original plant and make an angled cut at the

Taking root cuttings of Oriental poppies

1 *Lift the plant using a spade, and dig up as much of the root system as possible. Any roots left behind may grow.*

2 *Wash off the soil, then cut off lengths of young healthy roots about the thickness of a pencil. Replant the plant.*

3 *Cut the roots into 5cm (2in) lengths, making a straight cut at the top of each one with a slanting cut at the base.*

4 *Insert each cutting vertically with the straight cut at the top, cover with sand, and place in a propagator or cold frame.*

end nearest the root tips. These cuts will help you identify the top and bottom of each cutting. When a large enough number of cuttings has been taken the plant can be replanted, but try not to take more than a third of its roots for cuttings.

In some cases, you can take root cuttings without digging up the parent plant. Simply scrape the soil away from the roots using a hand fork and your fingers, cut off one or two roots for propagation, and replace the soil. Put the cuttings vertically, no less than 2cm (¾in) apart, in 12.5cm (5in)

pots of proprietary potting compost with the flat cut level with the compost's surface. Cover the cuttings with 6mm (¼in) of compost and a further 6mm (¼in) of grit. Label the pot and stand it in a propagator, with the thermostat set at about 13°C (55°F), or in a cold frame.

Shoots may appear quite soon but, as the roots often have sufficient reserves of nutrients to produce shoots before growing new fibrous root, do not be tempted to pot them on at once. However, when both new roots and new shoots are growing well, the young plants can be potted individually into 9cm (3½in) pots, then grown on during the summer for planting out in the autumn.

PLANTS WITH FIBROUS ROOTS

Plants with fibrous roots, such as phlox, can also be raised from root cuttings, but a variation in technique is required. The plants should be dug up in late winter and the soil then washed off so that the roots are clearly visible. Snip off sections of root 5–7.5cm (2–3in) long for use as cuttings. These may have a few fine, fragile roots attached, and these can be left in place.

The simplest way to deal with these fibrous cuttings is to fill a seed tray with potting compost and lay them out flat on the surface. Cover them with a fine sprinkling of compost and 6mm (¼in) of grit. Next place the tray in a propagator or frame. Pot up the young plants into 9cm (3½in) pots later in the spring.

There is an alternative for plants with fibrous roots if space is tight: group lengths of roots together in a small bundle of 10–20 roots with their tops level, tied loosely with twine, and insert them vertically in the centre of a 12.5cm (5in) pot of compost. The top of the bundle should be level with the surface. Cover it with a little compost and 6mm (¼in) of grit. When the shoots grow, remove the bundle from the pot, gently tease it apart, and pot up the root cuttings individually in 9cm (3½in) pots of potting soil.

Plants suitable for raising from root cuttings include *Acanthus*, *Anemone* (autumn-flowering types), *Catananche*, *Echinops*, *Eryngium*, *Geranium* (some), *Papaver orientale* varieties, *Phlox paniculata*, *Pulmonaria longifolia* varieties and *Pulsatilla*.

SEED

There are two substantial advantages to raising perennials from seed. The first is that growing from seed enables you to acquire a large number of plants for a very modest outlay, as a packet of seed often costs less than would a single plant of the same variety. This is especially important when planting out a new garden on a tight budget. The second great advantage is that you can order unusual varieties from seed catalogues without having to travel to specialist nurseries to find them. But there are also disadvantages. Many of the top varieties are not available as seed, so must be propagated by other means. Another problem is that some popular types, such as Michaelmas daisies, are available only as mixtures. The final drawback, although some would see it as an interesting bonus, is that when you raise perennials from seed the plants may not always be the same. Of course, some may be unusually good, but others may be poor.

Achillea 'Summer Pastels' flowers well in the same year as the seed is sown.

SOWING SEED OUT OF DOORS

The most basic method is to sow seed outside during the summer months. This approach, however, is not suited to varieties whose packets contain only a small number of expensive seeds; to ensure an adequate number of seedlings in such an instance, more care and cosseting are advisable. But where large numbers of seeds are supplied the plants can be raised out of doors very successfully.

Sowing technique The best time is usually early summer, when the soil has warmed up well and when there is still a good part of the growing season remaining for the plants to become established. Choose a sheltered, open site with good, fertile soil. A site protected from the heat of the midday sun is best but rarely available; avoid sites overhung by trees and where the soil is heavy and badly drained. If the soil is in good shape, ensure that the site is well weeded and forked over, trodden lightly and raked level.

Check the instructions on the packet before going any further, as varieties differ in spacing and depth of sowing requirements. The packet may give advice on how thickly to sow, but the thinner the better is usually the best advice. Aim to sow seeds 1–2.5cm (½–1in) apart. After cutting open the seed packet with a pair of scissors, check the contents. Then, keeping in mind whether you require only half a dozen plants or wish to raise much larger numbers, make a rough estimate of the length of row required. Using the point of a cane, draw a drill in the soil to the depth specified on the packet and of a length that seems suitable for the number of plants you wish to raise. Always use a longer row to raise more plants in preference to sowing

Sowing lupin seeds outside

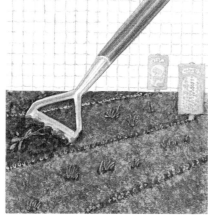

1 *Make a drill 1–2.5cm (½–1in) deep, sow the seeds about 2.5cm (1in) apart, then cover them carefully.*

2 *In good seasons most seeds will germinate, and when they do, hoe between the rows to control weeds.*

3 *As the seedlings develop, thin them to about 7.5cm (3in) apart to prevent overcrowding and spindly growth.*

4 *As they continue to grow and again become crowded, transplant the seedlings 15–23cm (6–9in) apart.*

drill. Then firm gently with the flat part of the rake. If a long spell of hot weather follows sowing, water well to encourage germination.

When seed germinates When the seed germinates, the row can be hand weeded as the seedlings develop. This will allow you to see how many seedlings have germinated. If germination has been good, the seedlings will need to be thinned to give them more space to develop. The seed packet will usually offer guidance, but in general the aim should be to thin the seedlings to about 7.5cm (3in) apart. The unwanted seedlings can be discarded, given away or planted out elsewhere. If germination has been poor, little or no thinning may be required.

As they develop, the seedlings of different plants perform in different ways. Some grow quickly, and can be lifted and replanted at a spacing of 15–23cm (6–9in) by the autumn. Others grow more slowly and are best left undisturbed until the spring; again, the seed packet will give guidance. Finally, remember that plants of many perennials raised from seed will not necessarily be identical, so it is advisable to see the plants actually in flower before you choose which individuals to transfer to your border.

thickly, and do not be tempted to sow all the seed if it is not necessary.

In dry weather it pays to water the drills before sowing. Fill the watering can, remove the rose, and, with one finger partly covering the spout to lessen the flow, gently fill the drill with water along its length. There are a number of ways of actually sowing the seed, everyone has their preferred method. One of the simplest is to pour some seed from the seed packet into the palm of your left hand (if you

are right-handed) then take a pinch in the fingers of your right hand and gently release it as you move your hand along the drill. Watch carefully to see that the seed is evenly distributed and spaced as recommended on the packet as far as possible. Large seeds, like those of lupins, can then be moved individually to a more accurate spacing. Once the seed is sown, insert a label at the end of the row and, with the back of the rake, draw a little soil from the sides to cover the

SOWING SEED IN PROTECTION
Sowing seed in a protected environment is a more efficient way of raising perennials than sowing outside, but you need the right facilities. Some gardeners are successful in raising perennials using a propagator on a windowsill in the house, but the low light levels and the difficulty of controlling the temperature make it more difficult than is often suggested. A cold frame or a greenhouse is far more likely to ensure success.

Cold frame

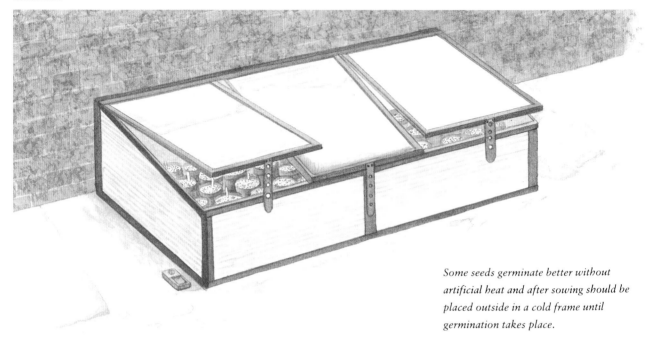

Some seeds germinate better without artificial heat and after sowing should be placed outside in a cold frame until germination takes place.

Cold frame A cold frame, which is usually rectangular in shape, serves as a box in which plants can be grown under cover, or protected during winter. It has a plastic or glass lid, and some types also have transparent side-walls. A frame is an important asset, for it provides sufficient protection to ensure that germination of seed and growth of seedlings are good, yet it is inexpensive, easy to manage and requires little space. In particular, it provides an opportunity to give expensive seed better conditions than those found in the open garden, and this is especially important when the packet contains only a small number of seeds. The added protection of a cold frame also allows plants to reach greater maturity before the end of their first growing season. The majority of perennials can be raised in this way. For some, like hellebores, primroses and pulsatillas, sowing in a frame in summer is the only way to ensure germination. However, a few plants, such as perennial lobelias, require not only the warmth of a greenhouse but also a long growing season following a spring sowing.

Most cold frames are suitable for raising seed. You can build a wooden or aluminium structure from a kit or you can make your own model using old floorboards or tongue-in-groove boards. The cold frame is best sited in an open position where it is not overhung by trees; if the only place available is in full sun, then shading will be necessary to prevent the temperature inside from rising too high.

Seed for perennials is best sown in summer, when most other plants, like half-hardy annuals, have been taken from the frame for planting out. Always check the seed packet for specific advice, but most varieties can be sown thinly in 9cm (3½in) plastic pots using a coir- or peat-based seed compost. It is usually advisable to add 20 per cent extra grit or perlite to the compost to improve drainage. Perennials vary enormously in the time they take to germinate so, after sowing, it is good practice to cover the seed with coarse grit to deter the growth of moss. Water the pots of seed thoroughly and place them in the cold frame, which is closed to keep the temperature high enough to encourage germination. Do note that some plants, especially primroses and other primulas, particularly dislike hot conditions, and for them it usually pays to site the frame in a place that gets no sun whatsoever.

It is important to prevent the frame overheating, or seedlings may be scorched. Thus, unless the frame is sited in a naturally shady place, you usually need to open it partially. In many areas the frame will also require shading with plastic netting during the warmest months. It is also vital to ensure that the seed and seedlings never dry out, so check them daily and water them when necessary. Because seedlings are vulnerable to slug damage from the moment they germinate, pellets or some other form of control should always be used. Some seedlings may be vulnerable to being eaten by mice, so a mousetrap or poison should also be placed in the frame.

After germination, the seed pots should be moved to an unshaded part of the cold frame. When the first true leaves have developed, prick the seedlings out into a proprietary potting compost. They can be moved into seed trays; or the more vigorous types can go straight into individual 9cm (3½in) pots. Then grow them on for planting later in the year or the following spring.

Finally, a number of perennials require either cool conditions or frost to promote germination. These include gentians, hellebores, pulsatillas and some primulas. These, too, are best sown in a cold frame, but they may not germinate until early in the winter after sowing or even until the following spring. The most practical approach is to sow the seed as soon as it becomes available from the seed company, then place the pots in a cold frame in a cool place and wait, ensuring that they never dry out. After germination they can be treated like other seedlings.

Greenhouse The greenhouse can be employed in much the same way as the cold frame, but it can be put to better use for sowing in spring. Quite a few perennials flower in their first year if sown in spring and raised in much the same way as you would raise half-hardy annuals. The sowing routine is the same as for seed sown in a cold frame, but sowing in early spring in a warm environment ensures prompt and more complete germination, so expensive seed is used to the greatest advantage by this method. A temperature of 16–18°C (60–65°F) is ideal; while this can be

provided in a heated greenhouse, a thermostatically controlled propagator is much more economical.

After germination, remove the seedlings from the propagator and place them either on the greenhouse bench or in a propagator set at a cooler temperature. After pricking out they can be grown on at quite a cool temperature, minimum 7°C (45°F) and then finally hardened off in an unheated cold frame to accustom them to outdoor conditions, before planting out in late spring. Many perennials are sufficiently tough to allow them to be planted out before the last frost if they are hardened off.

There is one disadvantage to raising perennials in this way, but two great advantages. The main difficulty is that in spring there is often competition for space in the greenhouse and propagator, as half-hardy annuals and greenhouse vegetables require sowing at the same time. Conversely, a major advantage is that many

perennials, sown early, will provide a good display in their first year (although sometimes a little later than their usual flowering season). The second advantage of early sowing is that plants available from seed only in mixed colours can be planted out in a spare piece of ground for the summer, and those plants with especially attractive flower colours can be selected for transplanting to the border the same autumn.

Perennials that flower in their first year The following plants flower well in their first year provided they are sown in warm conditions in early spring: *Achillea* 'Summer Pastels', *Centranthus ruber*, *Coreopsis* 'Early Sunrise', also *Delphinium* 'Southern Noblemen', *Geum* 'Lady Stratheden' and 'Mrs Bradshaw', *Lobelia* 'Compliment Scarlet', *Lupinus* 'Band of Nobles' and 'Gallery', *Polemonium caeruleum* and *Salvia* × *sylvestris* 'Blue Queen' ('Blaukönigin') and finally 'Rose Queen'.

Types of propagator

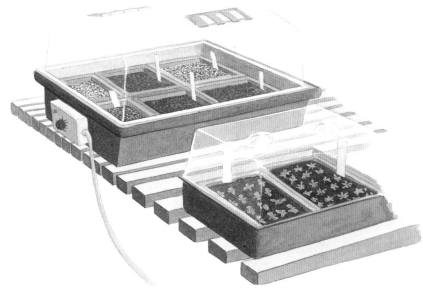

Seedlings raised in a heated propagator (left) should be acclimated to normal greenhouse conditions by giving them an intermediate stage in an unheated propagator (right).

USING
PERENNIALS

Perennials can be used effectively in many settings, from traditional perennial borders to patio containers but, whatever the scale, every situation benefits from a thoughtful approach. Many elements contribute to the success of these varied plantings, and you can organize them in many styles. The single most important factor in ensuring success is simply to think first and plant afterwards. Rushing ahead with no plan is usually a recipe for disappointment.

The upright spikes of delphiniums and lupins with Oriental poppies are fronted by bushier hardy geraniums.

Planning does not always mean drawing a plan to scale on a piece of paper and then transferring it to the patch of land outside. It also means thinking carefully about the desired effect and making sure that this effect will look appropriate in the space available.

Choosing the plants that are most likely to create the effect required and ensuring that they will thrive in the soil and situation available to you is also an important factor when planning the border. Once all this has been thought out, the way in which the plants are arranged and juxtaposed within the border is crucial. Selecting colours that complement each other or contrast attractively, and considering factors such as the plants' height on maturity, foliage colour, habit and flowering season, should ensure a successful planting.

Most important of all, as you enjoy the beds and borders you have created, look critically at them, and think about how you can improve them. Gardens change continually: make sure yours changes for the better.

Left: This skillfully planned herbaceous border in mid-summer is graded in height from the tall rudbeckias at the back to the shorter sedum and artemisia at the front. The colours link up along the border, with yellows and pinks repeated in different plants, and foliage colours calming any clashes.

PLANTING STYLES

Traditionally perennials were grown in formal herbaceous borders in large gardens, where tall plants and plants with a short season were easily accommodated. In cottage gardens, a jumble of perennials was grown alongside herbs, fruit trees and bulbs. Town house gardens tended to be reduced versions of grander gardens. As gardens became smaller, mixed borders became more popular. Today perennials are grown with a variety of other plants.

Many different ways of growing perennials have developed to cater for the range of gardens and individual tastes. Island beds, for example, were introduced as a response to the need, in the confined conditions of smaller gardens, for shorter, self-supporting plants. At the same time, imaginative gardeners began to adapt their planting ideas to their own situations and tastes. Collections of specific perennials are again becoming more prevalent; individual specimen plants are now used more often; more naturalistic plantings and wild gardens are gaining in popularity; and many gardens now feature permanent plantings of perennials in containers.

Above: This spectacular mid-summer border is split into two colour-themed sections. In the foreground the flowers are mainly bright yellow with an occasional red highlight; in the distance they are red with some bronzed foliage.

Above: This cool and restful tapestry of purples, lavenders and lilac, with occasional white high-lights, contrasts well with the darker, shadier area beyond. The planting is kept low to allow a view of the distant shade from the top of the path that looks down to the clipped holly, and is softened by billowing perennials.

Above: In seasonally themed borders, plants with the same flowering time are concentrated together to provide a colourful display. Here, tall white daisies of *Leucanthemella serotina* tower over other autumn-flowering perennials.

HERBACEOUS PLANTINGS

There was a time when almost every large country house had a herbaceous bed or border, which was intended to be one of the glories of the year's displays. Certainly, this is the most spectacular way to grow perennials, but they can also be organized to good effect on a much smaller scale.

TRADITIONAL HERBACEOUS BORDERS

The herbaceous border was usually a long straight border, sometimes up to 3–3.7m (10–12ft) deep and it could be up to 100m (325ft) long, depending on the size of the garden as a whole. The border was normally backed by a wall or by a hedge of yew or other evergreen, which provided shelter as well as offering an attractive neutral background against which to view the plants.

In many grand gardens it was usual that a pair of parallel borders was planted, with a broad grass walk between them which terminated in a view of the surrounding countryside, the house, a garden feature or some highlight of the distant landscape.

Generally these grand herbaceous borders were summer features. In displays of this scale the plants had to be colourful if they were to make any significant impact, so among the most popular perennials were groups such as delphiniums, Shasta daisies, phlox, lupins and Oriental poppies – all are summer-flowering plants.

The fact that the main display was deliberately concentrated into perhaps as little as two or three months of the year increased the intensity of the colour: for the period that the border was in flower there were no spaces where earlier plants had faded.

Displays for different seasons could be accommodated in other parts of what were normally extensive grounds.

These traditional borders were usually managed in a fairly straightforward way. Individual varieties were planted in broad groups, scaled in proportion to the overall size of the border. The tallest plants were placed at the back, graduating down to the shortest at the front. Bold clumps of individual varieties were sometimes repeated at intervals along the length of the border to create a more coherent feeling. Where a double border was planted, the two sides were often carefully planned as mirror images of each other.

Most of the plants grown were chosen for their colourful flowers. Foliage plants were used much less frequently, and then perhaps only to separate clashing colours. In fact, foliage plants in general were relatively uncommon compared with the wider selection available today.

THE DECLINE OF THE HERBACEOUS BORDER

Large-scale herbaceous borders were labour-intensive. The necessary tasks such as weeding, staking and deadheading would involve many hours of work for a team of gardeners. It was also customary for one-quarter or even one-third of the border to be replanted each year; this involved removing the plants, digging the border, incorporating large quantities of rich organic matter, then dividing the plants and replanting them.

Times changed: gardens became smaller and labour more costly. Setting aside a large area of the garden for a short seasonal display became difficult to justify – for much of the year there was very little to see, and in winter the soil was almost bare.

At the same time, with labour more expensive, it became impossible to provide all the regular attention such borders require.

As a result, the grand herbaceous borders began to disappear. They are still to be found in some public and historic gardens, but most gardeners now adopt a different approach to growing perennials.

MODERN HERBACEOUS PLANTINGS

In recent years there has been a revival of the herbaceous border, though in a style radically adapted to modern gardens. Many gardeners now plant small herbaceous borders but, by choosing varieties carefully, they ensure that the borders make a significant contribution to the garden as a whole.

One approach is to position the plants much closer together, so that more varieties can be grown in the same space; this is the opposite of the traditional approach, where plants were grown in their own individual clumps and regular lifting and replanting kept them from growing into one another. Though the choice of plants is crucial in the modern method, planting tightly, even allowing just two varieties to mingle, ensures that, as one variety finishes flowering, another is just coming into its own. This is almost impossible to manage on a large scale, but in a small space it is both manageable and effective.

Another way of adapting the traditional herbaceous border to smaller gardens is to choose perennials with an unusually long flowering period. This ensures that, instead of providing a few short weeks of summer splash, the border is colourful from early summer until the middle of autumn. A group comprising as little as a dozen varieties can make a very impressive, long-season display. The scale of such plantings can be reduced even further, so that perhaps as few as six carefully chosen varieties make a feature in a special place.

Alternatively, you can choose varieties that have valuable features in addition to their flowers. At its most basic, this means growing plants (such as pinks) that have evergreen foliage. Plants with colourful or unusually handsome foliage are particularly valuable as they provide a very long season of interest before and after the main flowering period.

Varieties that have colourful fruits or attractive winter stems are another good choice. In addition, there has been a strong trend towards growing perennials alongside other plants such as shrubs and bulbs, which provide colour and interest outside the perennials' flowering season.

The herbaceous border

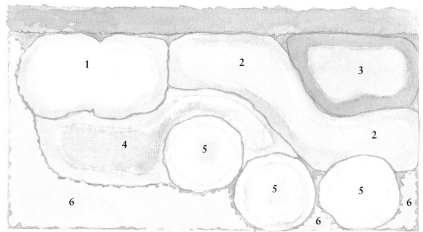

Key

1 *Delphinium* 'Blue Bird' × 1
2 *Anemone* × *hybrida* 'Queen Charlotte' × 2
3 *Echinops ritro* × 1
4 *Aster* × *frikartii* 'Mönch' × 1
5 *Sedum* 'Autumn Joy' × 3
6 *Stachys byzantina* 'Primrose Heron' × 3

COTTAGE STYLE

In contrast to the formal herbaceous borders that developed in the gardens of large houses belonging to affluent families, cottage borders originated in humble circumstances and in a much smaller space. Their creators had limited resources and were often under the day-to-day pressures of a basic rural existence. They saw little need to separate different types of plant, and simply planted what they liked. The result was a joyful jumble.

Lifestyles have changed, attitudes have become more sophisticated and cottage gardens today are usually more consciously planned. A disorganized appearance is now less natural and more the result of thoughtful foresight. The style has been adapted to an age in which resources may be more plentiful but the time available to spend on gardening more limited.

TRADITIONAL COTTAGE STYLE

The views of cottage gardens in Victorian paintings, while often idealized, give an idea of the way they were: billowing colour in a rural setting, unexpected combinations of plants with the cottage as a backdrop, and often work, rather than relaxation, in progress. Towards the back of the border, fruit bushes or even large fruit trees were to be found with rows of vegetables; access paths were

The cottage border

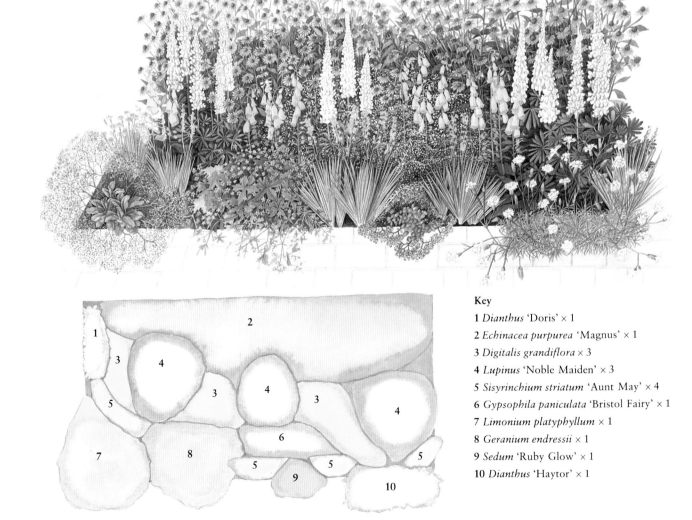

Key

1 *Dianthus* 'Doris' × 1
2 *Echinacea purpurea* 'Magnus' × 1
3 *Digitalis grandiflora* × 3
4 *Lupinus* 'Noble Maiden' × 3
5 *Sisyrinchium striatum* 'Aunt May' × 4
6 *Gypsophila paniculata* 'Bristol Fairy' × 1
7 *Limonium platyphyllum* × 1
8 *Geranium endressii* × 1
9 *Sedum* 'Ruby Glow' × 1
10 *Dianthus* 'Haytor' × 1

often of cinders or bricks. The beds might be edged with box hedges to keep the hens from scratching among the plants, or there could be a line of garden pinks or mossy saxifrages fringing the path.

The planting consisted of an apparently chaotic mix. Useful plants were set close to hand, where they could be looked after and picked easily, and ornamental plants were placed where they would grow well. So climbing or rambling roses, sweet peas and honeysuckle might grow up trees, shrubs, fences or cottage walls alongside runner beans. Annuals like love-in-a-mist and godetia and biennials like sweet rocket and forget-me-nots self-sowed where they could, flowered in unexpected places and made colourful combinations with perennial neighbours. Bulbs like daffodils and lilies grew steadily into ever-expanding clumps.

Holding all this together were the perennials, spreading steadily into fat clumps, only to be split and replanted in smaller groups whenever they began to occupy too much space. The varieties commonly grown were resilient – they had to be tough enough to survive. They were also usually easy to propagate; divisions were passed around the village, so it often happened that many of the gardens in a locality featured the same varieties. Anything and everything could be cut and taken indoors to brighten the house in a jar of water.

The care the cottage-garden plants received was generally rather unsophisticated. Manure provided the nutrients, waste water was tipped over plants that seemed to need it, pruning was done when there was time or not at all, and the plants that grew well in the soil and climate of the area survived the best.

Lupins, delphiniums, and self-sown foxgloves make spires in the early summer cottage garden.

Traditional cottage-garden perennials
These are traditional favourites and are still popular choices in today's cottage garden:

Aquilegia Columbines or granny's bonnets self-sowed in many colours.

Aster Michaelmas daisies of the past suffered from mildew. Many modern varieties are more resistant.

Dendranthema Tough garden chrysanthemums like 'Clara Curtis' are still grown today.

Dianthus Every cottage garden had its scented pinks. Many more recent varieties have no scent.

Iris Flag irises provided a sumptuous display in the months of early summer.

Lathyrus latifolius The perennial pea often scrambled over tough shrubs and fences.

Leucanthemum Bold white Shasta daisies are now more often seen in short, characterless forms.

Lupinus The slim spikes of the older varieties were less overpowering than today's tall, fat spikes.

Paeonia Left alone and manured occasionally, peonies flowered ever more prolifically.

Primula Primroses in particular were happy in the shade of taller, later-flowering perennials.

MODERN COTTAGE GARDENING

While the unaffected gardens of the past can still sometimes be seen, cottage gardening has in recent times, as rural life has changed, become more sophisticated. Although many gardeners concentrate on the traditional cottage-garden varieties, rather than growing the more up-to-date ones, the results tend to be planned: we strive more consciously now for the confused effect.

Gardeners in towns and cities recreate cottage gardens in unlikely situations, while both urban and rural gardeners try nostalgically to copy a style that derived from the circumstances of a different age. In these modern adaptations of the old-style cottage garden, fruit trees, except perhaps trained forms like cordons, or dwarf trees grown on dwarfing root-stocks, are seen much less frequently, while flowers and vegetables tend more often to be confined to their own areas.

PERENNIALS IN MODERN COTTAGE GARDENS

At the beginning of the 20th century the choice, highly bred varieties of perennials were cultivated in the large formal gardens and simpler forms, including wildflowers, were grown in cottage gardens. Sometimes plants from grander estates found their way into village gardens, but as they often required more careful attention they did not always thrive.

The perennial plants best suited to today's informal cottage style must be tough; we now try to pack even more varieties into our beds and borders, so there is vigorous competition among the plants. Short, stocky varieties with disproportionately large flower heads should be excluded in favour of varieties with a more open habit. Those which, through continuing development, produce bold blocks of colour should be passed over in favour of those with a less dominant style.

Perennials with a tendency to run were once appreciated, and this open growth allowed other plants to seed among them. This is still not necessarily a bad thing, but a balance must be struck between, on the one hand, allowing plants to spread and mingle and, on the other, preventing them from swamping their neighbours.

Modern cottage-garden perennials

These perennials have become more popular in recent times yet fit well into cottage-style borders:

Alchemilla The green-flowered plant *A. mollis* is now seen in many cottage-style gardens.

Allium Once these were merely a question of kitchen onions running to seed, but today many ornamental forms are grown.

Astrantia Generally rather demure, these can self-sow all too well.

Crocosmia Newer, brilliantly coloured forms still retain a certain elegance.

Eryngium The open habit of these ideally suits cottage-style plantings.

Geranium Hardy geraniums, rarely grown a century ago, are excellent cottage-garden flowers.

Helleborus Lenten roses, in particular, now come in many clear colours, with or without spots.

Linaria The wild yellow form, with its running root, was once a favourite. Today the slender pink 'Canon Went' is more common.

Nepeta Many new catmints are today available to complement the traditional form.

Penstemon Though often short-lived, these fit well into cottage plantings.

The less chaotic style of modern cottage gardens, with salvias and a range of penstemons.

MIXED PLANTINGS

The mixed border, in which perennials are grown alongside a variety of other plants, has become increasingly popular since the 1950s. It can vary from a few shrubs being used to make a background and provide protection for the perennials to a more fully integrated planting incorporating a wide range of plant types.

Deciduous and evergreen shrubs or even small trees serve as the main structure or backbone, of the mixed border. They also provide more early flowers, autumn leaf colour and fruits and a consistent presence throughout the season. Perennials usually provide the most colour and variety in both flowers and foliage, while annuals and bedding plants are carefully chosen to blend in rather than dominate. Bulbs are an essential constituent of the border, especially as they can grow through perennials and produce attractive colour combinations. Climbers scramble through shrubs and trees.

The scheme is planned so that the different constituents that make up the border knit together harmoniously. Choosing varieties that will not overpower each other, either in their vigour or their flower colour, ensures an attractive and balanced effect.

ADVANTAGES OVER HERBACEOUS BORDERS

Mixed borders have many advantages over borders composed entirely of hardy perennials. First, by adding shrubs and bulbs to perennials it is possible to have plants coming into flower for as much of the year as possible – indeed, in many climates, for the whole year. The majority of herbaceous borders tend to look rather empty between late autumn, when most of the plants are cut down, and

Perennials are now grown with other types of plants like these alliums and bedding pansies.

late spring, when the first full flush of flowers takes place. Shrubs, climbers, bulbs and biennials can be used to provide colour in that otherwise relatively colourless period.

Second, the enormous range of different plant types that can be included in mixed borders give you the opportunity to create the widest possible variety of interest. Shrubs, climbers and bulbs offer a diversity of both shapes and styles of growth that you cannot find among perennials alone. Perennials are grown primarily for their flowers, with foliage as a secondary attraction whereas shrubs,

in addition to their flowers and leaves, can provide a variety of barks, fruits and autumn colours.

But the single most important advantage of the mixed border over the herbaceous border is that, by choosing from the full palette of plants, a small garden can be made a great deal more colourful and more interesting for a great deal longer.

There are disadvantages, however, in replacing the traditional herbaceous border with the more modern mixed border, in that the latter, with its greater range of plant types, is less straightforward to look after.

PLANNING MIXED BORDERS

Mixed borders can be as simple or as intricate as you wish. In practice they are often organized in a fairly straightforward way at first, but they soon become more complicated as plants are added and self-sown seedlings appear.

You should choose the shrubs and small trees (if any) first. Some will make a solid presence at the back of the border, while smaller varieties will add substance towards the front. You can select climbers to clamber through them, either to flower with and complement the shrubs or to flower at another time of year so as to extend the season.

You can then consider your perennials, looking for both those that will associate well with the shrubs and climbers at flowering time and those that will extend the flowering season. Some should be long-flowering varieties, some should be good foliage forms and some should be chosen for their short but spectacular display.

Now you can plan spaces for annuals, summer bedding plants and biennials. The varieties of these that you choose can be changed from year to year to bring additional diversity, and bulbs can be selected to grow up

The mixed border

Key

1 *Clematis viticella* 'Madame Julia Correvon' × 2

2 *Tropaeolum peregrinum* × 1

3 *Aconitum carmichaelii* 'Bressingham Spire' × 5

4 *Nicotiana langsdorfii* × 5

5 *Spirea* 'Goldflame' × 1

6 *Stachys macrantha* 'Superba' × 4

7 *Cosmos atrosanguineus* × 7

8 *Kniphofia* 'Bressingham Comet' × 4

9 *Aster amellus* 'Violet Queen' × 4

10 *Heuchera macrantha* 'Palace Purple' × 1

11 *Helichrysum petiolare* 'Limelight' × 2

○ Spring flowering bulbs underplant the aster

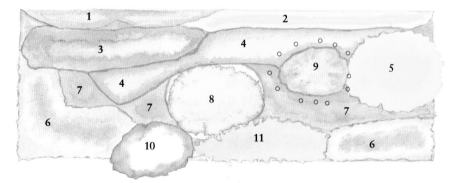

among the perennials, so more than one plant flowers in a single place during the course of the year.

PERENNIALS IN MIXED BORDERS IN SMALL GARDENS

The most important advantage of using perennials in mixed borders in small gardens is that being able to choose from such a wide range of plants allows you to do a great deal of interplanting, so that every inch of the border remains as colourful as possible for as long as possible.

Perennials and shrubs Although shrubs provide the backbone of the mixed border, perennials are generally the most important plants. Tall perennials that might otherwise require elaborate support, such as the white daisies of *Leucanthemella serotina*, can benefit from the shelter of large shrubs at the back of the border. Perennial climbers, such as peas (*Lathyrus latifolius*) or herbaceous clematis, can be planted under shrubs to scramble up through them.

Perennials and bulbs Some perennials are effective when interplanted among bulbs. Spring bulbs such as wood anemones can be planted in a carpet among summer-flowering perennials such as *Salvia × sylvestris*. Evergreen perennials like bergenias can make an excellent background for spring crocuses, while the very attractive foliage of hostas can mask the leaves of ornamental onions, which tend to shrivel when their flowers are at their best.

Perennials and annuals Annual climbers like canary creeper (*Tropaeolum peregrinum*) and sweet pea can be planted to climb into shrubs, but they will also trail very attractively through perennials and will often provide welcome colour after early perennials have been deadheaded.

Summer bedding plants that offer good foliage, such as the silver-leaved *Helichrysum petiolare*, can be used to hide the bare basal stems of some perennials, such as phlox, while at the same time they can provide a harmonious association of colour.

Dual-season perennials Perennials that have more than one attractive feature are especially valuable in mixed borders. For example, a plant such as

Geranium renardii starts the season with a new flush of sage-green leaves, which look delightful covered in dewdrops on spring mornings and make a good background for late-spring bulbs; then, in summer, its purple-veined white flowers appear, and finally, in early autumn, the mature mound of its leaves makes a good background to the pink or white chalices of colchicums.

Self-sown annual opium poppies mingle with delphiniums, salvias and potentillas in this most manageable of mixed plantings in which hardy bulbs are used for the main spring display.

ISLAND BEDS

Three important trends have altered the ways in which we grow perennials in recent decades. First, gardens have become smaller and beds and borders have correspondingly decreased in scale, so many larger perennials, such as delphiniums and rheums, are less easy to accommodate. Second, gardeners are now willing or able to spend less time looking after their gardens. Third, there has been a drift away from formality to a more informal style of garden and border design. The combination of these three factors has led to the development of the island bed.

WHAT ARE ISLAND BEDS?

Island beds are free-standing beds, made in lawns or in gravel or paving. They are usually designed in informal flowing curves around which it is easy to mow. A number of beds may be cut out of an area of lawn, their size depending on the scale of the garden, with grass walks between them.

The traditional border is usually viewed from only one side but island beds are intended to be seen from all round. This introduces a greater variety of view into a small area. If a number of island beds are created together it is possible to give each a different colour or seasonal theme, and so introduce yet greater variety.

Island beds are often unsuitable sites in which to grow taller plants, as their more open position, away from hedges and walls, exposes the plants to gales. Besides, you don't want to spend more of your limited time on staking than you have to.

A further reason to be wary of tall plants is that they are likely to be out of proportion to the scale of the beds themselves. Many of the stately traditional perennials are therefore not suitable for island beds; you need plants that are shorter, stockier and bushier. With the increase in enthusiasm for island beds many new, dwarf varieties have been developed to meet these requirements.

These island beds cut out of a well-kept lawn are densely planted to help keep down weeds.

ADVANTAGES OF ISLAND BEDS

This radical change of approach to using perennials in the garden has created many advantages:

- Small beds fit more effectively into today's smaller gardens.
- The all-round view creates more variety in a small space.
- Smaller plants with stockier growth allow more varieties to be grown in the available space.
- Dwarf, bushy varieties require little or no time-consuming staking.
- The informal design suits today's tastes and allows scope for composition to be viewed from all sides.
- Island sites create favourable conditions for a wide variety of plants.

PLANNING ISLAND BEDS

The traditional one-sided herbaceous border is usually a long rectangle set against a background. Island beds are often kidney-shaped or laid out in flowing curves, and are set in an open situation. In the traditional herbaceous border the tallest plants must go at the back, scaling down to the smallest at the front; in island beds the tallest plants go in the middle.

Taller plants look too formal if just planted in a line along the backbone of the bed; they are far more effective if set in clumps interspersed by groups of smaller plants. The clumps are best situated where the bed is at its widest and with smaller plants grouped around them. Only where big, sweeping island beds are created in large gardens is a strong backbone of substantial plants likely to be effective. Otherwise, it is often more successful to use shrubs for this instead, so that in effect you create two one-sided borders back-to-back. These two sides can be made very different in character, not least because one will probably be sunny and the other shady.

The key feature plants The taller, more substantial plants will set the main theme for the planting in terms of either colour or season, and will also influence the choice of nearby plants. Key plants should have a long

The island bed

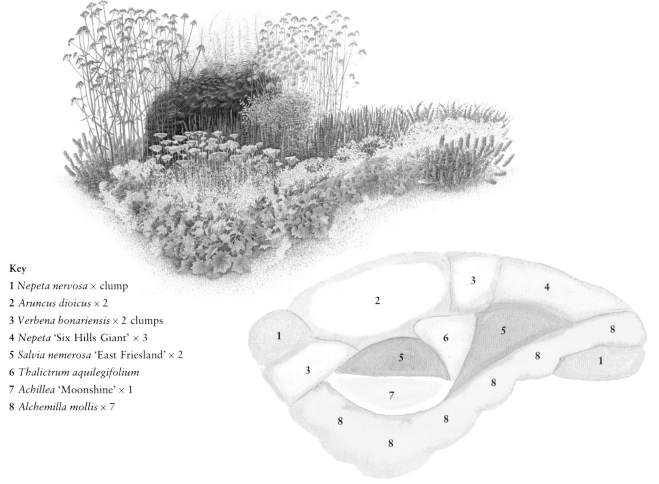

Key

1 *Nepeta nervosa* × clump
2 *Aruncus dioicus* × 2
3 *Verbena bonariensis* × 2 clumps
4 *Nepeta* 'Six Hills Giant' × 3
5 *Salvia nemerosa* 'East Friesland' × 2
6 *Thalictrum aquilegifolium*
7 *Achillea* 'Moonshine' × 1
8 *Alchemilla mollis* × 7

season or good foliage and, when their flowers are over, should provide a background for other plants. Some gardeners choose flowering and variegated shrubs rather than perennials for these positions, as they offer a greater selection of varieties that combine the relevant features.

There are other ways in which to deal with these key plants in the border, although they do involve more work. Instead of planting bold, long-season perennials or using shrubs, you can opt for a relatively tall early-season plant such as a delphinium, interplanted or surrounded by tall late-season plants such as asters; the delphinium flowers can be cut down when they are over, leaving the aster to develop and fill the space later in the season. Yet another approach is to construct a wigwam of canes or stakes and use it to support climbers, whether perennial, such as *Lathyrus latifolius*, or annual.

The infill planting Planning the planting around these key plants is more difficult than for one-sided borders, with their single viewpoint. Not only must the varieties chosen associate well with the key plants, whatever the angle of view, they must also associate well with each other, follow the planting theme (if there is one) and be suitable for the different conditions around the key plants. As an example of this latter consideration, substantial long-season feature plants cast shade, so that an infill plant may be well enough suited to the sunny side but languish on the shady side.

Your planning of an island bed must also reflect the fact that the bed has no solid backbone, so that it is often possible to look right across the whole planting from one side to the other. You must therefore pay attention to the colour and character of plants that will appear in the same view, even though they may actually be set some distance apart.

As with the other plants in the bed, you can extend the season of the infill through interplanting.

SMALL GARDEN, SMALL SCALE

There are two other features of island beds to consider, especially those made in small gardens. First, as beds are reduced in size, so the size of the plants must be reduced in proportion. Second, in a small garden the plants and plantings are examined far more closely and more regularly than in larger gardens. It is therefore worth keeping in mind the following points:

• Try to choose the best varieties.

• Replace any plants which do not thrive, or which for some other reason prove inappropriate.

• Choose varieties with secondary features (such as attractive foliage or fruits) in addition to their main display, so that their period of interest is much longer.

• Deadhead and tidy the plants and bed frequently.

• Avoid gaps – if a plant is slow to become established or dies, fill in temporarily with foliage annuals.

Small island beds like this can contain a good range of varieties and still fit the scale.

WILDFLOWER PLANTINGS

The increasing enthusiasm for wildflowers has developed along two distinct lines. First has been the increasing interest in growing perennials whose natural grace has not been destroyed by plant breeders trying to 'improve' them. Second, many gardeners find that growing perennials in a naturalistic way is a more satisfying approach than applying formal and highly planned strategies.

WILD SPECIES

The attractions of wild species over their more highly developed descendants are that such plants often have a greater elegance of habit, are less gaudy in colour, and display a simple charm that is missing from modern, highly bred varieties. Not having been developed in and for gardens, they also enjoy that intimate connection with the natural world which appeals to today's environmentally conscious gardener.

But they also have disadvantages. Some wild perennials are exceptionally vigorous and may overwhelm less rampant neighbours. Some produce too many self-sown seedlings, which can be a nuisance. Some, while undeniably charming, suffer from features which would not be considered deficiencies in the wild but are less desirable in the garden, such as tall growth, small flowers or a brief flowering season.

In short, while some wild species integrate well into herbaceous garden plantings in many styles, others are better used in deliberately planned wildflower habitats.

Native and wild There is a definite distinction between wild species and native plants. Wild species are simply unchanged species found growing in natural habitats around the world. Native plants are wild species that grow in and are particularly suited to a given area – a country, region or county. Just as gardeners have become more interested in wild species generally, so there has been an expansion of interest in native species. Beds and even whole gardens are given over to them.

In addition to their aesthetic attractions and their associations with unspoilt nature, native plants have one particular advantage. As the natural plants of the area they are also best adapted to the local conditions and most likely to attract insects, birds and other creatures. Many gardeners find this the most important reason for growing them.

WILDFLOWERS IN THE GARDEN

Creating garden habitats that replicate the natural environments in which wildflowers thrive is perhaps the most appealing but also the most challenging way to grow them.

Natural habitats Creating replicas of natural habitats is the opposite of the usual approach to gardening, which is inherently an artificial process. First you prepare the site in

Cornflowers, field poppies, corn marigolds and other cornfield annuals make a sparkling summer display and thrive in poor soil while perennials become established and take over the following year.

Wild primroses and anemones make an attractive spring group in a shady corner.

a way unheard-of when planning more conventional plantings (see p.29), in that you must strike a balance between letting the habitat settle down to develop in its own natural way and preventing weeds or aggressive species taking over. What you are attempting to create is something of a contradiction in terms: an artificial natural environment.

• Prepare the site carefully (see p.36) to ensure that the plants have the most appropriate habitat in which to grow and to minimize the chances of weeds smothering them.

• Check the balance of the different species regularly. If one tends to dominate, deadhead it in order to prevent self-seeding, or restrict its spread by digging up some of its roots.

• Some species may prove to be short-lived. This may be natural or it may be the result of inappropriate growing conditions. In either case, regular re-introduction may be the answer.

• Invasive weeds can quickly become established in plantings that are not managed in a conventional way. Keep a careful watch for them and remove any that appear as soon as possible.

• At the same time, keep an eye out for welcome arrivals of desirable native species.

• Pay attention to the health of native plants. They may be attacked by pests or diseases which, because they rarely strike garden plants, are unfamiliar.

Wild species in beds and borders
Some wild species are sufficiently colourful, accommodating and well behaved to be grown with other perennials in traditional beds and borders without requiring special treatment. Many such wild species can be found in the Plant Directory (see pp.142–227). Relatively undeveloped varieties of wild species can be integrated in the same way; they may just be uncommon colour forms.

One way to encourage traditional border plantings to develop a less managed, more natural look is to space the original plants more widely than usual and then interfere as little as possible with their natural spread by root and seed, thereby allowing much more mingling and integration. When you let plants spread relatively freely to cover any patch of bare earth, it is a good idea to put some stones in the bed to serve as access points when you want to tend the plants. Borders of this sort cannot just be left to run wild, of course: they require careful and detailed management to give a good balance of varieties and look pleasing from different viewpoints.

Recently a new approach has been developed. This integrates selected forms of wild species and suitable garden varieties into natural-looking stands of plants. Individual plants or clumps of plants growing in just one place, separate from one another, as in herbaceous beds and borders, is a circumstance rarely seen in the wild. Though individuals can certainly occur in the wild, usually there is a far more uniform mingling of species, often in broad swathes covering whole fields or mountainsides.

This style is now being replicated in gardens. Gardeners plant broad drifts that comprise a number of different wild species or garden varieties mingled intimately together. These may flower successively to give a series of sweeps of colour through the season, or they may flower together, providing an intensely rich and sometimes dramatic effect.

This kind of approach to planting requires not only space but also careful management, to ensure the balance of different plants is kept. It can, however, create a very satisfying area, combining the best features of natural wildflower habitats with

Right: Moisture-loving perennials, both wild and cultivated, can be allowed to grow naturally and to spread and self-sow freely.

SHOW BEDS

Many gardeners have groups of plants which are special favourites, and like to build up collections of these together. There are at least two popular ways of accommodating collections of perennials.

The first is simply to plant the individual varieties where they naturally grow well and look best; this is the way in which collections are usually built up initially. Integrating a collection into a garden works well only if the plants are relatively small and not too bright or overpowering; for example, if you spread a collection of delphiniums around the garden they will, when in flower, attract such attention that the garden

will seem to contain little else. By contrast, a collection of hardy geraniums, smaller in size and softer in colour, can be integrated with far greater success. They are adaptable enough to grow in a variety of situations, so spreading them around the garden will cause few problems. Collections of primroses or water irises, by contrast, need special conditions.

COLLECTIONS IN SHOW BEDS

Show beds are a second way of accommodating a collection of perennials. If the collection is grouped in one place, the particular conditions the plants require are more easily provided, looking after them is less demanding, and it is easier to compare the different plants in the

collection. The collection becomes a feature in its own right. A planting of delphiniums or phlox, for example, would be spectacular in early summer; a collection of hellebores would be intriguing and beautiful in early spring, and hostas are interesting for more than half the year.

But there are several problems associated with presenting plants in this way. First, you need a substantial area throughout which the conditions suit the plant in question. Second, if one individual is attacked by a pest or disease, this quickly spreads to the others. Third, and most important, when the collection is not at its peak there may be little to see.

Clearly it would be foolish to try to grow plants whose requirements cannot be met in your garden. However, in some instances you may decide it is worth indulging in a degree of special soil preparation – for example, if your chosen group has unusual members that are fussier than the more common ones. If a group of plants is prey to a particular pest, it may be no bad thing to grow them together because at least, when spraying for that pest, you need concentrate on only a single area of the garden.

SHOW BEDS OUT OF SEASON

The problem of out-of-season interest can, with some collections, be solved relatively easily. You can interplant with other varieties whose main interest comes at a different season. This interplanting is best kept very simple, so that the bed does not have various different care requirements. Bulbs are often the most suitable choice. For example, collections of summer or autumn perennials such as peonies, phlox or Michaelmas daisies, can be interplanted with

Hostas, with their harmonious leaf tones, make a good collection in a bed of their own.

species of crocus; these will often self-sow throughout the bed, making a delightful spring carpet before the summer plants come into their own. Winter and spring plants such as hellebores can be interspersed with lilies, or an easy hardy annual like love-in-a-mist can be allowed to self-sow among primroses or irises.

COMBINED COLLECTIONS

Sometimes two collections can be integrated to make a display in a single bed that provides conditions both plants enjoy. Both hostas and ferns like similar cool, shady situations, and the broad hosta leaves make a happy combination with the feathery ferns. Hellebores and primroses also look good together and appreciate similar conditions.

It can be difficult to give some plants the care they require when their companion plants are in the way, so collections that need a great deal of staking, deadheading and spraying, not to mention regular replanting, are best grown in isolation; examples include asters and delphiniums. Plants that have a tendency to run at the root, such as anemones, are best grown either on their own or widely separated by other plants.

THEMATIC DISPLAYS

There is another way of planting attractive show beds. An unusually spectacular display can be created with a substantial planting of just a few carefully chosen varieties. Instead of planting a small bed or border with a mixed range of perennials, using perhaps just one plant of each, you can restrict yourself to three or four varieties planted in larger numbers to create an impressive show. You can opt for plants that produce

A collection of asters makes a fine feature as their colours blend well.

a short but brilliant flash of colour, perhaps to coincide with a regular anniversary party, or you can select unusually long-flowering plants to bring constant colour to an important part of the garden, such as the view from the kitchen window.

Many other themes are possible. You could select varieties to reflect family names – *Dianthus* 'Diane' and *Sisyrinchium* 'Aunt May', for example. A Silver Wedding planting could be developed using silver foliage plants; or plants bought in a regular holiday area could be grown together. Such themed collections can provide a great deal of pleasure and ensure that your garden is unique.

FEATURE PLANTINGS

Some perennials can be used very effectively as a feature in their own right, rather than as just part of a bed or border. They may be large or colourful, such as *Gunnera manicata* and rheums. Like specimen shrubs or small trees, these plants are often better viewed from a distance and without surrounding distractions. Alternatively, they may be smaller, elegant plants like some of the larger hostas. Or they may be intimate specimens, plants which, in isolation, better display an especially attractive feature or combination of features such as habit, foliage and flower.

There is one problem. Unlike shrubs, most perennials die down in the winter, so you are left with an uninteresting gap in your garden's display. This must be planned for, either by ensuring there are winter attractions in other parts of the garden or perhaps by underplanting winter or spring bulbs or a low evergreen ground-cover.

DRAMATIC SPECIMENS

Some perennials are so bold and imposing that a long view is needed in order to appreciate their structure, habit or brilliant colour. They may be best used as focal points in beds or borders of other plants; this is the case with, for example, tall varieties such as *Leucanthemella serotina*, which may lose their lower leaves or whose attraction is mainly towards the top of the plant.

Others, such as the pampas grass *Cortaderia selloana*, can look superb in a more solitary situation. They can be used to fill a prominent angle between fences or walls, as the focal point at the end of a path or grass walk, or in splendid isolation towards the edge of broad gravel drives. In larger gardens they can be used in a more traditional manner in beds cut out of a lawn, although some may benefit from an edging of low ground-cover plants.

When plants are deployed as dramatic specimens it is especially important to look after them. A plant in a prominent position can look magnificent, but if it is poorly cared for or planted in unsuitable conditions it will languish, creating a far worse effect than if it had been grown among the rest of the border.

Plants to grow as dramatic specimens: *Cortaderia selloana*, *Cynara cardunculus*, *Eryngium* (tall species), *Foeniculum vulgare* 'Purpureum', *Gunnera manicata*, *Kniphofia* 'Prince Igor', *Macleaya cordata*, *Miscanthus sinensis* varieties, *Rheum* and *Stipa gigantea*.

INTIMATE SPECIMENS

Moving further down the scale, a number of smaller plants derive particular benefit if grown in isolation from distracting neighbours. These too can be grown in spaces made in paving or in gravel; some can also be grown in containers. Choose plants that look attractive in the scale and setting in which they are to be grown, and of course it is vital that the plants have an elegant habit, or at least one that is not ungainly. But the pre-eminent factor is that the plants should repay close inspection.

Such varieties may have especially interesting flowers, such as double primroses, or flowers that are delicately veined or spotted. They may have nodding flowers which reveal a surprise when turned up, like some of the hellebores, or possess an especially intriguing scent, like many pinks. Foliage whose delicate colouring is especially attractive at close quarters might be the special feature, as with the Japanese painted fern *Athyrium niponicum* var. *pictum*.

Plants to grow as intimate specimens: *Ajuga reptans* 'Variegata', *Aquilegia viridiflora*, *Athyrium niponicum* var. *pictum*, *Bellis perennis* 'Prolifera', *Campanula punctata* varieties,

A bed devoted entirely to delphiniums makes a spectacular summer feature.

These bold clumps combine to make a striking feature, with the iris in the wettest soil, and the hosta and euphorbia in slightly drier soil.

Dianthus (laced and scented types), *Geranium renardii*, *Helleborus*, *Primula* (particularly double primroses) and *Saxifraga fortunei* 'Wada'.

ELEGANT SPECIMENS

Perennials which are not exceptionally large but which nevertheless develop into specimens with a strong, distinctive character can be effective when grown on their own. You can do this in various ways.

You can remove a single slab from an area of paved terrace or patio to make space for the plant; the neutral paving surrounding it often makes an ideal background. The space can be in a corner of the patio or towards the side, or the plant can be sited more prominently as a focal point. In these situations you must ensure that the light is even so that the plant develops in a balanced way. If the paving is strongly coloured, choose your variety carefully: flowers or foliage in equally strong colours may clash with the background.

Gravel is another good background for elegant specimens, and it has the additional advantage of suppressing weeds. However, it also encourages self-sown seedlings to appear, and these may need to be removed so that the original specimen is left in splendid isolation.

Plants to grow as elegant specimens: *Acanthus*, *Agapanthus*, *Dryopteris erythrosora*, *Euphorbia characias* varieties, *Hakonechloa macra* 'Aureola', *Hosta* (larger varieties), *Iris pallida* (variegated varieties), *Molinia caerulea* 'Variegata', *Polystichum setiferum* varieties and *Zantedeschia aethiopica* 'Crowborough'.

A single planting of Euphorbia characias subsp. wulfenii develops into an imposing specimen for winter and spring.

CONTAINERS

There is no doubt that the majority of perennials are best grown in the open garden, where their roots can spread freely and they can develop naturally. However, some are better suited to the use of containers.

WHY USE CONTAINERS?

Your soil, particular features of your garden or specific problems with the plants themselves may encourage you to explore the use of containers.

Soil If you cannot transform your garden's natural soil sufficiently for favourite plants to grow well, containers may provide the answer.

• On unusually wet soil, containers can be used to provide free-draining conditions for plants that require drier soil. Examples include: *Arabis*, *Asphodelus*, *Dianthus*, *Gaillardia*, *Iris* (many types), *Paeonia*.

• On dry soil, containers can provide damper conditions for moisture-loving plants. Examples include: *Astilbe*, *Caltha*, *Dicentra*, ferns, *Hosta*, *Houttuynia cordata* 'Chameleon', *Iris ensata*, *Trollius*.

GARDEN SITUATIONS

Containers can provide additional planting options in parts of your garden where perennials could not otherwise be grown successfully. They are invaluable in small paved yards where there may be little soil available for planting perennials.

Carefully chosen varieties can be planted in window boxes and hanging baskets to bring perennials to unexpected sites. A specimen plant in a large container can make an arresting feature or focal point.

Solving problems Containers can be used to solve problems that prevent the successful cultivation of some perennials. For example:

• Hostas are easier to keep free of slugs when planted in containers.

• Some perennials which are too rampant for the open border, such as the variegated ground elder *Aegopodium podagraria* 'Variegatum', and *Houttuynia cordata* 'Chameleon', can be easily restricted in containers.

• In cold areas slightly tender plants, such as agapanthus, can be grown in the open in containers and then moved into a protected place in the autumn. (In very cold areas, move containers into the greenhouse or porch for the winter.)

USING CONTAINERS EFFECTIVELY

Planting in containers requires thoughtful planning. To ensure the best display you must choose suitable plants, containers and sites.

PLANTS FOR CONTAINERS

Good plants for containers fall into a number of categories.

• They should make elegant specimens in their own right and not be so tall or ungainly as to look out of place; low, rounded or broad plants are often very effective. Examples include: *Aegopodium podagraria* 'Variegatum', *Carex* (many), ferns, *Geranium* (some), grasses (many), *Hosta* (most).

• Low, trailing varieties are natural container plants as they soften the edges of tubs and boxes and, because their growth habit leaves some free surface, allow additional plants to be grown in the container. Examples

Containers are invaluable for paved areas where little soil is available for perennials.

include: *Ajuga*, *Dianthus*, *Geranium* (some), *Lamium*, *Malva sylvestris* 'Primley Blue', *Nepeta* (some), *Verbena* 'Homestead Purple'.

• Evergreen perennials are invaluable in containers as they maintain interest all year round. Examples include: *Ajuga*, *Bergenia*, *Carex*, *Dianthus*, *Heuchera*, *Lamium*, *Luzula*.

SITING CONTAINERS

In small paved gardens, where most of the plants must be in containers, different styles can be used in different ways to create the best effect:

• Position large wooden boxes along the bottoms of walls.

• Smaller boxes can go on low walls or beneath windows.

• Baskets can be hung along fences and from walls.

• Collections of pots in different sizes can be set in corners.

• Elegant individual pots can be used as focal points.

• Low boxes or broad tubs can cover drains or manholes.

In larger gardens, where most perennials are grown in the open ground, only a few containers may be in use but these must be positioned to ensure they blend into the garden setting. Points to bear in mind:

• Large single tubs or groups of tubs look more effective than a scattering of small ones.

• Use containers as focal points at the ends of narrow paths or in alcoves.

• Pairs of large tubs can frame doors or gateways.

• Pots of any size can look badly out of place in beds or borders.

The attractive foliage of ferns makes them ideal plants for containers.

Euphorbia characias subsp. wulfenii is a striking plant to grow in a container, and it remains handsome in all seasons.

Right: The dark evergreen hedge makes a good background and sets off pale cephalarias and slim delphinium spires well. The grey foliage balances the strong colours of the geraniums, and plants with tall stems are mixed with bushier varieties.

BEDS AND BORDERS

The planning of new beds and borders is one of the most exciting aspects of gardening. It is the stage at which good foundations are laid for long-term success, but it is also the time when you can make mistakes that may be difficult to put right later. It is a highly challenging aspect of gardening to group perennials so that the whole is more than simply the sum of the parts. There are so many factors to consider over and above the style in which the plants are to be arranged. What is the scale of the border, and how does it fit in with the existing house and garden? Should you adopt a formal or informal approach? What are the heights and habits of the plants themselves? What are the flower and foliage colours? Should you confine the planting to perennials, or incorporate shrubs, bulbs and other plants?

Fortunately there are some useful guidelines to help you plan successfully. You will find, incidentally, that many of the ideas and principles discussed in relation to perennials are relevant also to other plantings.

Above: This truly mixed border is planted in red and orange with complementary bronze foliage. The shrubs form a background to solidagos, monardas, heleniums, phlox and other perennials interplanted with dahlias, verbenas and other tender plants.

Above: This spectacular planting of Russell lupins makes a wonderful feature planting for early summer. It will also work well on a smaller scale but is best isolated by a fence or hedge from other borders.

STARTING FROM SCRATCH

An empty area of garden – perhaps a whole new, empty garden – presents a wonderful opportunity, but can also be daunting.

While there are perennials suitable for every situation, it makes sense not to fight against nature but to let the characteristics of each individual situation indicate the best style of planting and the most suitable plants. It cannot be stressed too strongly that it is a great mistake to decide where to place specific beds or borders or even a particular plant and then try to fit the other garden features around them. This is the way to create a muddled and disarrayed garden. Every herbaceous planting should be considered not in isolation but as part of an overall garden plan.

There is no need to plan every feature in detail from the start. However, when presented with an empty garden and the chance to design everything without the constraint of existing features, you should take the opportunity to make a coherent general plan. Even in an empty garden, though, there are indications of the best places for different types of herbaceous plantings.

ASSESSING SURROUNDINGS

Evaluate the external factors affecting the garden and how perennials will respond to them.

Local climate The local climate will significantly influence your choice of perennials. Are the winters unusually harsh, the summers unusually hot and dry, the winds unusually scorching? Choose plants accordingly.

Wind and shelter From which direction do the prevailing winds come? Is there any shelter, particularly from a fence or wall? (If there is, the fence or wall could make a backing for a traditional herbaceous border.) Are there hedges? If so, are they sound? If not, can a solid fence be erected or an evergreen hedge planted? (If this is not possible you might be better off with island beds of shorter plants or a mixed border in which the shrubs can provide shelter.)

Light and shade – trees Are there mature trees overhanging the garden? Are they evergreen or deciduous? (Few perennials thrive under evergreen trees.) Do they shade the whole garden, or are some areas lighter? Are they planted within the garden? If so, can the branches be thinned or lower branches removed to admit more light? (The thin shade of tall deciduous trees is the ideal cover for a woodland garden of shade-loving plants. If there is no consistently light place for sun-loving varieties, make a feature of the shade-lovers.)

Light and shade – buildings Do tall buildings overshadow the garden? Is the sun completely excluded, or are the buildings on the side of the garden that is naturally shady? Shade from tall buildings is less restricting than that from trees – they cast no overhead shade and have no hungry roots – so a wider range of plants

Ferns thrive in this shady bed and are brightened by the flowers of Stachys macrantha.

can be planted. It is very important to remember, though, that the soil immediately alongside a building's wall may be drier than in the rest of the border. Relatively short varieties should be chosen, as they will naturally lean less towards the light. The taller the building, the less light the plants will receive, so the more shade-lovers you should choose.

WITHIN THE GARDEN

The property's own features will influence the siting of garden features, the choice of plants and planting styles.

Views Short seasonal plantings are not an appropriate focus for a much-used view from the house (for example, from the kitchen) unless the view is sufficiently broad to include other features or is itself seasonal (for example, spectacular summer-season plantings can be the visual focus from a sitting area used only in summer). Specimens with a long season should be made the focal point of walks or paths. Check the views from upstairs windows as well as those from the ground floor.

Neighbours Do remember that your neighbours, too, may have a view of your garden. When planning an area for relaxation, especially one in which you might sit and enjoy scented and aromatic perennials, assess to what extent it is overlooked.

Garden features Relating one feature to another is a mark of good garden design. A herbaceous border makes a good view from a terrace, for it will be at its best at a season when the terrace is most in use. The planting along a path to a garage or front gate should be less intensely seasonal, as it will be used all year round. A path is more interesting if it runs along a richly planted border than if it simply cuts across a lawn.

This richly planted herbaceous border of silver stachys, pinks, campanulas, and Oriental poppies with its neat mowing edge forms an intriguing view from the garden terrace.

CULTURAL FACTORS

A new and unplanted garden gives you the opportunity to investigate soil conditions in some detail before you start.

Soil Test for pH and nutrients (see p.27). In an empty garden, make tests over the whole area; you may find that there is a pattern of barren and fertile areas that could influence the overall design. Patches of particularly barren or intractable soil could be sites for a sitting or paved area, a shed or greenhouse.

Debris Soil is often moved during building work. Before you start to draw plans in any detail, dig holes at regular intervals across the garden (see p.25) to find out where infertile subsoil may have been brought to the surface, rubble or other debris has been buried, and to reveal any hidden features. A detailed plan of your findings will be an invaluable start-point for the garden plan itself.

Previous cultivation Digging trial holes may also reveal unusually fertile areas, perhaps where vegetables were once grown or animals kept. Such soil should be valued. An area like this could be the best site for a herbaceous border.

RENOVATING AN EXISTING PLANTING

Often, however, your new garden will already have been cultivated, so you don't have the opportunity to plan new borders from scratch: instead beds and borders must be improved or entirely renovated. Established borders may have been neglected by a previous owner, or you yourself may have allowed the plantings in your garden to deteriorate.

After several years of neglect, vigorous plants may have outgrown their space and invaded their neighbours, and small, compact varieties may have suffered by being smothered by nearby plants. Many plants may have become crowded and spindly. Because no one has done any deadheading, self-sown seedlings of some varieties may have overwhelmed others. Some plants may be suffering from lack of nutrients. Perennial weeds may have moved in, or annual weeds formed suffocating carpets.

ASSESSING EXISTING PLANTINGS

Moving to a new garden If you have moved house and taken over a border whose history is unknown, your best plan is to do almost nothing to it for a year while the plants in the border reveal themselves as the seasons go by. This is the only practical way to discover exactly which plants are in the border, especially if, in addition to perennials, it contains bulbs which remain dormant or difficult to identify for much of the year.

You should not leave the border entirely alone during this period, however. For a start, it is important to keep control of weeds. By spot-treating perennial weeds using a systemic weedkiller you can make some valuable improvements. You

Wait for a year when taking over new gardens; these *Allium sphaerocephalon* would not be visible for much of the year and could be damaged if the more obvious liatris and campanula were removed

can also test the soil and generate some overall ideas about possible planning approaches.

As each plant comes into its season, you need to decide whether it is worth retaining; at this stage the plant's position is not important. Plants you do not want should be consigned to the compost heap; often they will be superabundant self-sown seedlings of good plants (for example, astrantias, lamiums and hardy geraniums). Don't leave unwanted plants in place after they have flowered.

Occasionally you may find a good plant is struggling to grow. In this case it is often wise to lift it at once. Pot it up, then keep it in a cold frame until it is growing strongly again and is ready to plant out. Otherwise, plants you want to keep should be labelled, preferably, if they are unfamiliar to you, with full details of

height, colour and flowering time. You might take a photograph to aid identification during the winter. Plants that have grown into one another need careful labelling to ensure that the correct variety is retained.

It is important at this stage not to be seduced into the idea that only a few changes need be made because the border already has lots of large clumps of mature plants. Be prepared to remould plantings thoroughly to your own taste, rather than change only a little and be sorry later.

In your own garden Plantings in your own garden that have deteriorated through neglect are easier to deal with: you don't need to spend a year watching and waiting to discover exactly what the border contains. Dealing with the weeds by spot-treatment, deadheading and the removal of self-sown seedlings should be your priorities until the time comes for soil improvement and replanting.

The scale of renovation will depend on the period of neglect, the degree to which the plants have deteriorated and the extent to which you feel you require a new plan rather than a simple restoration of the original planting.

IMPROVING EXISTING PLANTINGS

Moving to a new garden After a year you will have assessed all the plants and know the extent to which the planting needs renovating and changing. It may be that the plan and the plants are basically good, in which case you have little to do beyond the usual seasonal tasks plus adding favourite varieties. On the other hand, the border may contain both overgrown clumps and large spaces, so you will have to carry out a more substantial renovation.

By now you should have developed some ideas for the future of the area. It is usually a mistake to be over-influenced at this stage by the size and position of the plants you wish to retain. You should instead be concerned with how the area can best be used within the context of your garden as a whole. Most perennials can be lifted, divided and replanted in the place that suits them best, and this has the additional advantage that it provides an opportunity to improve the soil. That said, plants which look their best after many years' developing into substantial mature clumps – hostas, hellebores and peonies, for example – can sometimes most usefully be left in place if they fit well into the overall scheme.

Once you have decided on the general plan of the border and discarded any unwanted plants, you can set

Tired, mature plantings can be improved in a short time by adding quick-growing plants like this anthemis, which will flower well in its first season.

about planning in more detail. First consider the shape of the border; you should make any changes in its size, shape or outline before you start improving the soil. Next spring or autumn you can remove the plants you want to keep, improve the soil, and then plant a mixture of retained plants and new acquisitions.

In your own garden Restoring your own borders can involve either a radical overhaul or a more modest revival. Where the deterioration has been substantial – clumps have grown

into one another, others have all but faded away and weeds have moved in – you need to take strong action. Remove most of the plants, kill or remove weeds, improve the soil, and then replant the healthiest pieces of the old plants.

If the neglect has been less drastic, a blitz on the weeds, plus lifting and replanting plants that appreciate regular division, like asters and achilleas, may be enough. Having carried out these measures, you need to follow them up with regular care.

BORDER SCALE AND STRUCTURE

Scale is important in two respects when planning for perennials. First, the overall dimensions of beds and borders must be in proportion to the size of the garden as a whole and the existing features within it. Second, the size and spread of the individual plants must match the scale of the border in which they are located.

BORDER AND GARDEN

It is difficult to give definitive advice on the best sizes for beds and borders. However, guidance can be given for plantings of different types.

One-sided borders As a general principle, the ideal depth of a border that is set against a wall, fence or hedge depends on the height of the background and the length of the border: the taller the background and the longer the border, the greater the depth required if the proportions are to look balanced.

Many backgrounds are about 1.8m (6ft) high; in such a case a formal border restricted to perennials will rarely be successful if less than approximately 1.5m (5ft) deep. A mixed border needs to be deeper than this in order to accommodate the greater size of its shrubs.

If for some reason the depth of a border along a wall or fence is restricted, it is often better not to attempt a sophisticated planting of perennials. A collection of special plants, well suited to the soil and aspect and likely to repay close inspection, can be grown instead. Alternatively, clothe the background with climbers and plant the strip at the base with ground-cover plants.

At the other extreme, a large size garden may require borders 3m (10ft)

This one-sided mixed border backed by a hedge has tall groups of shrubs at the back grading down to smaller perennials at the front.

deep or more if they are going to look in proportion. Such borders need to be thought about in terms of a distant viewpoint, from which they can be regarded in their entirety, as well as somewhere closer, from which individual plants can be appreciated. For a large one-sided border you will need to leave space for a path along the back to allow yourself good access for maintenance.

The front edge of a border is often made parallel to the background, but in many situations it is more appropriate to draw it in sweeping curves, especially if you plan an informal arrangement of beds within a formal structure of walls and/or hedges. In such a case, parts of the border can be made narrower than would otherwise be ideal, although this should not be done arbitrarily. If the front line sweeps back towards a wall at a point where there is a fragrant climber to smell or where a seat can be sited in a sunny place, this gives a rationale for the change of line.

Island beds Island beds are similarly less likely to be successful unless made at least 1.5m (5ft) wide; it is difficult to prevent narrower strips from developing a strongly linear look. One or both ends of an island bed can, however, be made narrower, especially if the beds are a little broader than 1.5m (5ft) in the centre or towards the other end. When shrubs or small trees are added to the perennials to create a mixed planting, the beds should be made substantially wider; otherwise, once the shrubs mature, there will be little room for the perennials. The majority of the shrubs and trees can be used to form the spine of the bed, providing both shelter and a background, with the planting on either side being more dominated by perennials. Each side will have its individual conditions and so can be planted differently.

Right: This mixed border uses shrubs for height and bulk, conifers for emphasis and perennials and bulbs for frontal colour.

PLANTS IN BORDERS

There are two aspects to choosing plants of the appropriate size for beds and borders: the height that they reach, and the breadth of the clumps in which they are grouped.

Plant height The standard rule is that the height of the tallest plants in a border should not exceed half its depth. In one-sided borders set against a wall, fence or hedge, the plants can be a little taller, but remember that, where light is partially cut off by the background, plants at the back are apt to stretch a little towards the light. Other useful guides are that the tallest plants in a long border should be slightly taller than those in a short one, and plants in a one-sided bed backing onto a tall background can be slightly taller than those backing onto a lower background.

Do not line up the tallest plants side by side along the back of a one-sided border or along the centre of an island bed; to avoid a regimented look, separate them by groups of lower plants. It is worth remembering that delphiniums and other plants with tall flower spikes need space if they are to be shown off effectively. Taller plants also look especially dramatic when silhouetted against a neutral background.

Many interesting variations can be created by occasionally extending groups of tall plants towards the front of the border and allowing drifts of shorter plants to extend towards the rear. Put shorter, early-flowering plants near the front and taller, spreading plants behind them; these will then open out into their space later in the season.

In areas where strong or icy winds restrict your choice of plants, you can divide one-sided mixed borders almost into individual compartments by positioning bold evergreen shrubs among and between the more delicate plants. These give valuable shelter as well as varied backgrounds.

Plants in clumps The size of the individual clumps of plants is something else you need to consider. A whole border, however narrow it is, usually looks messy if planted entirely with single plants unless they are especially chosen for their capacity to intertwine and knit together well. An arrangement of fewer, bolder clumps usually looks better.

The number of plants needed to fill a given space varies enormously, according to the habit and form of the plant. For example, a single plant of a bold and naturally expansive species, such as *Crambe cordifolia*, may fill the same space as six or eight plants of a delphinium of similar height. In general, in a 1.5m (5ft) border, a mix of individual plants and groups of three or five will usually be most effective.

On a larger scale, a one-sided border 3m (10ft) deep may require ten plants of some varieties. It is wise, however, to create interest by ensuring that the clumps are not all the same size.

One of the most successful and effective approaches here is to allocate different spaces to each of the different varieties. You can do this by varying the number of individuals of each variety you plant, while taking into account their growth habit.

Finally, remember that no two gardens are the same. Many of these guidelines should be adapted according to the style of the individual garden and your own inclinations.

Hostas are best left to grow into bold clumps; the geraniums can be split regularly.

HOUSE AND GARDEN

Perennial plantings should be planned to fit in with existing garden features and also with the style of your house to create a harmonious whole. This coordination of plantings, house and general garden environment depends partly on the matching of the permanent features themselves: any new stonework, paving or fencing should be executed in a similar style and with similar materials if possible, and furniture should be sympathetic in both style and colour. But, in gardens where plants are important, the design of planting must also be appropriate to the overall tone.

ARCHITECTURE AND GARDEN PLANNING

The style of your perennial plantings should to some extent match the style of the house. If this proves impossible or conflicts with your own tastes, at least make a definite decision to make the style different rather than just allow your plans simply to drift until you find yourself with a garden that has no clear relationship at all with the house.

Old houses Traditional cottages or those with thatched roofs prompt ideas of rambling cottage gardens. This juxtaposition is likely to be very successful, although it is by no means an easy effect to achieve.

Take, for example, a front garden with a path from the gate to the door. This setup can be dealt with in two ways. The path can be edged with box or pinks while the rest of the garden can be planted with the full range of cottage plants, even including vegetables towards the back. (You will also need access paths.) The alternative approach is to place alongside the path a strip of low planting, with pinks and bulbs, then an area of lawn behind and a broad border at the back. The size of the lawn can be varied according to the time you want to spend looking after the borders. If your time is limited, the style of planting can shift from the organized

Cottage garden flowers such as these delphiniums are well suited to the garden surrounding this traditional-style thatched cottage.

Asters, lavatera and crocosmias crowd the windows of this country cottage, giving a cosy rural feel.

chaos of the old-fashioned cottage garden towards a more modern mixed border, with broader drifts of plants and effective ground-cover, but do include some classic cottage plants, like foxgloves and peonies, to keep the theme alive.

If the house is especially attractive you might choose to treat the garden around it in a more modern way. Gravel or stone chippings, in a colour chosen carefully to match or complement the building, can make an attractive weed-suppressing surface across which the house can be appreciated without the clutter of plants. Then borders, or specimen roses with underplantings, can be sited in strategic corners, and poppies, foxgloves and verbascums can be allowed to self-sow into the gravel (though don't let them take over). You can use rustic containers for features, again ensuring their colour and style are in keeping with the house, and choose some old-fashioned timber or metal garden furniture.

A main reason that cottage-style gardens usually go so well with cottages is that the wealth of detail in the planting matches the degree of detail often seen in the design of the house itself. Such complexity might look amiss in a garden attached to a larger, bolder house; here you would probably opt for more expansive planting on a bigger scale, with larger clumps of plants intermingling rather less, and with plantings in other styles confined to small areas subdivided from the overall prospect by hedges.

The narrow gardens of small town houses might seem very restrictive but they, too, frequently provide a range of opportunities. For a Victorian house you might adopt a Victorian pattern, perhaps even using Victorian-style materials like terracotta edging, old brick paving and wrought iron. You could have a straight brick path edged with tiles, and regular borders with perennials or colourful bedding. A more interesting compromise might be achieved by creating a

Victorian structure as a basis for a more modern and varied planting.

An alternative approach is to divide a long, narrow garden widthwise into a series of compartments using hedges, trellises or fencing. The area immediately beside the house can be closest in style to the house itself, with the other compartments being treated more freely.

Modern houses These demand a different approach. The stark lines, clean look and unweathered squareness of many modern houses often demand, to maintain the balance, a corresponding boldness in the garden. A structure of solid evergreen shrubs, especially if used to soften the angles of the building itself, is often helpful. The shrubs have a 'presence' which can match that of a modern building, but they are also twiggy and leafy. Because this detail connects visually with perennial planting, the evergreens can provide a link between the house and your perennials. Climbing roses on the house's walls can have a similar effect.

A garden made up of sweeping curves, planted in informal groups, with island beds of perennials cut out of the grass, will tone down the angularity of the building. This works very well even with smaller houses, as long as there is room in the garden for the beds to be developed.

A large house needs space as balance, and the most difficult gardens to plan are the disproportionately small plots so often attached to large modern houses. Here the focus is often best turned away from the house to the boundaries – the fences or walls – which are usually in a more appropriate scale. If the garden of a large house is likewise large, it is often best to adopt a formal style (see p.112). Plan a formal structure in relation to the house, and then plant it formally – perhaps with a traditional herbaceous border. Different and potentially conflicting styles can be segregated by walls or hedges into self-contained compartments.

Single-storey houses are easier to manage than more substantial buildings. Although their height – or lack of it – restricts your opportunities to grow climbers on the walls, it also fits in better with the scale of garden plants and, indeed, of people. The fact that single-storey houses do not dominate the garden to the extent that larger houses do, and set the tone less rigidly, allows you to explore a greater range of styles.

EXISTING GARDEN STYLE

Relating a new border to an established garden is easier. The style is set: all you have to do is ensure the new planting fits in with the old. Formality goes with formality; an extra island bed is made; more containers are bought and a bed is developed with a new colour theme. However, perhaps the reason you want a new planting is that you seek something entirely different, in a new style.

Fitting an island bed into a formal setting or a formal planting into a cottage garden is more difficult. The solution is often to isolate the different styles, which can be done in a number of ways. In a very small property the only method might be to plan the front garden in a different style from the back, so that the house itself serves as a division between the two of them. Where more space is available, different styles can be blended by gradually changing from one to another, although in practice this may be difficult to manage successfully; one effective solution is to give large island beds a backbone of

The mature trees cast shade that provides an opportunity to plant shade-loving plants and maintain the woodland style of the garden.

shrubs and then plant in a different style on each side. However, the most reliable way to accommodate different styles in the garden is often, as already implied, to segregate them using screens, hedges, fences or walls. This has two great advantages: different styles are separated effectively and cannot clash, and visitors to the garden are treated to visual surprises as each area is discovered.

What overall layout might you devise for the garden of a modern house? An area of gravel could open out at the rear and drift into a group

of containers near the house and in a sunny area, Mediterranean plants, which need warm conditions and well-drained soil. A rustic summerhouse might be set in a hedged area planted in a cottage style, with an arch leading through to a colour-theme garden or vegetable plot. A hedge planted to shelter the terrace might open onto a path leading to a gate with a mixed border on either side. These individual areas need not be large. Even small gardens can be subdivided, perhaps using trellises rather than hedges as divisions between separate themes.

SEASONS

In recent years, and especially as gardens have become smaller, gardeners have turned to the idea of all-year-round gardens as a way to generate the maximum amount of colour and interest from a limited space. There are two ways of developing this theme. One is to plan each border so that there are always plants of interest to see. The other is to plan for different seasonal highlights in different parts of the garden.

THE SEASONAL BORDER

The other approach to creating year-round interest involves planning in exactly the opposite way. The idea is to arrange the garden so that different parts are at their best at different times of the year. Plants with the same flowering time are concentrated together, so that at one period of the year they create a small but very colourful display. As one seasonal planting begins to lose its attraction, another is coming into its most colourful period. Throughout the year you enjoy a succession of displays in different parts of the garden. Such plantings do not rely so much on shrubs and bulbs, although these can add to the spectacle.

Planning these highlights is easier than working out an all-year-round border, and much less daunting if you have never planned borders before.

Advantages and disadvantages of the seasonal border The two important advantages of the seasonal border are that in season it provides a far more colourful display than an all-year-round border ever does, and that it is easier to plan. The disadvantage is that, when its season of glory is over and interest moves elsewhere, that space in your garden becomes dull.

Bugles and primroses mingle with phlox and other easy alpines in this bright spring garden.

In summer, borders should be bursting with a wide range of colourful perennials.

Summer plants linger but autumn eupatoriums and heleniums are taking over.

THE ALL-YEAR-ROUND BORDER

When winters are not too harsh you can plan a perennial border so there are always plants of interest to enjoy; foliage plants in particular will provide much of the winter colour. But it is easier to create an all-year-round effect if the border also includes shrubs and bulbs to fill in during the months that are devoid of perennials.

If at the planning stage you choose plants from a variety of flowering seasons, while keeping factors like height and colour in mind, you will go some way towards achieving the effect you require. Other ways of avoiding seasonally empty areas in the border include:

• Allowing long-season foliage plants to intermingle with flowering plants, rather than keeping them separate.
• Choosing evergreen varieties wherever possible and mixing them with deciduous ones.
• Placing late-flowering varieties close by early-flowering ones so that, as the early ones die away, the later bloomers fill the space.
• Using climbing perennials on free-standing supports.
• In mixed plantings, adding plenty of shrubs for winter and bulbs for late autumn and spring.

The choice of plants is crucial. Perennials with a fortnight of fleeting glory are obviously unsuitable for all-year-round borders; instead include plants with characteristics that extend the season in some way. Look for plants with the following features:
• Unusually long flowering season.
• Attractive foliage.
• Autumn fruits or berries.
• Autumn-colouring leaves.
• Attractive winter stems.
• Evergreen foliage.
• Striking habit of growth.
• Attractive or interesting buds.

Leave the dead stems of perennials in place all winter to catch the morning frost.

111

Advantages and disadvantages of all-year-round borders The great benefit is that there is always something colourful – or at least interesting – to see. Particularly in a small garden, blank spaces can be especially noticeable, so it makes sense to avoid them.

However, achieving an effective all-year-round planting using only perennials is not easy. The winter effect will largely depend on evergreen foliage plants such as bergenias, lamiums and hellebores, but, if you include enough of these to make the winter attractive, you will have little space left for summer plants – with the result that, at the very time when flowering perennials are expected to be at their peak, the display is not very dramatic. This is the real problem with these borders: while you can plan them to ensure there is always something to see, at no time do they ever become really spectacular. So, almost inevitably, you have to slip in spring bulbs, lilies and tricyrtis and tender summer annuals to supply a burst of colour when the long-season border may be looking rather dull, with foliage its only attraction.

Silver and yellow foliage will provide colour for months before and after these summer flowers.

REALISTIC OPTIONS
Two compromise approaches can go some way towards providing the best of both worlds.

One is to plan as before for a succession of colourful displays, season by season, in different parts of the garden, but in this instance to choose the varieties very carefully so that, when their flowers are over, they display some other feature of interest, particularly foliage. Although the impact from a given area is reduced when flowering is over, the space remains interesting.

The second approach can be combined with the first. This is simply to underplant each area of perennials with bulbs for a different season. For example, a planting of perennials whose display is concentrated in the main summer season can be interplanted with clumps of daffodils, in either a single variety or a range, to extend the area's season of interest by providing fresh colour in spring.

In this way, even though the main spring display is in another part of the garden, the summer planting area provides additional spring colour from these companion plants.

Long-flowering perennials: *Alstroemeria* ('Princess' hybrids), *Aster × frikartii* 'Mönch', *Aster × frikartii* 'Wunder von Stäfa', *Clematis integrifolia*, *Dianthus* (modern pinks), *Penstemon*, *Geranium wallichianum* 'Buxton's Variety', *Geranium × riversleaianum* 'Russell Prichard', *Salvia farinacea*, *Scabiosa* 'Butterfly Blue'.

Flowering perennials with good foliage: *Achillea* Clypeolata Hybrids, *Anthemis punctata* ssp. *cupaniana*, *Aquilegia vulgaris* 'Vervaeneana', *Astilbe simplicifolia* 'Sprite', *Dianthus* (pinks), *Dicentra* (woodlanders), *Eryngium*, *Euphorbia × martinii*, *Lychnis coronaria*, *Pulmonaria*.

FORMAL AND INFORMAL

Borders and/or entire gardens can be planned in a formal or informal style. The choice depends partly on the nature of the house, partly on the degree of formality displayed by existing garden features, and partly on your own preferences.

HOUSE AND GARDEN
The age and style of the house are important. An older house with a symmetrical appearance will suggest a formal garden, perhaps with box hedges or a pair of herbaceous borders. The elegance of such a house may itself be an important feature of the garden, and the planting must not detract from it. Conversely, a modern house in a less symmetrical style will suggest a less formal approach, with more curves, a relative lack of symmetry, and planting in a less ordered style; the planting may even clothe the house walls, so the house becomes part of the garden.

In many cases you will want to tailor these general principles so that the parts of the garden close to the house match it in style, with more distant areas developed in different styles. You can do this in two ways, either by instituting distinct styles in separate, self-contained parts of the garden or by creating a steady transition to a contrasting style.

WHAT ARE FORMAL AND INFORMAL STYLES?
In theory the distinctions between formal and informal styles are very clear. In practice, however, they can become blurred.

Formal style Formal styles are based on strong, straight lines; these are stressed in the obvious boundaries of

In a formal setting with evergreen hedges, double perennial borders look superb.

the garden as a whole, in the divisions within the garden, and in the shapes of the beds and borders. These lines are frequently emphasized by the planting of bold, often cleanly cut evergreen hedges, such as tall yew hedges or short box edging.

Symmetry is important. Matching borders may be created on opposite sides of a straight path, with a clear focal point in the distance. This focal point may be part of the house, a garden building, a specimen tree, a piece of statuary or, in large gardens, a feature of the landscape which actually lies beyond the garden boundary. Within the borders, individual specimen plants may be either repeated or duplicated opposite each other to create an additional feeling of regularity.

Other elements of formal gardens can include:
• Rectangular beds.
• Square areas which are subdivided into smaller squares, perhaps with the corners marked by matching specimen plants.
• Matching pairs of ornamental urns, seats, fountains or plants.

A planting that features perennials is always less strongly formal because perennials are by their nature soft and relaxed in their growth. While it is always possible to trim a hedge in a formal manner, perennials cannot be treated in the same way. It is more important when aiming to establish a formal style to think carefully about the manner in which the plants are arranged. Here are some guidelines:

• Grow perennials separately from other plants.
• Use pinks and other low plants as a linear edging.
• Keep the tall plants firmly at the backs of the borders and grade the plants evenly down to shorter varieties at the front.
• Plant in substantial groups that are well supported and cleanly separated from their neighbours.
• Pay timely attention to the details of cultivation, such as deadheading and cutting down, so that plants always look well tended.

Informal style Informal styles are based on a more natural look. This does not mean that the gardener stands back and lets the plants look after themselves, although in some settings this may be possible. The same degree of organization and planning is required, but directed towards a different objective.

Informality depends on a softer and less rigid approach to both gardens and planting. Curves, rather than straight lines, may predominate.

An asymmetrical layout gives a more appropriately relaxed feeling. Use sweeping curves that wherever possible reflect the contours of the garden and take in existing natural features like mature shrubs.

Whereas symmetry and line are emphasized in the formal approach, here they are played down, softened and – in more extravagant informal plantings – lost altogether; differences rather than similarities should be accentuated. Use a less definite division between the planting and any neighbouring paving or grass. Tough

perennials can be naturalized in rough grass, while creeping varieties can be allowed to escape from the border across gravel or along the cracks in paving.

You can relax the rule whereby tall plants are placed at the back of the border and short ones at the front. You can let plants mingle with each other, even plant them so that their clumps overlap. If their seed heads are interesting you do not need to cut the plants down the moment the flowers fade.

Plants such as campanulas and achilleas can be allowed to self-sow and their seedlings encouraged to create occasional surprises among other plants. Of course, you may have to remove many of their seedlings to prevent prolific varieties swamping others, and sometimes you may need to cheat a little and move a seedling

to a better spot where it will look as if it has turned up by chance, but the principle still holds. Staking can be less rigid, and plants can be allowed to fall into each other a little – though you will need to keep a watchful eye on them to ensure that shorter varieties are never overwhelmed.

COMBINING STYLES

Many successful gardens set informal plantings within a more formal layout characterized by bold lines, symmetry and a strong relationship with the house. This design gives the garden a clear, strong structure, but permits a more informal, relaxed planting style.

A rectangular border may be backed by a yew hedge and even edged with a low box hedge, but the perennials planted there can be organized in a more relaxed and informal way and cared for without the precision required by more formal plantings. In particular, you can break the straight lines by having low plants (such as hardy geraniums) growing over and through the box edging or billowing out over paving. The occasional self-sown seedlings that find their way into the path may be left in place.

For many gardeners this combination of a formal structure with an informal planting is the most satisfying approach. It allows a transition from the solidity of the house to the natural feeling of the garden; it provides some structure within which to work, yet still allows opportunity for personal expression in the choice and arrangement of the plants.

A formal boxwood hedge encloses a tumbling cascade of colourful flowering perennials.

Right: Allowing low-growing plants to spread onto the path and placing tall plants at random in the border creates an informal and relaxed garden scene.

COLOUR PLANNING

Most gardeners grow perennials mainly for their colour but, while the colours themselves are obviously important, using them effectively can be a challenge. There are three main ways of using colour when planning beds and borders:

• Colour contrasts can create a bold, eye-catching border.

• Cooler pastel shades can be used to create a more harmonious effect.

• Different strengths of the same colour will make a subtle show.

You can use these techniques singly or in any combination in different places within a border to create a highly sophisticated display.

SINGLE-COLOUR BORDERS

Borders in which the flowers and much of the foliage are in the same colour range can be the most effective and satisfying of all. It might seem that creating a border based on a single colour theme should be a simple proposition; if you plan a border composed largely of yellow flowers, for example, and ensure that all the varieties flower at approximately the same time, you will indeed create an interesting display. But with a little more planning you can produce something altogether more striking.

As a first step, select plants of a single basic colour, but choose varieties whose flowers or foliage varies from the rich and dark to the pale and pastel. If you planted these on their own you might achieve the ultimate in colour harmony but still produce a fairly dull display. To add variety, consider the other features of the plants. The overall habit of a plant, its foliage, the shape of the flowers, and the way they are held on the plant – all become more important when the colour range is relatively narrow.

You must decide where to define the boundary between one colour and another. When planning a border of yellow flowers, should you include varieties whose flowers are closer to orange or cream? Bending the rules may cause awkward clashes – or add the spark that lifts the whole border.

White agapanthus and fragrant white tobacco plants create a cool summer border.

COLOUR CONTRASTS

Bold colour contrasts create the most striking borders: scarlet and white, for example, or purple and yellow. However, while these are undeniably brilliant, eye-catching combinations, they are not restful.

Sometimes, unless the shapes of the plants are well chosen, they can look strangely unplanned. Such borders are best sited where the spectacle can be admired from a distance. They can be so bold and overpowering that they need to be positioned in areas separated from other parts of the garden: by trees, a lawn, a hedge, fence or perhaps a fruit garden, otherwise they will dominate and in effect nullify any cooler combinations nearby.

In practice you are unlikely to want to create a whole border of contrasting perennials. Contrasts on a smaller scale, however, can work well, offering endearing and very effective surprises in containers or small corners.

HARMONIOUS COLOURS

Borders with broader colour themes, such as two or three harmonious flower and foliage colours used together in a single bed or border, are simpler to plan and more likely to be successful than not.

Bringing together harmonious colours creates a more restful and relaxing feel. The softness of pastel colours such as blush-pink and pale sky-blue, linked by grey foliage, is best suited to a modest scale. Large plantings, seen from a distance, may enhance the atmosphere of the garden as a whole and draw the eye, but are too subtle to be impressive features. Harmonious colour combinations are most rewarding when you inspect them closely as this allows you to appreciate the subtlety.

Pink, mauve, and white perennials harmonize well in a cottage garden.

SOPHISTICATED COLOUR BORDERS

Bringing all these themes into one planting is a real challenge. It is often wiser to start with more limited objectives, and then to build on early successes in planning your borders, as you feel your confidence develop.

Planting to coordinate both contrast and harmony in colour, plus all the other variables of season, flower, foliage, shape and texture, not to mention the possibility of including shrubs, climbers, annuals and bulbs alongside the perennials, is a great adventure. When it works well it can be a triumph; the very fact that so much care has gone into the planning ensures that the end result far surpas

Purple lupins, salvias, and catmints look superb with fresh green foliage.

PLANT
COMBINATIONS

The ultimate success of planting schemes for beds and borders depends not only on how well the plants are grown but also on the way in which individual plants are grouped together. Putting the right colours of flower and foliage side by side; creating interesting juxtapositions of plant habit, form and texture; and integrating other features such as fruits into the overall planting scheme can transform a border from a muddle to a work of art.

Above: Careful colour harmonization in this mixed border sees purple echinops and hibiscus and bluish perovskia grown with silver-leaved stachys and artemisia, pale mauve phlox and white highlights from antirrhinums.

Left: In this summer-long perennial border the blue spikes of delphiniums are echoed in the purplish salvias and yellow thalictrums providing a lightening effect. Behind the salvia, crocosmias and heleniums will continue the display into autumn.

Left: A simple grouping of just two plants can create a most impressive effect. Here the yellow leaves of Catalpa bignonoides 'Aurea' provide the perfect background for the mahogany red flowers of 'Stafford', an old variety of hemerocallis but still one of the best.

FLOWER COLOUR

Grouping flower colours effectively is fundamental to creating a satisfying perennial display in the border; while there are planning guidelines that can help the newcomer, personal taste must always be paramount. The principles involved in the three basic approaches to colour planning were outlined earlier on page 116; here we discuss more detailed ideas, with popular plants as examples.

COLOUR CONTRASTS

Bold contrasts are best seen from a distance – the full effect is at its most impressive when seen across a lawn. However, while the choice of contrasting colours is the first priority, they can be emphasized if you pay attention to other types of contrast.

A clump of a delphinium, such as the bright 'Blue Nile' with its distinct white eye, stands out well and reaches 1.5–2m (5–6ft) in height, so the flat, deep butter-yellow heads of the rather shorter *Achillea* 'Coronation Gold' can be set slightly to one side. Here more than colour is involved: the flat heads of the achillea contrast with the upright spikes of the delphinium. The feathery, brick-red plumes of *Astilbe* 'Red Sentinel', a variety that also has unusually dark foliage, can go alongside the achillea. At the front you could add smaller summer varieties such as *Leucanthemum* 'Snowcap', with its bright, yellow-eyed white daisies, alongside the long-lasting slender spikes of *Salvia* 'East Friesland' in bluish-violet and, in a foam of greenish-yellow, *Alchemilla mollis*. If there is space, you might complete the picture with

Left: Contrasting white and blue campanulas with purple lythrum work well in this damp bed.

short edging plants like the salmon pink *Dianthus* 'Doris', the vivid red and yellow daisies of *Gaillardia* 'Kobold' or the multicoloured foliage of *Houttuynia cordata* 'Chameleon'.

This is a grouping of strikingly dissimilar flower colour, but there are also contrasts in the habits and forms of the individual flowers. The result is an undeniably colourful assemblage, but because of the careful choice of plants it avoids any of the garish clashes of colour that can sometimes result from juxtaposing varieties in strong shades.

HARMONIOUS COLOURS

The use of softer, more harmonious pastel shades creates a cooler, more restful atmosphere; while from a distance the effect may seem hazy, it is very satisfying close up.

Asters and anemones are two of the most important perennials of beds and borders in the autumn. *Aster × frikartii* 'Wunder von Stäfa' is a very attractive long-flowering soft lavender-blue aster with yellow eyes. Of the anemones, the pretty, pure white single-flowered *Anemone × hybrida* 'Honorine Jobert', also with yellow eyes, is especially lovely. If you set silver foliage in front of both, this will help tie the two shades together and connect them with the rest of the planting. Artemisias are always useful in this role, but here *Anaphalis margaritacea* var. *yedoensis* is a better choice; its downy foliage is slightly whiter, and it has the added bonus of small, silvery white everlasting flowers, while its slightly running habit helps it link up well with its neighbours. In front of the aster you could put the white pompom chrysanthemum 'Purleigh White', which develops pinkish tinges as it ages. On the other side of the anaphalis why not try

Phygelius × rectus 'Pink Elf', which has crimson-tipped pale pink tubes held in elegant open sprays.

The net result is that the use of silver forms a link between the lavender blue, pure white, blushed white and pale pink. This might look too pale and watery, so, running along the very front, you could have the dwarf, double, darker blue *Aster* 'Professor Anton Kippenberg', which fits in well with the flat heads of the rich, reddish pink ice-plant *Sedum* 'Autumn Joy'. These two plants, in slightly more definite colours, will also link in well with the many other, stronger autumn hues. As a bonus, this group should prove attractive to butterflies, which are particularly fond of the asters and the sedum.

SINGLE-COLOUR BORDERS

Choosing the majority of the plants in a border from a narrow range of flower colours may seem too restrictive. In fact, single-colour borders offer a straightforward way of creating an interesting planting. Where it

is possible to include foliage in the same range, a continuity of colour is maintained throughout the season.

Red borders There are two important questions to answer before tackling a red border. First, what exactly is red? You must decide whether or not to include rich crimson shades and how far to go in the direction of orange, ginger and gold.

To some extent your answer to the first question depends on just how you answer the second: should bronze and copper foliage be included in the selection? Red flowers and bronze foliage go together well; indeed, plants like *Lobelia* 'Queen Victoria' combine the two colours in a single plant. However, if you bring red flowers and bronze leaves together the result is a border which is very dark in both colour and atmosphere. Hence the relevance in this context of your response to the first question: a red border could easily include brighter, fierier shades of ginger and orange which will add a refreshing sparkle to the single-colour effect.

A single-colour border mixing red and bronze perennials with dahlias and other tender plants.

The best advice, if you decide to use a narrow range of brilliant red flower colours, is to restrict the foliage colours mainly to green; this creates a bright and effective planting. However, a far more satisfying planting can be created by adding bronze foliage. It then pays to incorporate additional varieties with yellow and orange flowers to create a wonderfully hot and fiery display.

Yellow borders Yellow is such a cheerful colour that borders of perennials selected from yellow-flowered varieties are very popular. There are other reasons. Flowers of this colour sit well with green foliage, and there are many yellow-leaved perennials which can be used to carry the colour theme when flowering varieties are out of season.

It is sometimes said that too many yellow flowers belong to the daisy family and flower in late summer. However, in spring there are primroses, euphorbias and irises, and in summer there are more hemerocallis, irises, kniphofias and achilleas, so there is a sufficiently wide range of other varieties to choose in creating an effective long-season border.

Although many flowers come in clean, pure yellows, some lack richness. The addition of gold- and even orange-tinted varieties can give the border extra substance and provide a greater depth of colour.

White borders White flowers look cool and seem very refreshing in sunny places particularly on sultry summer days. They are also valuable in darker areas of the garden. It is hardly surprising that white borders represent the most popular single-colour approach. White flowers have the great advantage of being set off especially well by foliage: they form an effective contrast with green leaves or a softer effect with silver foliage.

Once you have assembled a few white-flowered varieties you will soon notice some are much whiter than others. In part this may derive from colour changes as the flowers age: some are greenish or slightly blushed in bud, others may blush as they age. Still other flowers are never pure white but always have a hint of cream. When the varieties are planted together, the differences show. Some gardeners enjoy this slight variability and design to exploit it. If you intersperse foliage plants that have a creamy variegation, like *Symphytum* 'Goldsmith' or *Hosta* 'Shade Fanfare', among the flowering plants, you can achieve very pleasing effects.

So you can choose varieties with clean white flowers and use them with fresh green foliage; or you can add creamier shades and select foliage to match.

Blue borders Unfortunately there are comparatively few blue-flowered perennials, and a disproportionate number of them are delphiniums and salvias, which tends to unbalance the selection. Also, you have to take care when choosing among the purplish-blue varieties, like various darker penstemons, as their coloration may not sit happily with the clearer, sharper blues of some of the bushy Belladonna delphiniums.

By way of compensation, blues look especially good against fresh, bright green foliage, and indeed foliage in general can be a great help. In particular, the blue-leaved hostas make excellent companions for blue flowers and, as long as the soil does not dry out, will often grow more successfully in full sun than other hostas. From small varieties like 'Halcyon' and 'Blue Moon' to the more substantial *Hosta sieboldiana* 'Elegans' and the enormous 'Krossa Regal', all make good companions for blue flowers and can contribute considerably to the overall effect.

Yellow flowers create a sunny effect and are at their best in late summer.

SOPHISTICATED COLOUR BORDERS

Bringing all these different elements of colour planning together into a single, sophisticated planting is not easy to carry off successfully. The result, however, is an extremely satisfying display, and so most gardeners will want to make the attempt.

Starting with an evergreen hedge behind, a group could be built up with a background of a huge cloud of the slightly creamy white flowers of *Crambe cordifolia*. In front of these, and contrasting in habit, you could put the solid upright heads of the pink border phlox 'Eva Callum' and, alongside it, the Belladonna delphinium 'Peace', whose strong blue contrasts boldly with the phlox in colour but whose open, airy habit is similar to that of the crambe at the back. In between the phlox and the delphinium you could tuck creamy yellow daisies of the variety *Anthemis* 'E. C. Buxton', whose colour would connect with that of the crambe at the same time as contrasting with the phlox and delphinium.

Central to the next rank of shorter plants could be the silver foliage of *Artemisia* 'Silver Queen', which will fall into all its neighbours slightly and thereby serve to link them up. On one side, in front of the phlox, could go the flat yellow heads and pewtery green foliage of *Achillea* 'Moonshine', while on the other you could grow the pretty white bells of *Campanula persicifolia* 'Hampstead White'.

For the front rank of smaller plants you might choose to grow the neat-looking *Agapanthus* 'Lilliput', with its rounded heads of blue flowers; bronze-leaved *Heuchera* 'Palace Purple', with its rich purple foliage and white flowers; a pair of border pinks such as the highly scented white *Dianthus* 'White Ladies' and the pink and deep red 'Houndspool Ruby'; and the long-flowering, pink-petalled *Geranium endressii* 'Wargrave'.

Your border, a blend of mainly early-summer-flowering plants whose colour continues into autumn, would be a wonderful display of contrast, harmony and interesting shapes.

Brilliant flower colours are softened by looking through *Verbena bonariensis* and by pale yellow golden rods and limy tobacco plants.

FLOWERING AND GROWTH HABIT

Flower colour may be the first feature you consider when planning perennial borders, but other factors are just as important. The shapes of the plants and the ways in which the flowers are carried on them have a significant effect on the liveliness of any planting.

Plants come in six main growth styles: upright, arching, flat-topped, rounded, sprawling and spreading.

Upright plants Many tall perennials such as delphiniums, macleaya and lupins and shorter ones such as *Salvia × sylvestris*, plus kniphofias, which come in many sizes, have noticeably straight stems with a strongly vertical

Harmony in colour and variation in plant habit create an interesting planting.

look. They create a bold, military impression, although this is sometimes softened by the shapes of the flowers themselves. Planting too many upright plants together can look ridiculous especially if they are aligned in rows instead of growing in more natural looking clumps. But they are excellent for setting behind varieties such as achilleas, which have flat-topped flower heads. This creates interesting angles between the vertical stems of one and the horizontal heads of the other which are very pleasing.

Arching plants There are relatively few arching perennials, and many are ornamental grasses. The taller sorts, like the grey-leaved grass *Helictotrichon sempervirens*, have a special elegance best revealed when they are not cluttered by other plants nearby; only varieties which hug the ground make suitable neighbours. Smaller grasses with an arching, fountain-like habit, such as *Hakonechloa macra* 'Alboaurea', are excellent plants for growing in containers and look good hanging over low walls.

Flat-topped plants As with arching perennials, there are not many flat-topped varieties. In most of them it is the flower head rather than the whole plant which is flat. Achilleas and autumn sedums are the most frequently seen, along with *Lychnis chalcedonica*. Among the plants that do develop a flat-topped habit of growth are some of the shorter asters, while clumps of hostas often develop into a plateau of foliage as they mature. Plants with vertical stems contrast well with both groups, while rounded, billowing plants like gypsophilas can soften the strong horizontal line effectively.

Rounded plants Many perennials have a generally rounded look, although some are tighter in growth

than others. Border pinks in many colours, the shade-loving *Geranium macrorrhizum*, the spring-flowering *Lathyrus vernus* and the yellow *Euphorbia polychroma* create a fairly solid, rounded look – although, as a single plant spreads into a large group, the effect may change so that the clump becomes flat-topped and rounded at the edges. Gypsophilas and *Alchemilla mollis* develop a softer, more foamy look.

Sprawling plants These have a looser, more open habit, and their stems perform the invaluable function of naturally spreading into neighbours to create attractive informal associations and perform a useful linking function, drawing plants together into a cohesive group. These are the natural blenders among which you could consider the pretty red bells of *Campanula punctata* 'Elizabeth', the angular, upright shoots of *Malva sylvestris* 'Primley Blue', the long-flowering *Geranium* 'Johnson's Blue' and the more vigorous magenta of *Geranium* 'Ann Folkard'.

Spreading plants Perennials with almost flat growth are for the front of the border. They will knit in around the crowns of more upright plants, make flat mats at the border edge, and creep out across gravel or paving (they must be restrained from creeping out across the lawn). These are plants such as ajugas, with their variety of coloured foliage and most often blue flowers; the almost white-leaved *Artemisia stelleriana*; *Potentilla tonguei*, with its crimson-centred apricot flowers; and *Stachys byzantina* 'Silver Carpet', which produces an attractive silvery mat.

Right: Billowing, greenish yellow alchemilla fronts the contrasting spikes of Sisyrinchium striatum, yellow lupin spikes and bushy roses.

FOLIAGE COLOUR

Foliage makes its contribution to the border for a far longer period of the year than most flowers, so it is especially important to choose foliage plants carefully. Most foliage does not cause colour clashes: green, the natural colour of leaves, always provides a reliable background, and even leaves in other shades share an underlying green tint.

Foliage comes in the following main colour groups: green; green with variegations; yellow and gold; blue and greyish blue (sometimes with variegations); grey and silver; and bronze, red and purple.

This planting of hosta, ligularias and ferns shows a variety of green shades.

GREEN FOLIAGE

The natural colour of leaves creates a uniquely restful background for flowers and associates well with most other foliage colours. But green comes in a variety of shades, from the deep green of a background yew hedge to the brighter shades of young hosta leaves. Furthermore, the leaves of an individual plant may change colour as the months go by, and many yellow-leaved perennial plants become green as the season progresses. If you have made the decision to incorporate few other foliage colours, you can create visual variation by selecting varieties with different leaf-shapes and textures (see p.128).

YELLOW AND GOLD FOLIAGE

The words 'yellow' and 'gold' are often used indiscriminately to cover a wide range of yellow shades. In fact there are very few genuinely gold-leaved plants, but the colour category 'yellow' does cover a wide spread of shades, from deep cream through primrose to deep, rich yellow.

Yellow-leaved perennials bring light and brightness to the border, but you have to be careful how you position them. In some varieties the leaves scorch in full sun: the edges turn brown and crisp and the beauty of the plant is ruined. The degree of scorch depends to some extent also on the moisture content of the soil, with plants in moist soils being more tolerant. Conversely, many yellow varieties, when planted in areas of shade, lose their strength of colour and become greener; numerous hostas change in this way.

Despite these difficulties, yellow foliage can be used effectively with plants that have orange flowers or blue flowers and, even, cautiously, with red flowers. It also looks good with green or bronze foliage in contrasting shapes.

BLUE FOLIAGE

Few plants have leaves that are truly blue; rather more, especially hostas and grasses, show shades of bluish-green and greyish-blue, or have a waxy blue sheen to the leaves. Often these plants are sun-lovers and associate well with flowers of many shades, especially yellow, blue and white. A contrast of shapes seems to allow more opportunities; for example, a bold yellow leaf next to a bold blue one may look garish, but the blue-leaved *Hosta* 'Halcyon' looks very effective with yellow-leaved grasses trailing across it.

A few bluish-leaved plants, mainly hostas such as 'Frances Williams', which has foliage broadly, but irregularly edged with cream, are also variegated in cream or yellow. This combination can look very good, but it can be difficult to find pleasing groupings with other plants. Use such varieties either as isolated specimens, or with green foliage, or with pale yellow or pale blue flowers.

GREY AND SILVER FOLIAGE

The majority of grey- and silver-leaved plants originate in hot climates. The coating of hairs on the leaf, which gives them their colouring, helps protect the leaf from scorching sun and also reduces evaporation. In the garden many are highly drought-resistant and are good in sunny, well-drained borders.

Silver and grey have the great advantage of associating well with most other flower and foliage colours, while their neutralizing effect ensures that they clash with very few. So plants like artemisias and anaphalis are invaluable both for creating harmonious links between pastel shades and for preventing bold, primary colours from seeming too garish.

BRONZE, RED AND PURPLE FOLIAGE

Foliage in these dark shades must be deployed carefully: over use can make beds and borders seem too dark and create an unnecessarily heavy atmosphere. In general, brilliant blue flowers and hot-coloured flowers make good companions, together with grey and silver foliage; but it is in fiery borders with scarlet, crimson, rusty, gingery and orange flowers that bronze, red or purple foliage is most effective, adding valuable depth to the fiery sparkle.

Heuchera 'Palace Purple' is a rich colour.

VARIEGATED FOLIAGE

Variegated leaves – striped, edged, speckled or blotched with white, cream or yellow – are, after green, the most widespread type of foliage seen in gardens. As a general rule,

you should use variegated foliage sparingly; too much can look artificial without simple greens for contrast.

The degree of variegation varies enormously, from the narrow, clean white leaf edge of the Solomon's Seal *Polygonatum falcatum* 'Variegatum', to the bold cream streak of *Hosta undulata* 'Univittata', which fills most of the leaf. In some plants the brightness of the variegation creates a stark contrast with the basic leaf colour. In other plants the effect is more subtle. From a distance many variegations merge to create a haze of pale colour; only close up do you discover the details of the markings.

Some variegated perennials, like *Pulmonaria rubra* 'David Ward', scorch in full sun; this is also the case with many yellow-leaved plants. Some produce occasional plain green, stronger-growing shoots which will swamp the variegated ones unless completely removed.

The leaves of Houttuynia cordata 'Chameleon' are brighter than many flowers.

FOLIAGE FORM AND TEXTURE

Colour is not everything. While most perennials die down for the winter, some are evergreen, and this adds interest to the garden in winter. In these and other perennials the shape and texture of the foliage are also important. If you use these two features imaginatively you can add enormously to the success of your plantings, both large and small. Most often, the interesting shape and texture of foliage is more apparent from close up than from a distance, when such details may be invisible.

FOLIAGE FORM
Leaves vary in shape from the 'elephant ears' of the bergenias and the bold, circular leaves of *Darmera peltata*, each mounted on its own, individual central stalk, to feathery ferns and the long, hair-like strands of sedges such as *Carex comans* 'Bronze Form'.

Size as well as shape is important. At one extreme are the vast rhubarb-like leaves of *Gunnera manicata*, while at the other are the short, slender threads of *Coreopsis verticillata*. In between is the vast array of oval and divided shapes, from the tiny to the huge, which are so often overlooked in favour of flowers when planning borders.

The important rule to remember is: don't group together too many plants whose leaves are all more or less the same size and shape; as always with foliage, the starkest contrast is often the most successful. Delicate lacy ferns, broad heart-shaped hosta leaves and the narrow arching leaves of *Carex pendula* provide three contrasting shapes to make a group in a shady corner.

Grasses, bold hellebore leaves, and arching polygonatums make an attractive foliage combination.

Foliage shape can also be used very effectively with flowering plants. Divided foliage, especially when carried on lax stems (as with many hardy geraniums), will fit neatly among the vertical stems of plants like campanulas and help knit the planting together. As another example, dense bold foliage, like that of the larger hostas, can be used to hide the stems of *Aster novi-belgii* varieties, which often lose their lower leaves by late summer.

This intermingling of foliage and flowers is especially valuable when planting mixed borders, where the foliage of perennials can be used both to mask the leafless stems of bulbs and to make a strong and effective angle with their upright growth.

FOLIAGE TEXTURE
Leaves vary enormously in texture, a fact which can be used to great advantage in the border. For example, bearded irises are stiff but have a matt finish; the beautiful lobed leaves of *Geranium renardii* are soft and veined like those of culinary sage; and the marsh marigold *Caltha palustris* has leaves that are unusually glossy. Mixing these different textures usually works well – the contrast can be quite effective even when the shapes are similar. With many perennials it is the combination of shape and texture that creates the effect; for example, the soft leaves of many catmints are so small and neat that an overall impression of colour and delicacy is all that is apparent.

FRUITS

Most flowering perennials produce fruits after they flower. Attractive fruits can add a great deal of interest to borders many months after the main display of flowers is over.

Fruits can be divided into two groups: fleshy fruits, such as berries, and secondly, the various more familiar seed heads which turn dry and brown in the autumn. Neither will form if the plants are deadheaded, so the costs of retaining the fruits may be a reduced flowering display and unwanted self-sown seedlings.

PERENNIALS WITH BERRIES

Many berry-bearing plants do not have very colourful flowers. The clusters of white berries of *Actaea alba* and the corresponding red of *A. rubra* follow relatively dowdy creamy white flowers, but they bring a real surprise to a shady border long after all the spring flowers are over. The orange lanterns of *Physalis franchetii*, with their orange berries inside, are a different case; here again the flowers are less important, but the wandering roots often invade other vigorous

These red fruits of Actaea rubra are preceded by spikes of creamy flowers.

plants such as *Aster ericoides* 'Golden Spray' and yellow-leaved shrubs, among which the inflated orange fruits look pretty.

OTHER PERENNIAL FRUITS

The dried pods are the main fruiting attraction of some perennials. These are less colourful than berries, and need either a plain background to show them off or to be positioned near paths, where they will be more easily noticed.

The dark, slender stems of *Veratrum nigrum* last well, as do the spent pods of *Hosta sieboldiana*; when covered with the first autumn frosts they are particularly attractive. Grasses last, too; and, although the heads tend to fall to pieces as the weeks go by, the bleached stems and heads of

Miscanthus sinensis 'Silberfeder', for example, still look good in the middle of winter, especially if set against the background of a dark evergreen.

This illustrates another useful feature of perennials: their dead stems. Traditionally almost all perennials were cut down to the ground in the autumn but, if they are left in place, they provide not only protection for dormant overwintering buds at the base but also additional interest for many weeks. The structure of the bare dead branches can be attractive in itself, and in the depths of winter, when covered in white frost and with spiders' webs slung between the stems, they are a real delight. They are especially valuable in parts of the garden you pass as you go out or can see from the house.

The orange lanterns of physalis look good with their own yellow autumn foliage, though the plant's wandering roots mean that the lanterns sometimes appear among neighbouring foliage.

Left: In small borders plants can be allowed to mingle intimately. Here the silvery blue stars surrounding the green cones of this eryngium repay close examination as they emerge through reddish stems and pink spikes of Polygonium amplexicaule.

Above: The slender, creamy, vertical spikes of Kniphofia 'Little Maid' contrast well in shape and in colour with the flat pink heads of Sedum spectabile in this colourful autumn planting.

CHOOSING
PERENNIALS

There are so many perennials available that it can be difficult to select exactly which varieties to grow. Of course, personal taste must come first: there is no point growing plants you do not like. At the same time, there is little to be gained by trying to grow plants in soils or situations where they will never thrive, so choosing the right plant for the right place is vital.

Above: Rich, moist soil in partial shade provides ideal conditions for the brilliant blue Meconopsis grandis to stand tall above candelabra primulas and Hosta fortunei 'Aurea' with a dense cover of variegated hostas in the foreground.

THE ADAPTABILITY OF PERENNIALS

Perennials are highly adaptable plants, and fit well into a wide variety of garden situations. In recent years the range of varieties has increased in response to changes in gardening trends, so now more than ever, there is a plant for every place.

This adaptability reveals itself in two ways. First, because perennials come from such a wide range of natural habitats – meadows and forests, riversides and moors – there are species ideally suited to almost all soils and garden situations. Once adapted to gardens, these species have given rise to many more varieties in different colours or sizes and thus increased the range enormously. Second, some individual species of perennials are tolerant of a wide range of garden conditions. For example, many hardy geraniums will, within reasonable limits, grow in sun or shade, clay soil or gravel, dry or damp. It is, therefore, less easy to make mistakes when planting perennials than, for example, when planting alpines or annuals.

However, this certainly does not mean that perennials will grow in any and every circumstance. They do best and give their best display when planted in the soil and situation that suits them. The most important thing to remember is that you can improve conditions that are comparatively inhospitable to perennials until the widest possible range can be grown.

SPECIAL SOILS

It is impossible to change the fundamental nature of garden soil but often it can be made more favourable for a particular purpose. Improving the soil both allows you to grow a wider range of the more adaptable plants and provides conditions that will suit many of the more specialized plants.

HEAVY CLAY SOIL

Clay soil is sticky, often difficult to work, holds water, warms up slowly in the spring and may open into wide cracks in dry weather. It can be improved by drainage, and especially by adding large quantities of bulky organic matter. Every step taken towards reducing the negative effects of the clay will widen the range of plants you can grow in the garden, yet will have no adverse effect on the growth of natural clay-lovers. Clay soil which has been improved steadily over the years often turns out to be the most fertile of all soils, able to support a very wide range of plants.

Plants to grow Many of the best plants for heavy soils flower in summer or autumn: mauve eupatoriums, heleniums in yellow and rusty shades, and hemerocallis, now available in enormous diversity. Many of the yellow summer and autumn daisies are also good for growing in heavy soil. These plants all have strong root systems, which is why they are naturally content in heavy soil; thorough preparation (see p.26) will help them grow even more vigorously.

Strong-rooted spring flowers, such as *Helleborus orientalis* hybrids, usually succeed too, but spring-flowering woodland plants are less happy. Fortunately their root systems are

Helenium 'Moerheim Beauty' is one of many daisies which thrive in heavy soil.

relatively shallow so, to create the conditions they enjoy, you can raise the level of the bed and add leafy soil, or improve just the top few centimetres of the heavy clay with garden compost. Such measures will allow plants such as ajugas, asarums, ferns and primroses to thrive.

Plants to avoid Some plants find it hard to thrive in heavy clay, no matter how much it is improved. Surprisingly there are a few Mediterranean plants, such as *Euphorbia characias*, which grow well on heavy soil, but in general it is best to avoid Mediterranean and drought-loving plants, and the same rule applies for most plants which grow naturally on seaside shingle, although *Crambe maritima* is unexpectedly tolerant.

Plants with a tendency to rot at the crown, such as delphiniums, can be difficult to keep going. Gypsophila often grows well on heavy soils but may live for only a few years.

Dianthus, some silvery achilleas (such as 'Anthea' and 'Moonshine'), heucheras, species of peonies and scabious also dislike the wet conditions that heavy clay so often creates; it encourages them to rot off. Plants which are on the borderline of hardiness can suffer in clay soil in winter; in case the main plant is lost, take cuttings and overwinter them in frost-free conditions.

ROCKY SOIL

In some gardens there is solid rock only a few centimetres beneath the surface. If the rock is porous, the soil may be very dry. However, if the rock does not let water drain through, conditions may vary enormously from very wet – in some seasons and after rain – to very dry.

The most sensible solution in either case is to increase the depth of

the soil by building raised beds, as this lets you grow a greater variety of plants; in some instances you can even dig rock out from the beds to make the walls. Over porous rock, the extra soil will provide a water reservoir; over impermeable rock, raising the level will lift plants above the sodden soil after heavy rains.

Plants to grow Plants that appreciate good drainage but do not have deep, vigorous root systems are your best choice. In addition to alpines and heathers, many smaller perennials do well. In sunny areas plants like white arabis, the shorter artemisias, *Aubrieta*, *Dianthus* of all kinds, *Diascia*, blue-leaved festucas, *Platycodon* and *Pulsatilla* should thrive. A mulch of grit helps retain moisture.

In shady areas where the soil has been improved, many of the smaller woodland plants, like *Ajuga reptans*, asarums, *Corydalis flexuosa*, dicentras, epimediums, some of the smaller hardy geraniums and primroses, are a good bet. Here a mulch of bark is advisable. Where the shade is cast by trees whose roots invade the new bed, causing it to dry out, only plants suitable for dry shade (see p.135) are likely to succeed.

Plants to avoid Tall plants such as delphiniums and helianthus should be avoided, not only as their roots are vigorous but because, without the depth of soil the roots require to develop a strong anchorage, they are more likely to be blown over. Also, smaller plants with deep-growing roots, such as hellebores, hemerocallis and *Symphytum* × *uplandicum* 'Variegatum', may not thrive as they will not have the root space they need and, what is more, at the times when they should be growing strongly are unlikely to have access to the moisture they require.

Purple-flowered Pulsatilla vulgaris thrives well in rocky, well-drained soil in full sun.

WET SOIL

In parts of the garden where the soil is naturally wet, or if the whole of the garden is badly drained, the rule is to work with the soil rather than against it. Draining the garden can improve matters, but this is a huge undertaking, and not practicable along streamsides and in various other circumstances. So your best option is to choose moisture-loving plants. That said, you may want to reserve some small areas for plants less tolerant of moisture; you can create conditions suitable for a wider range of smaller plants by making a raised bed and filling it with gritty soil. You can use troughs and sinks to grow alpines, while containers of various kinds (see pp.96–7) filled with well-drained soil can make good homes for a wide range of other plants which do not enjoy damp conditions.

Plants to grow Many plants that grow naturally along the edges of streams and lakes or in boggy ground will thrive in wet places in the garden. Some of these plants, such as astilbes and perennial lobelias, are adaptable and will also grow in other borders as long as they do not dry out.

Moisture-lovers include ligularias, whose leaves have a tendency to collapse in warm weather if grown in drier situations, the elegant globeflowers *Caltha palustris* and irises. Irises are rather varied: some, such as varieties of *I. ensata*, *I. pseudacorus* and also *I. sibirica*, thrive in moist soil while others, such as *I. unguicularis*, prefer drier conditions.

Plants to avoid Obviously droughtlovers will not enjoy damp soil, but alpines and Mediterranean plants are not the only ones that hate the damp. Many other plants which thrive in ordinary border conditions will die in soil that is constantly wet, because the excess moisture encourages their roots to rot. Be cautious when choosing your plants.

STONY SOIL

Stony soil can be a problem for both gardener – cultivating soil containing too many rocks or stones is hard work – and plants. The net effect of a stony or gravelly soil is to make it drain more freely. This can be a great advantage if your main priorities are alpines and drought-lovers, but it may create difficulties for the many plants which like more moisture.

The addition of bulky organic matter is the most important measure to take, as this will build up the moisture-retentive capacity of the soil. Repeat this regularly in the form of a mulch – in dry soils organic matter tends to disappear fairly quickly.

Plants to grow Plants that hate wet soil and positively enjoy drier, well-drained conditions are ideal for open, sunny positions. These include plants such as *Arabis*, *Aubrieta*, *Campanula isophylla* and *Pulsatilla vulgaris*, which are sometimes classified as alpines, as well as *Agapanthus*, *Anthemis*, *Dianthus* and bearded irises, plus Mediterranean plants like *Asphodelus*, *Convolvulus altheoides* and *Euphorbia characias*.

In shadier sites, the more organic matter you can add over the years, the more small woodland plants and even the deep-rooted ones will enjoy the conditions. In the early years only the tougher varieties can be depended upon; these include ajugas, dicentras and forms of *Geranium* × *cantabridgense*. As the soil becomes richer in humus, you will be able to try less adaptable plants such as primroses and epimediums.

Plants to avoid Moisture-loving plants rarely thrive in stony soils unless some restriction in drainage keeps the soil unexpectedly damp. So do not choose bog irises, bog primulas and others similarly dependent

Not all irises thrive in wet soil but forms of Iris siberica like this 'Orville Fay' soon make tight, self-supporting plants.

on moisture. That said, apparently demanding plants such as hostas may thrive in shady places – although they would languish in the sun.

DRY SOIL

All plants need moisture, so dry soil presents an obvious problem. Fortunately it is possible in many cases at least partially to solve the problem and grow a reasonable range of plants. If the soil is dry because it is exceptionally well drained or unusually sandy, you can improve the growing conditions enormously by adding organic matter, both by working it into the soil and by mulching. Again, making a raised bed can help the situation, because you thereby increase the available depth to which soil improvers can act.

Where the reason for the soil's dryness is that tree roots are using the moisture, you have a more difficult problem: it may be impossible to take out some of the roots without harming the tree. Another difficulty is that the shade cast by the tree may further restrict the range of plants suitable to grow there. Raising the soil level and incorporating a vertical barrier in the soil to keep out roots can help.

Dry shade Dry shade is the most difficult situation for which to find good plants, as anything you try to grow will be deprived of both the things plants need more than anything else: moisture and light.

The first step is to improve the situation as much as possible using any of the ideas touched on above. When it comes to the actual selection of plants, start off by considering the evergreen perennials. These are able, all year round, to make use of what little light is available. The shield ferns *Polystichum* and particularly *P. setiferum* are especially valuable,

as is the surprisingly resilient fern *Dryopteris filix-mas*. Other good evergreen perennials for dry shade include the elegant sedge *Carex pendula* and the stinking hellebore *Helleborus foetidus*, with its boldly fingered leaves. You might be tempted to plant the choicer woodlanders, such as epimediums and primroses, but these are unlikely to thrive in such dry conditions.

Dry, sunny places Many plants that enjoy stony soils will also thrive in dry, sunny places, as the problems are similar. However, if you take the time to improve the soil you can grow a wide range of plants, including slightly tender varieties for which wet, cold winter conditions usually mean death. So, if the following plants are on the borderline of hardiness in your area and you have a bed

Polystichum setiferum is one of the few ferns that will do well in dry shade.

that is sunny and dry, improve the soil and then try them: agapanthus, diascias, the chocolate-coloured and chocolate-scented *Cosmos atrosanguineus*, and the two tuberous salvias, *Salvia patens* and *S. farinacea*.

Avoid plants that especially enjoy moisture, such as *Caltha*, *Trollius*, bog irises and bog primulas.

LIMY SOIL

In general, the lime content of soil has less influence on the choice of perennials than it does on that of shrubs: fewer perennials have definite preferences, although some plants are especially happy where the lime content is unusually high.

In most gardens it is impracticable to attempt to reduce the lime content of the soil. You can sometimes do it by regularly adding flowers of sulphur as an acidifying material, but generally it is better to work *with* the natural soil rather than *against* it.

Plants to grow A wide variety of plants will grow on limy soils, though beware of assuming that all will, particularly if the soil is especially high in lime. On lighter soils the many types of dianthus, including both modern and old-fashioned garden pinks, will do extremely well, as will scabious and campanulas. On richer soils bearded irises, in their vast variety, will thrive, along with hellebores and the delightful herbaceous clematis and peony hybrids.

Plants to avoid Few perennials have a particular objection to limy soil, though it is sometimes said that border phlox and lupins dislike it. However, it is more often the thin, dry conditions or the heavy clay associated with a high lime content which causes the problem.

SPECIAL SITUATIONS

Most gardens have places that are inhospitable to plants – on occasions whole gardens may pose a problem. This may be a result of difficult soils, or may be related to the climate or geographical situation. Fortunately, there are measures you can take to alleviate any difficulties, and there are always some plants which will tolerate or even enjoy the conditions.

NEW GARDENS

A new and empty garden is a special challenge. When you are developing a new garden it is heartening if attractive beds and borders can be built up quickly. At the same time, anything that requires unnecessary work or expense is best avoided – this is likely to be a busy and expensive enough period for other reasons.

In new gardens the soil is often poor, especially if it has been moved around and compacted by building machinery. Not all plants will succeed in such conditions, and those that are sufficiently robust may prove too vigorous later, once soil conditions have been improved.

Bargain plants Starting with plants that are not too expensive is always a good idea when you take over a new garden:

• Bring divisions from your old garden to get you started.

• Accept gratefully any presents of plants from family, friends or neighbours. At worst they can always be replaced in a few years' time.

Dianthus, diascias, lychnis and poppies thrive in this well-drained alkaline soil.

• When visiting garden centres in spring, look out for perennials which seem unusually cramped in their pots. These can often be split immediately into three smaller plants.

• Raise perennials from seed; sometimes the price of enough seed for hundreds of plants is no more than the price of a single plant from the garden centre.

Vigorous and tolerant plants Perennials that spread quickly to form a fat clump or become a bold specimen are very valuable in new gardens: they help make the garden seem more mature than it actually is. Unfortunately, plants that quickly spread into clumps often go on spreading and you may find that later they need curtailing or removing if they are not to swamp choicer neighbours.

Tough and resilient plants which grow well in the difficult conditions often found in a new garden may not be your special favourites. However, if they can tolerate poor drainage and poor soil, they may be valuable in the short term, so your best idea is just to live with them until your garden is ready for something you prefer.

Plants for new gardens: *Achillea* 'Summer Pastels', *Achillea ptarmica* 'The Pearl'; also *Ajuga reptans*, *Alchemilla mollis*, *Aquilegia* 'McKana Hybrids', *Geranium* × *oxonianum* 'Claridge Druce', and *Lamium maculatum*, *Lupinus*, *Persicaria bistorta* 'Superba' and *Phalaris*.

SLOPES

Sloping sites cause problems in gardens for a number of reasons. In dry areas slopes are often even drier than the rest of the garden, yet when rain comes it runs quickly across the surface without soaking into the soil. In wet areas the rain may soak in thoroughly but the volume of the precipitation may be so great that water also runs across the surface, carrying soil away.

Alleviating the problem Terracing is often the best way to improve a site. Build a series of low walls using stone, brick, timber or whatever material is available and fits well into the garden surroundings, then fill in the newly created space behind the walls with soil to produce a series of horizontal beds across the slope. Moisture will then drain into the soil without washing the soil away.

Choosing plants Once you have built your terraced beds, select the plants that would generally be suitable for such a situation. Since you have effectively created level beds on the slope you can treat them just like any other, although they are likely to be particularly well drained.

Where a slope itself must be planted, your main aims are to prevent rain washing the soil away – in fact, you need to encourage it to soak in. The way to achieve this is to avoid plants that have a tight central rootstock and opt instead for those with runners (which will root into the soil) or those plants which spread to make broad clumps (which will collect leaves, retain soil and slow down the flow of water). You may find that using carpets of ground-cover plants in place of the usual border perennials is the best solution.

Ajugas root from every leaf joint as they run across the soil, while diascias send up stems from an ever-

Clouds of Erigeron karvinskianus self-sow happily in this steep and stony bank.

extending root system. Vigorous dicentras such as 'Stuart Boothman' and 'Snowflakes' are good in the shade, while the many running grasses like *Glyceria maxima* 'Variegata' and *Phalaris arundinacea* 'Picta' are especially effective.

SEASIDE GARDENS

There are two difficulties associated with gardens by the sea: wind and salt. The problems created by wind are dealt with below, but if it carries salt it can be especially destructive, and many plants cannot tolerate it. When moist air carrying salt comes into contact with foliage or flowers, the moisture evaporates and the salt causes scorch. Salt is also washed into the soil and, while this suits some vegetables such as beetroot and cabbage, which are derived from seaside plants, it can be a problem for many perennial plants.

In some seaside gardens the soil may be unusually sandy. These gardens tend to drain rapidly, and as a result may be low in nutrients. Some plants, especially those that are used to growing in hot dry conditions – like *Euphorbia characias* and *Asphodelus fistulosus* – will thrive; but less tolerant plants will require generous applications of organic matter to improve the soil's moisture retention and fertility.

You can give your perennials valuable protection by planting shelter, though you must choose trees and shrubs that themselves tolerate the salt. In general you should rely on your choice of plants to solve the worst of the problems.

Choosing plants Plants that grow naturally by the sea are obvious choices, but rather few of these are in the top flight of perennials – although *Crambe maritima*, with bluish foliage and white flowers, is one. Otherwise it is largely a matter of choosing plants with sufficiently tough foliage and flowers to cope with the salt. Many of these, such as dianthus, eryngiums, *Elymus hispidus*, *E. magellanicus* and *Limonium latifolium*, have a waxy protective coating on the leaves; this not only sheds the salt-laden water quickly but also provides a barrier to any salt that might be left after moisture has evaporated.

WINDY SITUATIONS

Wind can be very destructive: it can physically batter plants, scorch or tear the foliage, blow plants over or loosen them at the roots, so that they die a slow death.

The problem falls into two categories. There are gardens which are in windy parts of the country; and there are parts of individual gardens which suffer particularly from exposure to wind.

Windy gardens Gardens in windy areas or in unusually windy sites benefit enormously from protection, but protecting a whole garden can be a large undertaking. Hedges and shelterbelts of trees and shrubs are generally more effective than walls and fences because they are sufficiently flexible to filter the wind yet not be damaged by it. When wind hits a wall or fence it swirls over the top, sometimes causing damaging eddies on the leeward side; this can be especially destructive to a herbaceous border planted with a wall as a background. Unfortunately, trees and shrubs take up a significant amount of space by comparison with a fence or wall, and their roots can rob borders of moisture and nutrients.

Within the garden Sometimes a combination of features creates an unusually windy area within a garden – often this occurs in a passage between two walls, such as a house wall and a boundary wall. The result is effectively a wind tunnel, and the gusts generated can do a lot of damage to your plants.

In some situations this problem can easily be resolved. You could fit a gate to a passage to ameliorate the tunnelling effect. Alternatively, you might set up a trellis screen, removable if necessary; this will filter the wind so that it does less damage. Tough evergreen shrubs or short hedges can be planted at those strategic points within the garden where shelter is especially necessary.

Choosing plants Perennials for windy sites need one of four special qualities:
• Some are sufficiently strong and flexible to be grown in an exposed site and bend in the wind without breaking. Many of the grasses, especially forms of *Miscanthus sinensis*, fall into this category. Clearly plants which are naturally rather fragile, like dicentras, should not be risked.
• Another useful feature is slender foliage which doesn't damage easily; the smaller grasses, *Dianthus* and kniphofias and some of the smaller irises score here.
• Flowers that allow air to blow through them are less easily damaged. Grasses, centaureas and perovskias can cope with wind far more effectively than peonies, poppies, large kniphofias, delphiniumns and large double chrysanthemums.
• Shorter plants, both because of their lower profile and because they tend to be sheltered by their neighbours, are obvious contenders in windy situations. Ajugas, arabis, aubrietas and lamiums are worth trying.

Right: Hedges shelter the borders in this windy garden and also support perennial sweet peas.

GUIDE TO CHOOSING PERENNIALS

Listed below are plants especially useful in particular situations, or with features of value in the garden. All are described in the Plant Directory (pp.142–227).

Clay soils

Anemone, Doronicum orientale 'Magnificum', *Eupatorium, Helenium, Hemerocallis, Hosta, Inula, Ligularia, Monarda didyma, Persicaria.*

Limy soils

Bergenia, Campanula, Clematis integrifolia, Dianthus, Eremurus robustus, Iris (tall and dwarf bearded forms), *Knautia macedonica, Linaria, Paeonia* (not species *Paeonia*), *Scabiosa.*

Wet soil

Astilbe, Caltha palustris 'Flore Pleno', *Darmera peltata, Filipendula purpurea, Gunnera manicata, Iris* (*I. pseudacorus* and *I. sibirica*), *Ligularia dentata, Lobelia, Primula japonica, Trollius.*

Dry shade

Acanthus mollis, Alchemilla mollis, Carex pendula, Dryopteris filix-mas, Epimedium × versicolor, Helleborus foetidus, Lamium, Liriope muscari, Polystichum setiferum.

Damp shade

Dicentra (woodlanders), *Epimedium, Gentiana asclepiadea, Helleborus* (Orientalis Hybrids), *Hosta, Primula vulgaris, Pulmonaria, Saxifraga fortunei, Smilacina racemosa, Tricyrtis hirta.*

Windy sites

Achillea 'Coronation Gold', *Ajuga reptans, Anemone, Campanula portenschlagiana, Centaurea montana, Festuca glauca, Miscanthus sinensis* 'Silberfeder', *Nepeta × faassenii, Phalaris arundinacea* 'Picta', *Stipa gigantea.*

Sloping sites

Aegopodium podagraria 'Variegatum', *Ajuga reptans* 'Silver Shadow', *Convolvulus altheoides, Diascia* 'Ruby Field', *Dicentra* 'Snowflakes', *Geranium macrorrhizum, Glyceria maxima* 'Variegata', *Phalaris arundinacea* 'Picta', *Symphytum* ('Goldsmith', 'Hidcote Blue' and 'Hidcote Pink'), *Waldsteinia ternata.*

Seaside gardens

Artemisia, Catananche caerulea, Crambe maritima, Dianthus, Dierama pulcherrima, Eryngium, Euphorbia characias, Kniphofia 'Atlanta', *Limonium latifolium, Persicaria bistorta* 'Superba'.

Cold gardens

Achillea millefolium, Cimicifuga simplex, Coreopsis verticillata, Echinops ritro, Iris sibirica, Malva moschata, Osmunda regalis, Phlox maculata, Primula vulgaris, Tiarella wherryi.

Hot and dry sites

Achillea ptarmica 'The Pearl', *Alstroemeria* 'Ligtu' hybrids, *Anthemis punctata* ssp. *cupaniana, Cynara cardunculus, Dianthus deltoides* 'Brilliant', *Epilobium canum, Eryngium, Euphorbia characias, Malva alcea* var. *fastigiata, Sedum* 'Ruby Glow'.

Deer-resistant plants

Agapanthus, Aquilegia, Cordateria, Delphinium, Digitalis, Helleborus, Kniphofia, Leucanthemum, Lupinus, Rheum.

Rabbit-proof plants

Acanthus, Aconitum, Agapanthus, Alchemilla, Anaphalis, Aquilegia, Aster, Astilbe, Bergenia, Brunnera, Delphinium, Digitalis, Euphorbia, Helleborus, Hemerocallis, Iris, Kniphofia, Liriope, Lupinus, Papaver.

Quick-growing perennials

Achillea ptarmica 'The Pearl', *Aegopodium podagraria* 'Variegatum', *Alchemilla mollis, Convolvulus altheoides, Dicentra* 'Snowflakes', *Geranium × oxonianum* 'Claridge Druce', *Houttuynia cordata* 'Chameleon', *Lamium galeobdolon* 'Florentinum', *Persicaria bistorta* 'Superba', *Tanacetum vulgare* 'Crispum'.

Specimen perennials

Aruncus dioicus, Cortaderia selloana, Crambe cordifolia, Delphinium 'Southern Noblemen', *Eremurus robustus, Gunnera manicata, Helianthus salicifolius, Hosta* 'Krossa Regal', *Kniphofia* 'Prince Igor', *Macleaya cordata.*

Perennials attractive to butterflies

Aster amellus, Centranthus, Cynara, Echinops, Erigeron, Nepeta, Phlox paniculata, Scabiosa, Sedum, Solidago.

Perennials attractive to bees

Anchusa, Anemone, Asclepias, Centaurea, Galega, Helleborus, Inula, Origanum, Salvia, Sedum.

Perennials for containers

Aegopodium podagraria 'Variegatum', *Agapanthus, Cosmos atrosanguineus, Dianthus, Diascia, Dryopteris wallichiana, Hakonechloa macra* 'Aureola', *Hosta, Lamium maculatum, Penstemon.*

FLOWERS BY SEASON
Spring-flowering

Aquilegia, Dicentra, Doronicum, Epimedium, Euphorbia characias, Geranium, Iris (dwarf bearded types), *Primula, Pulmonaria, Viola.*

Summer-flowering

Astilbe, Delphinium, Dianthus, Hemerocallis, Iris (*I. sibirica* and tall bearded types), *Kniphofia, Lupinus, Paeonia, Papaver orientale, Penstemon.*

Autumn-flowering
Anemone, Aster, Boltonia,
Cimicifuga, Dendranthema,
Eupatorium, Helenium, Leucanthemella
serotina, Liriope muscari, Sedum.

FLOWERS BY COLOUR
White flowers
Anemone × *hybrida* 'Honorine Jobert',
Aster novae-angliae 'Herbstschnee',
Campanula persicifolia 'Hampstead White',
Dianthus 'White Ladies', *Dicentra*
spectabilis 'Alba', *Paeonia* 'White Wings',
Papaver 'Black and White', *Penstemon*
'White Bedder', *Primula vulgaris*
'Alba Plena', *Pulmonaria officinalis*
'Sissinghurst White'.

Pink flowers
Anemone × *hybrida* 'Königin Charlotte',
Aster novi-belgii 'Little Pink Beauty',
Dendranthema 'Clara Curtis', *Dianthus*
'Doris', *Geranium* × *oxonianum*
'Claridge Druce', *Paeonia* 'Bowl of
Beauty', *Papaver orientale* 'Cedric
Morris', *Penstemon* 'Evelyn', *Phlox*
paniculata 'Mother of Pearl', *Sedum*
spectabile 'Brilliant'.

Red and orange-red flowers
Aster novae-angliae 'Septemberrubin',
Astilbe 'Fanal', *Dianthus* 'Houndspool
Ruby', *Geum chiloense* 'Mrs J. Bradshaw',
Kniphofia 'Atlanta', *Lobelia* 'Compliment
Scarlet', *Paeonia* 'Inspecteur Lavergne',
Papaver orientale 'Beauty of Livermere',
Penstemon 'Chester Scarlet', *Pulmonaria*
rubra 'Redstart'.

Yellow flowers
Achillea filipendulina 'Gold Plate',
Anthemis 'E.C. Buxton', *Aster ericoides*
'Golden Spray', *Caltha palustris* 'Flore
Pleno', *Doronicum orientale* 'Magnificum',
Helianthus 'Lemon Queen', *Hemerocallis*
'Stella d'Oro', *Kniphofia* 'Little Maid',
Lysichiton americanus, Paeonia mlokose-
witschii, Rudbeckia 'Goldsturm'.

Blue flowers
Aquilegia vulgaris 'Adelaide Addison',
Aster × *frikartii* 'Mönch', *Campanula*
carpatica 'Blue Clips', *Delphinium* 'Blue
Nile', *Geranium wallichianum* 'Buxton's
Variety', *Iris* 'Jane Phillips', *Iris sibirica*
'Cambridge', *Polemonium reptans, Viola*
'Ardross Gem'.

Purple, mauve or lilac flowers
Aster amellus 'Veilchenkünigin',
Campanula latifolia 'Brantwood',
Geranium phaeum, Lobelia 'Tania',
Penstemon 'Alice Hindley', *Polemonium*
'Lambrook Mauve', *Primula* 'Miss Indigo',
Salvia × *sylvestris* 'Mainacht', *Verbena*
bonariensis, Viola 'Maggie Mott'.

Scented flowers
Asphodeline lutea, Astilbe 'Deutschland',
Clematis × *jouiana* 'Praecox', *Crambe*
cordifolia, Dianthus 'Mrs Sinkins',
Hosta 'Honeybells', *Iris unguicularis,*
Paeonia 'Duchesse de Nemours', *Phlox*
carolina 'Miss Lingard', *Phlox paniculata*
'White Admiral'.

PERENNIALS WITH
GOOD FOLIAGE
Variegated leaves
Ajuga reptans 'Variegata', *Aquilegia*
vulgaris 'Vervaeneana', *Astrantia*
'Sunningdale Variegated', *Carex morrowii*
'Variegata', *Hakonechloa macra* 'Aureola',
Hosta 'Shade Fanfare', *Iris foetidissima*
'Variegata', *Lamium maculatum,*
Phlox paniculata 'Norah Leigh',
Symphytum 'Goldsmith'.

Gold or yellow leaves
Acorus gramineus 'Ogon', *Centaurea mon-*
tana 'Gold Bullion', *Deschampsia caespi-*
tosa 'Goldschleir', *Filipendula ulmaria*
'Aurea', *Hosta* 'Zounds', *Milium effusum*
'Aureum', *Origanum vulgare* 'Aureum',
Stachys byzantina 'Primrose Heron',
Tanacetum parthenium 'Aureum',
Valeriana phu 'Aurea'.

Silver, grey and bluish leaves
Anaphalis margaritacea var. *yedoensis,*
Anthemis punctata ssp. *cupaniana,*
Cynara cardunculus, Euphorbia myrsinites,
Helictotrichon sempervirens, Hosta
'Halcyon', *Nepeta* × *faassenii, Stachys*
byzantina 'Silver Carpet'.

Purple leaves
Ajuga reptans 'Braunherz', *Bergenia*
'Bressingham Ruby', *Foeniculum vulgare*
'Purpureum', *Heuchera micrantha* 'Palace
Purple', *Imperata cylindrica* 'Rubra',
Lobelia 'Queen Victoria', *Rheum*
palmatum 'Atrosanguineum', *Veronica*
peduncularis 'Georgia Blue'.

Bold foliage
Acanthus mollis 'Latifolius', *Bergenia*
'Ballawley', *Brunnera macrophylla, Crambe*
cordifolia, Darmera peltata, Helleborus
(Orientalis Hybrids), *Hosta* 'Krossa Regal',
Ligularia stenocephala, Lysichiton ameri-
canus, Rodgersia podophylla.

Lacy foliage
Achillea ('Millefolium' hybrids), *Artemisia*
canescens, Aruncus dioicus 'Kneiffii',
Athyrium filix-femina, Corydalis flexuosa,
Dryopteris filix-mas, Foeniculum vulgare
'Purpureum', *Polystichum setiferum,*
Thalictrum delavayi.

Narrow foliage
Carex, Dianthus, Festuca, Iris, Kniphofia
'Little Maid', *Liriope muscari, Miscanthus*
sinensis, Molinia caerulea 'Variegata',
Morina longifolia, Sisyrinchium striatum.

PERENNIALS WITH
ATTRACTIVE FRUITS
Actaea alba and *A. rubra* (berries),
Clematis integrifolia, Dictamnus albus,
Hosta sieboldiana 'Elegans', *Paeonia*
mlokosewitschii, Physalis franchetii
(berries), *Phytolacca americana*
(berries), *Smilacina racemosa* (berries),
Veratrum nigrum.

A - Z
DIRECTORY

Above: *Sedum spectabile* and *Aster amellus*, two of the best autumn
perennials, make an attractive and long lasting combination.

Left: The bright yellow of *Achillea* 'Moonshine' and the bold magenta
of *Geranium psilostemon* are softened by clouds of blue catmint.

The hardiness zones

The climatic conditions of an area are of prime importance when deciding what to plant in the garden. The successful cultivation of a plant largely depends on its native climate and how easily it can adapt to a new one, if necessary. The hardiness zones on pages 228–31 indicate the degree of coldness a plant can tolerate.

ACANTHUS

Bear's breeches

One of the most statuesque plants grown in the perennial border. It creates a fountain of shiny, jagged leaves, topped by stiff spires of hooded flowers. These flowers appear in summer but remain attractive until the first frosts. They make excellent material for dried floral arrangements.

This large genus contains about 20 species, with six in cultivation. They are easy to grow in any fertile garden soil, preferably well-drained, and can be used in sun or light shade. The main problems are slugs and snails. Propagate from seed or from root cuttings when dormant.

Acanthus mollis

A. mollis (above)

This is the most popular species of the genus. The deeply lobed leaves are a dull mid-green, and the flower spikes rise to 1.5m (5ft), carrying pink or white flowers with purple hoods. 'Latifolius' has large, shining leaves.

Acanthus spinosus

A. spinosus (above)

This plant is similar to *A. mollis* except that the shiny, dark green leaves are distinctly spiny. The flowers are white with mauve-purple hoods carried on 1.2m (4ft) spikes. 'Spinosissimus' has an even greater number of spiny leaves whose spines have a silvery-white sheen.

ACHILLEA

Yarrow

These tough, vigorous plants have very attractive ferny foliage and flat heads of short-petalled, daisy-like flowers. Most have yellow flowers, but an increasing range of pastel and brighter colours is being introduced. The cut flowers are useful for drying.

These are good border plants in a variety of heights. They spread to form large clumps; some varieties do so a bit too readily, and can become invasive.

Any good garden soil is suitable but it should be well-drained. Yarrows are drought-resistant. A sunny position is needed. Propagation is best carried out by division and, although yarrows can be grown from seed the results are unpredictable.

A. clypeolata hybrids

These have a beautiful silvery grey foliage and bright yellow flowers on 60cm (2ft) stems. They are short-lived and need regular replanting.

'Anthea' has very silvery leaves and paler flowers, while 'Moonshine' has similar leaves but brighter flowers.

A. filipendulina

Fern-leaf yarrow is the tallest of the yarrows, and makes an attractive grouping towards the back of a border. It has a ferny green foliage and large heads of golden yellow flowers. The tall, erect stems are up to 1.2m (4ft) high and need staking.

'Cloth of Gold' has abundant golden yellow flowers. 'Coronation Gold' is deservedly one of the most popular: its flower heads are about 7.5cm (3in) across and are a bright yellow, and the foliage is greyer than in other varieties. 'Gold Plate' has large heads, up to 15cm (6in) wide, and a greener foliage; it is one of the tallest of these forms.

Achillea millefolium 'Cerise Queen'

A. millefolium hybrids (above)

Common yarrow is a coarse plant, but there are excellent hybrids. Up to 75cm (2½ft) tall, they have a ferny foliage and flat heads 5cm (2in) or more wide. 'Apfelblüte' ('Appleblossom') has pale pink flowers, 'Cerise Queen' deep pink, 'Fanal' ('The Beacon') bright red, 'Forncett Fletton' orange-brown, 'Hoffnung' ('Hope', 'Great Expectations') creamy yellow and 'Lachsschönheit' ('Salmon Beauty') salmon-pink.

A. ptarmica (below)

Sneezeweed can be invasive, so ensure that you position it carefully. It is 60cm (2ft) tall with dark green leaves and looser heads of flowers than other varieties. The white flowers are double in most cultivars. 'Boule de Neige' and 'The Pearl', both with pure white flowers, are very similar and often considered to be the same plant.

Achillea ptarmica 'The Pearl'

ACONITUM
Monkshood

The monkshoods form a very large genus of about 200 species, of which a dozen are in general cultivation. They are grown for their attractive, curiously shaped flowers, which have a large upper petal shaped a bit like a helmet or hood. The colour is generally a wonderful dark blue, but there are also paler blue forms, as well as white and creamy yellow varieties. They flower in summer and autumn.

The majority are stiff, erect plants, up to 1.5m (5ft) tall, with the flowers held in spikes, but some are scramblers and need shrubs for support.

Monkshoods will grow in any soil that has been enriched with plenty of well-rotted organic material to make it moisture-retentive. The taller forms may need staking when sited in exposed positions. Propagation is by division or by seed. All parts of the plant are poisonous.

Aconitum 'Bressingham Spire'

Blue forms (above)

Among the blue forms 'Bressingham Spire' has violet-blue flowers and is shorter than most. *A.* × *cammarum* 'Bicolor' is of medium height and has white flowers with a blue margin. *A. carmichaelii* 'Arendsii' has deep blue flowers, while 'Spark's Variety' is an early-blooming form, also with intense blue flowers. *A. c. wilsonii* is a taller and more vigorous variety. All these forms flower in autumn.

Aconitum 'Ivorine'

Cream forms (above)

There are two main cream forms. 'Ivorine' is a creamy off-white and early-flowering. It grows to only 75cm (2½ft). *A. lycotonum* subsp. *vulparia* is creamy yellow and taller, growing up to 1.5m (5ft) in the right position.

ACORUS
Sweet flag

Although flowering plants, these are grown more for their sword-like foliage than for their summer flowers. They grow well in shallow water, making them ideal for planting in drifts along the margins of pools and streams. The flowers are minute and carried in strange spikes, shaped like horns jutting out at an angle from the foliage.

They can be grown in mud at the edge of water or in pond baskets. They should have a sunny position. Propagation is readily achieved by dividing the plants.

Acorus calamus 'Variegatus'

A. calamus (above)

This species has iris-like leaves which grow to 90cm (3ft). They are dark green and often wavy at the margins. When crushed they smell of tangerines. 'Variegatus' has creamy yellow stripes that are flushed with pink at the base of the leaves.

A. gramineus

The foliage on this plant is much shorter and finer than in the other varieties, being more like blades of grass. The flower spike is more upright. *A. gramineus* is not as hardy as *A. calamus*. 'Variegatus' has cream stripes, while 'Ogon' has deep yellow stripes. 'Pusilus' is more tufty than the other cultivars.

ACTAEA

ACTAEA
Baneberry

The plants of this small genus are grown more for their coloured fruit than for their flowers. They make attractive foliage plants, with leaves made up of a number of leaflets. The flowers are carried in fluffy plumes. They appear in late summer and are followed by the distinctive berries, which are poisonous.

Baneberries are woodland plants and prefer a cool, humus-rich soil in light shade. Propagation is by division or from seed.

A. alba

Also known as *A. pachypoda*, this species has red stems carrying loose bunches of spherical white berries with a black 'eye'.

Actaea rubra

A. rubra (above)

The leaves on this species are more ferny than those of *A. alba*. The flowers are white and the elliptical berries a very attractive shiny red.

ADIANTUM
Maidenhair fern

These deciduous semi-evergreen and evergreen ferns are very garden-worthy. They are characterized by their black, wiry central stem with parallel leaflets on either side. They are always fresh-looking and have a delicate appearance.

They enjoy a moist, shady position. For the majority, the soil should be either neutral or acid, preferably with plenty of leaf mould or well-rotted humus in it. They can be propagated from spores in the late summer or by careful division in spring.

A. pedatum

The northern maidenhair fern is a superb plant. It is normally deciduous but can be semi-evergreen in milder areas. It spreads slowly, but is not a nuisance. It reaches about 45cm (1½ft) in height and the same across.

AEGOPODIUM
Goutweed

This small genus of plants is known in the garden mainly through *A. podagraria*, which can become a very invasive weed, spreading by underground shoots. In the past it was grown as a herb, but it is very rarely tolerated now except in its less vigorous variegated form. It will grow in any garden soil, in either sun or light shade. It can be easily propagated by division in spring or autumn.

Aegopodium podagraria 'Variegatum'

A. podagraria 'Variegatum' (above)

This plant is grown for its very attractive variegated foliage. It reaches only 25cm (10in) high and will soon cover a wide area, but not as invasively as its parent. It should be grown in a confined space as it has a tendency to spread. The insignificant white flowers, borne in summer, are not particularly attractive and should be removed.

AGAPANTHUS
African lily

An increasing number of varieties in this genus are becoming available to gardeners. The fleshy roots produce a fountain of strap-like leaves and balls of blue or white flowers, carried on long stems. Each flower is like a miniature lily; the flowers appear in late summer and are good for cutting.

Blue African lilies grow in most fertile garden soils, preferably moisture-retentive ones. They need a sunny position. Avoid transplanting as the roots are brittle and will take 1–3 years to re-establish. In colder areas, they can be grown in containers that can be moved inside or otherwise protected during winter. Propagate by careful division or by seed, although the latter is not suitable for named cultivars.

Agapanthus africanus

Blue-flowered forms (above)

Blue is the commonest colour for the flowers; it ranges from very pale to deep blue. *A. africanus* has deep blue flowers on erect stems with broad, dark green leaves. 'Blue Giant' is one of the 'Headbourne Hybrids' (see **Mixed forms**, next column). It is 1.2m (4ft) tall and has excellent blue flowers. 'Bressingham

Blue' is slightly shorter than 'Blue Giant' and has the darkest flowers of all the blue-flowered forms.

White-flowered forms

'Bressingham White' is as good as its blue counterpart. Not quite so hardy and much shorter, but well worth growing in a tub, is *A. africanus* 'Albus'.

Mixed forms

'Headbourne Hybrids' are the most famous form of *Agapanthus*. They are the hardiest and offer a wide range of blues and whites. Many are named cultivars, but there is also a seed strain.

Agapanthus 'Lilliput'

Dwarf forms (above)

While most *Agapanthus* forms are 75cm–1.2m (2½–4ft) tall, there are some very good dwarf forms that are suitable for the front of a border or rock garden. *A.* 'Lilliput', *A. campanulatus* 'Isis' and *A. africanus* 'Peter Pan' are all short cultivars worth considering. They grow to 30cm (1ft) in height, although 'Isis' is slightly taller.

AGASTACHE
Mexican bergamot, Giant hyssop

This is a genus of short-lived perennials, all with fragrant foliage and dense spikes of flowers resembling those of the mints, to which they are related. The leaves are nettle-like in shape. The fact that the plants are short-lived is not too much of a problem as they self-sow, offering plenty of seedlings to replace lost plants.

They need a free-draining soil and a position in the sun. They do not have strong stems and, except in sheltered spots, need staking.

A. foeniculum (below)

This is the most commonly seen species. The foliage smells strongly of fennel or aniseed (hence the synonym *A. anisata*, under which it is sometimes listed). It grows to 90cm (3ft). The flowers are mainly a dull violet colour, although there are some white forms, including 'Alabaster', which is an ivory white.

Agastache foeniculum

A. mexicana

This species is slightly shorter and produces flowers varying from pink to red in colour. It is short-lived and should be propagated each year.

AJUGA
Bugle

These low-growing, vigorous plants form a dense ground cover. They are grown both for their spikes of blue, pink or white flowers, which appear in spring, and for their very decorative foliage, which comes in a variety of colours. Some forms have year-round foliage.

Bugles are essentially woodland flowers, and prefer moist, humus-rich soil. They grow best in a lightly shaded spot, but will grow in full sun provided the soil does not dry out. Some of the coloured-leafed forms need the sun to maintain their colour. The plants are invasive, but are not difficult to control. Propagation is by division of the strawberry-like runners.

A. reptans

This is the common bugle. The species has green leaves and blue flowers carried on 15cm (6in) spikes. There are many desirable cultivars.

Dark-leafed forms

'Atropurpurea' has deep purple foliage and blue flowers. 'Braunherz' is similar except that the purple coloration is much browner, more a deep bronze. Both these forms can revert to green if planted in too dense a shade.

Ajuga reptans 'Multicolor'

Patterned forms (above)

There are an increasing number of variegated forms. 'Burgundy Glow' has leaves that are a mixture of pink and burgundy, edged with cream. The cultivar 'Multicolor' (also known as 'Rainbow' or 'Tricolor') is similar except that the colours are purple, red and cream, often with patches of green. 'Variegata' is pale green and cream.

Vigorous forms

Several forms are vigorous growers with large flower spikes. 'Catlins' Giant' is the biggest, 'Silver Shadow' has pale green leaves, and 'Jungle Beauty' has very large, glossy leaves.

ALCEA
Hollyhock

The best known of the hollyhocks is the stately *A. rosea*, but this is now generally treated as a biennial because it is prone to a debilitating rust disease. This and other species in the genus were, until recently, known as *Althaea*, and are still sometimes listed under this name.

Their flowers are shallow funnels in a variety of colours. Double varieties are available. The flowers appear on tall spikes from the summer onwards. There are now dwarf forms of some species. Hollyhocks will grow in any good garden soil and prefer a sunny position. The taller varieties need staking. They can all be propagated from seed.

A. rugosa

This has become a popular substitute for the rust-prone *A. rosea*. It is not so tall, reaching only 1.2m (4ft), and is bushy rather than single-stemmed. The flowers are a delightful clear yellow.

ALCHEMILLA
Lady's mantle

These plants are loved for both foliage and flowers. The leaves are round in outline; in some cases pleated, in others cut almost to the centre in individual leaflets. Both types are attractive. The flowers, greenish yellow and held in billowing clouds, are carried mainly in late spring and early summer.

Alchemillas will grow in any garden soil, including quite poor ones, but look particularly attractive when sited near water. They are happy in either sun or shade. Propagation is very easy from seed – in fact, they frequently self-sow.

Alchemilla erythropoda

A. erythropoda (above)

This species is a low-growing one that reaches 15cm (6in) high. It is excellent at the front of a border or as a ground cover in light shade. The blue-green leaves are partly cut.

A. mollis (below)

This is the most popular species. It has large, rounded leaves with scalloped edges and deep folds that hold the dew and raindrops in a most beautiful way. The foaming flowers are borne in spring, and again in autumn if the plants are deadheaded after the first flush.

Alchemilla mollis

ALSTROEMERIA
Peruvian lily

There are a surprising number of different species of Peruvian lily, about 60, but only a handful are in cultivation. They are among the most exotic-looking flowers for the perennial border. The flowers are trumpet-shaped, often comprising a fusion of different colours and much spotted. The plants are 90cm–1.2m (3–4ft) tall.

They need rich, free-draining soil and a site out of the hottest sun. Plant at least 15cm (6in). Some form of support is frequently required. Although the roots are brittle they can be divided to increase stock. They can also be grown from seed.

A. aurea

This is the hardiest of the species. The flowers are a brilliant golden orange, spotted in red. With spreading rootstock the plant can become invasive, needing to be kept in check. It grows well and attractively through bushes.

Alstroemeria 'Ligtu Hybrids'

A. 'Ligtu Hybrids' (above)

These hybrids offer the gardener a wide range of colours, including cream, yellow, orange, red and pink. They are floriferous and hardy, but do self-seed and can become invasive.

A. 'Princess Hybrids'

A group of hybrids bred specifically for the cut-flower trade and now making an appearance in the garden, these are based on *A. aurea*. They are available in a wide range of colours, both pastel and bright.

A. psittacina

The parrot flower has intriguing red-and-green flowers. It is shorter than most border forms, reaching about 90cm (3ft), and is less hardy.

AMSONIA
Blue star

This small genus is made up of species that carry starry blue flowers in loose heads. Flowers appear in early summer and contrast well with the green leaves. Up to 90cm (3ft) tall, the plants spread to form clumps and rarely outgrow their allotted space. They make good cut flowers.

They like a moist soil with plenty of well-rotted organic material. A position in either full sun or light shade is suitable. In windy positions they need staking. Propagation is either by division or from seed and is carried out in the spring.

A. orientalis

Also known as *Rhazya orientalis*, this plant is less hardy than other members of the genus. The flowers are a pale grey-blue, appearing darker while still in bud.

Amsonia tabernaemontana

A. tabernaemontana (above)

This is the North American equivalent of *A. orientalis*. It produces clusters of small, tubular pale blue flowers on slightly taller plants, but is otherwise very similar.

ANAPHALIS
Pearl everlasting

Even though these plants have attractive flowers, they are grown mainly for their grey-silver foliage. Unlike most silvery-leafed plants, they can be grown in moist, shady positions, which makes them extremely useful. The leaves are narrow and felted with hairs. The flowers are small buttons with yellow centres and white straw-like petals or bracts, and appear from the late summer onwards.

Although these plants are happy to grow in shade they also do well in a sunny position. A moisture-retentive soil is required, as the leaves will begin to wilt and droop if the plants become too dry. Propagation is readily achieved by division in winter or spring, or by seed in autumn.

A. margaritacea

This is an erect plant growing up to 90cm (3ft) tall. It spreads and can become very invasive. The leaves are grey-green or silvery grey with just a few hairs above, and are whiter on the underside.

A. m. var. yedoensis (below)

In many respects this variety of anaphalis is very similar to the species, but the leaves have a distinct silver edge to them. The flower heads are also larger.

Anaphalis margaritacea var. *yedoensis*

Anaphalis triplinervis 'Summer Snow'

A. triplinervis (above)

This species is so-named because of the three distinct veins that run down each leaf. The leaves are white, with hairs; the flowers white balls of stiff bracts with a tiny yellow centre. They are carried in profusion in late summer. The plant is clump-forming rather than spreading. The variety 'Sommerschnee' ('Summer Snow') is more of a dwarf form, only 25cm (10in) high, and is covered in white flowers. This is not so drought-resistant as *A. m.* var. *yedoensis*.

ANCHUSA
Anchusa

These coarse plants are welcomed because of their brilliant blue flowers which brighten the borders in early summer. The flowers are carried in long spikes that uncurl in a similar way to those of their relatives the forget-me-nots (*Myosotis*).

They need a deeply cultivated, fertile soil, but resent those that are too wet or heavy and will die out after a year. They also need a sunny position. The stems are stiff and can snap in wind, so staking is necessary at all times. For named cultivars, propagation is by root cuttings. For the species, seed is also possible.

A. azurea

Italian bugloss is the most commonly grown species. This is a tall plant, reaching 1.5m (5ft). The stems and long leaves are clothed in coarse hairs. There are a number of cultivars. 'Dropmore' is deep blue, flowering later than other forms. 'Little John' grows to only about 45cm (1½ft) and is useful for exposed borders. 'Loddon Royalist', of intermediate height, has rich purple-blue flowers.

ANEMONE
Anemone

This very large genus includes woodland species such as *A. nemorosa* and bulbous ones like *A. pavonina*. These, along with such plants as *A. narcissiflora* and *A. rivularis*, make good border plants, but the Japanese anemone and its relatives are most commonly used in the border. These can grow to about 1.2m (4ft) and spread underground to form large clumps. They flower from late summer well into autumn. The saucer-shaped flowers are white or rose-pink, each with a yellow central disc of stamens. There are also double forms.

Anemones will grow in full sun or light shade, but do best in the open. They prefer a rich soil, but will also grow in relatively dry alkaline conditions. No staking is required. Propagation is by division or by root cuttings taken in early winter.

A. × *hybrida*

Of the several species and hybrids of Japanese anemones A. × *hybrida* is the principal group, although varieties of *A. hupehensis* and *A. japonica* are also regularly seen.

Single white forms (next column)
White-flowered forms are particularly good at brightening up dull corners. It is often difficult to distinguish between the various forms. A. × *hybrida* 'Alba' is a general name represented by 'Honorine Jobert' in the UK and its seedling 'Lady Adilaun' in the USA; both are excellent whites. 'White Giant' has particularly large flowers.

Anemone × hybrida 'Honorine Jobert'

Anemone hupehensis 'Bressingham Glow'

Single pink forms (above)
The pink forms are more variable in colour. The flowers of *A. hupehensis* 'Bressingham Glow' are rosy pink, 'Hadspen Abundance' a deeper pink, A. × *hybrida* 'Königin Charlotte' ('Queen Charlotte') larger and medium pink.

Double forms
There are several double forms. A. × *hybrida* 'Wirbelwind' ('Whirlwind') is a semi-double white, while 'Margarete' is a semi-double pink.

ANTHEMIS
Anthemis

This genus offers the gardener a very good range of daisies. The flowers are of typical daisy shape, with a central yellow disc surrounded by ray petals of either white or various shades of yellow and orange. The finely cut, aromatic leaves also help to make these good border plants. Their only drawback is that they are not long-lived, especially on wet soils, and so need yearly propagation to keep them going.

Anthemis plants need a well-drained soil and a sunny position to give of their best. The taller varieties need to be staked. Stock can be increased by taking cuttings in the spring, and some can be grown from seed sown at the same time of year.

A. punctata subsp. cupaniana

This sprawling plant, easy to grow, roots as it spreads, but can easily be cut back and so is not invasive. It has white flowers, in spring and early summer, and silver foliage.

A. sancti-johannis

For gardeners who like hot colours this plant is an essential for the border. The combination of strong golden orange flowers and delicately-cut foliage in this form is very attractive.

Anthemis tinctoria 'Grallach Gold'

A. tinctoria (above)

The golden marguerite has yellow flowers. However, it is mainly grown as its several cultivars. 'E. C. Buxton' has pale lemony flowers, while 'Wargrave' and 'Sauce Hollandaise' have creamy yellow ones. As a contrast, the flowers of 'Grallach Gold' are golden yellow and those of 'Kelwayi', bright yellow.

AQUILEGIA
Columbine

The columbines are an old-fashioned favourite. The flowers, like miniature ballet dancers with frilly skirts and arms held high, are available in a very wide range of colours and exist as doubles as well as singles. There is also a wide range of heights, from about 7.5cm (3in) to 90cm (3ft), suiting all positions in the border.

They will grow in any fertile garden soil and in either full sun or light shade. They do not generally need staking. They tend to self-sow. Old flowering stems should be cut down before seed is shed. Because they cross easily, self-sown seedlings do not necessarily come true, although they frequently produce exciting new forms. Propagate from seed sown in spring, or preferably in summer when fresh.

Aquilegia viridiflora

Species (above and next column)

A number of straight species are suitable for the border. *A. alpina* is a medium-height species with nodding blue flowers, often with a white inner skirt, while *A. canadensis* is slightly taller and has small flowers of red and yellow. *A. formosa* is similar. *A. chrysantha* is a much taller

species, this time with yellow flowers; many of the long-spurred hybrids are derived from this beautiful plant. *A. fragrans* is a medium-height plant with pale blue, slightly fragrant flowers and purple stems. *A. viridiflora* is one of the most intriguing; it is very short – rarely more than 30cm (1ft) – and has beautiful lovat-green flowers. *A. vulgaris* has been grown in gardens for generations and has produced many good varieties, mainly in blues and purples, including some delightful doubles (see below).

Aquilegia alpina

Old-fashioned forms

Many old short-spurred varieties, mainly derived from *A. vulgaris*, are still in existence. 'Adelaide Addison' is a nodding blue columbine with double white skirts. 'Nivea', known also as 'Munstead White', has pure white flowers and pale green leaves. 'Nora Barlow' is a curious double with spiky petals in cream, red and green. 'Hensol Harebell' is a wonderful rich violet-blue. 'Vervaeneana' is of mixed colours and the leaves are splashed with golden variegations.

Modern hybrids

Modern hybrids, many with long spurs, have been created out of a number of species. 'Crimson Star' has red flowers with white lower petals. 'Dragonfly Hybrids' are long-spurred columbines in

a mixture of red, blue and yellow, some in a single colour, others bicoloured. They look spectacular but tend to be short-lived – plants may have to be replaced after two or three years. 'McKana Hybrids', also long-spurred, come in a similar range of colours.

ARABIS
Rockcress

This is a very large genus, many of whose 100 species should be considered weeds due to their general appearance. There are, however, a number that are suitable for the garden. The generally low-growing, carpeting plants are most suited to the front of the border. The flowers are four-petalled, small and usually either white or pink. These plants are spring-flowering, but in some species the leaves are sufficiently attractive for them to count as foliage plants for the rest of the year.

Rockcress will grow in most garden soils but prefers those that are well-drained. A sunny position is required. After flowering, trim the plants over with shears to prevent them from becoming leggy. Propagate by division or cuttings.

Arabis caucasica 'Variegata'

A. caucasica (above)

Sometimes listed as *A. albida*, this is the most commonly grown species of rockcress. It forms low mats of rosettes that spread rapidly, yet are not invasive. The leaves are grey-green. The flowers are pure white, appearing in spring. 'Flore Pleno' has double flowers. 'Snow Cap' is particularly floriferous and 'Variegata' has cream variegations on the leaves.

A. ferdinandi-coburgii

This is a much more refined version of A. caucasica. It forms a ground-hugging carpet with narrow green leaves and short spikes of small white or occasionally pink flowers. 'Old Gold' has golden yellow variegations on the leaves, while 'Variegata' has cream-striped leaves.

ARTEMISIA
Mugwort

Of the 400 species in this genus, only a handful make good garden plants. They range considerably in character and height, with most being grown more for their foliage than their flowers. Those with silver foliage are useful, especially in creating white borders or associated with soft pinks and purples. The foliage is often aromatic. The flowers are generally very small and a dirty yellow. Many gardeners remove them on sight as they can destroy the beautiful foliage effect.

All artemisias need a well-drained soil and a sunny site. Many of the taller species benefit from being staked if they are in a windy position. They should be cut back in early spring, once the new growth can be located. Propagation can be carried out either by careful division or, more easily, by taking cuttings in spring.

Tall forms (next column)
A. absinthium 'Lambrook Silver' is one of the best silver-leafed plants. It grows to 75cm (2½ft) and has finely divided leaves. A. lactiflora is different from all the other species in that it has green foliage and attractive spikes of creamy yellow flowers. In the form 'Guizhou'

the leaves are flushed with purple. In A. ludoviciana var. latiloba the leaf segments are much broader than in the other tall forms and are pewter in colour. In the form 'Silver Queen' the leaves are a beautiful silvery colour.

Artemisia absinthium 'Lambrook Silver'

Bushy forms
The A. canescens forms are low bushy shrubs, 45cm (1½ft) high, with finely divided silvery foliage. They make good ground cover. A. pontica, with grey-green foliage, is slightly taller and not so bushy, being more upright. It also makes a dense cover but can become invasive.

Prostrate forms
Some forms that make excellent cover for the front of a border. A. schmidtiana creates a compact, low-growing hummock whose flower stems reach 15–30cm (6in–1ft). 'Nana' is one of the most compact forms. A. stelleriana can grow a little taller than A. schmidtiana. 'Mori', however, is a prostrate variety and has very white foliage; it is also known as 'Silver Brocade'.

ARUNCUS
Goat's beard

The goat's beards are double-value plants in that they are grown for both their foliage and flowers. The foliage is deeply cut and produced in great fountains. The

tiny flowers are held in large fluffy sprays and are either white or cream.

These plants are not fussy about their soil and will grow in either sun or shade. If in a sunny position, however, they do better in a moisture-retentive soil. They are clump-forming but not invasive. They need staking only if grown in an exposed position, and can be increased by division.

A. aethusifolius

This is a less commonly seen species. It is low-growing, reaching only 20cm (8in) high. It has finely cut leaves and spreads to form a non-invasive carpet. The cream flowers appear in short spikes.

A. dioicus (below)

This is the species most frequently grown in gardens. It is tall, reaching up to 2m (7ft) in fertile conditions. The leaves are composed of a number of oval leaflets. In the form 'Kneifii', however, these are very deeply cut, producing the impression that they are lacerated. This form is only half the height of its parent.

Aruncus dioicus

ASARUM
Wild ginger

These plants are grown for their foliage, which is rounded or heart-shaped and shiny green. Low-growing plants, rarely rising above 23cm (9in), they spread underground to make a dense ground cover. The flowers are of a curious shape and are deep purple in colour, but unfortunately they usually appear beneath the thick covering of leaves and are not easy to see. These are very good plants for growing in a shady border.

The wild gingers are woodlanders that thrive when allowed to creep around in a moist, humus-rich soil in light to deep shade. They do not tolerate very dry conditions. Propagation is by division in spring. They self-sow easily.

A. canadense
Canadian ginger has large heart-shaped leaves. It is deciduous.

A. caudatum
This is a semi-evergreen species with dark green leaves. The flowers have tail-like lobes.

Asarum europaeum

A. europaeum (above)
This is a smaller-leafed form than the others, but the foliage is a very attractive glossy green and remains on the plant throughout the year.

ASCLEPIAS
Milkweed
Native to North America, this large genus of plants offers a few very garden-worthy species, but others can sometimes become troublesome pests (*Asclepias syriaca*, for

example), as they tend to spread invasively Milkweed flowers form a wonderful spread of colour, with flat heads of bright red, pink or orange that will brighten up any border. The flowers are carried on erect stems that are strong enough to stand without extra support; the seeds that follow have tufts of silky hairs. The stems ooze a milky sap when broken – hence the common name.

Milkweeds will grow in any garden soil, but prefer a sunny position. They can be propagated from seed or by division.

A. incarnata
This attractive plant has pink flowers that appear in summer on 90cm–1.2m (3–4ft) stems. It likes a moister soil than do the other garden species.

A. tuberosa (below)
In late summer this species has bright orange flowers that make a valuable contribution to a border based on hot colours. It is shorter than *A. incarnata*, growing to a height of 75cm (2½ft), and prefers a drier soil.

Asclepias tuberosa

A. tuberosa 'Gay Butterflies'
This is a seed strain producing mixed colours, including pink, red, gold and orange. The 'butterflies' in the name refers to the fact that butterflies are attracted to this plant.

ASPERULA
Woodruff
Woodruff is a large genus of plants. Most of its garden forms are grown mainly in the rock garden. There are, however, a few that are suitable for a shady border and especially good as ground cover under shrubs or trees. They produce a mass of sprawling stems, each carrying whorls of narrow leaves and heads of tiny, starry, white or pink flowers.

Although these are primarily woodland plants, they will grow in a sunny position if the soil is moisture-retentive. After flowering they can become untidy and may need cutting back. Propagate by division.

Asperula odorata

A. odorata (above)
Also known as *Gallium odoratum*, this plant is a woodlander. Its white flowers can be used to brighten up a shady spot during early summer. It will climb through shrubs and reach a height of 45cm (1½ft). The stems and leaves have the scent of fresh hay.

ASPHODELINE
Jacob's rod
These fascinating plants are excellent for growing in a sunny border. From clumps of untidy, grass-like foliage emerge tall stems carrying star-like yellow flowers. The flowers have six or seven narrow petals and measure over 2.5cm (1in) across. The

flowers open successively up the spike and are followed by attractive seedpods, giving the plant a long season of interest. These plants make dramatic clumps when seen in the middle of a border and go especially well with blue-flowered plants.

They need to have a well-drained soil and a sunny position, sheltered from strong winds. They can be easily propagated by division or from seed.

A. lutea (below)

This is the main species in cultivation. It grows to 1.2m (4ft) high. The bright yellow flowers are fragrant and emerge from buff-coloured bracts. The plants are in flower from late spring through early summer.

Asphodeline lutea

ASPHODELUS
Asphodel

This genus is often confused with *Asphodeline* because of the similarity not only in name but also in general appearance. The leaves are slightly wider than those of Jacob's rods, but just as untidy. The spikes are much denser but they produce the same kind of starry flowers as do the Jacob's rods, although they are white or pink in colour rather than yellow.

Asphodels like a well-drained soil and a sunny position. Propagate by division or from seed in autumn.

A. aestivus

Also known as *A. microcarpus*, this is one of the less common asphodels. It grows to about 90cm (3ft) high and, in late spring, carries dense spikes of white flowers that often display flushes of pink when in bud.

Asphodelus albus

A. albus (above)

This is the most common species in cultivation. It is much taller than *A. aestivus*, reaching 1.5m (5ft) if grown in good conditions. The flowers are white but sometimes tinged with pink.

A. fistulosus

This is the shortest of the three species, reaching only 45cm (1½ft). It has narrow green leaves and, in the summer, spikes of white stars, flushed with pink.

ASPLENIUM
Spleenwort

This is a very large genus of ferns. The fronds, their main feature, range considerably in size, shape and texture from species to species. Many have deeply divided leaflets while in others the leaf is whole. They nearly all have a leathery appearance and all are evergreen.

The majority prefer to be grown in a cool, shady position, preferably in a humus-rich soil, although others are happy to grow in the barren conditions of stone walls.

A. scolopendrium (below)

Sometimes listed as *Phyllitis scolopendrium*, the hart's tongue fern is so-called because its strap-like, undivided fronds look like tongues. The colour is a shiny light- to mid-green. These ferns will grow in cool, shady conditions and make a good contrast to clumps of other ferns with the more usual cut-leafed fronds. There are many forms of this plant, of which a number have been in cultivation since Victorian times. 'Cristatum' has curious forks at the tip of the blades. 'Crispum' has wonderful undulating margins, while 'Undulatum' also has undulating margins but less pronounced than in 'Crispum'.

Asplenium scolopendrium

ASTER
Aster

Aster is understandably a popular genus with gardeners. Among its species are a wide range of plants – from dwarf ones, for the front of the border, to stately ones, to go at the back. They flower from early summer onwards, with some cultivars flowering as late as late autumn, offering a long period of colour in the garden.

Most have a yellow central disc, surrounded by narrow petals, mainly in blues and purples, although there are also pinks, reds and whites. Flower size varies from 5cm (2in) or more to less than 10mm (⅓in), but the small size of the latter is made up for by the large quantity in which they appear. Most make good cut flowers.

Asters will grow in any good garden soil, but do best in those that are not allowed to become too dry. An open sunny situation suits them best. The taller forms need staking if grown in windy, exposed situations. Their main problem is mildew, which can be treated with a fungicide spray. Propagation is readily achieved by division in autumn or spring.

A. amellus varieties (below)
The flowers of this species are among the largest in the genus. The many varieties make superb border plants with a very long season, from late summer onwards. The asters can reach a height of 75cm (2½ft). 'King George' has large purple flowers, 'Nocturne' dark blue and 'Veilchenkönigin' ('Violet Queen') rich violet flowers.

Aster amellus 'King George'

A. × frikartii
This series of hybrids between *A. amellus* and *A. thomsonii* are excellent border plants with a long flowering season. The best include 'Mönch', with lavender-blue petals, and 'Wünder von Stafa', which is taller and slightly paler.

A. novae-angliae varieties
These Michaelmas daisies are less prone to mildew than the *A. novi-belgii*

varieties. They are also generally taller, reaching up to a height of 1.5m (5ft). There is a wide choice of cultivars, all of which flower in the autumn. 'Andenken an Alma Pötschke' is a superb plant with bright rosy pink coloured flowers. In 'Herbstschnee' ('Autumn Snow') the flowers are pure white, in 'Harrington's Pink' they are clear pink, 'Lye End Beauty' cerise-lilac, 'Purple Dome' purple, 'Rosa Seiger' mauve-pink, 'Treasure' ('Hella Lacy') deep violet and in 'Septemberrin' ('September Ruby') they are red-purple.

Aster novi-belgii 'Little Pink Beauty'

A. novi-belgii varieties (above)
New York asters make up the largest group of Michaelmas daisies. Within this group there are several hundred varieties to choose from. They vary considerably in height from 15cm–1.2m (6in–4ft). The recommended varieties include 'Audrey' which has lavender flowers, 'Bonningale White' (white flowers), 'Climax' (light violet), 'Coombe Violet' (violet), 'Crimson Brocade' (purple-red), 'Eventide' (violet), 'Goliath' (mauve), 'Jenny' (bright red), 'Lady in Blue' (blue), 'Little Pink Beauty' (pink), 'Marie Ballard' (light blue, double), 'Professor Anton Kippenberg' (mid-blue), 'Purple Dome' (violet-purple), 'Royal Ruby' (ruby-red) and 'Schneekissen' ('Snow Cushion') white.

Small-flowered forms (below)
There are a number of asters that produce small flowers which are insignificant in themselves but create a beautiful hazy effect when seen in quantity. *A. divaricatus* has very interesting wiry black stems and myriad white flowers. *A. ericoides* produces clouds of flowers: 'Golden Spray' is a tall form, reaching a height of 1.2m (4ft), with creamy white petals and a large golden central disc; 'Pink Cloud' is a haze of pale pink. On *A. laterifolius* 'Horizontalis' the branches stick out at right angles to the main stem. It has mauve flowers. *A. pringlei* 'Monte Cassino' (previously considered to be a form of *A. ericoides*) has white flowers. In *A. spectabile* the flowers are violet-blue.

Aster laterifolius 'Horizontalis'

ASTILBE
Astilbe
Astilbes are colourful plants and valuable for brightening up a border over a long period. The flowers are produced in fluffy pyramids and come in a range of bright reds, purples, whites and creams; some seem almost luminous. They are summer-flowering. When not in flower they have attractive ferny foliage, often tinged with purple. Most grow to 60cm–1.2m (2–4ft) tall but there are also some dwarf forms.

These are versatile plants: they will grow both in the sun and in light shade.

It is important, however, to give them a moisture-retentive soil; they grow best if placed next to a pool or stream. They do not need staking. Propagate by division.

A. × arendsii

The species are rarely grown; it is the hybrids, in particular those known as *A.* × *arendsii*, that are usually seen. A wide range of colours, both of flowers and foliage, is available.

White forms (below)

The white forms need deadheading as soon as the flowers are over, as they fade to an unattractive brown. The foliage is mainly bright green. 'Brautschleier' ('Bridal Veil'), pure white, grows to 60cm (2ft). 'Deutschland' is similar but flowers earlier. 'Ellie' is creamier and taller than the other white forms.

Astilbe × arendsii 'Brautschleier'

Pink forms

These vary in intensity of colour. 'Bressingham Beauty' is a rich pink for late in the summer. 'Erica' is a bright pink and flowers earlier. 'Straussenfeder' ('Ostrich Plume') has large plumes of coral-pink in mid-season. 'Peach Blossom' flowers at a similar time but is a pale pink and shorter than the others. 'Rheinland' is similarly compact, reaching 60cm (2ft), and has deep pink flowers that appear early in the season.

Astilbe × arendsii 'Feuer'

Red forms (above)

These are the brightest of the hybrids, and need careful placing not to clash with other colours. They frequently have purple foliage. 'Fanal' has bright red flowers carried in short, dense spikes and flowers early. 'Feuer' ('Fire') has coral-red flowers and is taller; it flowers late. 'Red Sentinel' has deep carmine-red flowers on tall stems, and flowers earlier.

A. chinensis

This is rarely grown as a species but is commonly seen in its varieties. *A. c.* var. *pumila* is a dwarf form that grows only 30cm (1ft) tall. It has pretty mauve-pink flowers. As a contrast *A. c.* var. *tacquetii* 'Superba' grows up to 1.2m (4ft).

A. simplicifolia

This species is known for its form 'Sprite'. It is a dwarf species with pink flowers and particularly fine, delicately cut foliage.

ASTRANTIA
Masterwort

Masterworts have an old-world charm that makes them ideal for cottage and similar gardens. The character of the tiny flowers is given by the green bracts that surround the central dome of the flower, giving the impression of a pincushion. In most species the bracts and the centre are a pale green,

giving the plant a cool appearance. In some of the cultivars, however, these are pink or even red. Masterworts come into flower in early summer and some forms continue until late summer or early autumn. They are 60cm (2ft) in height.

Masterworts are suitable for positions in either full sun or light shade, and are especially useful in the latter. A moisture-retentive soil, enriched with plenty of well-rotted humus, is needed. Although the plants are moderately tall, they do not require staking. Propagation is by division or by sowing seed.

Red forms

The red forms are becoming increasingly popular and new, better forms are constantly being sought. They often take longer to form a good-sized clump than the normal green forms. *A. carniolica* 'Rubra' is an old variety with green and crimson flowers. It is being challenged for depth of colour by two newer varieties, *A. major* 'Hadspen Blood' and the red-stemmed 'Ruby Wedding'; both have deep, rich wine-red flowers.

Astrantia maxima

Pink forms (above)

The pink forms are very charming and make excellent cut flowers. *A. major* var. *rosea* is a green form flushed with pink. *A. maxima* is a magnificent plant with rose-pink triangular bracts around the flower, which is also rose-pink in colour. *A. major* 'Buckland' is another good green-and-pink form.

White forms

There are no true white forms: all are a very pale green, usually flushed with a slightly darker green. The species *A. major* is very pale green and makes an excellent plant for a shady spot. Even better are the extremely large heads of the pale coloured 'Shaggy' (which is also known as 'Margery Fish'), named for its long bracts.

Variegated forms (below)

There is one excellent form with creamy variegations on its leaves. This is *A. major* 'Sunningdale Variegated'. The leaves become greener as the season progresses. The greeny-pink flowers are usually removed as they detract from the appeal of the foliage.

Astrantia major 'Sunningdale Variegated'

ATHYRIUM
Athyrium

This is a genus of graceful ferns that make a wonderful contrast with other plants. They include some of the most popular species for growing in a shady spot. They vary in height but most garden forms are 60cm (2ft) tall.

These ferns are woodland plants and they prefer a moist soil with lots of leaf mould or humus in it. However, they will grow in drier conditions if necessary. Light dappled shade, such as that provided by deciduous shrubs and trees, is a suitable situation. They can be increased either by sowing spores or by division.

Athyrium filix-femina

A. filix-femina (above)

This is the famous lady fern, and a species of great refinement. The pale green fronds are finely dissected and arch gracefully from a gently creeping rootstock. It is deciduous.

A. nipponicum var. *pictum*

The Japanese painted fern is as desirable as *A. filix-femina*. The name is derived from the 'painted' appearance of its red-flushed stems, and its fronds are washed with a silvery grey. It spreads gently, not invasively, to form a moderate-sized colony.

AUBRIETA
Aubrieta

Aubrieta is one of the colourful signs that spring is under way. The plants form low hummocks that are suitable for the front of a border or for hanging over the edge of a wall. The foliage sets off the colours of the flowers, which include blue, purple, pinks, reds and white. The flowers are short-stemmed and lie close to the foliage, in a good season covering it completely.

Aubrieta will grow in nearly all garden conditions, even dry ones. However, they are more floriferous and compact if grown in an open sunny position. For the best results trim the plants with shears once flowering is finished; this will keep them compact. Propagation can be achieved by taking cuttings from new growth or by sowing seed.

Cultivars (below)

There is a wide range of colours from which to choose. The selection is further widened by the existence of some cultivars with double flowers and others with variegated leaves. The following list is a selection of the best: 'Aureovariegata' has gold-variegated leaves and lavender-blue flowers; 'Bob Saunders' is a purple-red double; 'Greencourt Purple' is a double purple; 'Bressingham Pink' is a double pink; 'Doctor Mules' has deep violet flowers; 'Red Carpet' is the best of the reds.

Aubrieta 'Dr. Mules'

BAPTISIA
False indigo

This North American genus provides a few excellent garden plants. They are members of the pea family, and the flowers strongly resemble those of the pea. There is a range of colours including blue, yellow and white. These are tall plants, reaching up to 1.2m (4ft), and, although they are not invasive, they can take up a great deal of room and are therefore not suitable for use in small borders.

Baptisias are deep-rooted plants that like a deep, rich soil. They are, however, drought-resistant and will succeed in poorer conditions, and grow in either sun or light shade. In a windy position they need staking. Being deep-rooted, they resent disturbance of any kind. Propagation is carried out from seed or by careful division.

B. australis (below)
This is the main species in cultivation. Its popularity stems from the wonderful blue flowers it produces in early summer. It grows up to 1.2m (4ft).

Baptisia australis

BEGONIA
Begonia
This genus includes nearly 1,000 species, which mainly come from the tropics and subtropics. The majority of begonias are thought of as annuals. Most of the tender forms are perennials but they are best overwintered in a greenhouse or raised every year from cuttings or seed.

B. evansia (next column)
Often listed as *B. grandis* var. *evansia*, this species is hardy in many areas. It is a tuberous plant with pointed, heart-shaped leaves and drooping clusters of pink flowers in summer. It likes a moist, humus-rich soil and in hotter areas light shade. It is not long-lived, but mulching with straw helps it through a cold winter. Propagation is by division.

Begonia evansia

BELLIS
Daisy
Some daisies are considered irritating weeds, others, usually with double flowers, are thought of as desirable border plants. These plants have been grown by generations of cottage gardeners and are often used to line paths. Uniform in height and colour, they are often used as bedding plants, although they are perennial.

Bellis perennis 'Dresden China'

B. perennis forms (above)
This is the weed of lawns, but there are any number of very good varieties. The flower stems grow only 15cm (6in) high and the plants form neat rosettes of leaves. If you keep them permanently in the border, make certain they do not self-seed and produce unattractive hybrid forms. Some varieties have large flowers, usually white with touches of red or pink, but the best varieties are neat button-like doubles, such as the excellent soft pink 'Dresden China'. 'Prolifera' (also known as 'Hen and Chickens') is a curious plant, growing secondary flower heads that appear out of the first.

BERGENIA
Elephant ears
As ground-cover plants, few can surpass elephant ears, yet they are also very attractive in their own right. Their common name derives from the large, rounded leaves, leathery in texture and often glossy. They come in various shades of green but many also turn red or purple during the winter. The flowers appear in short, bold spikes up to 45cm (1½ft) in height, with the predominant colour pink in various shades, though there are also white forms. These flowers appear from spring through into early summer. All in all, these are good all-year-round plants.

Not only are they versatile in their foliage and flowering, they are also very accommodating in their requirements. They grow in either sun or shade and tolerate both dry and moist soils. Some gardeners like to dig them up every 5 years, improve the soil and then replant them, but many gardeners find they can leave them in the same position almost indefinitely – another factor in their favour. They can be propagated by division or by taking sections of their rhizomes as root cuttings.

Foliage types (next column)
Although elephant ears all have good foliage, some are certainly better than others. *B.* 'Bressingham Ruby' has a ruby foliage throughout most of the year and

bright pink flowers. *B. cordifolia* 'Purpurea' has very large leaves that take on an attractive purple coloration in winter. It has bright magenta flowers. *B.* 'Perfect' (also known as 'Perfecta') has purple leaves and deep pink flowers on long stems.

Bergenia cordifolia 'Purpurea'

Pink-flowered forms

There are several varieties that are especially noted for their fine pink or pinkish flowers. *B.* 'Abendglut' ('Evening Glow') is one of the best, with rich purple flowers and small leaves that turn purple in winter. *B. cordifolia* has deep pink or magenta flowers and large leaves. 'Red Beauty' has red flowers, while 'Ballawley' has bright crimson flowers and a good purple foliage in winter.

White-flowered forms

White forms are less numerous, and some are tinged with pink. However, *B.* 'Bressingham White' is an almost pure-white form. *B. stracheyi* 'Alba' is a short form, reaching only 25cm (10in) high, with good white flowers.

BLECHNUM

Blechnum

There are about 200 species of this fern, most of them from tropical or subtropical regions. A few, however, are hardy and make good garden plants. They slowly

spread to create large colonies. The fronds are deeply cut and are mainly evergreen, although those that have produced spores fade and become unattractive, and should be removed.

These plants like moist, humus-rich soil, preferably in a shady position, and look particularly attractive when planted next to water. Blechnums do best in a soil that is slightly acidic. They are not completely hardy, and in colder districts need a winter mulch to protect them. Propagation is by division or from spores.

B. penna-marina

This fern has very slender dark green fronds, giving it a delicate appearance. It spreads to form a dense ground cover, but is the least hardy of the group.

B. spicant

This is known as the hard fern and is a larger version of *B. penna-marina*, growing to as much as 75cm (2½ft) in height. It is a hardier plant and will grow in drier conditions. Its leaves are dark green and glossy.

B. tabulare

This species is very similar to *B. magellanicum*, with which it is often confused. It has large fronds, reaching up to 90cm (3ft), and leathery leaflets. It forms substantial colonies.

BOLTONIA

Boltonia

This genus is often overshadowed by its similar-looking relations, the Michaelmas daisies (*Aster*). Boltonias are attractive plants, however, and, well worth growing in their own right. The flowers are typical daisies, with a yellow central disc and rays of white, pink or lilac petals. These are only 2cm (¾in) across but are carried in large numbers in loose clusters. The heights of the varieties range between 60cm (2ft) and 2m (7ft).

Boltonias will grow in any good garden soil, but they prefer it to be well-drained, though not too dry. They grow best in full sun, although they will tolerate very light shade. They need supporting only in exposed places. Increase by dividing the plants in spring.

B. asteroides (below)

This is the main species in cultivation. It is tall, up to 2m (7ft), but has much smaller cultivars. The colour of the flowers varies, with a choice of white, pink or lilac. In *B. a.* var. *latisquama* they are lilac and relatively large. 'Snowbank', on the other hand, has white flowers and is one of the shorter varieties, reaching only 1.2m (4ft) in height. 'Pink Beauty' has pink flowers.

Boltonia asteroides

BORAGO

Borage

This genus is best known for its annual culinary herb, *B. officinalis*, but there are two other species, one of which, *B. pygmaea*, is suitable for the border.

B. pygmaea (next page)

Until recently this species was known as *B. laxiflora*. It is a loose-growing plant with rough leaves and small nodding flowers. These flowers are a beautiful soft blue. Unfortunately, it is rather a lax plant and is unable to support itself, but it does particularly well when grown through a low shrub. It is a tap-rooted plant that resents disturbance. It will grow in any garden soil as long as it is not too dry, and grows equally well in either sun or light shade. It is easily propagated from seed, and there are usually plenty of self-sown seedlings that can be transplanted.

Borago pygmaea

BRUNNERA
Brunnera

This is a small genus, containing three species, of which only *B. macrophylla* is generally grown in gardens. These plants originate in southwest Asia and are delightful for their loose spikes of blue, forget-me-not-like flowers.

They will grow in any good garden soil, but prefer ones that are moisture-retentive. These woodland plants grow best in light shade, but can be grown in sun if the soil is not allowed to dry out too much. They can be easily propagated by division.

B. macrophylla (next column)

This species, sometimes known as Siberian bugloss (although it does not come from Siberia), grows to 45cm (1½ft) high and spreads to make an effective ground cover with its large, slightly hairy leaves. Although it spreads rapidly it is not invasive, as it can easily be controlled by pulling it up. The blue

flowers make a magnificent display in spring, when they are held in airy sprays well above the leaves. Once they are over, the leaves are attractive enough to maintain the plant's interest. Several cultivars are widely grown. 'Betty Bowring' is a beautiful, white-flowered form. 'Dawson's White' (previously known as 'Variegata') has variegated foliage with wide, pale cream, almost white margins. 'Hadspen Cream' is similar but the variegations are creamier in colour. 'Langtrees' has silver spots on the leaves. The variegated forms have a tendency to brown if exposed to strong sunlight.

Brunnera macrophylla 'Dawson's White'

BUPHTHALMUM
Buphthalmum

This is a small genus of European plants of which only one, *B. salicifolium*, has entered general cultivation. Another plant, *B. speciosum*, which can become an invasive pest, is now known as *Telekia speciosa*. All the species have yellow, daisy-like flowers, but their foliage is often coarse and unattractive, which is why only *B. salicifolium* is grown to any extent.

Buphthalmum will grow in any garden soils, including quite poor ones, and will be happy in either sun or light shade. They are not strong, however, and should be staked in any but the most sheltered positions. They can be propagated either by division or by seed sown in the spring.

B. salicifolium (below)

This is so-called because of its willow-like leaves, *Salix* being the willow genus. It grows to 60cm (2ft) and carries masses of rich, golden yellow daisies throughout summer and into autumn. It makes a very good plant for a border based on hot colours. It slowly spreads to form large clumps, but is not invasive.

Buphthalmum salicifolium

CALAMINTHA
Calamint

The plants of this genus are best suited to the front of a border. They belong to the mint family, and have loose heads of typical lipped, tubular flowers, which are usually pink or white. The plants are short, they can reach 60cm (2ft) high when grown in rich conditions but are often much shorter. The flowers provide an effective contrast with the dark to light green foliage, which is aromatic when it is crushed.

They all need a well-drained soil and an open, sunny position. They dislike winter wet and may die if the conditions are too damp during that time of the year, so protect them if necessary. Propagate in the spring by cuttings or by careful division.

C. grandiflora (next column)

This forms a small bush with dark green, coarse-toothed aromatic leaves. The flowers are deep pink and smother the plant in summer and autumn. In the form 'Variegata', the leaves have a speckled creamy variegation.

Calamintha grandiflora 'Variegata'

C. nepeta

This is a smaller plant than the previous one, reaching only 45cm (1½ft) high. It has lighter green leaves, which have a particularly fine scent, and the flowers are white or blue. It is hardy but dislikes winter wet, so you must grow it in a well-drained soil.

CALTHA
Marsh marigold

These plants are the glory of the spring. They produce a mass of golden, buttercup-type flowers that brighten up even the dullest of days and which show up well against the dark green of the large rounded leaves. They are spreading plants that can grow to 60cm (2ft) tall.

As their name implies, these plants enjoy wet, marshy conditions, and although they will grow in ordinary border soil, if it is not allowed to dry out, they do best if planted on the margins of a pond or stream. They thrive in a sunny position but are equally at home in light shade, especially under deciduous trees or shrubs that have yet to come into leaf when the marsh marigold flowers. Propagation is from seed, which should be sown while it is still fresh, or by division.

C. palustris (below)

This species is very widespread from the Arctic to the Himalayas and from North America to Europe and on to Japan. Some authorities go so far as to say that many other members of the genus are in fact this species in slightly different guises. It is equally as widespread in gardens as in the wild. The main species has golden yellow flowers, but there are forms with paler petals; the variation *alba*, for example, has almost white flowers. There is also a superb double-petalled form, 'Flore Pleno'.

Caltha palustris 'Flore Pleno'

CAMPANULA
Bellflower

This is a large genus, with 300 species, of which a surprising number are in cultivation. They range in height from those that are ground-hugging to those that reach up to 1.5m (5ft) or more. The flowers that give them both their Latin and common names are bell-shaped. In most species they hang down, but in some they are held up so that you can see right into the bell. The predominant colour is blue, but this varies from very pale to very dark and includes some purples. As with nearly all blue-flowered plants, there are also white forms of bellflowers available.

Most bellflowers thrive in a well-drained soil enriched with well-rotted organic material. Most will grow in either full sun or light shade. The white forms of some species look especially good when planted under trees. The majority do best, however, if they are planted in an open site. The species can be propagated by seed or from cuttings, but the varieties must be propagated vegetatively (for example, by leaf cuttings or division) if they are to come true to their colour and form.

Campanula portenschlagiana

Short forms (above)

There are a number of low-growing bellflowers that make admirable plants for the front of a border. *C. carpatica* is a bushy plant growing to about 30cm (1ft) high. It has open saucer-shaped bells, that mainly face upward, and come in various shades of blue, such as 'Blaue Clips' ('Blue Clips'), which has mid-blue flowers. White forms include 'Alba'. The evergreen *C. isophylla* bears smaller, shallow, upward-facing flowers; it is not so hardy. *C. lactiflora* 'White Pouffe' has white flowers on a short form that reaches only 30cm (1ft). There are both white and blue forms available. *C. portenschlagiana* is a rampant ground coverer with blue flowers; the form 'Resholt' has larger, lighter blue flowers. An even more rampant spreader is *C. poscharskyana*. It is only approximately 15cm (6in) tall but will scramble up through shrubs. It carries masses of starry blue flowers.

Campanula glomerata 'Superba'

Medium forms (above)
There are many good garden species that fall within this group. *C. alliariifolia* has distinctive heart-shaped leaves and attractive blue flowers. In the form 'Ivory Bells' they are creamy white. The species *C. glomerata*, known as the clustered bellflower, has its flowers grouped together in clusters. The best form is 'Superba', which can reach up to approximately 90cm (3ft) tall; the others mentioned are only half this height. *C. punctata* can spread invasively by underground runners but the form 'Elizabeth', with reddish bells, is better behaved. *C. takesimana* is another runner, but its large pink bells, flushed with reddish purple, make it well worth growing and controlling. It needs support. *C. rotundifolia* varies considerably in stature and can be used as a rock or border plant. It has delicate hanging bells carried on slender stems. The form 'Alba' has white bells.

Tall forms (next column)
The tall forms add colour and substance to a border. Most need staking to prevent them falling over under the weight of flowers. *C. lactiflora* is one of the most spectacular, with large heads of upward-facing bells on 1.5m (5ft) stems. The form 'Loddon Anna' has pink flowers instead of the more usual blue.

C. latifolia grows to 90cm (3ft) and has spikes of blue flowers. 'Brantwood' is one of the best cultivars, offering deep blue flowers over a long period. The form 'Gloaming' is a smoky blue. *C. latiloba* likewise has spikes of flowers, but they are denser than those of *C. latifolia* and the flowers are more open and saucer-shaped. They are generally blue in colour but in 'Hidcote Amethyst', for example, they are lilac-pink. 'Highcliffe' is a strong plant with lavender-coloured flowers. *C. persicifolia* is very similar in general appearance to *C. latiloba*, but the flowers are carried on short stalks attached to the main stem and the plants are less robust. There are a large number of cultivars: 'Alba', as you would expect, has white flowers; 'George Chiswell' has a pretty white flower edged with blue; while the equally charming 'Hampstead White' has semi-double white flowers; 'Telham Beauty' is a single with very large flowers of lavender-blue.

Campanula latifolia 'Brantwood'

CAREX
Sedge

Sedges are very similar to grasses in both appearance and garden use. Grasses have hollow stems while sedges' are solid, but the most obvious difference is that the sedges' stems are triangular. Another noticeable difference is that the leaves of the sedge form a cylinder round the stem, whereas in the grasses the leaves wrap round the stem with overlapping edges. In general appearance sedges look like clumps of grass with fountains of narrow leaves. The various species of *Carex* are grown mainly for the colours of the leaves, which range from green to bronze and can be variegated.

Sedges will grow in any good garden soil, but do best in those that are moisture-retentive. Many look especially good when grown next to water. They can be increased by division in the spring.

Carex buchananii

C. buchananii (above)
Buchanan's sedge, from New Zealand, grows to about 45cm (1½ft) high and erupts in a fountain of narrow leaves that are bronze on the undersides. It looks well when grown towards the front of a border.

C. comans 'Bronze Form'
This is another New Zealander, this time forming a lax clump that grows up to 60cm (2ft) tall. The bronze-coloured leaves are very fine and hair-like.

C. hajijoensis 'Evergold'
This is a brightly coloured sedge with gold variegations running along the centre of its green leaves. The leaves are up to 45cm (1½ft) long. It is also known as *C. morrowii* 'Evergold'.

C. morrowii 'Variegata'

This plant is similar to *C. hajijoensis* 'Evergold' but with white variegation that runs down the edges of the leaves.

C. pendula

This is a large sedge with drooping flower heads hanging from long thin stems. In wet conditions the plant can grow up to 1.2m (4ft) tall. The leaves are broad and dark green. This is a graceful plant but it can self-sow too readily.

C. riparia 'Variegata'

The greater pond sedge is usually grown in its variegated form, which produces 60cm (2ft) high clumps of white-striped leaves. In some cases the variegation is so strong that the whole leaf appears white. This plant is attractive, but can become invasive through spreading roots.

CENTAUREA
Knapweed

This is a superb genus of plants, of whose 600 species only a fraction are in cultivation. They make excellent border plants, with flowers that can be cut either for arrangements or for drying. The flowers are thistle-like, with a central disc and an outer ring of petals that are frequently dissected and feathery. They come in a wide range of colours, from purples to yellows and whites. Most knapweeds flower in early summer. A distinctive feature is that the flowers are held in a hard, rounded calyx. The foliage is not especially attractive, although in some varieties it creates a good foil for the flowers.

Knapweeds like a well-drained soil and do particularly well on limy ones. Staking is often necessary. Propagation is either by division or from seed, although many will also propagate from root cuttings.

C. bella

This is one of the smaller species, growing to only 30cm (1ft). The foliage forms a mat of finely cut silvery leaves which are attractive in their own right. The flowers are a soft purple that contrasts superbly with the foliage.

Centaurea dealbata 'Steenbergii'

C. dealbata 'Steenbergii' (above)

This form of the Persian cornflower has light green leaves that are grey on the underside. The flowers are large and a rosy purple. Unfortunately, the plant is floppy, and needs support to give of its best. It grows to about 60cm (2ft) high. Its tendency towards underground invasion can be a problem.

C. macrocephala

The yellow hardhead has magnificent, golden yellow flowers opening from large papery buds. The yellow looks good against the large, mid-green leaves. It grows to 90cm (3ft) or more.

C. montana

The mountain knapweed is one of the first knapweeds to flower. It is a rather lax plant that needs some form of support. The flowers are like large cornflowers, with blue or purple outer petals surrounding a red centre. They suffer badly from mildew and should be cut down after flowering to stimulate the growth of new foliage. 'Alba' is a good white form and 'Gold Bullion' is distinguished by its yellow leaves.

CENTRANTHUS
Red valerian

Although there are a dozen species in this genus, only one of them is usually grown. This is *C. ruber* (below), sometimes listed as *Kentranthus ruber*. It is fleshy, with grey-green stems and foliage and pyramidal heads of red flowers. It has long been a favourite with cottage gardeners and often looks best when it is left to seed at will, although it can be kept in a neat clump in the border. There is a white form of this plant, *alba*, which is sometimes listed as 'Snow Cloud'.

Although *C. ruber* grows best in garden soil, it will also thrive in poor conditions, where the plants are usually more compact. It does well in seaside gardens, and can often be seen growing wild on beaches and adjacent wasteland. It will also grow on walls. It self-sows prolifically, so cut back after flowering to prevent this and to promote a second flush of flowers. Propagation can be from seed or by taking cuttings.

Centranthus ruber

CEPHALARIA
Cephalaria

This is a genus of plants with scabious-like flowers. Indeed, many of them have been considered part of the genus *Scabiosa* in the past. They range considerably in size, from tiny plants suitable for rock gardens to the 2m (7ft) giant described overleaf.

The flowers are usually in soft colours, mainly yellow and lilac-purple, and are useful for pastel colour schemes.

Cephalaria will grow in any good garden soil and likes an open, sunny position. Propagation can be from seed or by division, if you can manage it with the larger plants, although it can be more difficult.

C. gigantea (below)

This is the giant member of the genus, rising to a height of 2m (7ft) or more when grown in rich soil. The flowers appear in early summer and are a soft lemon-yellow, well set off by the dark green leaves. The flowers are carried on tall, wiry stems but, in spite of its height, the plant does not require staking except in very exposed areas. It has a tendency to self-sow rather prodigiously, and should be cut back before this happens. It is tap-rooted and resents being disturbed once planted.

Cephalaria gigantea

CERATOSTIGMA
Plumbago

Strictly speaking, most members of this genus are shrubs rather than perennials, but they are usually considered along with the latter as they die back to the ground in the late autumn, like herbaceous plants. They are rather untidy shrubs, but their brilliant blue flowers are so appealing that this seems unimportant. Another point in

their favour is that they flower in autumn when good blues are in short supply. Their untidy habit can be overcome by growing them among other plants, through which they can clamber.

They need a fertile, well-drained soil and a sunny position. In warmer areas, where the frost does not do the job for you, they should be cut back almost to the ground after flowering. Propagation, done in spring, can be from cuttings or seed.

Ceratostigma plumbaginoides

C. plumbaginoides (above)

This is a low plant – only about 30cm (1ft) high – but it spreads, and will scramble up through other plants, given the opportunity. The blue flowers stand out against the reddening autumn leaves.

C. willmottianum

This plant is much taller than its sister plant, C. *plumbaginoides*, reaching 90cm (3ft). It too has blue flowers, but comes into bloom earlier.

CHELONE
Turtlehead

The intriguing common name of this plant originates from the resemblance between the shape of the flowers and that of the head of a turtle. The flowers are fat tubes with thick lips, and are generally pink, purple or white. The plants form clumps of stiffly erect stems, reaching up to 1.2m

(4ft), which makes them suitable for the centre of a border. They are generally late-flowering, filling gaps towards the end of summer and into autumn.

They will grow in any good garden soil, but prefer those that are moisture-retentive. They will grow in either sun or light shade, although the former is preferable. They can be propagated easily by dividing in autumn or spring, and can also be grown from seed.

C. lyonii

This is a pink-flowering species. The flowers are carried in dense spikes. In hot areas it grows better in shade.

C. obliqua (below)

This is similar to C. *lyonii* but is usually considered more decorative. The flowers are pink or white and appear over a long period. It has a strong constitution and will stand up to autumnal weather.

Chelone obliqua

CIMICIFUGA
Bugbane

Not only does this plant provide tall attractive spires of flowers late in the year, it offers plenty of ferny foliage for the rest of the season. The flowers are curious in that they have no petals but are, in fact, bunches of stamens, which when all seen together make a wonderful spire of fluffy flowers in either cream or white. The leaves are generally green, but some species have very desirable purple foliage. They are tall, reaching 1.8m (6ft) or more.

Bugbane grow in any fertile garden soils, but prefers those that are rich in well-rotted humus. A cool, lightly shaded situation is best, but they will grow in full sun as long as conditions are not too hot or dry. Stake if grown in an exposed spot. Propagation is by division or from seed.

C. racemosa
This tall species grows to 1.8m (6ft). It has white flowers in mid-summer and leaves in fresh green, deeply divided.

Cimicifuga simplex 'White Pearl'

C. simplex (above)
Although shorter than *C. racemosa*, only 1.2m (4ft), this is still an impressive plant, both for its flowers and for its foliage. It is the last bugbane species to flower, producing spires of white flowers in late autumn. 'Atropurpurea' has dark purple foliage, while 'Brunette' has bronze leaves. 'White Pearl' has pure white flowers carried in large numbers.

CIRSIUM
Thistle
Most gardeners treat thistles as weeds, yet, while some are pests, others are not only well behaved but also attractive. They usually have either pink or purple flowers and foliage that is tipped with spines.

Thistles are able to grow in any garden soil, even a poor one, but they do best in reasonably rich conditions. Sun suits them best. They can be readily increased by division or from seed, the latter in spring or when ripe.

Cirsium rivulare 'Atropurpureum'

C. rivulare 'Atropurpureum' (above)
This form of *C. rivulare* is the best thistle in cultivation. It has soft pin-cushion heads of the most sumptuous-looking crimson, which appear in early summer. The leaves look more prickly than they are. The plant grows to approximately 1.2m (4ft) high and spreads, although not invasively.

CLEMATIS
Clematis
Most gardeners tend to think of clematis in terms of woody, climbing plants, but a surprising number are herbaceous, dying back to the ground each year, and can be used in perennial borders. They might not be as spectacular as some of the climbing varieties, but they can still be very attractive. The flowers vary considerably in size and colour, but those suitable for growing in the border are mainly blue or white. The leaves in some species can also be very attractive.

Border clematis can be grown in any fertile garden soil, but it should be well fed with organic material. Clematis like to

have their roots cool and their tops in sunlight, so shade the base of the stems with other plants. Most border clematis are scramblers, and need something to climb through; they can be supported with pea-sticks or by shrubs that have finished flowering. Some make attractive ground cover if left to sprawl across the ground. Propagation is by taking cuttings.

C. crispa
This climbing species from the south-eastern USA dies back to the ground each winter. The single flowers, on long stems, are bell-shaped with reflexed petals. They are delightfully coloured: blue with a white stripe down the centre of each petal. These plants flower from summer onwards.

Clematis × durandii

C. × durandii (above)
C. × durandii is a hybrid between *C. integrifolia* and *C. jackmanii*. It is one of the larger-flowered herbaceous forms. The flowers are up to 12.5cm (5in) across and a wonderful rich blue in colour, appearing from late summer onwards. The plants will climb through shrubs or can be supported on sticks. They do best when cut all the way back to the ground each winter. If the plants are pruned to approximately 1.2m (4ft), however, they will act as climbing clematis, growing to 3m (10ft) or more.

C. × *eriostemon* (below)

This is a cross between *C. integrifolia* and *C. viticella*. It grows to about 2.5m (8ft) tall and requires a shrub for support. The flowers are nodding, open bells, coloured an attractive purple-blue. It flowers from late summer onwards.

Clematis × eriostemon

C. *heracleifolia*

This is among the most commonly seen herbaceous clematis. It is generally left to grow over the ground from its woody base. The flowers are very similar in shape and colour to those of a hyacinth. They are blue and scented, and appear in autumn. The foliage is large and rather coarse, making a good ground cover.

C. *integrifolia*

The beautiful flowers of this clematis are like loose, hanging bells, with four thin twisted petals. They are purple-blue in colour, with a prominent central boss of creamy white stamens, and appear in late summer. The narrow leaves are lance-shaped. In a very sheltered position, this plant is self-supporting, but it usually requires some form of support unless it is allowed to flop on the ground.

C. × *jouiniana*

This is a vigorous plant that will clamber over shrubs and fences. The flowers are quite small, but what they lack in size they make up for in numbers and, at times, the plant seems to be a haze of blooms. They are soft blue and appear from late summer onwards. There are several forms: 'Mrs Robert Brydon' has milky white flowers; 'Praecox' has soft blue flowers that come into bloom much earlier than those of any other form.

CODONOPSIS
Bonnet bellflower

The bonnet bellflowers are not spectacular plants in terms of their contribution to the overall appearance of the border, but looked at individually they are very attractive. They are members of the bellflower family, as can be seen from the shape of the flowers. The outside is usually blue, but when the flower is tipped up and the inside examined, an array of bright colours is exposed. These are mainly climbing plants, and need a low shrub for support.

Plant in any good garden soil, but preferably in moist conditions. Either sun or light shade will suit them. They can be propagated by seed.

C. *clematidea* (below)

This is the species most commonly grown. The outside of the 2.5cm (1in) bells is pale blue, while inside are orange nectaries and crimson veining. They flower in late summer and, under good conditions, will climb to 1.2m (4ft).

Codonopsis clematidea

CONVALLARIA
Lily of the valley

There is only one species in this genus, namely *C. majalis* (below). The fresh appearance and sweet scent of this plant have endeared it to generations of gardeners. It is an attractive, reliable plant. If it has any defect, it is that it can spread at a rate that makes it invasive, but it is not too difficult to control. In early spring, large, erect, oval leaves appear. These are soon followed by spikes of nodding bells that are held in the leaves like a posy. The flowers are pure white and wonderfully fragrant.

Lily of the valley is a woodlander and enjoys a moist, leafy soil and a cool root run in light shade. It spreads by underground shoots, which can be easily divided for propagation purposes.

Convallaria majalis

Interesting forms

There are several cultivars worth seeking out. *C. m.* var. *rosea* has soft lilac-pink flowers, 'Fortin's Giant' is an altogether larger form with broader leaves and large stocky bells. It flowers later than its parent or other forms, making it possible to extend the lily of the valley's flowering season in the garden.

CONVOLVULUS
Convolvulus

Many of the species of this genus and its close relatives are considered weeds by most gardeners. They tend to spread underground at an alarming rate, but they all have attractive flowers, even the worst pests. These are funnel-shaped, usually white, but also in pink and blue. *C. cneorum* (a shrub with white flowers and silver foliage) and the rock plant *C. sabatius* (blue flowers) are both safe plants to grow.

Convolvulus will grow in any garden soil, even quite poor ones. The plants prefer to grow in a sunny position, but many will scramble up into the light if planted in shade. Propagation is easily achieved either by division or by seed.

Convolvulus althaeoides

C. althaeoides (above)
If this were not such a beautiful plant, most gardeners would avoid it, but its soft pink flowers and grey, finely cut foliage are too much of an attraction. It runs vigorously underground, but is often cut back by frosts. Elsewhere it will be necessary to contain it in some way to stop it spreading.

COREOPSIS
Tickseed
Although there are over 120 species, very few of these plants are grown in cultivation. Those that are make a valuable contribution to both the summer and autumn borders. They have yellow, daisy-like flowers that appear over a long period. All species make good cut flowers. The foliage is bright green and sometimes finely cut. It contrasts well with the flowers.

Tickseeds will grow in any fertile garden soil, but they prefer a sunny position. The wiry stems are strong and need staking only if grown in a very exposed position. Slugs attack the young growth, stunting the plants. Propagation is either by division or by seed.

C. grandiflora (below)
This is one of the shorter species, normally reaching only about 60cm (2ft) high. They are not so hardy as other species and can die out in hot summers, so they are often treated as annuals. The flowers are golden yellow and 5cm (2in) or more in diameter. 'Brown Eyes' has a brown central disc. 'Early Sunrise' has frilly double flowers. 'Sonnenkind' ('Baby Sun') is a very popular cultivar that grows to a height of only about 40cm (16in) and is suitable for a rock garden or as bedding. 'Sunray' has very full double flowers.

Coreopsis grandiflora 'Early Sunrise'

C. rosea
Although most tickseeds like a well-drained soil, this species prefers moister conditions. It is also unusual in that it has pink flowers. It grows to about 60cm (2ft). 'American Dream' is a popular form which is slightly shorter and has light pink flowers.

C. verticillata (below)
Of all the tickseeds, this is the best species. It is taller-growing than the others, up to 90cm (3ft) in good conditions, and has very attractive filigree leaves. The 5cm (2in) flowers are golden yellow and appear over a long season from summer onwards. 'Grandiflora' has large flowers. In 'Moonbeam' the flowers are much paler than in the parent. 'Zagreb' is shorter, reaching a height of only 30cm (1ft) or so.

Coreopsis verticillata 'Moonbeam'

CORTADERIA
Pampas grass
This is a genus of large, stately grasses. They form huge fountains of narrow leaves from which rise tall stems that carry large white plumes of flowers in autumn. Being assertive plants, they are best used in isolation as focal points, although with care they can be incorporated into herbaceous or mixed borders.

Pampas grasses need a moist soil that never becomes too dry. They also require a sunny position. The edges of the leaves are very sharp and should not be planted in gardens where children play. They can cut your hands as you weed and may also badly damage nearby plants when blown by the wind. Cut them to the ground in spring. Propagation is by division, although this is heavy work because of their size and the compact nature of the clump.

C. selloana (below)

This is one of the best forms of pampas grasses, with thick fluffy plumes that appear in late summer and early autumn. It is available in a wide variety of forms, ranging in height from 1.5m (5ft) to 3m (10ft). As well as those with green foliage there are forms with gold-striped variegations. The flowers of *C. selloana* can be white or pink.

Cortaderia selloana

CORTUSA

Cortusa

The genus *Cortusa* is small, containing only eight species. These plants are closely related to the primulas and are often mistaken for them. The flowers and foliage are very similar. The flowers are either pink, purple or yellow, and are carried in drooping heads. The plants are approximately 30cm (1ft) high.

These are woodland plants and are not suited to hot, dry conditions. Plant them in cool, moist soil, with plenty of leaf mould or other humus in it, and a shady position. They can be increased either by division or from seed, the latter being sown as fresh as possible.

C. matthioli

This is the species of *Cortusa* that is most commonly grown. It has pink flowers and densely hairy leaves. The subspecies *pekinensis* has larger flowers

and deeply cut dull green leaves. The small, bell-shaped flowers are held in one-sided flowering stalks.

CORYDALIS

Corydalis

An increasing number of gardeners are discovering the delights of this genus of plants, of which there are now many species in cultivation.

Unfortunately, most types are too small or too difficult for the open border, but a few can be grown there. The flowers are tubular, each with a long spur and broad upper and lower lips. They come in a wide range of colours, those of the open border being blue, purple, pink, red, yellow and white. The majority of corydalises are short, bushy plants, although some do scramble up through other plants.

Most corydalis species prefer a moist, leafy soil and grow best in light shade. They can be increased from seed, sown as fresh as possible, but may also be propagated by division.

Corydalis flexuosa

C. flexuosa (above)

Many *Corydalis* come from China and this is one of them. It grows up to 30cm (1ft) and its bronze-green foliage is topped in spring with sprays of electric-blue flowers. Some forms have paler blue flowers than others.

COSMOS

Cosmos

Although this genus contains some 25 species, only one is cultivated in gardens as a perennial; the rest are either annuals or grown as such.

Cosmos are members of the daisy family and come from Mexico. They resemble a close relative, which also comes from that country, the dahlia.

Cosmos atrosanguineus

C. atrosanguineus (above)

Known as the chocolate plant because of the rich brown of its flowers and its chocolate fragrance, this is a valuable plant for the border as there are few plants of its colour.

The flowers very closely resemble those of the dahlia and appear from the late summer onwards. The foliage is also attractive. This cosmos reaches a height of 75cm (2½ft).

It needs a deep moisture-retentive soil and a sunny position. It is also similar to the dahlia in that many gardeners prefer to lift the tubers and store them under cover, in sand, over winter. They can be left in the ground in milder areas, but it should be remembered that this plant is often late appearing above the soil, sometimes not before early summer. Propagation is by taking cuttings of the young growth as soon as possible in the year.

CRAMBE
Crambe

These extrovert plants for large borders erupt, in early summer, in a cloud of small white flowers held in sprays often up to 2m (7ft) or more high and as much across. After they have flowered, crambe can be considered foliage plants as they form low hummocks of good foliage – if not attacked by slugs or insects.

Crambes like a well-drained soil; they will even tolerate quite poor conditions. In windy areas they will need some form of support. Taking root cuttings is the best method of propagation.

Crambe cordifolia

C. cordifolia (above)
This is the largest member of the genus, with enormous sprays of sweetly scented flowers. The leaves are large and dark green in colour.

C. maritima
Sea kale is a much shorter plant than *C. cordifolia*, growing to only 90cm (3ft). It is grown as much for its glaucous blue-green foliage as for its flowers. The foliage is particularly attractive when it first appears.

CYNARA
Cynara

A few species of this genus of thistles are in cultivation, partly for their beautiful flowers but also because of their decorative foliage. The flowers are typically thistle-like, with purple heads held in a large, scaly calyx. The foliage in the ornamental species is often silver.

Cynara will grow in any good garden soil, but prefer well-drained soil. They are increased by division or from seed.

C. cardunculus
The cardoon is one of the best of all foliage plants. It forms a magnificent fountain of silver leaves, from which rise tall stems bearing very large flowers that appear in summer. Both leaves and flowers are excellent when cut. It grows to 2m (7ft) or more.

C. scolymus (below)
The globe artichoke is mainly grown as a vegetable, but it too has silvery grey leaves that make it a valuable foliage plant. Shorter than *C. cardunculus*, it is neither so silver nor so graceful.

Cynara scolymus

CYNOGLOSSUM
Hound's tongue

This large genus contains 80–90 species of annuals and perennials, but only a few are suitable for the garden. The flowers are carried in spiralled spikes, much in the manner of forget-me-nots, and are mainly blue. The leaves are rough, being covered in stiff hairs.

These plants need a moisture-retentive soil, although it should not be too rich; they will grow in either sun or shade. Support will be needed as they are naturally rather floppy. Propagate from seed or by root cuttings.

Cynoglossum nervosum

C. nervosum (above)
This is the only perennial hound's tongue in general cultivation. It is valuable in the garden for its bright blue flowers, which appear in early summer. The plants grow to 75cm (2½ft) high.

DARMERA
Umbrella plant

This is a single-species genus, with *D. peltata* its sole representative. Until recently it was generally known as *Peltiphyllum peltatum*. The common name is derived from its large umbrella-like leaves. Each rounded leaf is dished in the centre, between 30cm (1ft) and 60cm (2ft) across and carried on a stem that can reach up to 1.2m (4ft) tall. The clusters of pale pink flowers are rather curious as they appear before the leaves and are carried on tall, sinuous stalks.

Umbrella plants must have a wet, marshy situation, such as next to a pond or stream or in a bog garden, but are happy in either sun or shade. They spread by rhizomes, which can be easily divided for propagation purposes.

DELOSPERMA
Delosperma

This genus of succulents is related to the mesembryanthemums. They are carpeting plants suitable for either the rock garden or a position at the front of the border. The leaves are thick and fleshy; the flowers are daisy-like and usually in very bright colours.

Delospermas need a free-draining soil and a sunny position. They are easily propagated from cuttings. They are not hardy and, in colder areas, you need to overwinter plants or cuttings under glass.

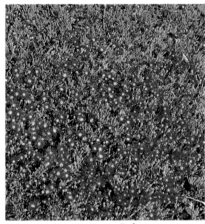
Delosperma cooperi

D. cooperi (above)
This is one of the hardier species. The daisy-like flowers have a white centre and bright magenta petals. The fleshy leaves are cylindrical. It grows to only 10cm (4in) high.

DELPHINIUM
Delphinium

The tall stately spires of blue delphinium flowers create some of the most romantic sights in an herbaceous border. However, delphiniums have a lot more to offer than this. There are a number of different species and hybrids that produce quite different-looking plants – ones that are short, with clouds of flowers rather than spikes. Garden delphiniums are no longer restricted to blue; there are purple-, pink-, white-, yellow- and now even red-flowered forms. There is also a wide range of blues, from the palest to the darkest shades. In addition, there are doubles as well as singles and those with black or violet 'bees' (eyes) in the centre. Even with all these variations, it is very difficult not to recognize a delphinium when you see one.

A fertile soil, enriched with well-rotted organic material, is required. Many smaller species will also grow in less rich, more free-draining soil. The taller forms are likely to require staking. In the border, plants can be supported as a whole, but flower spikes for cutting or exhibition are best staked using individual canes. Delphiniums can be grown from seed, preferably sown fresh, or by taking cuttings in the spring. Some can also be divided.

D. × belladonna (below)
These are hybrids between *D. elatum* and *D. grandiflorum*. They are not so heavy as the border hybrids, with many branching stems reaching up to 1.5m (5ft), but often as small as 90cm (3ft). They will produce a succession of flower spikes over a long period. Many different forms are available, and it is possible to buy mixed seed that provides a range of colours. Among the named forms, the best include 'Bellamosum' (dark blue), 'Pink Sensation' (white and pink) and 'Royal Copenhagen' (violet-blue).

Delphinium × *belladonna*

D. elatum hybrids
These hybrids are the tall, stately border varieties, some of which grow to 1.8m (6ft). They are available in a wide range of forms and colours.

D. grandiflorum
This was one of the original parents of the tall border cultivars, but its contribution to the hybrids is the size of its flower and not its height, as it grows to only about 60cm (2ft). It forms a loose, airy plant with dark blue flowers. There are several cultivars including 'Blue Mirror' (gentian blue) and 'Blue Butterfly' (bright blue).

Delphinium, mixed

Mixed – seed (above)
There are a range of seed strains that provide a mixture of seedlings. 'Blackmore & Langdon Strain' includes mixed colours and very large spikes. 'New Century Hybrids' are a mixture of blues and whites of medium stature. 'Southern Nobleman' is a tall strain, with high-quality spikes in a wide range of shades including purples. 'Magic Fountains' are short forms, only 90cm (3ft) tall, and include a wide range of colours, including purples.

Separates – seed
Many named forms of delphinium can be raised from seed. 'Astolat' comes in

various shades of pink. 'Black Knight' is dark blue with a black bee, 'Blue Bird' a clear mid-blue with a white bee, 'Cameliard' lavender with a white bee, 'Galahad' pure white, 'Guinevere' rosy lavender, and 'King Arthur' deep purple.

Separates – cuttings

Some forms can only be propagated vegetatively, by taking cuttings. 'Alice Artindale' is the most exquisite of all delphiniums. It has fully double flowers that are bright powder-blue in colour. 'Blue Nile' is mid-blue with a white bee, 'Faust' ultramarine, 'Fenella' gentian-blue with a black bee, 'Sungleam' deep cream, and 'Rosemary Brock' dusky pink with a brown bee.

DENDRANTHEMA

Chrysanthemum

When the genus *Chrysanthemum*, made up of some 200 annuals, perennials, and shrubs, was reclassified, the gardens' and florists' chrysanthemums were all moved to a new genus, *Dendranthema*. This large genus represents one of the most popular of all garden plants. The large variety of flowers, shapes and colours and the evocative fragrance of its foliage have given generations of gardeners much pleasure. Although there are no blues, there is a wide range of colours, some-times pure, sometimes mixed. The heads can be delicate singles or large, blousy doubles with innumerable petals.

Chrysanthemums like a rich moisture-retentive soil to which a good quantity of well-rotted organic material has been added. The tall forms with heavy flower heads, often used for cutting and exhibi-tion purposes, generally need staking, but the more stocky border forms are usually self-supporting.

Many of the border forms, such as the Rubellums, are hardy enough to be left outside over winter but other types, especially the exhibition forms, need to be

lifted and stored in frost-free conditions. They can be replanted in spring, or basal cuttings can be taken to start new plants.

Garden sprays (below)

These chrysanthemums are the ones most commonly grown by gardeners. They can be grown either in the border or in reserve beds for cutting. The flower heads come in a wide variety of forms, both single and double. There is also a wide range of colours, including all colours except blue. Each stem carries a 'spray' of five or six blooms and each plant is restricted to about five stems. The plant's height is 1.2m (4ft). 'Madeleine' has pink reflexed blooms. 'Pink Procession' is a prolific pink single. The Pennine series is a large collection of hardy spray chrysanthemums, each incorporating 'Pennine' in its name – for example, 'Pennine Oriel'. They vary greatly in form and colour.

Dendranthema 'Pennine Oriel'

Korean (next column)

This is a type of spray chrysanthemum, but one with far more flower heads than in the usual sprays. These plants have a very long flowering period. They are generally hardier than other spray types and may be left outside, provided the ground is not too wet. Lift and store under cover if there is any doubt about conditions. 'Brown Eyes' is a two-tone

brown double with small flowers. 'Tapestry Rose' is a single with deep pink petals and a green centre. 'Wedding Day' also has a green centre but the petals are white. 'Yellow Starlet' is a soft yellow single.

Dendranthema 'Brown Eyes'

Pompons

These are medium-height cultivars, reaching 90cm (3ft) at most, with masses of small, rounded heads of double flowers. 'Bronze Elegance', as its name suggests, has bronze flowers. 'Mei Kyo' is pink and 'Purleigh White', white.

Rubellums

These are the hardy types that can be left outside in most locations, as long as the soil is not too wet. They form bushy clumps up to 75cm (2½ft) high. The flowers, in a variety of colours, are single and daisy-like: 'Duchess of Edinburgh' is coppery red, 'Clara Curtis' pure pink, 'Emperor of China' silvery pink and 'Mary Stoker' apricot.

DENNSTAEDTIA

Cup fern

This is a large genus of 70 species of hardy deciduous semi-evergreen ferns, of which only one is in general cultivation. This is the hay-scented fern, *D. punctiloba*, which comes from eastern North America. It is an attractive light green fern with finely divided deciduous fronds reaching a height of 60cm (2ft).

Hay-scented fern likes a well-drained, dry soil as well as a shady situation. Its thin rhizomes can spread invasively, so care should be taken in choosing its site. Dennstaedtia can be propagated by division or from spores.

DESCHAMPSIA
Hair grass
This genus of 40–50 species of grasses includes both annuals and perennials. They are tufted grasses with flat leaves and showy, open plumes of flowers. They grow up to 60cm (2ft) tall.

Unlike many grasses, these will grow in both sun and light shade, and on a wide range of soils, including dry ones. They can be increased by seed or by division.

Deschampsia caespitosa 'Goldschleier'

D. caespitosa (above)
This evergreen species is the one that is most commonly grown. An evergreen grass that forms tufts, it has narrow, rough-edged, deep green leaves and pink or green flowers held in elegant spikes that appear in the summer. There are a number of cultivars to choose from, of which the best include 'Bronzeschleier' ('Bronze Veil'), which has light bronze flower heads, and 'Goldschleier' ('Golden Veil'), which has attractive gold-yellow flowers.

DIANTHUS
Pinks
Although carnations also belong to this genus, it is the smaller pinks that are mainly grown as border plants. These are mostly based on the species *D. plumarius*. They have been popular garden plants for as long as gardens have existed, and there are over 300,000 varieties recorded, with several thousand still in cultivation. The flowers are often fringed and vary from singles to full doubles. Besides white, the colour is usually a variation of pink or red. In most varieties the foliage is grass-like and bluish grey in colour, although there are some with green leaves. The flower stems rarely reach above 60cm (2ft), while the foliage makes mats no more than 15cm (6in) high.

Pinks perform best in a slightly alkaline or neutral soil, although they will grow in mildly acid conditions as long as the soil is not too wet. However, they do need a sunny position. Propagation is either from cuttings or from seed. They are usually hardy plants as long as the winter soil does not remain too wet.

Dianthus 'Doris'

Modern pinks (above)
These are varieties that have been bred since the beginning of the 20th century. They are usually repeat-flowering, with larger flowers and less scent than the old-fashioned varieties. The colours are often brighter and the leaves coarser in texture. 'Becky Robinson' is a double with a rose-pink ground and crimson lacing. 'Doris' is a heavily scented double with a pink ground and a darker salmon-pink central zone. 'Gran's Favourite' is a double with a white ground and narrow purple-pink lacing. 'Haytor' is a very good, double pure white with pronounced toothing to the petals. 'Houndspool Ruby' is a double with a bright pink ground and a ruby-red centre. 'Old Mother Hubbard' is a semi-double with a pink ground and stripes and flecks of a darker pink.

Dianthus 'Mrs Sinkins'

Old-fashioned pinks (above)
These are usually smaller and more subtly coloured than the modern pinks. The foliage is also finer. The majority were introduced before the beginning of this century, but a number have been raised since in the same style. 'Brympton Red' has large single flowers with a rich purple-pink ground and chestnut-red lacing. 'Dad's Favourite' is a double with a white ground and velvety, maroon lacing. 'Inchmery' is a double with the most delightful shell-pink colour that is strongly scented. 'Mrs Sinkins' is an all-time favourite that has fringed, double white flowers with a pale green centre. It is very sweetly scented. 'Sops-in-Wine' is reputed to date from as long ago as

medieval times. It is a blousy, double white with a crimson centre. 'White Ladies' is another fringed, double white that is also scented.

D. deltoides (below)

This species has very fine foliage, often flushed purple in colour, and a myriad of small flowers. These come in a variety of colours, including white, pink and cerise, but 'Brilliant' is the brightest, with double crimson flowers.

Dianthus deltoides 'Brilliant'

DIASCIA
Twinspur

These are some of the most useful plants in the garden. Their gay, colourful flowers appear from spring right through to the first frosts. Growing to 30cm (1ft) or more, they make excellent front-of-border plants, especially where they are allowed to scramble up through their neighbours. The flowers from the different species and varieties are very similar to each other, with only subtle differences in the shade of pink and size of bloom.

Twinspurs need a moisture-retentive soil, but if it is too rich they will become loose-growing and produce few flowers. They do best in a sunny spot but will tolerate light shade. Propagation is very readily achieved by taking cuttings at any time during the growing season. Most diascias tend to be short-lived.

D. barberae

This is one of the least hardy of the diascias, but has beautiful rose-pink flowers and is well worth the effort of taking cuttings each autumn and keeping them frost-free over the winter.

Diascia 'Ruby Field'

D. 'Ruby Field' (above)

This superb hybrid is hardier than its parent, *D. barberae*. It has purple-pink flowers and mid-green leaves.

D. 'Salmon Supreme'

This is a marvellous introduction. The salmon-pink flowers are larger than in many other forms, and the flowering season is just as long. It has the hardiness of *D.* 'Ruby Field', one of its parents.

DICENTRA
Bleeding heart

Bleeding hearts have long been popular garden plants. Generations of gardeners have been intrigued and charmed not only by the curious shape of the flowers but also by the finely cut foliage. The flowers, in varying shades of pink and white, are shaped like a heart. The leaves are either a fresh green or silver-grey in colour, making dicentras attractive foliage plants when they are not in flower.

They are extremely easy plants to grow – sometimes too easy, as they have a tendency to spread rather rapidly, though

rarely to the point of becoming invasive. They will grow in any good garden soils, but prefer those that are reasonably moisture-retentive, such as woodland soils. Most can be grown in either sun or light shade, but in hot areas they grow better in shade. They can all be divided at planting time for propagational purposes.

Border plants (below)

In the open border the larger – up to 90cm (3ft) – *D. spectabilis* makes an excellent plant. It has long, arching stems from which dangle large pink lockets, white in the variety *alba*, appearing from early spring onwards. This species forms clumps and is much slower-spreading than the smaller varieties. While still attractive, the foliage is not as fine and dainty as that of the woodland forms.

Dicentra spectabilis var. *alba*

Woodlanders

Although most species and varieties will grow in the open border, many prefer a little light shade, especially in areas where the sun can be fierce. These varieties are low-growing, up to 30cm (1ft), and quickly spread to form large clumps. They flower from spring on into the summer. 'Bountiful' has deep pink flowers, while 'Snowflakes' has pure white flowers that contrast superbly with the crisp, mid-green foliage.

DICTAMNUS
Burning bush

This intriguing plant gets its name from the fact that the plant exudes a volatile oil that on hot days can be lighted with a match to produce a spurt of flame. There is only one species in the genus, namely *D. albus*, which in early summer has white flowers. These are held in loose spikes that rise up to 90cm (3ft) high. The leaves are deeply cut and smell of lemons when crushed or bruised. The variety 'Purpureus' has pink-mauve flowers with darker purple veins. Both make excellent plants for the centre of the border.

Burning bushes can be slow to establish but, once this is done, they are easy to grow and will last for many years in the same position. Disturbance and transplanting, however, are resented. They will grow in any fertile garden soil, but do better in those that are enriched with well-rotted organic material. A sunny position is preferable. In spite of their height they are strong enough not to require staking. Propagation is best achieved by sowing seed in spring.

Dictamnus albus

DIGITALIS
Foxglove

Foxgloves are a much-loved genus of plants, especially for the informal or cottage garden. The most common species is *D. purpurea*, generally treated as a biennial although it will often act as a short-lived perennial. All foxgloves are characterized by tall spires of tubular flowers, usually of soft colours that make them suitable for pastel border schemes. The flowers appear from early summer onwards.

Foxgloves will grow in most garden soils, even dry ones, although they do best in soil that is not allowed to dry out completely. They will grow in either sun or shade, the latter being preferable in hot districts. There is generally no need to support them, though in windy positions some of the taller species may need to be staked. Few foxgloves are very long-lived, but each plant produces masses of seed which can be allowed to self-sow or be sown in pots in spring.

Digitalis ferruginea

D. ferruginea (above)

This is a very attractive short-lived foxglove with dumpy, pouch-like flowers borne in mid-summer that are a rusty yellow inside with noticeable brown-red veins. It grows up to a height of approximately 90cm (3ft).

D. grandiflora

The large flowers of this species are a soft yellow with traces inside of a brown veining. The flowers are slightly hairy. The leaves are oval to oblong in shape. This evergreen, clump-forming plant grows to 75cm (2½ft).

D. × mertonensis (below)

This cross between *D. grandiflora* and *D. purpurea* more closely resembles the second species. It produces large flowers which are pink suffused with a yellow-buff colour. The oval leaves are large and held in a rosette. They are covered in coarse hairs. The plant grows to about 90cm (3ft).

Digitalis × mertonensis

DORONICUM
Leopard's bane

The spring garden would not be complete without the bright yellow flowers of the leopard's banes. Each flower is a perfect daisy-shape held on a swaying stem above the fresh-green foliage. There are 35 species, of which several are in cultivation. All produce excellent flowers both for the border and as cut blooms.

They will grow in any well-drained garden soil, although they will not thrive if conditions are too dry. Leopard's banes will grow in either sun or light shade, but in hot areas are best in the latter. The plants often die back below ground as summer progresses, but can be easily propagated by division.

D. orientale 'Magnificum'

This is one of the best of the leopard's banes. It grows to about 75cm (2½ft) tall and carries masses of very large heads of bright yellow flowers.

DRACOCEPHALUM
Dragon's head

The dracocephalums are often confused with the nepetas, which they closely resemble, and some species are often listed under the other genus. Their flowers, generally blue, are tubular with flared lips and carried in short spikes. The foliage is a mid- to dark green and is mint-like in shape. The different species vary in height. While not spectacular they make good plants for the front or middle of a border.

They will grow in any free-draining garden soil, preferably in full sun. They can be propagated from seed, by taking basal cuttings in spring, or by simple division.

Dracocephalum ruyschianum

D. ruyschianum (above)
This commonly grown species has violet-blue flowers, but it can also be found with pink or white blooms. It grows up to 60cm (2ft) tall.

DRYOPTERIS
Shield fern

The originally very large genus of this name has been much divided botanically, and there are now only 150 species left within it, the remaining 1000 or so having been put into other genera. Of those that remain, about 60 species and varieties are in cultivation. They are tall, graceful ferns with elongated, triangular fronds that are deeply divided. They can be used as foliage plants in their own right or in combination with other plants, providing a cool-looking background for flowers or attractive contrasting foliage.

These shade-loving ferns like to be grown in woodland conditions of dappled shade and in moist, humus-rich soil. In cooler areas they can be grown in full sun as long as the soil is not allowed to dry out. Propagation can be easily achieved by sowing fresh spores on sterile compost in summer or by division in autumn.

D. erythrosora
This is known as the Japanese shield fern or the copper shield fern. The latter name derives from the colour of the young fronds which, when mature, become a dark, glossy green. These very graceful fountain-like plants are about 75cm (2½ft) tall.

Dryopteris filix-mas

D. filix-mas (above)
The male fern is a very common plant throughout much of the world, but its frequency does not detract from its beauty. The deeply cut fronds are grouped into a fountain or vase shape, and in favourable conditions can reach up to 1.5m (5ft).

D. marginalis
The marginal shield fern is a slow-growing plant grown more by collectors than by those gardeners who like using ferns as part of a decorative border. The species can reach a height of approximately 60cm (2ft).

D. wallichiana (below)
This is an evergreen fern with dark green, glossy fronds. It is very attractive and in good conditions can grow up to 1.8m (6ft).

Dryopteris wallichiana

ECHINACEA
Coneflower

Related to *Rudbeckia*, the plants of this genus all carry daisy-like flowers with large cone-shaped centres. They are rather coarse plants, with rough, hairy leaves and stems, but the flowers are attractive and they make very colourful border plants for the latter half of the season as well as excellent cut flowers. They are much loved by butterflies and bees.

Coneflowers are easy to grow in that they are not particular about soil, as long as it is reasonably fertile. They prefer a sunny position. Except in exposed sites, the stems are strong enough to support the flowers without staking. Propagation, done in spring, is easy, either by division or from seed.

E. purpurea (next page)
Although there are several species in the genus, this is the only one in general

cultivation. It has large flower heads, up to 15cm (6in) across, carried on stems up to 1.2m (4ft) tall. The flowers mainly have purple outer petals and a bronze central cone. The several cultivars of *Echinacea* available include 'Bressingham Hybrids', a seed strain in which there is a slight variation in the shade of the purple outer petals. 'Magnus' has very large flowers with deep purple outer ray petals, 'Robert Bloom' is similar, and 'White Swan' has white outer ray petals.

Echinacea purpurea 'Robert Bloom'

ECHINOPS
Globe thistle

Of over 100 species in this surprisingly large genus, only a handful are in general cultivation. The common name originates from the shape of the flower, which is completely spherical. Although the leaves are generally coarse and often prickly, they make an attractive foliage feature, especially when they first emerge. The plants do well at the middle or rear of a border.

They like a deep, well-prepared soil, but will also thrive on poor, even dry soils. They must have a place in full sun to look their best, and in windy positions need staking. Later in the season they may suffer from mildew, which disfigures the foliage. Propagation is mainly from seed, but special forms can be raised from root cuttings or by careful division.

Echinops ritro

E. ritro (above)

This magnificent plant grows to about 1.2m (4ft) tall, and has steely blue balls of flowers and dark green leaves that are grey on the reverse (this contrast often shows, particularly in a breeze). The flowers are much loved by bees and butterflies.

ELYMUS
Elymus

Although this is a large genus of grasses, only a couple of species are in cultivation. These plants are occasionally invasive, so they may have to be dealt with firmly or they can take over the whole border. They can be beautiful, so it is worth the effort to keep them under control. They are grown for their wonderful blue-grey foliage, which makes them attractive not only in their own right but also when planted in combination with a wide range of other colours.

The main problem with these plants is that some of them tend to run underground, which makes them valuable for stabilizing sand dunes but a bit of a nuisance in the border! To contain their questing shoots, plant them in a bottomless bucket and sink this into the border. Alternatively, they can be planted in a wilder part of the garden, where they can spread unchecked without becoming a nuisance to other plants.

Elymus grows in any garden soil, including a dry one, but like most grasses, it grows and looks best in a sunny spot. Propagate it by division in spring.

E. hispidus

This has beautiful blue-grey upright foliage reaching 90cm (3ft) in rich conditions. The leaves are prominently veined. It is mainly clump-forming but still has a tendency to wander.

Elymus magellanicus

E. magellanicus (above)

If anything this species has an even more magnificent colour than *E. hispidus*. The leaves are smooth. It grows to a similar height, but as it can spread too vigorously it is more invasive and must be contained in some way.

EPIMEDIUM
Barrenwort

These are increasingly popular plants for both their foliage and their flowers. The heart-shaped leaves range in colour from light green to bronze and, in some forms, are flushed with red. Attractive throughout the year, they are at their best when the new foliage is just beginning to unfurl in late winter. The small, curiously shaped flowers are carried in decorative airy sprays well above the leaves, usually in spring; they range in colour from pink to white and yellow. In addition to being attractive, the foliage creates a dense ground cover through which weeds find it difficult to grow.

These woodland plants like a moist, humus-rich soil and light shade, although they can be grown in a more open position as long as the soil is not allowed to dry out. All species should be cut back in mid-winter, including the evergreen forms, so that new growth can easily be seen and appreciated. Propagation is by division in spring or autumn.

Epimedium perralderianum

E. perralderianum (above)

This is another yellow-flowered species, this time with shiny leaves which make it an excellent ground-cover plant. It grows up to 30cm (1ft).

E. × rubrum

This cross between *E. grandiflorum* and *E. alpinum* is worthy of attention for both its attractive red flowers and its foliage, which is distinctively marked with red when young.

E. × versicolor

This is another cross, this time between *E. grandiflorum* and *E. pinnatum* subsp. *colchicum*. The result is a good foliage plant that carries yellow flowers and reaches a height of 30cm (1ft). The form 'Sulphureum', with pale yellow flowers, is one of the best.

E. × youngianum

This cross between *E. grandiflorum* and *E. diphyllum* has produced hybrids with white or pink flowers and pale green leaves. It grows up to 38cm (15in) tall.

EREMURUS
Foxtail lily

The foxtail lilies are among the most spectacular of herbaceous border plants. The flowers are borne in towering spires, sometimes reaching 2.5m (8ft) or more.

Epimedium alpinum

E. alpinum (above)

This European species of barrenwort has yellow petals and red sepals, which appear in spring. The finely toothed, glossy foliage is deciduous. The plant grows up to 38cm (15in) tall.

E. grandiflorum

Up to 45cm (1½ft) tall, this barrenwort has deep pink flowers with white spurs; there are also white and red forms. It has toothed evergreen foliage.

E. × perralchium

This evergreen barrenwort has sprays of large yellow flowers and glossy, deep green leaves. It was originated as a cross between *E. perralderianum* and *E. pinnatum* subsp. *colchicum*. The form 'Frohnleiten' has golden yellow flowers and grows up to 30cm (1ft) high.

Each spire is formed from a solid column of small starry flowers, which may be white, pink, yellow or even bright yellow-orange. The foliage is a fountain of strap-like leaves. Foxtail lilies are wonderful plants for the back of a herbaceous border, where they can appear above or between other plants and then die back into obscurity.

It is important to give these plants a rich but free-draining soil and a sunny position. The taller varieties are likely to require staking. Propagation is by careful division of the crowns, although the species may also be grown from seed.

Eremurus robustus

E. robustus (above)

The giant desert candle, as it is sometimes called, is one of the best of the 50 or so species of *Eremurus*. It grows up to 2.5m (8ft) tall and carries dense spikes of pink flowers for a long period.

E. 'Ruiter Hybrids'

Compared with *E. robustus*, these plants are short, reaching a height of only 1.5m (5ft); they are nonetheless spectacular plants, with pastel-coloured spikes of pink, yellow or golden blooms.

ERIGERON
Fleabane

The fleabanes are a genus of attractive daisies suitable for a variety of positions in the border. They are typically daisy-like, with an outer ring of two or more rows of narrow ray petals and an inner disc of usually yellow florets. The ray petals are white, blue, purple, pink or red. The plants range in height from just a few centimetres to as much as 75cm (2½ft).

Fleabanes will grow in any garden soil that is reasonably free-draining. Some grow in poor soils, but they need a sunny position. The taller need support of some sort. They can be propagated by division in early spring or autumn or from seed in autumn. Alternatively, many can be grown from basal cuttings taken in spring.

Erigeron 'Quakeress'

Border varieties (above)
The border forms vary in height and so can be used at either the front or the back of the bed, although the taller ones will certainly need staking. They remain in flower for a long period. 'Quakeress' has pale lilac-pink flowers. 'Darkest of All' has very dark violet flowers, as does 'Schwarzes Meer' ('Black Sea'), the latter being slightly shorter. 'Pink Jewel' has pale pink flowers.

E. karvinskianus
The Mexican daisy, still known by many as *E. mucronatus*, flowers continuously from spring until the first frosts. An airy-looking plant covered with small white and pink daisies, it is suitable for the front of a border.

ERYNGIUM
Sea holly
The members of this species are attractive as both flowering and foliage plants. Although belonging to the cow parsley family, they often bear more resemblance to thistles, with their prickly leaves and spiky domes of flowers. The flowers are usually blue, but can be white or pale green. The foliage is attractive long before the flowers appear, with leaves that are often heavily veined or marbled in white. Some have sharp spines on their margins, making them dangerous plants among which to weed.

Sea hollies have taproots so do best in a deep, well-drained soil, preferably in full sun. They are strong plants and rarely need staking. Most can be propagated from seed; root cuttings are a good alternative.

Eryngium agavifolium

Tall forms (above)
There are a number of tall species, some reaching 1.8m (6ft), although the majority are shorter than this. *E. agavifolium*, one of the taller forms, has impressive, sharply toothed sword-like leaves and flowers shaped like small, pale green globes. *E. proteiflorum* is shorter, with similar leaves and grey-blue flowers.

Medium forms (next column)
There are a large number of medium-sized species that are suitable for the

front half of the border. *E. alpinum* is very attractive, with large heads of intense blue flowers surrounded by frilly ruffs of similar-coloured bracts. While its pale green flowers, surrounded by silvery bracts, are attractive, *E. bourgatii* is grown mainly for its white-veined leaves. *E. planum* grows to a height of about 60cm (2ft) tall and bears heads of light blue flowers, which are accentuated by pointed silver bracts. *E. variifolium* has beautiful rounded foliage with pronounced white veins. The small thistle-like flowers are grey-blue and produced in late summer. They are surrounded by pointed silver bracts.

Eryngium variifolium

EUPATORIUM
Boneset
These are mainly tall, clump-forming plants suitable only for larger borders. They are grown not only for their flowers but also for their coloured stems and leaves, which are often a very attractive purple. The flowers, carried in fluffy heads, are very enticing to butterflies, bees and flies.

Eupatoriums like a moisture-retentive soil and do best if situated near a pond or in a bog garden, but they can be grown happily in any good garden soil as long as it is not too dry. They prefer a sunny position but will also grow in light shade. Propagation can easily be achieved by dividing the plants in spring or autumn.

E. cannabinum

Hemp agrimony is a native of British ditches and is suitable only for wild gardens. The form 'Flore Pleno', however, has beautiful, soft-pink, double flowers and is well worth growing in the border. It reaches a height of 1.2m (4ft).

Eupatorium purpureum

E. purpureum (above)

Joe Pye weed is one of the most important flowering plants for the latter end of the year. Its tall purple stems grow up to 2m (7ft) and carry fluffy sprays of rose-pink flowers.

EUPHORBIA

Spurge

The spurges comprise one of the largest genera, with up to 2000 species and many subspecies and cultivars. Many of these, however, are tropical, and they include trees as well as plants best treated as house-plants. Nevertheless, many of them make excellent border plants. These are grown for their attractive foliage and for the colourful bracts surrounding the petal-less flowers. The leaves are usually a cool green, although some are flushed with red or purple. The bracts are yellow-green, sometimes gold, and fresh-looking. The plants range in height from around 10cm (4in) to 1.5m (5ft).

Spurges will grow in any garden soil, and most are suitable for shade as well as

sun. A few need staking, but the majority are self-supporting. They can be grown from seed in early spring or increased by division or cuttings of basal shoots in late spring.

Deciduous forms (below)

Some forms are deciduous and die back completely during the winter. They need to have all the old vegetation removed before the new growth starts to appear in spring. *E. dulcis* 'Chameleon' is an extremely attractive plant with bronze-purple foliage. It is short-lived but comes readily from seed. *E. griffithii* 'Dixter' and 'Fireglow' are two taller forms that have red-tinged foliage and bracts. Unlike *E. dulcis* they run freely and soon form large colonies. *E. polychroma* is one of the earliest to flower, creating a rounded mound of bright yellow in early spring. In contrast, *E. schillingii* and *E. sikkimensis* both flower in late summer; they are tall and slender with large bright yellow-green flowers. The latter species is liable to spread, thus forming large colonies.

Euphorbia griffithii 'Fireglow'

Evergreen forms (next column)

Despite not dying back each year, many of the evergreen forms benefit from having the old stems cut back to the ground in early spring. The attractive red foliage of *E. amygdaloides* 'Rubra', for example,

often becomes mildewy by early summer and so is best cut back to promote fresh growth. *E. characias* and its subspecies *E. c. wulfenii* need to have their flowering stems removed once they go brown. Both plants produce tall, club-like spires of green-yellow flowers in spring, with the latter being the yellower of the two. *E. × martinii*, a cross between *E. amygdaloides* and *E. characias*, is a very attractive spurge, halfway in height between its two parents and with noticeable red 'eyes' in the spring flowers. *E. myrsinites* is low-growing, with grey leaves arranged in spirals around its prostrate stems. It flowers in spring.

Euphorbia × martinii

FESTUCA

Fescue

The fescues are a large genus of grasses, some of which are used in lawns and grass paths while others, more ornamental, are employed in the front areas of borders. These clump-forming tufted plants are grown for their fine blue or green blades.

Fescues grow on any well-drained soil, including poor ones, but avoid rich, moist sites. They like a sunny position. To keep them vigorous, divide every few years. Propagate by seed or division in spring.

F. glauca

This is popular because of its incredibly striking blue foliage. One of the best forms is 'Blauglut' ('Blue Glow'), which is a wonderful silver-blue. It grows to a height of about 30cm (1ft) tall.

Festuca valesiaca 'Silver Sea'

F. valesiaca (above)
This is another blue-leafed form, mainly grown in its variety 'Silbersee' ('Silver Sea'), which has a silvery sheen. This compact plant grows to no more than 20cm (8in), with intensely blue foliage.

FILIPENDULA
Meadow sweet
The meadow sweets are a plant group whose common name is partly derived from the sweet fragrance the summer flowers give off. These flowers are small, carried in flat, fluffy heads, and usually white or pink. The plants range in height between 60cm (2ft) and 2.5m (8ft), which makes them suitable for the middle or back of a border.

The majority of meadow sweets prefer a moist position and do particularly well next to a water feature or in a bog garden. They will grow in either full sun or light shade. They can easily be divided to increase stock.

F. palmata
This is one of the medium-height species of meadow sweet, at about 1.2m (4ft). It has pale pink flowers that fade to white as they age.

F. rubra
Known as queen of the prairie, this species is one of the tallest, reaching 2.5m (8ft) or more if grown in favourable conditions. It has pink flowers. Avoid planting in a small or crowded border as it spreads vigorously. The form 'Venusta' has darker pink flowers.

F. ulmaria (below)
The European meadow sweet is perhaps not as attractive as some of the other species. In its form 'Aurea', however, the leaves are a lovely golden yellow; it should be planted in light shade so that the foliage does not burn. Remove the pink flowers: they spoil the foliage effect and may, if left, produce self-sown green-leafed seedlings.

Filipendula ulmaria 'Aurea'

F. vulgaris
Dropwort is one of the meadow sweets that prefers a dry soil and can be grown in chalky conditions. It has small heads of white flowers. The form most widely grown is the one with double flowers, 'Multiplex' (also known as 'Flore Pleno'), which grows to only about 30cm (1ft).

FOENICULUM
Fennel
Fennel is well worth growing both for its foliage and for its flowers. It is a stately plant, often reaching 1.8m (6ft) or more, with arching branches of very fine, filigree leaves. In late summer, flat heads of small yellow flowers appear; these are extremely attractive to bees and wasps. The plants can either be used by themselves as a feature in the garden or be planted towards the rear of a border.

Fennels will grow in any garden soil, even a poor one, but do best in those enriched with humus and in an open sunny position. Cut back as soon as flowering is over or they will self-sow everywhere. Although tall, fennels do not need staking. Propagation is achieved by division or by sowing seed in spring or when ripe.

Foeniculum vulgare 'Purpureum'

F. vulgare 'Purpureum' (above)
This is the most popular form. It has delicate foliage that takes on a delightful purple colour when young, and then becomes bronze as the season progresses and the plant ages.

FRAGARIA
Strawberry
Strawberries are not normally associated with herbaceous borders, but some are decorative in either their leaves or their flowers. One of the most popular is 'Pink Panda' (next column), which has attractive bright pink flowers instead of the usual white. These bloom on and off throughout the summer and into the autumn; as an

added bonus, edible fruit is produced. The plants are good for growing at the front of the border in full sun or even light shade, and may be used as ground cover.

Decorative strawberries will grow in any soil that does not become too dry. They can be increased, as with all strawberries, by dividing off the rooted runners.

Fragaria 'Pink Panda'

GAILLARDIA
Blanket flower

If a splash of bright colour is required in a border, then blanket flowers are just the thing. Their blooms consist of large daisies, either red or yellow or sometimes a mixture of both. The centre of the flower is a red-brown domed disc. The plants are hairy and somewhat sticky, and normally grow to about 90cm (3ft) in height. 'Burgundy' is bright red with yellow tips to the petals. 'Kobold' ('Goblin') is a short form (next column), reaching only about 23cm (9in) high, with red flowers and a yellow margin. 'Monarch' is a good seed strain, producing flowers of various colours.

Blanket flowers will grow in any soil, but do best in those that are not too rich. They are able to stand drought well and a position in the sun is essential. They have a somewhat straggly growth habit and need to be staked if you require them to look neat. Propagation is by division or, provided you do not mind getting colour variations, from seed.

Gaillardia 'Goblin'

GALEGA
Goat's rue

Goat's rue is a large, bushy plant which, as well as being attractive in its own right, is useful for creating hazy patches of colour in the border, perhaps as a background to other plants. The flowers, produced on a myriad of spikes, are pea-shaped and usually blue. The fresh-looking leaves grow in pairs on either side of the stem.

These deep-rooted plants will grow in any garden soil, including a dry one. They prefer a sunny position, but will also grow in light shade, especially in hot areas. They are not very sturdy plants, and often scramble through other vegetation in the wild, therefore needing to be staked except in the most sheltered of positions. They can be increased by careful division or from seed.

G. officinalis

This is the species normally grown in gardens. It has pale lavender-blue flowers. Equally popular is 'Alba', a form with white flowers. Both bloom profusely around mid-summer and reach a height of 1.5m (5ft). They can be cut to the ground after flowering is over.

GAURA
Gaura

Although there are a number of species in this genus, *G. lindheimeri* (next column) is

the only one in general cultivation. When in flower it resembles a host of white butterflies. The upright stems carry loose spikes of dainty flowers, each with somewhat reflexed petals and prominent stamens. These contrast well with the narrow fresh green foliage. The flowers appear over a long period during summer and autumn. The plants can reach 1.2m (4ft) and are excellent for the middle of a border, especially if they are set against a dark background.

Gauras grow in any fertile garden soil, although they do not grow well in one that is too wet or heavy. They do best in full sun, but will also thrive in light shade. They need no staking. Increase by taking cuttings (in spring) or from seed (sown early).

Gaura lindheimeri

GENTIANA
Gentian

The intense blue of many gentians has entranced gardeners for centuries. This large genus contains about 400 species, the majority of which are more suited to the alpine bed than the open garden. However, one or two, larger than the rest, can survive in competition with border plants. Surprisingly, not all gentians are blue – some species are yellow or white – but all have the characteristic trumpet-shaped flower.

Gentians grow best in a soil that does not dry out, so plenty of humus should be added to it. They grow in full sun or shade. Propagation is by division or from seed.

G. asclepiadea (below)

The willow gentian, so-called because of its willow-shaped leaves, is the main species grown in the herbaceous border. It reaches about 90cm (3ft) and has long, gracefully arching stems from which the blue trumpets emerge in late summer and autumn. It is a very useful shade plant. There is a white form, 'Alba'.

Gentiana asclepiadea

G. lutea

Felwort is an upright-growing gentian for an open position. Its flowers are a remarkable pale yellow. Do not cut back after flowering as the seedheads are also attractive. It grows up to 1.2m (4ft) tall.

G. septemfida

The crested gentian is a lower-growing plant – it reaches only about 30cm (1ft) – with clusters of dark blue flowers appearing in late summer at the ends of its sprawling branches. An ideal position is at the front of a border in a slightly shady position.

GERANIUM

Geranium, Hardy cranesbill

The geraniums form the backbone of any flower garden. There are several hundred different species, cultivars and hybrids in cultivation, presenting the gardener with plants for all manner of situations and colour schemes. They range in height from only about 10cm (4in) up to 1.2m (4ft), and the flower colours cover a range of blues, pinks and purples as well as white. Most are happy in either sun or shade. Many have a very long flowering period; those that have a shorter one often make good foliage plants when not in bloom.

Geraniums will grow in most garden soils, but do best in those that are reasonably moisture-retentive; extra humus added to the soil will help achieve this. Most will grow in either sun or light shade, although on the whole the shorter varieties prefer sun. The taller forms need support. Geraniums can be increased by division or, if you do not mind variation in the resulting plants, by sowing seed.

Geranium pratense 'Mrs Kendall Clark'

Blue forms (above)

'Johnson's Blue' is an extremely good violet-blue-flowered form for the early summer. It grows to about 30cm (1ft) high, soon forming a good-sized clump. G. himalayense, one of its parents, itself makes a good border plant, especially in its purple-blue double form 'Plenum' (also known as 'Birch Double'). One of the most attractive blue geraniums is G. pratense 'Mrs Kendall Clark', in which the flowers are soft blue, veined with silver. This grows to 75cm (2½ft)

and needs support. For later in the season, G. wallichianum 'Buxton's Variety' is ideal. This rambling plant creeps over other vegetation without being invasive.

Geranium 'Ann Folkard'

Magenta and purple forms (above)

'Ann Folkard' has purple flowers with a darker centre. It spreads out uninvasively, clambering over other plants. G. phaeum is a more upright plant, forming a 75cm (2½ft) dome of foliage surmounted by sprays of reflexed dark purple flowers. One of the brightest-flowering geraniums is G. psilostemon; it forms a rounded plant 1.2m (4ft) tall and covered in summer with bright magenta flowers, each with a very dark purple centre. At the other extreme, G. procurrens is unable to support itself and spreads out over an area of 1.2–1.8m (4–6ft), clambering through bushes and other plants. It can become quite invasive but nevertheless is very attractive, with pink-purple flowers suffused with very dark purple and produced late in the season.

Pink forms

G. × cantabridgense 'Cambridge' forms a good ground cover of shiny leaves and pink flowers from spring onwards. G. dalmaticum, one of its parents, is a low-growing plant suitable for the front of a border. G. endressii 'Wargrave' is a much taller plant, growing to 60cm (2ft). Upright at first, it soon flops over and needs support. A similar plant with brighter flowers is G. × oxonianum 'Claridge Druce'. G. macrorrhizum is an excellent ground-cover plant with fragrant, evergreen foliage. The form 'Ingwersen's Variety' has soft pink flowers. G. × riversleaianum 'Russell Prichard' has silver foliage and purple-pink flower. G. sanguineum 'Striatum' is a low-growing plant with large, pale pink flowers veined with red.

Geranium clarkei 'Kashmir White'

White forms (above)

G. × cantabridgense 'Biokovo' has shiny leaves and white flowers, and grows to approximately 30cm (1ft) tall. G. clarkei 'Kashmir White', slightly taller, has white flowers veined with pink. G. phaeum 'Album' has white flowers and paler leaves than the usual purple form known as the mourning widow. G. renardii has attractive, white flowers veined with purple and produced in the spring, but is grown mainly for its rounded silver foliage.

GEUM
Avens

These clump-forming plants add a touch of gaiety to the front of a border. The flowers of many of the species and cultivars are brightly coloured in strong reds, oranges and yellows, but there are also some forms that have a subtle coloration more suitable for pastel borders. The plants grow to about 60cm (2ft).

Avens will grow in any good garden soil. They tolerate light shade, but do best in an open, sunny position. Propagation can be by division at planting time, or stock can be increased from seed sown in spring or when ripe.

Geum 'Lady Stratheden'

Varieties (above)

Among the best of the brightest forms is 'Borisii', 30cm (1ft) high, with brilliant orange single flowers that can span up to 2.5cm (1in) across. Two choices that are twice as tall and that have semi-double flowers 4cm (1½in) across are 'Lady Stratheden' (yellow) and 'Mrs Bradshaw' (bright red). On the softer and smaller side is 'Leonard's Variety', which is a coppery version of the pink-flowered plant G. rivale.

GILLENIA
Indian physic

This is a small American genus of two plants, of which only G. trifoliata (next column) is widely grown in gardens. It looks shrubby, with reddish brown woody stems and an open bushy shape. It is, however, herbaceous, dying back to the ground each winter. In summer it is decorated with delicate white flowers that seem to flutter over the plant's surface like tiny butterflies, the white of the flowers being emphasized by the red calyces. It grows to 1.2m (4ft) in ideal conditions, and is a good choice for the middle part of a border.

Indian physic will grow in any good well-drained garden soil, although it has a slight preference for acidic ones. In most areas it is best grown in sun, but in hotter districts a light shade is preferred. It is best propagated from seed, but with care it can also be divided.

Gillenia trifoliata

GLYCERIA
Glyceria

There are 16 species of this grass but only G. maxima, in its variety variegata, is cultivated to any extent. G. maxima itself is a green-leafed grass growing to about 1.8m (6ft) in height; it is rather invasive, spreading about by creeping rhizomes. The variety has cream and green stripes on the leaves and creates a wonderful fountain effect, especially when topped by the greenish-flowering stems. It does not grow so tall as G. maxima, reaching at best a height of 1.5m (5ft) and is not so invasive, though it can still become a nuisance.

Glyceria can be grown in ordinary soil, but does best when planted in wet ground next to a water feature. It can even be planted in the water, as long as this is no deeper than about 20cm (8in). Increase is carried out by division.

GUNNERA
Gunnera

The 35 species of gunnera range from prostrate plants no more than 2.5cm (1in) high to giants 2.5m (8ft) tall with leaves 1.8m (6ft) across. It is one of the latter plants that is normally grown in gardens: the spectacular *G. manicata* (below), with its large, pleated leaves held like giant umbrellas on prickly stems. The flowers are carried on thick, club-like stems up to 60cm (2ft) tall. Although it can be grown in a border, it is best beside water or in a damp spot, where it forms a focal point.

Gunneras must be grown in a wet or moisture-retentive soil, which should be richly laden with well-rotted humus or compost. They can be raised in either full sun or light shade, but as they are not completely hardy, the dying leaves should be cut and placed over the crown to protect it during the winter. Propagation is by division or from seed.

Gunnera manicata

GYPSOPHILA
Baby's breath

The intriguing common name of these plants refers to the tiny flowers carried in light, airy sprays above the leaves, creating a misty cloud. Although there are 125 species in this genus, very few are grown in the garden – many that are would be better in the rock garden than in the herbaceous border.

Baby's breath needs light, free-draining soil and a sunny position. It is tap-rooted and resents disturbance, so avoid transplanting. Support is required for the taller plants. Propagation is from seed, with named forms being grown from cuttings.

G. paniculata (below)

The main species grown in the open border is *G. paniculata*. This is a tall bushy plant, up to 1.2m (4ft). The flowers are generally white, but there are varieties in shades of pink. 'Bristol Fairy' has double flowers and is particularly attractive. 'Perfecta' is similar but it is taller and has larger flowers. 'Flamingo' also has double flowers, but in lilac-pink. 'Rosenschleier' ('Rosy Veil') is much shorter, growing to approximately 30cm (1ft) high, and carries beautiful, semi-double flowers in pale pink.

Gypsophila paniculata 'Bristol Fairy'

HAKONECHLOA
Hakonechloa

The single species in this Japanese genus is *H. macra*. Although occasionally grown in gardens, it is best known in its form 'Aureola' (next column), a superb grass with fountains of narrow blades coloured a rich gold and highlighted with narrow green stripes. It grows to about 30cm (1ft), and spreads slightly to form a good-sized clump. This highly decorative plant well deserves a particularly prominent place in the border, especially where it can impart its radiance to a dark corner.

This grass grows in any good garden soil, but prefers a moisture-retentive one. It also likes a little light shade, making it an ideal subject for a woodland border. It can be increased by division in the spring.

Hakonechloa macra 'Aureola'

HELENIUM
Sneezeweed

Heleniums are among the mainstays of the summer and autumn border. They form large drifts of daisy-like flowers that remain in bloom over a long period. Both the outer petals and the central disc are yellow or brown, or a mixture of both, with the browns often quite reddish. The plants are generally tall, reaching up to 1.5m (5ft), although some are much shorter. They are not invasive; they slowly form large clumps, and are suitable for creating drifts of colour.

Heleniums will grow in virtually any garden soil, but do best in soils that do not dry out completely. They prefer a sunny position. In spring, as the plants are starting into growth, slugs can cause a lot of damage to the young shoots and may have to be controlled. Heleniums are generally strong enough to do without support, but if grown in exposed positions staking will probably be required. Propagation can easily be accomplished by division in autumn or in spring.

Varieties (below)

There are many varieties to choose from, with more being created all the time. A few, however, stand out. 'Bressingham Gold' has bright yellow flowers, while those of 'Brilliant' are brown. The flowers of 'Coppelia' are a coppery orange. 'Moerheim Beauty' is an old variety and still one of the best, with reddish brown flowers that fade to dark orange as they grow older.

Helenium 'Coppelia'

HELIANTHUS
Sunflower

The perennial sunflowers are rather coarse, brash plants, but nonetheless have a place in the border, even if they are only there to create a splash of colour (yellow or orange-yellow) towards the back. There are by some estimates 150 species of sunflowers, and about 20 of these plants, with their daisy-like flowers, are in cultivation. They are usually rather lanky in habit, growing up to 1.5m (5ft), and they spread rather vigorously by rhizomes. The leaves and stems have a rough, hairy surface. Most sunflowers bloom in late summer or autumn.

They will grow in any soil and are particularly suitable for poor conditions, though a sunny position is needed. In exposed situations, stake the taller forms. These plants are most easily propagated by division in autumn or spring.

Varieties (below)

Of those available the best include the pale yellow single-flowered 'Lemon Queen', and 'Loddon Gold', an old variety with golden double flowers. *H. salicifolius*, with narrow leaves and yellow flowers, is very tall, growing to about 2.5m (8ft).

Helianthus 'Loddon Gold'

HELICTOTRICHON
Helictotrichon

Of this large genus of grasses only one species, *H. sempervirens*, is widely cultivated. It is a well behaved grass that does not spread invasively but forms a dense clump about 1.2m (4ft) tall when in flower. Its beauty lies in its blue foliage, the individual blades of which are erect and slightly hairy. The foliage reaches only 60cm (2ft) high, but is over-topped by graceful stems of the grey-blue flowers.

This grass will grow in any garden soil, including dry ones, and like most grasses it needs a sunny spot. Remove dead leaves to maintain the overall effect of this plant's colour. Propagation is by division in spring.

HELIOPSIS
False sunflower

This genus is closely related to the true sunflowers, *Helianthus*, and the species look very similar, although the false sunflowers are usually considered a little more refined in habit, and make good border plants. The similarity is reflected in the name of the species most commonly seen in cultivation, *H. helianthoides*. This grows to 1.2m (4ft) or 1.5m (5ft), with flowers that look like large yellow daisies. It has a long flowering period, starting in summer and going on well into the autumn.

The false sunflowers will grow in any garden soil, including a poor one, and are reasonably drought-resistant; a sunny position is required. Their stems are strong, and they do not usually require staking. Propagation is by division.

Heliopsis helianthoides 'Goldfieder'

H. helianthoides (above)

The species itself is rarely seen in cultivation, being usually represented by one of its varieties. The variety *scabra* has rough leaves and yellow flowers. 'Goldfieder' ('Golden Plume') has large deep yellow double flowers, while the even bigger flowers of 'Sommersonne' ('Summer Sun') are more orange in colour than those of the other varieties.

HELLEBORUS
Hellebore

Hellebores are among the few perennial plants that flower in the winter and, as such, are important in providing colour and interest at that time of year. Their saucer-shaped flowers are mainly white-green or plum-coloured, although there is an increasing range of variants. They can be grown at the back of a border, where they will show up in winter but be covered by other plants during the summer, when they are not so interesting.

Hellebores like a moist, humus-rich soil and a lightly shaded position, so they make excellent candidates for a woodland border. They can be propagated from seed or, if you wish to perpetuate a particular colour strain, by division.

Helleborus argutifolius

H. *argutifolius* (above).

Until recently this species was better known as *H. corsicus*. It is a bushy plant that grows up to 60cm (2ft) tall. The leaves are coarse and noticeably toothed, and the clustered flowers are pale green or yellow.

H. *foetidus*

This is one of the tallest species, reaching up to approximately 60cm (2ft). It has finely divided leaves and bunches of pale green flowers, often tipped in red. 'Wester Flisk' is similar except that the stems are tinted red.

H. *niger*

The Christmas rose is a popular species that has white flowers with an attractive boss of yellow stamens in their centres. They usually start to appear in midwinter. It tends to prefer a slightly alkaline soil.

Helleborus orientalis

H. *orientalis* hybrids (above)

A great number of forms based mainly on *H. orientalis* have been produced. They appear in a variety of colours, many of them plum-coloured. Some are very dark purple while others are white, green, pink or yellow, often speckled with purple spots.

Helleborus × sternii

H. × *sternii* (above)

This hellebore is a cross between *H. argutifolius* and the slightly tender *H. lividus*. It is an excellent plant having smoky-pink flowers and blue-grey leaves. Some forms are better than others.

HEMEROCALLIS
Day lily

The day lily has been popular since the Victorian times, and there still seems to be a constant flow of new varieties. Its common name comes from the fact that each flower lasts for only one day, though there are sufficient buds to ensure a succession for many weeks. The other part of its common name refers to the shape of its flowers, which are similar to those of the trumpet lilies. Their colour varies from yellow through orange and pink to very dark red-brown. The plants are clump-forming, with fountains of strap-like leaves from which rise the leafless stems bearing the flower buds. Although the majority flower in summer, some species flower earlier and some later, so that with careful selection you can have day lilies in bloom for much of the summer.

Day lilies will grow in most garden soils, although they prefer those with plenty of added organic material and reasonably free drainage. They are happy in either full sun or light shade. The clumps can become congested after a few years, and it revitalizes them if they are lifted, divided and replanted. Propagate by division.

Hemerocallis 'Cartwheels'

Cream, yellow and gold forms (above)

This colour range probably presents the largest choice of plants. Among those to be recommended are the pale orange 'Bonanza', which has a dark red centre. 'Canary Glow' has bright yellow flowers, while 'Cartwheels' is a similar colour but has very large, open flowers.

'Corky' has small flowers that are rich brown on the outside and yellow inside. 'Cream Drop', as its name suggests, has cream flowers. 'Golden Chimes' has flowers in a pure deep yellow. 'Marion Vaughn' is bright lemon-yellow. 'Stella de Oro' is dwarf in habit and has full petals that are golden yellow in colour. 'Whichford' is a primrose-yellow colour, and is scented. Finally there is the form *H. dumortieri*, from Japan and China, which has narrow, golden yellow flowers that emerge, unlike those of other forms, from green bracts.

Pink forms

'Catherine Woodbury' has subtle colouring that includes shades of lilac-pink, with a yellow throat. 'Varsity' is a buff-peach with a red eye. 'Luxury Lace' is lavender-pink on an orange-buff ground. 'Pink Damask' is pink suffused with red.

Hemerocallis 'Buzz Bomb'

Red and purple forms (above)

There are some wonderful forms in this colour range. 'Buzz Bomb' is red-brown with a yellow throat. 'Little Wine Cup' has dark wine-red petals, while 'Cherry Cheeks' is rose-pink suffused with red. It also has a distinct yellow throat. 'Stafford' is mahogany-red with a creamy-white strip in the middle of each petal. 'Chicago Royal Robe' is rich purple with a yellow-green throat.

HEUCHERA
Alumroot

Heucheras are among the best of border plants. They have attractive flowering stems, and also make excellent foliage plants. The tall airy flower spikes contrast well with the rounded leaves. The individual flowers are mostly insignificant, mere dots of colour, but when floating above the foliage they can be very attractive. The foliage varies both in its background colour, with some green and others various shades of purple, and in its markings, which can be brown or silver. These make excellent plants for the front parts of borders, and are especially useful in areas that are lightly shaded.

Heucheras like a rich soil, provided it is well-drained. They are happy in either full sun or light shade, the latter being preferable in hot areas. After four years or so it is a good idea to divide the plant and replant the outer parts, discarding the woody central portion. Propagation is by division in autumn or spring.

Flowering types (below)

'Bressingham Hybrids' produce flowers of mixed colours but mainly reds and pinks. 'Firefly', as its name might suggest, has bright red flowers, as does *H. sanguinea*, although the latter does have some white forms. 'Schneewittchen' has pure white flowers.

Heuchera sanguinea

Heuchera 'Snowstorm'

Foliage types (above)

Some forms are noted more for their interesting foliage than for their flowers. These include 'Pewter Moon' (purple foliage splashed with silver, and white flowers), 'Rachel' (purple foliage and pink flowers) and 'Snowstorm' (green leaves spectacularly speckled with creamy white and red flowers). *H. micrantha* has produced two notable seedlings: 'Palace Purple' (rich purple foliage and white flowers) and 'Bressingham Bronze' (brownish leaves and white flowers).

× HEUCHERELLA
Heucherella

This genus has been created by crossing *Heuchera* and *Tiarella*, resulting in some very beautiful, delicate-flowered plants, displaying characteristics from both of the parents. The airy sprays of flowers are particularly attractive, and the marbled foliage is also worthy of attention. Heucherellas can make excellent plants for the front of the border, being only 45cm (1½ft) tall when in flower.

A rich, well-drained soil is what is needed to produce the best from these plants. They can be grown in sun or light shade, although the plants prefer the latter. Divide them every few years in order to increase the stock and to keep the plants vigorous.

Main varieties (below)

'Bridget Bloom', one of the oldest varieties, has delicate pale pink flowers. 'Rosalie', a newer hybrid from Canada, has soft pink flowers and red-brown veined leaves.

× Heucherella 'Bridget Bloom'

HOSTA

Hosta

There can be few gardens that do not have at least one hosta, as these are among the most popular foliage plants. They provide a wide range of colours, textures and shapes, the colours ranging from glaucous blues through many greens to yellows. Often the leaves are variegated, splashed or striped with white-yellow. The texture varies: the light being reflected back from those with shiny surfaces or absorbed by those with a glaucous bloom. Some leaves are more heavily textured with veins than others, while the shapes can be anything from narrow and willow-like to huge, almost circular plates. The flowers are often considered only as an afterthought, but they can be extremely attractive, especially when seen *en masse*. They are funnel-shaped and carried on tall spikes held well above the foliage. The colour of these flowers is mainly pale blue, but other shades of blue and purple, as well as whites, occur.

Hostas need a rich, moisture-retentive soil to show of their best. They can be grown in full sun, in which case special attention should be given to ensure that the soil is kept moist. Hostas generally do better in light to mid-shade. Slugs can be a problem, and may have to be controlled. Propagation is by division.

Blue-leafed forms (below)

'Big Daddy' has very large, deep blue leaves, with distinctly puckered surfaces. 'Blue Moon' has glaucous blue leaves which are small and rounded. 'Hadspen Blue' is one of the bluest-leafed hostas, while the popular 'Halcyon' is not far behind. 'Krossa Regal' has very large blue-green leaves, which erupt in an attractive fountain. 'Wide Brim' has rounded blue-green leaves with a wide creamy margin – hence the name. *H. fortunei* var. *hyacinthina* has leathery grey-green leaves but also has several variegated forms. *H. sieboldiana* var. *elegans* has enormous glaucous leaves with a seersucker texture.

Hosta 'Halcyon'

Green-leafed forms

'Colossal' is so named because of its large leaves. 'Honeybells' spreads very quickly, as does the very similar-looking 'Royal Standard'. 'Sum and Substance' has enormous, yellow-green leaves. *H. lancifolia* has narrow shiny leaves. *H. plantaginea* has plantain-shaped, glossy pale green leaves.

Yellow- and gold-leafed forms (below)

'August Moon' has large golden leaves that have a slightly wrinkled texture. They are pale green when they first open but then mature to an attractive golden colour. 'Gold Edger' is a small-leafed gold form. 'Gold Standard' opens green but turns to a wonderful bright gold colour if given enough sun. 'Golden Sunburst' is a golden form of the variegated 'Frances Williams'. 'Little Aurora' has tiny golden leaves and is suitable only for the front of a border. 'Piedmont Gold' has shiny gold leaves that are slightly twisted. 'Zounds' has some of the largest leaves of all the golden forms; they are puckered.

Hosta 'Gold Standard'

Variegated-leaf forms (next column)

'Francee' has rounded leaves that are a deep green with a regular white margin. 'Frances Williams' is one of the most popular of all hostas. It has glaucous blue-green leaves irregularly edged with cream; and it should not be grown in full sun. 'Ginko Craig' is another popular variety, with lance-shaped leaves and narrow white margins. 'Shade Fanfare' has light green leaves with yellow margins. In 'Thomas Hogg' the leaves range from oval to lance-like in their shape and have broad cream edges which continue as a narrow cream stripe down the leafstalk. *H. undulata* var. *albo-marginata* has wavy leaves with irregular white margins, while *H. u.* var. *univittata* is less wavy than the previous species and has central variegations.

Hosta 'Frances Williams'

HOUTTUYNIA

Houttuynia

This single-species genus is represented by *H. cordata*, a plant that grows up to approximately 45cm (1½ft) and rapidly spreads to form a large colony. Since it has large heart-shaped leaves, this tendency makes it useful as ground cover. The flowers are shaped like small crosses, with four white petals and a central yellow-green boss. The leaves are normally green, but in one very popular cultivar – 'Chameleon' (sometimes known as 'Variegata' or 'Tricolor') – yellow and red variegations are overlaid on the green. The other variegated form, 'Variegata', is less dramatic in its colouring. 'Chameleon' (next column) is too vigorous for most formal borders, but can be used wherever ground cover is required. It also makes a very fine container plant but must be watered well and not be allowed to dry out.

Houttuynia will grow in any garden soil but prefers those that are moist, even to the extent of being boggy. It grows in either sun or shade. Planting is carried out from autumn to spring, and propagation can be achieved by dividing the plants in the spring.

Houttuynia cordata 'Chameleon'

IMPERATA

Imperata

This is a genus of eight or so species, of which only one, *I. cylindrica*, is in cultivation. It is grown in the form known as 'Rubra' (although this does not vary greatly from the species itself). Of all the grasses this must be one of the most beautiful. The leaves grow upright to a height of about 45cm (1½ft). They are a light green, flushed with a brilliant red towards the tips, an effect seen at its most spectacular when sunlight shines through the blades. The foliage is complemented by silvery spikes of flowers. This is a rhizomatous plant, but spreads slowly and does not usually become a nuisance except if grown in hot areas.

Imperata will grow in any garden soil, and can be sited in either a sunny or a lightly shaded position. It can be propagated by division in spring.

INCARVILLEA

Incarvillea

The characteristically flared, trumpet-shaped flowers of incarvillea add a touch of exotica to the border. These plants originate from the Himalayas and China; an increasing number of species and varieties are now grown in the West. The trumpets are pink or rose-pink, with the flared bell of the blooms usually darker than the tube. The leaves are

very attractive in their own right and are arranged in pairs on either side of the stems.

Incarvillea can be grown in any well-drained soil. In most areas they prefer a sunny position, but they should be given light shade in hot regions. Protect from slugs. Planting is best undertaken in autumn or spring. Increase by division or from seed in a greenhouse.

Incarvillea delavayi

I. delavayi (above)

This is one of the more commonly grown species. It can reach 60cm (2ft) tall and flowers in summer, with large trumpets in dark rose-pink. Some protection may be needed in winter.

INULA

Inula

Not everybody likes yellow daisies, but this genus contains some of the better specimens. They have a deep golden central disc and a ring of narrow outer petals in bright yellow. Their height ranges considerably, from no more than 20cm (8in) up to 1.8m (6ft) or more. The leaves also vary, from narrow, willow-like ones to huge broad leaves that are rough to the touch. Where you position these plants will differ according to their size, but all make good border plants – although some can be a little invasive.

Inulas will grow in any garden soil, but preferably one that is reasonably well-drained. The majority of inulas prefer a sunny position. The easiest method of increase is to divide the plants in spring.

Inula ensifolia

I. ensifolia (above)

This medium-sized species grows up to 60cm (2ft). It has narrow leaves and flowers up to 5cm (2in) across. It will grow in light shade. A similar plant is *I. orientalis*, which has larger, deeper-coloured flowers, and hairy leaves.

I. magnifica

As its name suggests, this is the largest species in cultivation, often growing to 1.8m (6ft) or more. The flowers, too, are large, up to 15cm (6in) across. If grown in an exposed position, it needs staking.

IRIS

Iris

Few perennial gardens can be without at least a few irises. In spite of the basic similarity between the species and all the hybrids and cultivars, there is surprising variation, particularly in flower colour. The characteristic flowers are made up of three standards (the upright petals) and three falls (the lower petals). They usually appear in early summer and, in many cases, are fragrant. The sword-like leaves are useful for creating foliage contrasts in the border. Because irises tend to finish flowering by mid-summer, some gardeners prefer to create special iris beds which can be ignored once the flowers are over.

Irises will grow in most garden soils, but some species need to have a moist soil and will even grow in shallow water. They are mainly sun lovers, and in particular the rhizomatous types should be planted where their rhizomes can bake in the sun. The most practical way to increase stock is by division, but they can be grown from seed if the resulting colours are not considered important.

Iris ensata 'Rose Queen'

I. ensata (above)

This species, previously classified as *I. kaempferi*, has produced a wealth of varieties. Called Japanese irises, these forms like to be grown in shallow water or very moist soil. In ordinary borders, add plenty of moisture-retentive humus. They grow up to approximately 90cm (3ft) high and the sword-like leaves have a pronounced midrib. 'Eleanor Parry' has blue flowers with purple markings. 'Great White Heron' has pure white semi-double flowers. 'Moonlight Waves' has white flowers with a green throat. 'Nara' has violet double flowers. The flowers of 'Nikko' are pale blue with purple markings. 'Pink Frost' has large soft pink flowers. 'Rose Queen' has rose-pink petals. 'Variegata' has purple flowers but is mainly grown for its white-striped foliage.

Iris sibirica 'White Swirl'

I. sibirica (above)

The Siberian irises form large clumps of narrow leaves. They grow well in any border soil. 'Caesar's Brother' has deep purple flowers with a velvety texture. 'Cambridge' has light blue petals. 'Ego' has rich blue flowers. 'Flight of Butterflies' has small pale blue petals with a much darker blue veining. 'Little White', as its name suggests, has small white flowers. 'Orville Fay' has large blue flowers with purple veining. 'Showdown' has deep violet petals with white and yellow markings. 'White Swirl' has white ruffled petals and a gold throat.

Dwarf bearded forms

These bearded irises, that are based mainly on *I. × germanica*, grow up to approximately 70cm (2¼ft) high. They are best suited to areas from the front to the middle of the border because of their size. 'Cherry Garden' has cherry- or wine-red flowers with a contrasting dark purple beard. 'Green Spot' is white with green spots on the falls. 'Lemon Flare' has creamy white flowers. 'Lilliwhite', as its name suggests, bears white flowers. 'Orange Capers' has orange-yellow flowers. 'Pogo' has rich yellow petals with rusty markings. 'Tinkerbell' has bright blue flowers with slightly darker markings.

Tall bearded forms (below)
These are similar to the dwarf bearded irises but taller, above 70cm (2¼ft). Among the thousands available the following have been selected for special attention: 'Berkeley' has deep yellow petals. 'Frost and Flame' is white with a hint of purple and a yellow beard. 'Jane Phillips' is soft blue with a white beard, and 'Pearly Dawn' is a pearly pink. 'Stepping Out' is very distinctive, its large white patches contrasting with dark purple edges. 'Victoria Falls' is a light blue form.

Iris 'Jane Phillips'

Pacific Coast forms
These have been created by crossing *I. douglasiana* with *I. innominata*. They will grow in full sun but in hot areas, prefer shade. They are of medium height, growing up to 60cm (2ft). There are many forms from which to choose. 'Broadleigh Rose' and 'Broadleigh Sybil' are both members of the large Broadleigh series of Pacific Coast hybrids. The former is a deep rose-pink while the latter is brown-yellow with purple markings.

Species (next column)
As well as the thousands of cultivars there are several hundred species for the enthusiast to explore. *I. cristata*, the crested iris, is a low-growing form,

reaching only 25cm (10in) high. The flowers appear in spring and range in colour from pale blue to purple. This is one of the few species that will grow in shade. *I. pallida* is up to 1.2m (4ft) tall, has pale blue flowers and is known mainly in its 'Aurea Variegata' and 'Variegata' forms, the leaves of which have golden and cream variegations respectively. *I. pseudocorus*, yellow flag, will grow in wet conditions, including shallow water. It has bright yellow flowers on a 1.5m (5ft) plant. *I. tectorum*, Japanese roof iris, is a short plant reaching to 30cm (1ft) and has flat, open flowers in shades of blue and purple or white. *I. unguicularis* flowers during the winter and needs a well-drained soil and sunny position. The fragrant purple flowers are shorter than the leaves, which reach up to 45cm (1½ft) high.

Iris unguicularis

JASIONE
Jasione
Nearly all the jasiones make desirable plants for the garden, although the majority are too small for border use, except perhaps at the front. They have loose, untidy heads of blue flowers in summer, the colour ranging from pale blue to purple. The flowers are carried on wiry stems well above the mat of green foliage, and their colours make them particularly suitable for pastel-coloured borders.

Jasiones like a free-draining soil and a position in full sun. Snip off the flowering stems once blooming is over. Jasiones can be increased by sowing seed or by division.

Jasione laevis

J. laevis (above)
Previously known as *J. perennis*, this jasione is the species that is best suited to the perennial border. It forms a low mat of foliage above which the flower stems rise up to 38cm (15in) high, bearing pale blue flowers.

KALIMERIS
Kalimeris
Kalimeris is one of those odd genera that botanists regularly rename. Many people still consider it part of *Aster*, and its plants are still frequently found listed under this name. They are indeed not easy to distinguish from many of the Michaelmas daisies. The flowers are about 2.5cm (1in) across, with a central yellow disc and white or pale lavender ray florets. None are frequently grown, but *K. incisa* is one of the commonest; it grows to about 60cm (2ft). *K. mongolica*, less common, grows to 90cm (3ft) or even more. *K. yomena* 'Shogun' is the form most often seen; it has variegated foliage.

Not only do kalimeris look like asters, they also need the same kind of conditions. They will grow in any soil that does not become too dry. A sunny position is best, although they will grow in light shade if necessary. In exposed positions the taller ones need staking. Propagation can be carried out successfully by division in the spring.

KIRENGESHOMA
Kirengeshoma

This genus is represented solely by *K. palmata* (below). This unmistakable plant grows to about 1.2m (4ft), with black stems on which are borne soft yellow bells and large maple-like leaves. It is an especially useful plant as it flowers very late in the year, during late summer and autumn, and also tolerates shade.

Kirengeshoma is a woodland plant and as such likes a moist, humus-rich soil with plenty of leaf mould. It prefers a position out of the direct sun, although it will grow in the open provided the soil is not allowed to dry out. The young growth may be attacked by slugs. Propagate by division or by sowing seeds in spring.

Kirengeshoma palmata

KNAUTIA
Knautia

Although this is quite a large genus, very few species are actually grown in cultivation – in fact, only one is commonly seen: *K. macedonica* (next column), a splendid plant that forms a great mound of loose stems which seem to shoot off in all directions. These bear crimson, pincushion-like

flowers, which appear in early summer and continue well into the autumn, although the later flowers are much smaller than the earlier ones. It is about 90cm (3ft) tall and as much across.

Knautia can be grown in any good garden soil, but prefers one that is reasonably free-draining. A sunny position is ideal. This floppy plant will need some support. Propagate by careful division or from seed.

Knautia macedonica

KNIPHOFIA
Torch lily, Red hot poker

Torch lilies are very distinctive border plants. Their bright flowers are held in club-like heads on tall stems that rise out of fountains of narrow grass-like leaves. Their height ranges from about 30cm (1ft) to over 1.5m (5ft). The colour of the flowers likewise varies. The more traditional varieties are bright red, often touched with yellow, but more subtle colours, including apricot, have been introduced, and there are also forms that have bright yellow or yellow-and-green flowers. The vertical nature of the flowering stems can offer a contrast with more rounded plants in the border. The upright flowering spikes and their bright colours tend to draw the eye, making these valuable plants for creating an interesting focal point.

Torch lilies will grow in any fertile garden soil, preferably one that is well-

drained. They should be given a sunny position. Since they are not completely hardy they may need protection in colder areas. Propagation is by division.

Tall varieties (below)

The taller varieties grow from 90cm (3ft) to 1.8m (6ft) high. 'Green Jade' has cool green flowers, fading to pale yellow, and broad leaves. 'Prince Igor', one of the tallest varieties, has large heads of bright red, fading to yellow at the base. 'Atlanta' grows up to 1.5m (5ft) and has heads that are bright orange-red at the top, fading to yellow at the base; it is one of the earliest varieties to flower.

Kniphofia 'Atlanta'

Medium-sized varieties

These forms grow to 60cm–1.8m (2–6ft). 'Royal Standard' grows 90cm–1.2m (3–4ft) high and has golden yellow flowers that emerge from red buds, giving the flower head a two-tone effect. 'Bressingham Comet', which flowers later, is shorter, at 60cm (2ft), and is orange-red and yellow.

Short varieties

These grow up to 60cm (2ft). 'Little Maid' is one of the finest of all short pokers. It has narrow, upright leaves and creamy white flowers. 'Sunningdale Yellow' has light yellow flowers.

Mixed varieties

'Border Ballet', a seed strain, produces plants up to 90cm (3ft) tall which carry red or yellow flowers.

LAMIUM
Dead nettle

The dead nettles are excellent plants for creating blocks of colour as ground cover. They are very easy to grow, and most will tolerate shade. They are cultivated for their attractive leaves and flowers, which are hooded and carried in whorls around the stems. The flowers vary in colour from white to yellow, pink and purple. The leaves are often delightfully variegated with splashes of silver.

Dead nettles will grow in any garden soil, but tend to do best in those that are moisture-retentive. They grow particularly well in shade and will also grow in the open as long as the soil is not allowed to dry out too much. Propagation is easily achieved by division.

Lamium galeobdolon

L. galeobdolon (above)

This species shuttles back and forth between *Lamium*, *Lamiastrum* and *Galeobdolon*, and may be found listed under any of these genus names. It has yellow flowers. It can be invasive and should therefore be sited with care. 'Herman's Pride' has beautiful silver leaves that are veined in a contrasting dark green. 'Florentinum' ('Variegatum') is particularly invasive, but makes good ground cover in suitable situations. It has larger leaves than 'Herman's Pride', and they are splashed with silvery white.

L. maculatum (below)

This is a low, ground-covering species reaching a height of approximately 38cm (15in). It is available in several varieties with attractive leaves. 'Beacon Silver' has silvery white markings and pink flowers. 'Pink Pewter' has grey leaves and pale pink flowers. 'White Nancy' is one of the best varieties, with fresh green leaves that are liberally splashed with silver markings. These leaves dramatically set off the pure white flowers.

Lamium maculatum 'Beacon Silver'

LATHYRUS
Pea

This large genus includes a number of species grown in perennial borders. Many are climbing plants that need support, but there are also several clump-forming species. All have typical pea-shaped flowers. The colours are mainly pink and purple, but there are also golden and white forms.

Lathyrus will grow in any garden soil; most prefer a sunny position. They can be increased either by division or by sowing from seed in spring.

Lathyrus vernus

L. vernus (above)

This low-growing species reaching a height of just 30cm (1ft), has purple-blue flowers that appear in the spring. It is usually grown in full sun, but in the wild it grows in deciduous woodland, and therefore it can be grown in a similar situation in the garden. The variety 'Albo-roseus' displays beautiful white and pink flowers.

LEUCANTHEMELLA
Leucanthemella

The name of *L. serotina* (next page) has been changed several times and can still be found in catalogues as *Chrysanthemum serotinum* or *C. uliginosum*. It is typical of the chrysanthemums, its daisy-like flower having a yellow central disc and white outer petals. It is a tall plant, growing to 1.8m (6ft) or more. The flowers are carried at the top of these tall stems and have the curious habit of turning on their side and following the sun throughout the day. They appear in late autumn, when little else is in flower, but since the plants are tall – and somewhat boring when out of flower – it is best to plant them at the back of the border.

Leucanthemellas will grow in any fertile garden soil, but do need a sunny position. They slowly form a large clump, and this can be easily divided for propagational purposes. The eventual flowering height of the plant can be reduced by cutting back the developing shoots by about one-third in early summer. Unfortunately, this may delay the flowering time until later on in the autumn.

Leucanthemella serotina

LEUCANTHEMUM
Shasta daisy

As a result of the break-up of the genus *Chrysanthemum*, the shasta daisies have been renamed *Leucanthemum* × *superbum*, but they may still be found under the older name, *Chrysanthemum* × *superbum*. These are splendid plants, both as cut flowers and when grown in the border for display from summer onwards. They are typical daisies, with a yellow central disc and a ring of white outer petals, but there are also forms which have pale yellow outer petals. In the main they grow to about 90cm (3ft) and have thick stems and dark green leaves.

Shasta daisies will grow in any good garden soil, but do best in those that are moisture-retentive. A sunny position is best, though they will grow in light shade. Taller forms need support. Shasta daisies slowly form large clumps, and can easily be divided to increase stock. Some strains can also be propagated from seed.

Varieties (next column)
There are a number of variations on this plant, in both height and doubleness of the flower. 'Polaris' is a good cut-flower strain grown from seed. It has very large flowers. 'Silberprinzesschen' ('Silver Princess', 'Little Princess'), which can be grown from seed, is a dwarf strain, reaching a height of only 30cm (1ft). 'Snow Lady' is an even smaller dwarf seed strain. 'Snowcap' is a perennial form, somewhat taller, reaching 45cm (1½ft) or so. 'Wirral Supreme' is one of the many taller, double forms and grows to a height of approximately 90cm (3ft).

Leucanthemum 'Snowcap'

LIATRIS
Blazing star

The flower spikes of the blazing stars make a positive contribution to the late summer border, in terms of both the upright nature of the plant and the bright flower heads. These heads form columns of purple flowers; those at the top of the spike usually open first (instead of those at the bottom, as with most other plants). There is not a great deal of difference between the various species in cultivation.

Blazing stars will grow in any good garden soil, but need a sunny position. They can be propagated by dividing the corm-like rhizomes.

L. pycnostachya
This is very similar to other forms in cultivation, differing mainly in its densely clustered leaves and softly hairy stems. It grows to 1.5m (5ft). There are both purple and white forms. It flowers over a long period.

L. scariosa
This species is the same height as *L. pycnostachya* but has wider leaves and more open flower spikes. It has a white flowered form, 'Alba'.

Liatris spicata

L. spicata (above)
This is the main species in cultivation. It grows to 75cm (2½ft) and has glabrous stems. 'Floristan Violet' is a violet-purple seed strain which is is grown for cut flowers. 'Floristan Weiss' ('Floristan White') is the white equivalent. 'Kobold', one of the main perennial varieties, is only 45cm (1½ft) high and has dense spikes of bright purple flowers.

LIGULARIA
Ligularia

Yellow daisies can add a touch of brightness to a border, especially a shady one. Ligularias are particularly useful for this. They flower from late summer onwards and, unlike most other plants with similar flowers, many have interesting foliage.

Ligularias prefer to be grown in a moisture-retentive soil. If the soil dries out, the leaves will soon begin to flag, indicating that they require watering. They will grow in either sun or light shade, but if they are to be planted in the sun, it is extremely important that the soil is moist. Propagation can be achieved either by division at the time of planting or by sowing seeds in the spring.

L. dentata

This plant is 1.2m (4ft) tall and has loose, untidy heads of large golden yellow flowers. The species and cultivars are often grown for their foliage, which in 'Desdemona' is a rich purple. The foliage is prone to slug attack.

L. 'Greynog Gold'

This hybrid has loose spikes of large orange-yellow flowers that stand out well above the green foliage. The plant is 1.8m (6ft) tall.

Ligularia 'The Rocket'

L. 'The Rocket' (above)

This is one of the best of the ligularias. It is a hybrid, although sometimes attributed to the species *L. stenocephala* and sometimes to *L. przewalskii*. It has tall, slender spires of bright yellow flowers carried on dark stems 1.5m (5ft) high. The leaves are decoratively toothed.

LIMONIUM
Statice, Sea lavender

Statice, or sea lavender, is a large genus of plants that contains a number of garden-worthy species, several of them annuals.

They are characterized by having dense heads of colourful flowers which not only make decorative garden features but also work particularly well as dried flowers.

They need a well-drained soil and a sunny position. They are tolerant of salt-laden winds and so make good plants for maritime gardens. Propagation is from seed or by division.

Limonium platyphyllum

L. platyphyllum (above)

Until recently this species, the most popular, was known as *L. latifolium*, and it is still sometimes found under that name. It produces an airy cloud of tiny mauve flowers in late summer. It grows to only 45cm (1½ft), and so is suitable for the front of the border.

LINARIA
Toadflax

The toadflaxes produce tall, slender spikes of antirrhinum-like flowers, mainly in soft colours. The flowers are often quite small, and the colour effect depends on their being produced in great quantity. They are useful plants for infilling between other, more solid-looking plants.

They will grow in any garden soil, but do particularly well on light, well-drained soils, where they will happily run or self-sow, sometimes invasively. They like a sunny position. Propagate by division or from seed.

Linaria dalmatica

L. dalmatica (above)

This species is much larger in all its parts than *L. purpurea*, and is a much bolder plant; the detail of the individual bright yellow flowers is easy to see. The stems and leaves are a glaucous grey-green. The plant flowers from mid- to late summer and grows to 90cm (3ft). It tends to run invasively, so position it with extra care.

L. purpurea

This plant produces slender spikes of tiny flowers from mid- to late summer. In the species they are purple, but in the form 'Canon Went' they are a delicate pink. A good white form, 'Springside White', is also widely available. All grow to 90cm (3ft) high.

LINUM
Flax

The flaxes produce beautiful blue flowers. Shallowly funnel-shaped, they are held on gracefully arching stems in summer. Each flower lasts only a day, but there is a constant succession of new ones. Although well worth growing in the garden, they are short-lived, needing to be renewed every 2–3 years. They should be planted towards the front of the border, where their fountain of stems is not constricted by other plants. Flaxes grow to about 60cm (2ft) tall.

Flaxes do best when planted in a light, well-drained soil in a sunny location, preferably in a sheltered position. They can be readily increased by sowing seed in autumn or by taking cuttings in summer, and they often self-sow.

Linum narbonense

L. narbonense (above)

This is the larger and stronger-growing of the two main species, and the longer-lived. The flowers vary slightly in colour from a pale to a rich blue.

L. perenne

This is very similar to *L. narbonense*, with which it is often confused, but it is slightly smaller in all its parts and is not so long-lived, needing to be replaced about every 2 years. There is a white form, 'Diamant' ('Diamant White').

LIRIOPE

Lilyturf

Liriopes come into their own during the autumn, when many other perennials have died back; the fact that the flowers are violet-blue is an added bonus for this time of year. They appear in spikes that erupt from the clump of narrow, strap-like leaves. The plants usually grow to only about 45cm (1½ft) high, which makes them candidates for the front of the border. Another bonus is that these plants will grow in either sun or shade.

They thrive in any fertile garden soil, including dry. Propagation is by division.

L. muscari (below)

The flowers, small balls of violet-blue clustered round the stem, look like those of the bulb *Muscari* (grape hyacinth), hence the botanical name. The form 'Majestic' has large spikes of flowers.

Liriope muscari

L. spicata

This species is very similar in appearance to *L. muscari*. The big difference is that it spreads rapidly and can become invasive. It does, however, have a very good white-flowered form, 'Alba'.

LOBELIA

Lobelia

Although the flower shape has much in common, border lobelias are quite different from the trailing, bedding lobelias frequently grown. The perennials are stiff, upright plants with spikes of red, blue or purple flowers that appear in late summer and grow up to 90cm (3ft) tall.

They look finest when planted next to a water feature, and must have a moisture-retentive soil to give their best. Either plant lobelias near water or add plenty of humus to the soil. They will grow in either sun or shade but, since some are on the tender side, may need winter protection in colder areas. Propagate by cuttings or division.

Lobelia 'Compliment Scarlet'

Red varieties (above)

'Bees' Flame' has deep purple foliage and scarlet flowers. *L. cardinalis* has green leaves and scarlet flowers, and is one of the hardier species. 'Compliment Scarlet' is a seed-raised scarlet-flowered form, while 'Queen Victoria' is an old variety with red foliage and bright red flowers.

Blue and purple varieties

L. siphilitica has blue flowers, though it has also a white form, 'Alba'. The variety *L. × gerardii* 'Vedrariensis', a cross between the red *L. cardinalis* and the blue *L. siphilitica*, has deep purple flowers. 'Tania' is a similar cross but with redder flowers. 'Russian Princess' has purple leaves and flowers.

LUPINUS

Lupin

Lupins have been much loved by many generations of gardeners. The large spikes of colourful flowers, with their peppery smell, are perfect for the cottage or traditional garden. The individual flowers are pea-like and come in a very wide range of colours; some are a single colour, while others are bicolours. The leaves, made up of many narrow leaflets arranged in a circle, are carried on plants which, when in flower, are up to 1.2m (4ft) high. They bloom in early summer and will go on to produce a second flush later if they are cut back.

Lupins will grow in any good garden soil, but do best in reasonably rich, free-draining ones. They prefer full sun, but will tolerate light shade. They can suffer badly from the grey lupin aphid. Most garden hybrids are short-lived, and are best replaced every few years either from seed or from basal cuttings taken in the spring.

Lupinus 'Band of Nobles'

Mixed colours (above)
Seed is the easiest method of obtaining lupins. Several strains will provide a mixed selection of colours. 'Band of Nobles' is a good mixture of 'Russell Hybrids' offering the full range of lupin colours. 'Gallery' offers a similar range of colours but on much smaller plants.

Separate colours
Individual colours are available as named forms or as seed strains, but in the latter case the shades may vary. Plants derived from seed include 'Chandelier', which includes various yellows, and 'The Pages', which are carmines. There are bicolours available, 'Noble Maiden' (white and cream) and 'The Governor' (blue and white).

LUZULA
Luzula
This genus of grass-like rushes contains some 40 species, of which about half are in cultivation. They are not particularly

spectacular, but are useful because they will grow in the shade. The leaves are flat and strap-like, often with white hairs. The plants form either tufted clumps or spreading carpets.

They will grow in any garden soil, including dry ones. Either a sunny position or shade will be suitable. Propagate by division in spring.

L. sylvatica
A woodland plant that slowly spreads to form a large colony, giving good ground cover. A flowering stem carrying brown flowers appears in spring and early summer. The form 'Marginata' also grows slowly. It produces attractive thick tufts of broad mid-green leaves that have hairy white edges.

LYCHNIS
Campion
The campions are easy to grow and very decorative. They tend to have very brightly coloured flowers and can be used to liven up a border with their bright reds, pinks or orange. The flowers are in some cases up to 4cm (1½in) across, while in others they are much smaller but they make up for it with quantity.

Campions will grow in any garden soil, but prefer well-drained ones. A sunny position is required; taller forms require staking. Propagation is mainly from seed, although division is possible. Most self-sow vigorously and need to be dead-headed to stop them becoming too invasive.

L. x arkwrightii
This short-lived plant has bronze-tinted foliage and large bright orange flowers. It grows to only about 30cm (1ft). Regular replacement will be needed, often yearly.

L. chalcedonica (next column)
The Maltese cross is so-called because of the cruciform shape of its bright scarlet

flowers. These are quite small but are carried in a dense, domed head and so make a definite splash in the border with their bright scarlet flowers. The plants are clump forming and grow to about 1.2m (4ft) in height.

Lychnis chalcedonica

L. coronaria
Rose campion, one of the most popular campions, has startling, carmine flowers that are well set off by its furry silver leaves and stems. 'Atrosanguinea' has even darker magenta flowers. The form 'Alba' has pure white flowers, while those of 'Oculata' have a pink eye that forms as they age. The plants grow up to 75cm (2½ft) tall.

L. flos-jovis
This is shorter than the previous species, reaching 45cm (1½ft) tall. Its silver stems and foliage are beautifully complemented by the sugar-pink flowers. 'Hort's Variety' offers a particularly clear pink.

LYSICHITON
Skunk cabbage
Previously known as *Lysichitum*, this small genus has just two species, one from each side of the North Pacific. The strange flowers, which appear before the leaves have developed in spring, are club-like and surrounded by either a white or a yellow spathe. Large leaves, much in the manner

of a cos lettuce's, soon develop and can be up to 1.2m (4ft) tall. In suitable conditions these plants can spread to make large colonies.

They should be grown in a moist soil, preferably in a bog garden or near a water feature. Either sun or light shade is suitable. Propagate by seed.

L. americanus

This, the bog arum, has large yellow spathes and green spadices. The flowers have an unpleasant smell. This species has the bigger leaves of the two, reaching up to 1.2m (4ft).

L. camtschatcensis (below)

Slightly smaller than L. americanus, this plant has pure white spathes and pale green spadices. The flowers have a faint, sweet smell.

Lysichiton camtschatcensis

LYSIMACHIA
Loosestrife

The loosestrifes are reliable rather than exceptional border plants. They produce tall spires of flowers in either white or yellow, and must be sited with care as they spread, possibly invasively, by rhizomes. They grow to a height of approximately 1.2m (4ft) and can be used in a block towards the rear of the border, often providing a background or companion for other plants.

They all like a moisture-retentive soil and do best in damp soil near water. They will grow in either sun or shade, flowering better in the former. Propagation is easily undertaken by dividing the clumps.

L. clethroides

These grow to a height of approximately 90cm (3ft), producing a neat clump, at the top of which the short white flower spikes seem to whizz like fireworks, each bending over part of the way up the flower head.

Lysimachia ephemerum

L. ephemerum (above)

This species has flower spikes that stand rigidly to attention. The flowers are white and more spaced-out than in L. clethroides, but are nonetheless well displayed against the glaucous blue-green stems and foliage.

L. punctata

Yellow loosestrife grows in ditches and wet places and can spread invasively. Its foliage is coarser and not so interesting as in the other species, but as if to compensate for this, it produces columns of larger flowers, bright yellow in colour. Unless rigorously controlled, yellow loosestrife is much better suited for planting in a wild patch than in a formal border. It grows to a height of about 90cm (3ft).

LYTHRUM
Purple loosestrife

Although this shares a common name and a liking for wet places with *Lysimachia*, the two are not related. Only two out of *Lythrum's* 35 species are in cultivation, but they have produced a large number of varieties. All are of similar appearance, producing tall spikes of bright purple flowers. They grow to 1.2m (4ft) high. The plants are clump-forming and are good plants for the middle to rear of a garden border.

Purple loosestrifes thrive in boggy soils or next to water, but will grow in ordinary soil, provided it contains a lot of moisture-retaining humus. They will grow in either sun or light shade, although the former is preferred. Propagation is by division.

L. salicaria (below)

This species has narrow leaves and large, solid spikes of purple flowers from mid-summer onwards. 'Feuerkerze' ('Firecandle') grows to 90cm (3ft) and has rose-red flowers. 'Robert', shorter, has pinker flowers.

Lythrum salicaria 'Robert'

L. virgatum

This particular species does not differ greatly from L. salicaria, but its appearance is more slender and dainty and the flowers are not quite so bright. Of its various cultivars, 'Dropmore Purple' has the richest-coloured flowers.

MACLEAYA
Plume poppy

The two species of plume poppies are superb plants for the large border. They grow up to approximately 2.5m (8ft) in height and rapidly spread to form large colonies. The tall stems and large, attractively lobed leaves are a glaucous, pearly grey. The pink or white flowers are small and petalless, but are carried in quantity in loose airy spikes. Although plume poppies are tall plants, and thus best suited to the back of the border, they should be planted so that the foliage as well as the flower heads can be appreciated.

Plume poppies will grow in any garden soil but seem to prefer light, well-drained conditions. They can be grown in full sun or partial shade. They are fully hardy and do not need staking even in exposed sites. Propagation can be achieved by taking root cuttings or by division.

M. cordata

This species has pale, almost white, flowers and is generally considered to be less invasive than *M. microcarpa*, although it still spreads rapidly. The variety 'Flamingo' has pinker flowers.

Macleaya microcarpa

M. microcarpa (above)

This plant is very similar to the clump-forming *M. cordata*, except that the flowers are a deeper pink. The form most commonly grown is 'Kelway's Coral Plume': as its name suggests, this has coral-coloured flowers.

MALVA
Mallow

Related to the hollyhocks, these plants have similar cone-shaped flowers. They are much smaller, however, and their colours are not so bright, yet this does not detract from their beauty. They are mainly upright, with lobed leaves; the species' variation in height makes these plants suitable for all parts of the border.

Mallows will grow in a wide range of garden soils, including dry and impoverished ones. However, some varieties will be noticeably smaller in undernourished soils. They prefer full sun. These plants are short-lived but some tend to self-sow, so are easily perpetuated. Increase is mainly from seed, although they can also be propagated by taking cuttings in spring.

Malva alcea 'Fastigiata'

M. alcea (above)

These tall forms reach 1.2m (4ft) and have large pink flowers. The old variety 'Fastigiata' has richer pink flowers than the species and a neater shape due to its upright growth.

M. moschata

The musk mallow is much loved in old-fashioned gardens. It has a bushy habit, reaching a height of about 60cm (2ft), and for a long period from summer onwards is covered with beautiful pink flowers. There is also a very attractive white form, 'Alba'. The leaves are deeply cut and very decorative.

M. sylvestris (below)

This is a completely different plant, with a sprawling habit and purple flowers that are noticeably veined. It is grown mainly in the form 'Primley Blue', in which the flowers are bluer and the plant shorter than in the species. It has round, lobed leaves.

Malva sylvestris 'Primley Blue'

MATTEUCCIA
Ostrich fern

This small genus contains only three species, all vigorous ferns that will soon form large colonies. Each plant produces a fountain of deeply cut fronds. The species most commonly seen in gardens is *M. struthiopteris*, which has pale green fronds and is a vigorous spreader. It grows up to 90cm (3ft) high. *M. pensylvanica* is very similar, though its fronds are a darker green and, when satisfied with its conditions, it can grow much larger. Both need space to spread.

These woodland ferns love a moist humus-rich soil and a dappled shade – next to a shady stream is ideal. Propagation is from spores or by division.

MECONOPSIS
Blue poppy

Meconopsis is a large genus consisting of about 40 species, most of which are in cultivation. Most are blue, but there are also yellow, orange and red species, as well as white varieties of the blue forms. The flowers have the same tissue-paper quality as poppies, and each generally has a large central boss of golden stamens. They can be used as specimen plants, but look best when planted in drifts.

Blue poppies must have a moist, lime-free soil, which can most easily be created by adding humus. They can be grown in the open in sun as long as the conditions are moist, but it is more common to grow them in light shade. Generally they are easist to grow in a moist, sheltered atmosphere. Propagation is mainly from seed, but they can also be divided.

M. betonicifolia

This is the original 'blue poppy' that first sparked interest in the genus. It grows up to 1.5m (5ft) tall. There is also a white form, 'Alba'.

M. grandis (below)

This grows to the same height as *M. betonicifolia* and is very similar – indeed, the two are often confused. It is generally a larger plant, with bigger flowers in a richer hue.

Meconopsis grandis

M. × sheldonii

This series of hybrids between *M. betonicifolia* and *M. grandis* manages to improve on both of them. Again the flowers are blue. One of the best forms available is 'Ormswell'.

MELISSA
Lemon balm

The three species that make up this genus are untidy plants; their rightful place is in the herb garden rather than in the border. The main species in cultivation is *M. officinalis*. In spring and early summer it has attractive fresh green leaves which smell strongly of lemon, but once the small white flowers have appeared it begins to become leggy and rather unattractive. In the form 'Aurea' (below) the green leaves are speckled with gold.

Lemon balm will grow in any garden soil and in either sun or shade, with the golden form changing to light green in the latter position. Plants should be dead-headed immediately after flowering, both to tidy them up and to prevent them self-sowing invasively. Propagate from seed or by division.

Melissa officinalis 'Aurea'

MENTHA
Mint

Mentha species are perhaps better grown in the herb garden than in the border, but there are some very attractive forms and, as long as measures are taken to prevent them spreading into other plants, they can make good additions to the front of the border. They are mainly grown for the scent and flavour their foliage provides, and it is the leaves that give them most of their appeal – the flowers generally go unnoticed except in borders where subtle, pale colours are required. They grow to a height of 45cm (1½ft).

Mints will grow in any garden soil, doing best in moist sites, and thrive in either sun or light shade. To prevent them spreading invasively, plant them in a bottomless bucket and remove the flowering stems before they have a chance to seed. Propagate by division.

Mentha × *gracilis* 'Variegata'

Variegated forms (above)

For the border, the variegated varieties are the most attractive. *M.* × *gracilis* 'Variegata' (also known as *M.* × *gentilis* 'Variegata') has dark green leaves which are veined with golden yellow. In contrast, *M. suaveolens* 'Variegata' has soft green leaves splashed with cream variegations. It seldom flowers.

MERTENSIA
Mertensia

This large genus of plants has an increasing number of species that are coming into cultivation, as the beauty of their often glaucous foliage is becoming more widely appreciated. *M. virginica* (below), the Virginia cowslip or bluebell, has been in cultivation a long time. It grows to 60cm (2ft), with beautiful blue-green foliage and nodding heads of bright blue flowers, pink in bud. Unfortunately it dies back after mid-summer, and then there is a long wait until spring once more brings forth the elegant foliage and flowers.

The Virginia cowslip needs a moist, humus-rich woodland-type soil to excel, as well as a cool, shady position. Propagation is either from seed or by division in spring.

Mertensia virginica

MILIUM

Millet grass

Of this small genus of grasses only *M. effusum* (in its form 'Aureum') is in general cultivation. This variety is popularly known as Bowles' golden grass and is a beautiful plant of some refinement. It is a clump-forming grass rather than a rapidly spreading one, and its narrow leaves make a low fountain of golden yellow from which arise delicate airy heads of pale green flowers. Millet grass is at its best in the spring, as later in the season it can become slightly greener, although it usually holds its colour well.

This grass will grow in any garden soil, but produces the best results in light shade. Propagation can be from division, but it also gently self-sows, providing ample seedlings for most uses.

MIMULUS

Monkey flower

This genus is a large one with a large number of species in cultivation. Many of the plants are treated as annuals and propagated afresh each year. One species that is usually treated as a perennial is *M. cardinalis* (below), the scarlet monkey flower. This has erect growth of about 90cm (3ft), downy foliage and the characteristic cheeky-faced flowers of the mimulus. As the name suggests, the flowers are mainly scarlet in colour, but there are also varieties in yellow and pink, and sometimes a mixture.

Since they like moist soil, these plants do best in a bog garden or next to a water feature. They also look best in this situation, particularly tumbling down a low bank to the water's edge. They will grow in the sun or in light shade. Cut back after the first flush of flowers to encourage the production of further blooms. Propagation can be carried out by taking cuttings, by division or by sowing seed.

Mimulus cardinalis

MISCANTHUS

Miscanthus

This is a genus of some 17 species of grass, of which a number are in cultivation. These are generally the tall, statuesque grasses that look so dramatic when seen across a lawn or at the edge of a pool, but they can equally well be used as part of a perennial border, giving it height and movement. These grasses are clump-formers, spreading only slowly. The leaves are flat and strap-like with a stiff, erect appearance. The decorative flower heads are usually supported on stiff stems that rise well above the leaves.

Miscanthus will grow in most garden soils, including dry ones, and like most grasses prefers to be sited in a sunny position. Cut back the previous year's stems in late winter before the new growth begins. Propagate by division in the spring.

Miscanthus sinensis 'Kleine Fontäne'

M. sinensis (above)
The Chinese silver grass provides most of the varieties in cultivation, the majority growing to 1.8m (6ft) high. 'Goldfeder' ('Gold Feather') has a golden sheen to its pink plumes, while 'Silberfeder' ('Silver Feather') has a wonderful silvery pink effect. 'Kleine Fontäne' has pink heads and grows to only 1.2m (4ft); 'Malepartus' has broad leaves with a silver central line; and 'Morning Light' has variegated leaves. The leaves of *M. s.* var. *purpurascens* change colour as the seasons progress, to purple-brown with a distinctive central vein; the plant grows to only 1.5m (5ft). 'Variegatus' has wide leaves variegated in white, while 'Zebrinus' is very distinctive, with its yellow variegations going across the leaves.

MOLINIA
Moor grass
Of the three species in this small genus of grasses, *M. caerulea* is the main one in cultivation. This is the purple moor grass, 60cm (2ft) tall with feathery plumes of purple flowers. 'Variegata' (below) is among the best known of its several varieties. Its arching leaves have cream variegations along their length, and in autumn take on light brown tints. It is a good plant for lighting up a dark corner.

Moor grass will grow in a wide variety of soils, including boggy ones, but needs a sunny position. Cut back the dead leaves and stems in late winter before new growth commences. Propagation is carried out by division in spring.

Molinia caerulea 'Variegata'

MONARDA
Bergamot
Bergamots are intriguing plants, with fascinating whorls of dead-nettle-like flowers in bright reds, pinks and purples. Bergamot looks better when planted in drifts rather than as a specimen plant. Many also have fragrant leaves, which have been used in tisanes and herbal teas for centuries. It is a good idea to plant monardas where you can reach a few leaves every time you pass, just to give you the pleasure of smelling them.

Most monardas like a sunny position and a rich, moisture-retentive soil; but they soon impoverish the soil and need to be dug up and divided, and the bed revitalized, before replanting. Many monardas can suffer from powdery mildew, especially in dry weather. Propagation is carried out by division.

Monarda didyma

Species (above)
Although the hybrids are most frequently grown, there are a few species that deserve a place in the border. *M. didyma* (bee balm or Oswego tea) grows to about 90cm (3ft), with strongly scented foliage and bright red flowers. This species, crossed with the more drought-resistant *M. fistulosa*, has been used to produce most of the hybrids. *M. punctata* has pale yellow flowers that are spotted with purple-brown and held in pink bracts.

Red varieties
M. didyma has provided some very attractive red varieties. 'Adam' is bright cherry-red. The old-fashioned 'Cambridge Scarlet' is slightly darker. Darker still is 'Mahogany', which has a touch of brown in it.

Purple varieties
'Blaustrumpf' ('Blue Stocking') is dark mauve, despite its name. 'Loddon Crown' is rich red-purple, while 'Prairie Night' is vibrant purple.

Pink varieties
Many of the pink forms have been in cultivation a long time. An old favourite is 'Croftway Pink', with its soft rose-pink flowers. 'Beauty of Cobham' is very pale pink. 'Pink Tourmalin' is darker.

White varieties
White-flowered forms do not seem to be quite as strong-growing as other colours. Good forms are 'Ou Charm' and 'Schneewittchen' ('Snow White'), with the former being shorter and having a hint of pink in the flowers.

MORINA
Morina
Although this is a fascinating genus of plants, only *M. longifolia* (below) is widely grown. It looks like a thistle, although not in fact related to the thistle family. It forms a rosette of long, dark green spiny leaves that are fragrant when crushed. From this rises a tall stem, up to 90cm (3ft) high, bearing a spike of tubular flowers that are pale pink initially and flush darker as they are fertilized. These eye-catching plants always command attention in a border.

Morinas can be short-lived if not planted well. They like a soil that does not dry out but is also well-drained. They will grow in either sun or shade and are normally propagated from seed, though with care they can be divided.

Morina longifolia

NEPETA
Catmint

The nepetas are valuable for providing hazy blue flowers for the summer border and are excellent in a soft and romantic colour scheme. They are floppy plants that carry whorls of blue or purple flowers, which appear mainly during the summer. The leaves are nettle-like, either green or a soft grey-green, and many are aromatic. Some of the larger forms are suitable for positioning further back in the border, but the majority are best when used as edging plants.

They all like a light, well-drained soil and the majority require an open, sunny position. Cut back after first flowering to promote a second flush of blooms or to encourage a crop of fresh leaves. Propagation is by division or, for non-named forms, by seed.

N. cataria

This rather untidy plant, catnip, has off-white flowers. It is very aromatic and much loved by cats, who nibble at the shoots and roll in it, making it a very difficult plant to maintain.

N. x faassenii

This is the most frequently seen form of catmint and is used as an attractive edging. With its grey leaves and pale lavender flowers, the whole plant has a soft, hazy effect. It can reach up to approximately 60cm (2ft) if the lax stems are adequately supported. 'Snowflake' is a white-flowered form.

N. govaniana (next column)

This is the sole yellow-flowered nepeta in cultivation, although in the wild it also frequently occurs in blue. It is tall, with airy stems that can reach up to 90cm (3ft) or more. It is the only species that will grow in shade and prefers a moister soil to that favoured by the other nepetas.

Nepeta govaniana

N. nervosa

This lower-growing species has dense spikes of bright blue flowers and leaves that are noticeably veined. Although growing up to 60cm (2ft), it is frequently shorter, and is thus a good plant for the front of a border.

N. sibirica

This is one of the forms of nepeta in which the flowers play a positive role. The plant grows up to 90cm (3ft) and carries relatively large blue flowers above fresh-looking green foliage. The form 'Souvenir d'André Chaudron' is shorter than the species and flowers on into the autumn.

N. 'Six Hills Giant'

This is an old variety that produces 90cm (3ft) stems of grey aromatic foliage and clouds of lavender flowers. It is larger than other similar varieties. If necessary its informal habit can be controlled by staking.

OENOTHERA
Evening primrose

These plants produce flowers that last only a day, or in many cases a night, but they are well endowed with buds and so bloom over a very long period of the summer and into the autumn. They produce large, dish-shaped flowers in yellow, white or pink; these appear luminous in the evening light. This glow, together with their scent, attracts night-flying moths, which carry out the pollination. The plants range considerably in size: some are prostrate and obviously best positioned at the front of a border; while others grow to 1.2m (4ft) tall or more so should be placed at the back of the border.

Evening primroses grow best in free-draining soil that is not too rich, and they must have a sunny position. The stronger species are able to stand by themselves; but the others prefer to scramble through neighbouring plants or have some other form of support. They are mainly propagated from seed or division in the autumn or spring, or by cuttings in late spring.

Oenothera fruticosa 'Fyrverkeri'

O. fruticosa (above)

This is mainly grown in two of its better known forms. 'Fyrverkeri' ('Fireworks') has bright yellow flowers (red in bud) and purple-flushed foliage. *O. f.* var. *glauca* (also known as *O. tetragona*) has yellow flowers over purple foliage that is glaucous on its underside. Both grow to about 45cm (1½ft) tall.

O. macrocarpa

Known also as *O. missouriensis*, this sprawling plant grows to 30cm (1ft), with large yellow flowers that open in the evening.

O. pallida

This species flowers in the evening. It grows to about 50cm (20in) and has fragrant white flowers that age to pink.

Oenothera perennis

O. perennis (above)

Also known as *O. pumila*, this has yellow flowers that appear during the day. It grows to about 45cm (1½ft).

O. speciosa

This plant spreads by underground rhizomes and can become invasive. It grows to about 45cm (1½ft), and has narrow greyish leaves and, during the day, beautiful white flowers. There is also a pink form, 'Rosea'.

OMPHALODES
Navelwort

Navelworts are worth growing because they introduce a bright, cheerful note to the spring: their charming bright blue forget-me-not-like flowers are always a welcome reminder that summer is near. Given time, these low-growing plants will create a carpet of green foliage. In the border they are useful for growing between other plants, especially at the front of the bed but also further back, where they will be hidden later in the season when they are no longer flowering.

Navelworts will grow in any garden soil, including quite dry ones. They prefer to grow in partial shade, provided by other perennials as well as by trees and shrubs. Propagation is by division or by seed.

O. cappadocica

This is the taller of the two species that are commonly in cultivation. It grows to 25cm (10in) and carries its blue flowers above the leaves in loose spikes.

O. verna (below)

Sometimes known as blue-eyed Mary, this is smaller in all its parts than *O. cappadocica*. It also produces fewer flowers, but still makes an attractive ground cover. It prefers a somewhat moister soil.

Omphalodes verna

ORIGANUM
Marjoram

Quite a number of marjorams are in cultivation, the majority being grown in either herb or rock gardens. But several are eminently suitable for the open border. While these are decorative plants, they still retain the aromatic qualities of the kitchen herb. The pink, purple or white flowers, held in loose clusters above the leaves, are much loved by butterflies during the late summer and autumn.

Marjorams like a well-drained soil and a sunny site. They can self-seed prolifically, so it is best to deadhead them after they flower. Propagation can be by division or from seed.

O. laevigatum

This superb border plant has upright stems that can reach a height of 45cm (1½ft) or more. The stems carry airy displays of purple flowers. There are several good forms; 'Herrenhausen', with its dark purple flowers, is one of the best.

Origanum vulgare 'Aureum'

O. vulgare 'Aureum' (above)

This is the golden-leafed form of the common marjoram. It creates a rounded mound of pure gold foliage in the spring; some clones remain golden, but most begin to change to green later in the season. The white flowers are often removed, as this variety is grown principally for its leaves.

OSMUNDA
Royal fern

The genus *Osmunda* is known by gardeners mainly for the royal fern, *O. regalis* (next column). A very distinctive, clump-forming fern, this has large fronds with wide, light green leathery segments. In the centre of the plant the fronds are of a different type: rusty-brown in colour and looking as if shrivelled up. These latter are the spore-bearing fronds. The whole plant reaches a height of 1.8m (6ft) or more when happy with the conditions.

The royal fern must be grown in a moist soil, as found in a bog garden or near a water feature. If conditions are moist enough it can be grown in the open; otherwise grow it in light shade. Increase is from spore or by division.

Osmunda regalis

PAEONIA
Peony

Peonies are among the mainstays of spring and early-summer borders. Their bushy growth adds substance and their flowers, colour. The flowers of the species and of many cultivars are single and bowl-shaped, with a distinct central boss of stamens. Other cultivars have double flowers; these have the same shape, but the bowls are filled with layer upon layer of frilly petals – sometimes the same colour as the outer petals, sometimes contrasting. The foliage is frequently attractive, especially in spring when it first emerges and again later in the year when it takes on autumn tints.

Peonies are not especially tall plants – 90cm (3ft) at most – and are best sited in the front half of the border, perhaps accompanied by plants that flower later in the season.

Peonies like a deep, rich soil with plenty of added humus. Do not plant them too deeply: the crowns should be no deeper than 2.5cm (1in) below the surface. Once planted, they will continue for many years without needing to be dug out. Peonies grow best in sunny positions. Propagation is by division at planting time, although species can be grown from seed.

Single varieties (below)
'Coral Charm' has coral-pink flowers that are darker in bud. 'Emblem' has maroon-red flowers. 'Patriot' is characterized by deep maroon-crimson flowers. 'White Wings' has large pure white flowers. The nearly unpronounceable *P. mlokosewitschii* is one of the earliest to flower; it opens to a beautiful clear yellow. For a dark red *P. tenuifolia* takes some beating, especially as it has attractive finely cut foliage.

Paeonia 'White Wings'

Double varieties
P. officinalis 'Alba Plena' and 'Duchesse de Nemours' are both white doubles; the latter is particularly strongly scented. 'Festiva Maxima' is a white flower flecked with crimson. 'Inspecteur Lavergne' is completely crimson. 'Felix Crousse' is carmine. 'Monsieur Jules Elie' is a soft silvery rose-pink. 'Rosa Superba Plena' is bright pink; 'Rubra Plena' is crimson. 'Sarah Bernhardt', a beautiful pink, is one of the most popular of all peonies.

Imperial or Japanese varieties
These forms all have anemone-like flowers. 'Bowl of Beauty' has large flowers that are deep pink on the outer petals and creamy white on the inner ones. 'Evening World' is similar except that the outer petals are a pale pink.

PAPAVER
Poppy

Poppies have long been very popular in gardens. The flowers may be transient but there is a great delight in their brief blooming. The majority are in bright colours, and even the more subtle pinks and whites tend to draw attention to themselves. Most of the border varieties are derived from *P. orientale*, the oriental poppy. These have large tissue-paper flowers, often with black or purple blotches in the centre. The flowers are further enhanced by a large central boss of black stamens.

They can be grown in most garden soils, but do best in rich, well-drained ones and they should be planted in full sun. Many need support. Cut them down after flowering to encourage a fresh flush of the coarse, hairy, deeply cut leaves. Propagate by taking root cuttings in early winter.

Papaver orientale 'Perry's White'

White varieties (above)
'Black and White' has white petals, each with a black blotch at its base. 'Perry's White' has white petals and a purple-maroon blotch.

Pink varieties
'Mrs Perry' has pale salmon-pink petals with black blotches. 'Cedric Morris' is pale pink with a very large central black area. 'Turkish Delight' is a pale salmon-pink with no blotches.

Red varieties

'Beauty of Livermere' has huge, bright scarlet flowers with black blotches. 'Patty's Plum' ('Mrs Marrow's Plum') is a dark purple.

Papaver orientale 'Curlilocks'

Orange varieties (above)

'Allegro' is bright scarlet-orange with coarse, hairy foliage. 'Curlilocks' has fringed petals and is a bright orange-red with black spots. 'Doubloon' is an early-flowering orange double.

PATRINIA

Patrinia

This genus contains about 15 species, of which three are occasionally seen in cultivation. They are closely related to the valerians, with loose flat heads of small flowers. Instead of being white or pink, however, patrinia's flowers are usually yellow. An attractive addition to a rock garden, these plants spread through the garden by creeping, forming either a large clump or a small colony.

Patrinias are normally grown in moist woodland soils in light shade. They can be increased by division or from seed.

P. scabiosifolia

This is one of the taller forms, growing up to 90cm (3ft) high. Yellow flowers are carried during the summer. It prefers to be grown in a more open and sunnier position than *P. gibbosa* and *P. triloba*, the other two similar species, which are more frequently seen in cultivation.

PENNISETUM

Fountain grass

The members of this large genus of annual grasses and perennials come mainly from tropical areas, but a few are suitable for cultivation in more temperate climates. They are grown not so much for their leaves as for their soft flower heads, which are cylindrical and look like bottlebrushes. They range considerably in height from about 45cm (1½ft) to 1.5m (5ft), making some suitable for the front of a border, where they can be stroked as you pass, and some for further back.

They like a light, free-draining soil and, like most grasses, an open, sunny position. They should be cut back in winter or early spring before new growth begins. Propagation is either by division in spring or from seed.

P. alopecurioides

This is one of the taller species, growing to 90cm (3ft). The foliage is not particularly remarkable, but the flower heads are delightful: bluish with a white tuft at the top. Unfortunately, they flower only after a warm summer. The whole plant turns a buff colour for the winter. 'Hameln' is a particularly good early-flowering form.

P. setaceum

This species is a less hardy one than *P. alopecurioides*. Its flower heads range from pink to purple. In the form 'Rubrum' they are rose-pink, with foliage the same colour. Both fade to light brown for the winter.

PENSTEMON

Penstemon

Penstemons are extremely valuable plants for summer borders. They have bright, cheerful flowers that continue blooming for a long period; they look good in drifts or in small groups and are easy to propagate. *Penstemon* is a very big genus, with a large number of species in cultivation. Many of these are small and are grown in the rock garden, but equally many are tall enough to be grown in the open border, and are a valuable addition. The flowers are tubular and range in colour from blues through purples to reds, and include whites. Most are bicoloured with a contrasting, usually white, throat. The leaves are pointed, and range from light to dark green, but they always have a fresh appearance which offsets the flowers beautifully. Penstemons range in height from 60cm (2ft) to 90cm (3ft).

They will grow in most garden soils but prefer a free-draining one. It is possible to grow them in very light shade, but most prefer a warm, sunny position. Propagation is easily achieved by taking cuttings, although with care some plants can also be divided. Not all penstemons are completely hardy, and it is good insurance to overwinter a few cuttings.

Penstemon 'White Bedder'

White varieties (above)

'White Bedder' is one of the few penstemons that appears as a single colour. As the name suggests, it is white, but it has dark anthers that give it a slightly spotted look.

Pink varieties (below)
'Beech Park' (also known as 'Barbara Barker') has large flowers that are cream and white, flushed with pink at the mouth. 'Hidcote Pink' has soft pink flowers, paling towards the throat, which is veined with red streaks. 'Mother of Pearl' has smaller flowers that are pearly pink and white.

Penstemon 'Hidcote Pink'

Red varieties
'Andenken an Friedrich Hahn' (also known as 'Garnet') has purple-scarlet flowers. 'Chester Scarlet' has scarlet flowers. 'Ruby' ('Schoenholzeri') has small flowers of bright scarlet.

Purple and lilac varities
'Alice Hindley' has large flowers in soft lilac, fading inside the tube. 'Sour Grapes' has small flowers with deep violet petals, paling in the throat. 'Stapleford Gem' is similar to 'Sour Grapes' but paler.

Species
Many of the species are also suitable for cultivation. *P. barbatus* has small red flowers with yellow beards and is grown in a number of cultivars, including the less common 'Elfin Pink', which has small pink flowers. *P. digitalis* is named for its resemblance to the foxglove. In the form 'Husker's Red' the foliage is

tinged dark purple-red and the flowers are very pale pink. *P. heterophyllus* is a shrubby plant with flowers that vary from purple to bright blue. *P. pinifolius* is a low-growing form that is suitable only for the front of the border or a rock garden. It has narrow needle-like leaves and small narrow flowers that are orange in colour. There is also a yellow form, 'Mersea Yellow', a very unusual colour for penstemons.

PEROVSKIA
Russian sage
This is a small genus of salvia-like plants which are, strictly speaking, shrubs or subshrubs. The only species in general cultivation is *P. atriplicifolia*. This is a woody sub-shrub that is usually treated as a herbaceous plant and cut back each winter. It has delightful feathery foliage which is covered in soft, white hairs, giving the plant a grey, ghostly appearance. The pale blue flowers, which appear from late summer onwards, are carried in whorls on the spreading branches, adding to the misty effect. The plant grows up to 1.5m (5ft) in height. 'Blue Spire' (below) has particularly finely cut foliage.

This is a plant that likes a well-drained soil and a warm, sunny position. In spite of the height that it reaches, no staking is required. Propagation can be achieved by taking basal cuttings in the spring.

Perovskia atriplicifolia 'Blue Spire'

PERSICARIA
Knotweed
To many gardeners this genus, which is made up of at least 150 widely varying species, may be more familiar as *Polygonum*, and its plants may still be found listed as such in most nurseries. It contains many excellent plants for the perennial garden, although some can spread rather rapidly and are more suited to growing in the wild part of your garden.

They range in height from low carpets, 30cm (1ft) high, to tall colonies, 1.8m (6ft) or more. The flowers, mainly held in tight, cylinder-like spikes or balls, come in a variety of shades of pink. In most cases the leaves make a dense ground cover.

Knotweeds will grow in most garden soils but do best in those that are slightly moist. They do well when grown in either sun or shade. Plant at any time between autumn and spring. Since most knotweeds spread, the easiest method of propagation is by division.

Persicaria amplexicaulis

P. amplexicaulis (above)
This is one of the best border forms. It forms a dense clump of dock-like foliage, from which rise wiry stems carrying narrow heads of pink or red flowers. It grows up to 1.2m (4ft). It does spread, but not at the alarming rate of some of its relations. 'Firetail' has large crimson flower spikes.

P. bistorta

This species can be grown in the ordinary border but comes into its own in a bog garden or beside a water feature. It grows to 75cm (2½ft). The bright pink flowers are well set off by the fresh green of the large leaves. It soon forms large colonies, 90cm (3ft) or more across. The form 'Superba' has bigger flowers.

P. campanulata

This plant spreads to 60cm (2ft) or more and can be very invasive; it carries a constant display of tiny bells. The foliage, too, is decorative, with distinct veins. Plant in a damp position. It grows to 1.2m (4ft).

P. virginiana

This species is often incorrectly listed as *Tovara*, usually under the form 'Painter's Palette'. It is grown mainly for its decorative foliage, which is a mixture of cream and brown-maroon as well as green. It rarely produces flowers. It reaches a height of approximately 60cm (2ft).

PHALARIS
Ribbon grass

Although there are 15 species in this genus, only one is grown: *P. arundinacea*, usually in the form 'Picta' (next column). Known as ribbon grass or gardener's garters, it is a very attractive grass with fresh-looking leaves that are green, striped with white; when young the shoots are pink. The widish blades give rise to the common name of this grass. It grows up to 90cm (3ft). Unfortunately, it is an extremely invasive species, particularly in rich, damp soil, and should be planted where it can spread at will, or in a position where it can be contained in some way.

This grass will grow in any garden soil but should be given a sunny position. Planting should be carried out in spring. Propagation is by division.

Phalaris arundinacea 'Picta'

PHLOX
Phlox

This genus provides gardens with popular plants that flower either in the spring or later in the year. Some of them are ground-hugging, some reach 1.5m (5ft), while others are in between. Some like to be in the open and others in shade. This great diversity of habits and requirements, coupled with the wide range of colours, means that there are at least some phloxes for every garden. The flowers are tubular, flaring out into a flat disc of five petals. The colours are predominantly white, blue, purple, pink and red.

Phlox like a humus-rich soil that never becomes too dry. Although they vary in their requirement of shade, border phlox mainly prefer sunshine. Propagation is best done by root cuttings, but phlox can also be grown from basal cuttings or divisions.

P. carolina

This species reaches 1.2m (4ft), flowers in early summer, and will grow well in light shade. The most popular variety is 'Miss Lingard', which has striking pure white flowers.

P. divaricata

This is a very useful species for a shady border. It grows to only 30cm (1ft) and forms a tight carpet of foliage from which the flowering stems rise in spring. The flowers are usually pale blue. 'Dirigo Ice' has light blue flowers, while in 'Fuller's White' they are so pale as to be almost white.

P. maculata (below)

This is like *P. carolina* except more slender and with the flowers held more in a spike than a cone. The plants are shorter, growing to only 60cm–1.2m (2–4ft) tall, and they flower earlier. 'Alpha' has mauve-lilac flowers and darker centres. 'Omega' is white with pink eyes; and 'Rosalinde' has deep pink flowers.

Phlox maculata

P. paniculata (next column)

This species provides most of the border phlox, which reach 1.2–1.5m (4–5ft) and have pyramidal flower heads. They require a sunny spot. In exposed areas the taller varieties need staking. White forms include 'Blue Ice', (pale blue ageing to white), 'Fujiyama', with large heads of pure white, and the similar, but later-flowering 'White Admiral'. Pink forms include 'Bright Eyes', (pale pink with a dark eye), 'Dodo Hanbury Forbes', with large heads of medium pink, and 'Eva Callum', which is pink with a dark centre. Lilac forms include 'Amethyst' (violet-blue), 'Blue Boy' (lilac-blue) and 'Franz Schubert' (lilac, with a darker centre). Orange-tinted forms include 'Brigadier' (salmon), 'Orange Perfection' (near-orange) and 'Prince of Orange' (deep salmon). Red forms include 'Aida' (violet-red) and 'Starfire' (cherry-red). Variegated forms include 'Harlequin', with red-purple flowers and cream marginal variegations, and 'Norah Leigh', with pink flowers, darker in the centre, and dominating cream variegations on the leaves.

Phlox paniculata 'Eva Cullum'

PHYGELIUS
Cape figwort

Two shrubby species from South Africa occupy this genus. From the summer onwards they produce tubular flowers in red or yellow. In optimum conditions and grown against a wall they can reach 6m (20ft) or more, but in the border they are normally confined to 1.2m (4ft) or below. They are attractive plants that flower over a long period.

Cape figworts will grow in any garden soil, although they do best in those that are moisture-retentive which allow excess water to drain away. They can be increased from cuttings or by careful division.

P. aequalis

This plant produces straight tubular flowers that open into a flared mouth. The species is dusky pink but another version, 'Yellow Trumpet', which has attractive creamy yellow flowers, is the form that is most commonly grown in the garden.

P. capensis

In this species the flowers curve back towards the stems and the tips of the tubes are reflexed. The flowers are orange-red.

Phygelius × rectus 'African Queen'

P. × rectus (above)

This is the name given to the hybrids between the two species. There are now a number of these, and they have become very popular. 'African Queen' is pale red with orange-red tips. 'Moonraker' is similar in colour to 'Yellow Trumpet' but the flowers are carried all round the stem. 'Pink Elf' has pale pink tubes with crimson tips and a yellow throat.

PHYSALIS
Chinese lantern

Physalis is a large genus, but only one species, *P. alkekengi*, is found in general cultivation. This is grown mainly for its seedheads, which look like inflated orange balloons. The white flowers that precede them are insignificant, but the foliage is a fresh green which contrasts well with the orange colouring. A sprawling plant, 45cm (1½ft) tall, this spreads to form a large colony. It is not a plant to be placed in a highly visible position.

Chinese lanterns grow in any garden soil and can be placed in either sun or shade. Planting can take place at any time between autumn and spring, and propagation is best achieved either by division or from seed.

PHYSOSTEGIA
Obedient plant

The odd name of this plant is derived from the fact that, if the individual flowers are pushed to one side, they will remain there and not spring back. The pink, tubular flowers are borne in spikes towards the end of summer on plants up to 1.5m (5ft) tall, which stand very erect. Though not a spectacular plant, it will fill a space in the border attractively enough and spread to form large clumps.

Obedient plants grow in any good garden soil but do best in those enriched with humus. Although they prefer a sunny position, they can be grown in light shade. They can be increased by division or from seed.

Physostegia virginiana 'Bouquet Rose'

P. virginiana (above)

This is the main species to be grown in gardens. The flowers range from pale to rose-pink. There is a particularly beautiful white form, 'Alba'. 'Bouquet Rose' ('Rose Bouquet') is a larger form with rose-pink flowers. The form 'Variegata' has pink flowers and cream-variegated foliage.

PHYTOLACCA
Pokeweed

This genus consists of bold, somewhat invasive plants better relegated to the wild garden than kept in the formal border, where they may become a nuisance. They are tall plants, up to 2.5m (8ft) when grown in suitable conditions, and have candle-like spikes of white or pink flowers that emerge from the large green foliage. They are attractive, but must be used with care, as all parts are poisonous. The species most commonly grown is *P. americana*, (below) which has white flowers. The more attractive *P. polyandra* (*P. clavigera*) has pink flowers.

They will grow in any garden soil and in either sun or light shade. Propagation is either by division or by seed. Self-sown seedlings are usually available.

Phytolacca americana

PLATYCODON
Balloon flower

This fascinating plant will cause much comment. The aspect that generates the attention is the buds: these are balloon-shaped, and inflate until they finally burst open to form beautiful cup-shaped flowers in a deep silky blue. These are carried at the top of the upright stems, which grow to 75cm (2½ft). As seen from the open flowers, these plants are closely related to the campanulas. The single species in the genus, *P. grandiflorus* (next column), is beautiful in itself, but there are several varieties. *P. g.* var. *albus* has, as its name suggests, white flowers, while *P. g.* var. *mariesii* has larger blue flowers.

Balloon flowers will grow in a rich, well-drained soil, and will tolerate a little shade, though they do best in full sun. The new growth emerges in late spring, so take care not to dig the plant up accidentally. Slugs like the new growth. Propagation is from seed, cuttings or by careful division.

Platycodon grandiflorus

PLEIOBLASTUS
Bush bamboo

This genus has recently been separated from *Arundinaria*, and its species are still sometimes listed in nurseries under that name. It has about 20 species, of which a surprisingly large number are in cultivation. Only two, however, are grown to any extent: *P. variegatus* and the more popular *P. auricomus* (*P. viridistriatus*). Both are variegated, the former with white stripes and the latter with deep gold ones, and both are considered the best variegated bamboos of their colour. Both run slightly, forming large clumps, but they are not generally invasive.

Plant them in any garden soil, but for the best results grow them in moisture-retentive conditions. They thrive in full sun, but will grow in shade; here, however, the golden form will lose its rich colour. Propagation is by division in the spring.

POLEMONIUM
Jacob's ladder

These delightful old-fashioned plants have been grown in gardens for generations. The curious name comes from the shape of the leaves, which are made up of a series of parallel leaflets, like the rungs of a ladder. The flowers are shallow funnels, mainly in various blues, though white forms are available. Jacob's ladders range in height from those which form loose plants only 30cm (1ft) or so tall to those that stand erect, reaching 90cm (3ft) or more. They are mainly spring- and early-summer-flowering, and it is a good idea to grow later-flowering plants next to them to cover their drabness during the rest of the season.

Jacob's ladders will grow in any good garden soil, but do best where the conditions are moisture-retentive. They like a sunny position, but will grow in light shade; in hot areas shade is preferred. Propagation is from seed or by division.

Blue forms

Blue is the main colour of many of the species. *P. caeruleum* is the tallest, at 90cm (3ft) or more, and has pale blue flowers. *P. foliosissimum* is very similar but tends to have darker flowers. *P. reptans* is smaller, growing to only 60cm (2ft), and is a sprawling plant with lavender flowers.

White forms

Both the taller blue species, *P. caeruleum* and *P. foliosissimum*, have white forms, known respectively as *P. c.* var. *album* and *P. f.* var. *alpinum* ('Album').

Lilac forms (next column)

As well as blue forms, several species and cultivars produce delicate lilac-pink shades. *P. c.* 'Hopleys' is an upright form while *P.* 'Lambrook Mauve', a hybrid from *P. reptans*, is a delightful low-growing sprawler.

Polemonium 'Lambrook Mauve'

POLYGONATUM
Solomon's seal

The Solomon's seals are among the most delightful of plants. They have a fresh, cool quality about them that always creates a tranquil mood, and are ideal for a shady position, especially in a dappled woodland setting. The plants have arching stems, from which opposite pairs of leaves stand out horizontally and from below which hang the white flowers. These are narrow bells, pulled in slightly at the waist and tipped in green.

The plants run underground and, once settled, can soon make large colonies. They are not invasive, however, as they can be easily controlled. There are about 30 popular species from which to choose, although the genus is more numerous than this.

Solomon's seals are essentially woodland plants, and like a moist humus-rich soil and a cool root run. Sawfly caterpillars can reduce the foliage to tatters by late summer, and need to be controlled. Propagation is easily achieved by division of the running rootstock.

P. biflorum

This is a smaller version of the common Solomon's seal. It grows to 90cm (3ft), but is often much shorter. As its botanical name implies, the flowers are carried in pairs.

P. × hybridum (below)

Also known as *P. multiflorum*, this is the commonest species of Solomon's seal. It is taller than *P. biflorum*, and the flowers are carried in clusters of between two and five. There is a creamy white variegated form, 'Striatum'. Another variegated form is *P. odoratum* 'Variegatum', with fragrant flowers and more delicate variegations than has 'Striatum'.

Polygonatum × *hybridum* 'Striatum'

POLYSTICHUM
Shield fern

This very large genus of ferns provides some extremely garden-worthy plants. The fronds are typically fern-like, often evergreen and with an appealing glossy, leathery appearance.

They should be grown in a moist, acid to neutral soil – one with plenty of humus or leaf mould would be ideal. They will grow in anything from light to deep shade. Propagation is by division in spring or from spores in autumn.

P. aculeatum

Known as the hard shield fern, this plant is delicately divided and light green when it first unfurls, darkening to a deep green. It is evergreen and grows to 90cm (3ft).

P. polyblepharum

The evergreen Japanese holly fern is a shorter plant than *P. aculeatum*, but no

less decorative, with delicately divided fronds of shiny dark green.

Polystichum setiferum

P. setiferum (above)

The evergreen soft shield fern is one of the tallest species, growing up to 1.2m (4ft) in optimal conditions. It is also one of the most elegant of all ferns, with finely divided fronds of a soft green. It tolerates quite dry soil. There are several varieties, of which 'Divisilobum' is among the most beautiful.

POTENTILLA
Potentilla

This genus sometimes causes confusion, as it provides the gardener with both shrubs and hardy perennials. The flower shape on both is the same – five petals arranged in a flat dish – but the underlying structure is obviously woody in the shrubs while the perennials are soft and die back each year. The wide range of colours, based on red and yellow, makes these plants a cheerful addition to any border. Some are double or semi-double, but all tend to be scrambling plants, never happier than when growing up through another plant – a low bush perhaps.

Potentillas will grow in any garden soil although they prefer those that are well-drained. Most prefer a sunny position. Propagation is by division or, in the case of the species, by seed.

Varieties (below)

'Flamenco' has bright scarlet flowers. 'Gibson's Scarlet' is a scarlet so bright it is difficult to look at. 'Monsieur Rouillard', a double, has deep red flowers touched with yellow. 'William Rollison' is a semi-double in orange splashed with yellow. 'Miss Willmott', a form of *P. nepalensis*, has flowers of cherry-pink, darker in the centre. 'Roxana', another variety of the same species, has deep pink flowers with a dark centre.

Potentilla 'Gibson's Scarlet'

Species and other forms

P. atrosanguinea, a parent of many of the hybrids, has red flowers. *P. a.* var. *argyrophylla* has yellow flowers, and leaves with silvery white hairs. *P. recta* has yellow flowers, while its form 'Warrenii' has flowers of the same colour but brighter. *P.* × *tonguei* is one of the few that will grow in light shade. Its flowers are apricot-coloured with a red centre.

PRIMULA

Primula

This is a large genus mainly consisting of low-growing plants. The majority belong in the alpine garden, but a few are strong enough to be grown among perennials. Many, such as the primroses, have been grown in gardens for centuries, and few spring gardens would be without them.

The flowers offer the entire range of garden colours, so they can be fitted into any colour scheme. In formal borders they make good plants for the front; the early-flowering ones can either be placed among plants that will cover them later in the year or moved to reserve beds. A more permanent position can often be found in shady borders and woodland gardens.

Primulas like a soil that does not dry out and with extra humus to help keep it moist and enrich it. Most prefer a shady position, but will tolerate full sun in cooler areas as long as the ground is moist. Propagation is by seed, sown as soon after ripening as possible, and by division.

P. denticulata (below)

These are the drumstick primulas, so-called because of their spherical heads, made up of many flowers and held on the top of a tall stem. They are typically mauve, but there are many variations, including 'Alba' (white) and 'Rubinball' (shades of red).

Primula denticulata

P. japonica

The Japanese primula is one of the candelabra varieties. These are tall, growing to 60cm (2ft), with whorls of flowers at intervals up the long stems, mainly in white or red. Some of the better forms are named. As its name indicates, 'Miller's Crimson' is red.

P. rosea (below)

This delightful primrose-type species has rose-pink flowers held on short stems above veined leaves. 'Micia Visser de Geer' ('Delight') has carmine flowers.

Primula rosea

P. vialii

In flower this extraordinary primula is often mistaken for an orchid. It has a tight, rocket-shaped head of mauve flowers, tipped with red buds. Unlike most primulas, it flowers in summer. It grows to approximately 60cm (2ft) in good conditions.

P. vulgaris

This is the beautiful English primrose, the yellow-flowered species usually considered the harbinger of spring. Many other coloured forms have been derived from it, including a whole series of attractive double-flowered forms. 'Easter Bonnet' has lilac flowers, 'Miss Indigo' has indigo petals delicately rimmed with silver, and 'Alba Plena' is pure white. Many single forms are just as attractive, including 'Guinevere' ('Garryard Guinevere'), a unique old-fashioned form with pale pink petals and a yellow centre, set against purple foliage. 'Cowichan Series' is a seed strain which produces some very richly coloured plants, many of which flower later than other varieties of primula.

PRUNELLA
Self-heal

This is an attractive ground-cover plant for the front of the border. It forms a dense mat of evergreen leaves, from which rise stubby spikes of purple flowers. The flowers are hooded and lipped, resembling those of dead nettles. Self-heals are mainly blue or purple in colour, although white forms are occasionally seen.

They grow in any garden soil, including dry ones; they prefer a sunny position but will also grow in shade. They can self-sow prodigiously, so deadhead after flowering. Propagation is by division.

P. grandiflora (below)

This is the main species in cultivation. It has large heads of purple-violet flowers. There is a series of varieties suffixed with the name 'Loveliness'. 'Loveliness' itself has lilac flowers, while 'Pink Loveliness', 'Purple Loveliness' and 'White Loveliness' are all named for their colours.

Prunella grandiflora

PULMONARIA
Lungwort

The common name of this plant is derived from the resemblance of the spotted leaves to a diseased lung. However, it is these spots which make this such a valuable foliage plant. Most species have rough, spear-shaped green leaves and some have silver spots that merge to make virtually the whole leaf silver. Once the plants have finished flowering in spring they can be sheared over and new foliage will appear, making a fresh-looking plant for the rest of the year. The tubular flowers are not very big but provide a carpet of colour in late winter and spring. They mainly occur in different shades of blue and pink, but there are a few white forms.

Pulmonarias do best in moist soils, with plenty of humus. They prefer a shady position. Propagate by division after flowering.

Pulmonaria rubra 'David Ward'

Foliage varieties (above)

Although the following are mainly grown for their foliage effects, the flowers have considerable attraction. The spotted-leafed *P. saccharata* produces several good foliage forms. In 'Argentea' the spots have merged to produce a silver leaf; the flowers are pink and blue. *P. rubra* 'David Ward' has pale green leaves, edged with cream.

Red-flowered varieties

True red forms have yet to be developed, but some are deep pink-red. One of the reddest is *P. rubra* 'Redstart', which has plain green leaves.

Blue-flowered varieties

Blue varieties range from very bright to pale. Some of the brightest come from *P. angustifolia*, and of these *P. a.* subsp. *azurea* is among the best. 'Blue Ensign' is another good form. 'Lewis Palmer' ('Highdown') displays its bright blue flowers on long stems.

White-flowered varieties

Most blue forms produce occasional white seedlings, but there is an excellent named variety, *P. officinalis* 'Sissinghurst White'. This pulmonaria has long, elliptical leaves that are spotted with a paler colour.

PULSATILLA
Pasque flower

This genus is often listed as *Anemone pulsatilla*. Pasque flowers make excellent plants for the front of a border. Their attraction lies not only in their beautiful cup-shaped flowers but in their finely cut foliage and their superb display of silky seedheads. They flower in the spring, with the seedheads lasting well into summer. The most commonly seen species is *P. vulgaris* (below). Typically this has mauve flowers, but a wide range of purples, reds and whites is available, possibly introduced from other species. These plants are clump-forming and up to 30cm (1ft) tall.

Pulsatillas grow in most free-draining soils but need a sunny position. Increase stock by sowing the seed as soon as it has ripened. Often pulsatillas self-sow.

Pulsatilla vulgaris

RANUNCULUS
Buttercup

A few species of this very large genus are grown in the perennial border and rather more in the rock garden. Although many have yellow flowers, some species carry white ones. Many of the yellow forms that are derived from native plants tend to be invasive, and so should be treated with care. Some of the safer ones, however, can be used to brighten up the border, while the more invasive ones can be relegated to the wild garden. The plant grows to 60cm (2ft) high.

Buttercups will grow in most garden soils. They prefer a sunny position but many will also grow in light shade. Increase can be by division or from seed.

Ranunculus aconitifolius 'Flore Pleno'

R. aconitifolius (above)

This is a bushy plant that in early summer produces white flowers carried on airy branches. It is best known in its button-flowered double form, 'Flore Pleno'. It is commonly known as fair maids of Kent.

RHAZYA
Rhazya

This small genus is sometimes included in *Amsonia* and listed as such in nurseries. It is represented in cultivation by *R. orientalis* (next column). In summer this produces heads of starry soft-blue flowers held on stiff, wiry stems. These are about 45cm (1½ft) tall and are clothed in narrow, grey-green leaves. The plants slowly spread to form a small colony.

Rhazyas will grow in any good garden soil, in either full sun or light shade. Propagation is best achieved by division, although plants can be grown from seed if obtainable.

Rhazya orientalis

RHEUM
Rhubarb

Rhubarb is often thought of only in culinary terms, but there are a large number of ornamental species can be grown in the perennial garden. They are mainly distinguished by their impressive foliage rather than by their flowers, although these can also be noteworthy. The leaves are large and umbrella-like. The flowers emerge from them on gigantic spikes, which can look as attractive in seed as in flower.

Rhubarbs need to have a deep, rich soil with plenty of well-rotted organic material added. They will grow in either full sun or light shade. Propagation can be either by division or from seed.

R. 'Ace of Hearts'

Unlike many of its big relations, this large-leafed form can be grown in a small garden as it reaches only 90cm (3ft) or so. The leaves are roughly heart-shaped; the flowers are pink.

R. alexandrae

This strange plant always becomes a conversation piece. The flowers are covered with large pale yellow bracts, like handkerchiefs, which protect them from the constant rain of the plant's native habitat in western China, Tibet and the Himalayas. In cultivation the plant needs a similarly moist atmosphere to survive. This species grows to a height of 1.2m (4ft).

R. palmatum (below)

This is the most commonly seen ornamental rhubarb, particularly in its form 'Atrosanguineum'. The large leaves are attractively lobed and toothed and, when young, are deep red. The tall flower spikes are red. These plants grow to a height of as much as 1.8m (6ft) when the conditions are ideal.

Rheum palmatum 'Atrosanguineum'

RODGERSIA
Rodgersia

All six species of this small genus are in cultivation. They are renowned for their handsome foliage and attractive flowers. Large clumps of plants are formed when conditions are right, creating attention-drawing features in borders or woodland gardens. The flowers are fluffy and held in loose heads, much in the manner of the astilbes; they appear in the summer and are held well above the foliage. The leaves are large, noticeably veined and often slightly shiny, the colour ranging from bronze to dark green. The foliage is very effective over the whole growing season, although some of the bronze forms slowly change to green.

Rodgersias must have a moist soil, preferably one enriched with plenty of humus. They can be planted in either a position of sun or shade. Propagation is carried out by division.

R. aesculifolia

This species has huge, very distinctive horse-chestnut-like leaves, which are very large and flushed with bronze. The flowers are cream. The plant grows to a height of approximately 1.5m (5ft).

R. pinnata

In this species the leaves are pinnate, made up of pairs of leaflets on opposite sides of the stem. In the species they are green but in 'Superbum' they are tinged with bronze; the flowers are pink. The plant grows to approximately 1.2m (4ft) in height.

Rodgersia podophylla

R. podophylla (above)

This species, like *R. aesculifolia*, has horse-chestnut-like leaves, but the margins of the leaflets are distinctly jagged and the flowers are cream. The plant grows to 1.2m (4ft).

RUDBECKIA
Coneflower

The attractive daisies in this genus flower in late summer and autumn. They all tend to have prominent central cones (hence the name) of black, brown or green and droopy yellow ray petals. The plants spread, generally non-invasively, to form large colourful groups. Some reach 60cm (2ft), while others grow to 2.5m (8ft).

Coneflowers will grow in any garden soil as long as it is not too dry, but they do need to be placed in a sunny position. Propagation is by division, although some seed strains are available.

Rudbeckia fulgida 'Goldsturm'

R. fulgida (above)

One of the main coneflower species, this plant has produced some excellent varieties. It has golden yellow flowers each with a very dark central cone – hence its common name, black-eyed Susan. *R. f.* var. *deamii* is a floriferous variety which is more drought-resistant than most. 'Goldsturm', one of the most popular varieties, has large flowers of a rich gold colour. All these forms grow to about 60cm (2ft).

R. 'Goldquelle'

This is a good plant for the rear of the border as it grows to about 1.8m (6ft). It has large, bright yellow double flowers from late summer onwards.

R. hirta

This annual or short-lived perennial species has produced a number of seed strains. 'Mixed Single Hybrids' produces large flowers in a variety of yellows and browns on plants of different heights.

SALVIA
Sage

Salvias are an extremely varied genus of plants for the flower garden, totalling some 700 species worldwide. They produce a range of different types of plants, varying from those treated as annuals to perennials and shrubs. Their flowers are mainly in shades of blue, but some of the more tender species produce a range of reds and reddish purples. Most have a long flowering season and are much loved by bees and butterflies. The foliage is often aromatic when crushed.

Sage needs a well-drained soil. A sunny position is essential. Slugs can severely damage the emerging shoots in spring. Planting should be carried out in either autumn or spring. Propagate either from cuttings or, in the case of the species, by sowing seed.

Salvia × superba 'Mainacht'

Summer-flowering varieties (above)

A group of salvias – *S. × superba*, *S. × sylvestris* and *S. nemorosa* – are all so similar that they are constantly being confused, with their cultivars frequently being attributed to the wrong species. They produce rounded bushes up to 90cm (3ft) tall, with dense spikes of blue or purple-blue flowers. 'Blauköningen' ('Blue Queen'), 'Mainacht' ('Maynight'), 'Rose Queen', 'Lubecca' and 'Ostfriesland' ('East Friesland') are all well worth growing. *S. verticillata* 'Purple Rain' is a distinctive plant, with arching stems on which purple flowers are carried in pronounced whorls. *S. pratensis* 'Haematodes' is short-lived and has airy branches of pale blue flowers.

Salvia guaranitica

Autumn-flowering varieties (above)
S. guaranitica is 1.5m (5ft) tall and carries deep blue flowers. An even taller plant, frequently requiring support, is *S. uliginosa*, which has pale blue flowers.

Less hardy varieties
Many sages are hardy but some succumb to a hard winter, and can be grown as perennials only in warmer districts. Elsewhere they should be overwintered under glass as cuttings or young plants. *S. patens* is one of the main examples. It has large blue flowers and comes in a range of varieties. 'Cambridge' is a pale blue and 'Chilcombe' a lilac-blue. *S. farinacea* is a shrubbier plant with a long flowering season; its most popular form, 'Victoria', has blue flowers. 'Porcelain' has white flowers.

SANGUISORBA
Burnet

The sanguisorbas, which include the species that used to belong to *Poterium*, are a very distinct group of plants. They are characterized by tall, swaying stems that in summer carry soft, bottlebrush-like flowers in pink, red or white. The mainly fresh green leaves are pinnate and, in some species, they have a distinct smell of cucumber when crushed. Even when out of flower these plants are attractive.

They will grow in any good garden soil but do best in moist ones. Most can be grown in either full sun or light shade. Some species need deadheading after flowering to prevent excessive self-sowing. Propagation can be successfully achieved by division or from seed.

S. 'Magnifica Alba'

There are a number of white sanguisorbas, of which this is a popular variety. Its origins are in doubt, but this does not prevent it from being a good choice of plant to grow in the garden. It grows to approximately 75cm (2½ft).

Sanguisorba obtusa

S. obtusa (above)

This species has beautiful grey-green foliage and thick bottlebrushes of pink flowers. It grows to 1.8m (6ft). It is often confused with a similar green-leafed species, *S. hakusanensis*.

SAPONARIA
Soapwort

This large genus is mainly of use to the rock gardener. There is, however, one species, *S. officinalis*, that makes a colourful if somewhat invasive plant for the open border and wild garden. This is known as soapwort, as the leaves were once used as a soap substitute; it also has the colourful name bouncing Bett. It is a 90cm (3ft) plant with glaucous stems and leaves and bears 2.5cm (1in) flower heads of clear pink. There are a number of varieties. 'Alba Plena' has double white flowers. 'Dazzler' has variegated leaves and pink flowers. 'Rosea Plena' is a pale double, while 'Rubra Plena' (below) is a darker double.

Soapworts will grow in any garden soil, often rather too vigorously: they may need to be contained. Either sun or light shade is suitable. Propagation is by cuttings or by division, and the species can be grown from seed.

Saponaria officinalis 'Rubra Plena'

SASA
Sasa

Bamboos add not only a touch of exotic foliage to a garden but also sound, as they are constantly rustling in the slightest breeze. They are not as popular as they once were, but are now more widely available. *Sasa* is a large genus with several species in cultivation. One of the most attractive is *S. veitchii* (next column). This has oval leaves that are dark green with a creamy white margin. It grows to about 1.5m (5ft). Its great drawback is that it is extremely invasive. For this reason, *Sasa* is best planted in a wild garden, or else contained in some manner.

Plant out in any garden soil. It is a shade-lover. Propagate by division.

Sasa veitchii

SAXIFRAGA
Saxifrage

Only a few saxifrages are large enough to be suitable for the open garden. The larger forms have graceful, arching flower stems carrying a myriad of tiny pink or white blooms in an airy spray. Their foliage usually forms close mats of ground cover, suitable for clothing the ground under shrubs or trees.

The larger saxifrages like a soil that does not dry out, but also one that does not retain excessive moisture; they do not like their soil too rich. Partial shade is best. Most naturally increase by producing runners in the manner of strawberries, and so are easy to propagate.

S. fortunei

This flowers very late, its white, dancing blooms not appearing until the autumn. Its shiny rounded leaves make an attractive ground cover. In the form 'Wada' the leaves and stems are a wonderful glowing red.

S. × geum

This is another ground-covering plant. It has rosettes of spoon-shaped leaves. In mid-summer it has sprays of tiny, white flowers with red and yellow spots all over them.

S. × urbium (below)

This is the popular flower London pride. When grown in ideal conditions it spreads widely, forming extensive carpets of rosettes with spoon-shaped leaves. It is a magnificent sight when in bloom, with its long-stemmed, tiny white flowers, rose-pink in the centre. The flowers appear in early summer.

Saxifraga × urbium

SCABIOSA
Scabious

Scabious produce long wiry stems, each carrying a pastel-coloured pincushion-shaped flower. There are species and varieties in pale blue, pale yellow, pale pink and white. In some varieties these can be quite large, up to 7.5cm (3in) or more, and the flowers are carried above delicately divided grey-green foliage. Altogether, these are plants for romantic-looking borders with soft colour schemes.

Scabious need a well-drained soil, on the alkaline side of neutral, and a sunny place in the border. Propagation is from division, and the species can also be grown from seed.

Blue varieties (below)

The most popular colour is light blue, and several varieties are available. 'Butterfly Blue' has lavender-blue coloured flowers, while *S. caucasica* has produced several good forms – including 'Clive Greaves', 'Blauseigel' and 'Fama' – all of which are similar in colour.

Scabiosa caucasica 'Clive Greaves'

White varieties

In keeping with the romantic image, there are no pure whites, but there are several subtle creamy whites. Again, *S. caucasica* has produced some fine forms, like 'Alba' and 'Miss Willmott'.

SCROPHULARIA
Figwort

Figworts are plants suitable only for the wild garden. With one exception they have little to offer the formal garden. That exception is the variegated form of *S. auriculata* 'Variegata' (next page). It is for this cream variegation that the plants are grown. The flowers look like miniature reddish brown frogs and, as they are not very distinguished, many gardeners cut off the flower stems, particularly as they have a tendency to self-seed everywhere and produce ordinary green-leafed plants. They grow to 90cm (3ft) tall.

These figworts appreciate a moist soil and will grow in either full sun or light shade. They must be propagated from cuttings. Plants that have been raised from seed and self-sown seedlings always produce plants with plain green leaves.

Scrophularia auriculata 'Variegata'

SEDUM
Stonecrop

Stonecrops are one of the few succulent plants grown as perennials. The genus is very large, with over 600 species, of which most garden forms are too small for border use. However, a few are suitable for ground cover and colour at the front of a border and other, taller varieties can be grown further back. The stonecrops all have clustered heads of starry flowers. The colour of the taller ones is mainly shades of pink, but yellow and white also occur, and they are much loved by bees. The fleshy leaves can also be very attractive and there are some very useful purple-foliaged stonecrops.

Stonecrops will grow in any garden soil, including dry, poor ones. Although they can be grown in light shade they always look best in sun. Propagation can be by division or cuttings. Seed can be used if obtainable.

White-flowered varieties

White is not a common colour among the taller varieties, but there are two that make good plants. 'Iceberg' and 'Star Dust' are forms of *S. spectabile*, the latter variety having a touch of pink in it.

Sedum 'Herbstfreude'

Pink-flowered forms (above)

There are many different pinks, ranging from very pale to dark rose-pink. 'Herbstfreude' ('Autumn Joy') is one of the best known. It has large flat heads of medium pink flowers that turn to copper as they age. *S. spectabile* 'Brilliant' has deeper pink flowers.

Yellow-flowered forms

Yellow is not a common colour in border sedums, but the flat heads of *S. aizoon* are able to provide a bright yellow. In the form 'Aurantiacum' they are a much richer orange-yellow colour and have red stems.

Purple-foliaged varieties

'Ruby Glow' has red stems and leaves. It sprawls and is one of the smaller forms. 'Vera Jameson' has purple foliage and is larger in size. It, too, has a tendency to spread. Bigger and more upright is the variety *S. telephium* subsp. *maximum* 'Atropurpureum'.

SENECIO
Senecio

Of this very large genus only a handful of the 3000 species are grown in gardens. The main one that is of interest to perennial gardeners is *S. cineraria*, which is used as a foliage plant. Often known as dusty miller, it has foliage and stems covered in soft white hairs, giving the whole plant a silvery white appearance. A good form of prairie mallow is 'White Diamond' (below). The flowers are yellow but are usually removed as soon as they appear. The whole plant only grows to 60cm (2ft) high. It is neither long-lived nor hardy.

Dusty miller must have a free-draining soil, as it will quickly die if planted in a wet position, especially in winter. A sunny position is essential. Propagation is carried out either from cuttings or from seed.

Senecio cineraria 'White Diamond'

SIDALCEA
Prairie mallow

Prairie mallows are attractive plants with spikes of softly coloured flowers like miniature hollyhocks. The main colour is pink, but there are also darker forms, almost purple, and white ones. When grown from seed, many have inferior-sized flowers, so it is best to choose one of the named forms with larger flowers. The blooms appear from summer onwards, with a second flush if the spent stems are cut back. The foliage forms a dense basal clump and makes good ground cover early in the season. The plants grow to 1.2m (4ft) in height.

Sidalceas will grow in any reasonable garden soil and, although they prefer a sunny spot, they will flower in light shade. Propagate preferably by division; they can also be grown from seed.

Varieties (below)

S. candida is the only white-flowered form. 'Brilliant' has very dark rose-pink flowers. 'Rose Queen' has medium rose-pink and 'Party Girl' pink flowers.

Sidalcea candida 'Rose Queen'

SILENE
Campion

Campions make a useful if not outstanding contribution to the border. Many in cultivation are low-growing plants that are useful for carpeting frontal areas of the border, while the taller forms are useful further back and for the wild or woodland section of a garden. Some forms flower in spring, some in summer, and some in autumn; others continue to bloom from spring through to autumn. Their flowers are usually simple flat discs of five petals, sometimes deeply cut. The red campion, *S. dioica*, has rose-red or pink flowers 2.5cm (1in) wide. They grow to about 60cm (2ft). The double forms 'Flore Pleno' and 'Rosea Plena' are more frequently grown, the latter having darker flowers.

These campions grow in any garden soil. Either sun or shade is suitable. Propagate by division. The species will come from seed.

SISYRINCHIUM
Sisyrinchium

These can brighten up a border. The round blue or yellow flowers are not very large but, in quantity, they seem to shine out among other plants. Not all gardeners love them, however, as they do tend to self-seed. The foliage is narrow and grassy or iris-like, and from these tufts arise the spikes of flowers in spring or summer.

Sisyrinchiums like a well-drained soil and a sunny position. Cut off the old flower heads before they seed. Propagation by division is best done in late summer; spring is the best time for seed. Planting should be carried out in either autumn or spring.

S. angustifolium

This is one of the toughest species, tolerating most conditions, including the cold. It has yellow-throated violet-blue flowers that appear in summer and dark green foliage. It grows to 20cm (8in) high. It is sometimes referred to as *S. bermudianum*.

S. idahoense (below)

This is similar to *S. angustifolium* in that it has blue flowers with a yellow centre, but it is twice the height and flowers earlier. It is known also as *S. bellum*.

Sisyrinchium idahoense

S. striatum

The most popular border form. It produces tall spikes, up to 75cm (2½ft) high, of soft yellow flowers, darkening towards the centre, which bloom for a long period during the summer. The form 'Aunt May' has cream variegations on the leaves.

SMILACINA
False Solomon's seal

This is closely related to the Solomon's seal and has inherited much of its fresh-looking appearance. The species mainly seen in cultivation is *S. racemosa* (below). It has the same kind of graceful, arching stems with opposite leaves as has Solomon's seal, but the flowers, instead of appearing along the stems, are gathered in a fluffy cluster at the tip. They are creamy white and appear in the spring. The plant grows up to 90cm (3ft) high. They spread to form a large clump but are not invasive. They make an attractive group for a shady spot.

Smilacinas like a moist, woodland-type soil, preferably on the acidic side, and a cool, shady position. Propagation is best by division or from seed.

Smilacina racemosa

SOLIDAGO
Golden rod

The golden rods are invaluable for creating drifts of yellow from summer onwards. The flowers are individually tiny but are carried in profusion in loose fluffy heads. The narrow leaves are not particularly attractive and in some varieties can suffer badly from mildew. Plants range in height between 30cm (1ft) and 1.5m (5ft), and slowly spread to form large clumps, creating solid blocks of colour when in flower.

Golden rods will grow in any reasonable garden soil and will tolerate either sun or light shade. Propagation is by division.

Varieties

There are many varieties of golden rod. 'Golden Baby' ('Goldkind') is a short golden yellow form. 'Goldenmosa' is a taller, bright golden yellow, and flowers early. 'Queenie' has bright yellow flowers on an 20cm (8in) plant.

× Solidaster luteus 'Lemore'

Hybrids (above)
Solidago has been crossed with an *Aster* to produce a new genus, × *Solidaster*, with flowers larger than those of *Solidago*. One of the most popular of these crosses is a variety called × *Solidaster luteus* 'Lemore'. This has soft yellow flowers and is sometimes listed under *Solidago*.

STACHYS

Betony

This genus gives the gardener a number of useful plants, many of which are so different it is hard to believe they are of the same genus. The difference arises from the fact that some are grown for foliage effect while others for their flowers. The flowers are similar to those of the dead nettles and mints: tubular, with a hooded upper lip.

Most betonies like a well-drained soil and although they prefer a sunny position will also tolerate light shade, especially in hot areas. Propagation is mainly by division, although seed can be used.

S. byzantina

Still also known as *S. lanata*, this species is grown as a foliage plant. Its densely felted leaves and stems give the whole plant a bright silver appearance. The flowers, carried on tall stems, are small and pink. Many gardeners dislike the flower spikes and remove them from the base so as not to spoil the foliage effect, but others feel the pink adds to the overall impression. 'Cotton Boll' replaces the flowers with what appear to be balls of cotton on the stems, while 'Silver Carpet' rarely produces flower stems at all. 'Primrose Heron' has flushes of yellow on the silver leaves.

S. macrantha (below)

Also known as *S. grandiflora*, this species contrasts with *S. byzantina*, as it produces large heads of purple-pink flowers above pleated green leaves. The best form, 'Superba', has extra-large purple flowers.

Stachys macrantha 'Superba'

STIPA

Stipa

This large genus consists of grasses that are grown mainly for their wonderful feathery flower heads. Some are quite short, but it is generally the taller species that are employed to make dramatic statements in the garden. While they are often used in conjunction with other plants in the border they are also eminently suitable as specimen plants. A good situation is one that catches the late evening sun.

Stipa will grow in any good garden soil, preferably one that is not too wet, but a sunny position is required. Planting should be carried out in spring. Propagation is generally by division in spring, but they can also be grown from seed.

S. gigantea

This is the species most commonly grown. It can be up to 1.8m (6ft) tall and carries open, airy heads of large purple flowers that turn golden as seed is formed.

Stipa tenuissima

S. tenuissima (above)

This is a much shorter plant, growing to only 60cm (2ft). It has soft feathery plumes in early summer.

STOKESIA

Stoke's aster

This is a single-species genus, with *S. laevis* (next column) as its sole representative. The plant is a member of the thistle family but is not at all prickly, nor does it have a tendency to become invasive. It is a good low-growing, sprawling plant, 45cm (1½ft) tall, with large, flat flowers comprising a central disc of small flowers and an outer ring of larger, strap-shaped, purple-blue petals. It flowers from late summer onwards. There are a number of cultivars. 'Alba', as one would expect from the name, has white flowers. 'Blue Danube' has deeper blue flowers and 'Blue Star' is distinguished by its larger flowers.

Stokesia likes a soil enriched with organic material, but it should be reasonably free-draining. It needs a sunny site. Increase by division.

Stokesia laevis

SYMPHYANDRA
Symphyandra

This small genus of plants is closely related to the campanulas. Unfortunately, these plants are not seen as frequently as they should be, perhaps because they are short-lived, but most produce copious amounts of seed and so are easy to propagate. *S. wanneri* is one of the most popular; it produces masses of nodding lavender-blue flowers in early summer on a pyramid-shaped plant. The oval-shaped leaves are hairy. This clump-forming species grows to only 25cm (10in), and is thus best suited to the front of the border.

Symphyandra will grow in any reasonable garden soil, although prefers one that is free-draining. A position in either sun or light shade is suitable. Increase by seed.

SYMPHYTUM
Comfrey

The flared tubular flowers of comfrey are carried in spikes that uncurl as the flower buds open. The flowers come in a wide range of colours, including blue, pink, red, white and creamy yellow. These are carried on thick, hairy stems above large coarse leaves. The leaves themselves can be decorative, and there are some variegated forms. The plants grow to a height of approximately 30–90cm (1–3ft) tall. Comfrey can become very invasive, spreading underground, and is difficult to extract once it has a hold. This means they are better planted where they can be contained or in a wild part of the garden rather than in a formal border.

Comfrey likes a deep, rich soil that does not get too dry. It will flower in either sun or light shade. Cut back after flowering to promote fresh foliage and also to prevent seeding. Propagation is from seed or by division. Any piece of root left in the soil will produce a new plant.

Symphytum 'Goldsmith'

Foliage varieties (above)

Some forms of comfrey are grown almost exclusively for their foliage. For example: 'Goldsmith' has cream and yellow variegations on dark green, while *S.* × *uplandicum* 'Variegatum' has cream variegations set against a grey-green background.

Flower varieties

Almost all species and varieties are worth growing for their flowers. Two of the best are 'Hidcote Blue', which has white bells touched with blue and opening from small red buds, and 'Hidcote Pink', in which the blue tinge is replaced by a pink one.

TANACETUM
Tansy

The tansies are a group of daisy-like plants, often quite dissimilar in their general appearance. The plant commonly known as tansy is mainly considered a herb and is too vigorous for the open border, but there are several other members of the genus worth considering. Their flowers range considerably in size from 7.5mm (⅓in) to 7.5cm (3in) and their colour can also vary greatly.

Tansies will grow in any garden soil but prefer a sunny position. Many will grow from seed, but named forms are best increased by cuttings taken in the spring or by division.

Foliage varieties

Tansies generally have attractive foliage and hold the attention even when not in flower. Feverfew (*T. parthenium*), in its golden-leafed form 'Aureum', is particularly attractive. It holds its colour for most of the season and can always be cut back to provide new growth. The plant is covered with small white and yellow daisies throughout most of the summer season.

Flower varieties (next page)

One species, *T. coccineum*, has been developed for its brightly coloured flowers that appear in early summer. More commonly known as pyrethrum, this makes an excellent border plant. They are not very tall plants, reaching only up to 60cm (2ft). 'Snow Cloud' is a good white form of tansy. 'Eileen May Robinson', 'Laurin' and 'Robinson's Pink' are all excellent pinks, while 'Brenda' and 'James Kelway' are strong reds.

Tanacetum 'Eileen May Robinson'

TELLIMA
Fringe cup

There is only one species of *Tellima*, *T. grandiflora*. This is extremely useful as a decorative ground cover for areas of light and medium shade. The foliage is dark green and similar to that of *Heuchera*, to which this plant is related. The flowers appear on tall thin stalks in late spring, and are small white-green bells that age to pink. With the flower stems the plants can reach up to a height of 60cm (2ft). The form 'Rubra' has a purple tinge to the leaves.

Tellimas needs a woodland-type soil that is moist and rich in well-rotted humus, and a cool, shady position. Propagation is carried out by division.

THALICTRUM
Meadow rue

In most meadow rues both the foliage and the flowers are very delicate, and create a wonderful hazy effect. The flowers do not have petals but are made up of a bunch of fuzzy stamens, the colour being provided by the sepals. The plants range in height considerably from smaller ones around 10cm (4in) high to tall, stately plants of 1.8m (6ft) or more.

They do not want too rich a soil, although they like plenty of humus to keep the conditions moist. They will grow in either sun or shade, the latter being preferable in hot areas. Some of the taller species will need support. Propagate from seed or cuttings, or by division.

T. aquilegifolium (below)

This species derives its name from the similarity of its foliage to that of *Aquilegia*; when out of flower the two plants could easily be confused. The flowers are lilac and carried in fluffy profusion. The seeds hang like massed earrings and are very decorative. There is a creamy white form, 'Album', and a more purple form, 'Thundercloud'. All grow to about 90cm (3ft).

Thalictrum aquilegifolium

T. delavayi

Also known as *T. dipterocarpum*, this is one of the most delicate of plants, with dainty foliage and airy heads of purple sepals filled with creamy stamens. It grows to a height of approximately 1.5m (5ft). 'Hewitt's Double' is possibly the gem of the genus, as its stamens are transformed into purple 'petals', creating double flowers.

T. flavum

This is a tall plant, reaching 1.8m (6ft) or more, and is heavier in all its parts than

the other species. It is a dramatic plant, especially when grown in large clumps, because of its strongly contrasting dark green leaves and yellow flowers. There is a better known form, *T. f.* subsp. *glaucum*, which has glaucous blue-green stems and foliage.

T. rochebrunnianum

This species is similar to *T. delavayi*, with purple flowers over glaucous blue-green foliage. It flowers a little later and grows to 1.8m (6ft).

THERMOPSIS
False lupin

Thermopsis are bright and cheerful plants with dark green foliage and bright yellow, lupin-like flowers. The flowers appear in the spring; for the rest of the year the plants can be used for their foliage. The big disadvantage is that they run underground and can be very invasive, so they need to be planted where they can run at will or where they can be contained.

The various species do not show a great deal of difference between them and they are difficult to tell apart. *T. montana* (below) is a good species to try. It grows to a height of 90cm (3ft).

Thermopsis will grow in most soils, including dry ones. Most will tolerate both sun and shade. Propagation is by division or from seed.

Thermopsis montana

TIARELLA
Foam flower

This is a small genus of plants that are ideal for creating ground cover in a shady place. Unlike most other ground covers, these plants have a wonderful charm about them. Their tiny flowers are held in loose heads above the foliage and are responsible for the plant's common name. The leaves are palmate and evergreen. Foam flowers grow to about 45cm (1½ft).

They like a cool, moist soil with plenty of well-rotted humus in it. They need a lightly shaded position. Propagation is usually carried out by division, but they can also be grown from seed.

T. cordata

This is the main species in cultivation. It has clusters of white flowers and the plant spreads by stolons, soon forming a large colony.

Tiarella wherryi

T. wherryi (above)

This is a more compact plant with the pink-tipped flowers in a more positive, pyramid-shaped spike. It is not so aggressively invasive as the other species as it does not spread underground.

TRACHYSTEMON
Trachystemon

This is a two-species genus and only *T. orientalis* is seen in cultivation. It is an odd plant as its flower stems always seem on the point of dying. This is mainly due to the way the blue flowers hang down while their petals curl back, almost as if they were wilting. In spite of this it is worth growing for the general effect the flowers give. The loose clusters of flowers appear in spring, before the leaves open, on rough stems that reach up to 45cm (1½ft). The leaves are also rough and, when fully open, form a good ground cover. This plant can become invasive and is not recommended for formal borders, but is useful for growing in large areas under trees or bushes.

Trachystemon enjoys woodland conditions which do not dry out too much. It is extremely easy to grow and needs no attention once planted. Propagation is by division after flowering.

TRADESCANTIA
Spiderwort

Spiderworts are mainly known through the species grown as house-plants, but *Tradescantia* is a large genus of some 60 species, a few of which make a valuable contribution to the garden. These tend to have a close resemblance to the pot-plants, with the strap-like foliage clasping the round stems and the characteristic three-petalled flowers held in clusters in the uppermost leaves. As well as white there is a range of very bright, almost luminous flower colours, mainly blues and pinks. The plants flower over a long season, from late spring onwards. When grown in the right conditions they tend to spread and make large, rather untidy-looking clumps, reaching approximately 60cm (2ft) high.

Spiderworts should not be planted in a rich soil or the foliage growth will be lush at the expense of the flowers. The soil should not, however, be allowed to become too dry. A sunny position is usually required. The best method of propagation is by division.

T. × andersoniana (below)

This is the main group of hybrids cultivated in gardens. *T. virginiana* is one of their parents, and a wide range of colours is available. The best pure white forms are 'Innocence' and 'Snowcap'. 'Iris Prichard' is white tinged with blue. 'Isis' is deep blue, while 'Zwanenburg Blue' is royal blue. 'Karminglut' ('Carmine Glow') is bright carmine and 'Pauline' lilac-pink.

Tradescantia × andersoniana 'Karminglut'

TRICYRTIS
Toad lily

Toad lilies are among the most intriguing of all border perennials. The flowers need to be examined closely for their full beauty to be appreciated. Each consists of six strap-like petals opened out into a shallow funnel, from which erupts a fountain of stamens and styles. The flowers are mainly white or yellow, heavily spotted in purple, red or brown; they are usually upward facing, rising from the rigidly erect stems of the plant, and come in autumn. The lanceolate foliage clasps the stem and is mainly a shiny green. Toad lilies have a running rootstock and soon form a large, trouble-free colony, up to 90cm (3ft) in height. When they have formed a big group they look their best in the border, since individual plants are hardly noticed.

Toad lilies need a moist, humus-rich soil and a cool root run. They can be grown in a shady border but look best in a dappled woodland setting. They resent being disturbed; slugs like the young growth. Propagate by division or from seed.

T. formosana (below)

This has flowers with a white ground flushed and spotted with mauve. The dark green leaves are often spotted as well. There are a number of cultivars, each varying slightly in colour. 'Stolonifera Group' is a collective name given to these variations.

Tricyrtis formosana

T. hirta

The foliage and stems of this plant are covered in short hairs, while the white flowers, which appear in the autumn are heavily spotted with purple.

TROLLIUS
Globe flower

Globe flowers are among the glories of the spring and early-summer garden. They produce great orbs of orange or golden yellow held well above the buttercup-like foliage. In some species the flowers are cup-like, similar to those of their close relative the buttercup, while in others the petals curve into a complete sphere. These are plants of boggy areas and do best in bog gardens or near water features. However, provided that there is enough humus in the soil to make it moisture-

retentive they are a perfectly good choice of plant to use to create an attractive border.

In most areas globe flowers grow in the open, but in hot regions they do better in light shade. Deadhead regularly. Propagation is by division or from seed, which should be sown fresh.

T. chinensis

This species is still also known as *T. ledebourii*. The outside petals open to a shallow dish filled with upright narrow petals, which are a rich golden yellow. The plant grows up to 90cm (3ft).

T. × cultorum

This is a series of popular hybrids with variously coloured flowers. 'Alabaster' is a very pale green-yellow. 'Feuertroll' ('Fireglobe') is deep orange. 'Golden Monarch' is golden. 'Lemon Queen' is lemon-yellow. They all grow up to 90cm (3ft) in height.

Trollius europaeus

T. europaeus (above)

This is the European native. It produces spherical globes of pale yellow flowers that are carried on stems up to 75cm (2½ft) high.

UNCINIA
Uncinia

Not many sedges are garden-worthy, *U. unciniata* certainly deserves attention. It

belongs to a large group of sedges that come mainly from New Zealand. It has beautiful brown leaves that are brightest when young. The plants are very variable in colour and it is best to see them in growth before acquiring one. They make fountains of evergreen foliage up to 45cm (1½ft) and are excellent foliage plants.

They like a moisture-retentive soil, and can be grown in either a sunny position or light shade. Propagation is by division in spring or from seed, although seed will not necessarily produce good colour forms.

UVULARIA
Uvularia

This is a curious but very attractive small genus of plants, related to the Solomon's seal, although this is not apparent at first sight. They form colonies of arching stems from which dangle yellow flowers that look like limp pieces of twisted rag; they flower in spring. The foliage is fresh light green and the plants can reach 60cm (2ft) in height. While most of the species are cultivated, only *U. grandiflora* (below) is regularly seen. This has flowers 2.5cm (1in) long and of a rich primrose-yellow; there is a much paler form, 'Pallida'.

Uvularias need a cool, moist soil with plenty of well-rotted humus in it. They will grow in sun but a shady position is preferred, especially in hot areas. They are perfect for the woodland garden.

Uvularia grandiflora

VALERIANA
Valerian

Valerians are pleasant but not particularly distinguished plants, and are better suited to the wild garden than to formal areas. They are tall, with clustered heads of small white or pale pink flowers, though one form is becoming increasingly popular for its foliage rather than its flowers: *V. phu* 'Aurea' (below) which forms a mound of brilliant gold leaves in the spring. Unfortunately, by summer they begin to turn green. The off-white flowers are usually removed before they open. Although the foliage makes a mound only 30cm (1ft) or so high, this is a plant to grow in the middle of the border so that it shows up when it is at its best but is covered by other plants later in the season.

Valerian will grow in most garden soils. While most species will grow in the open, they prefer a slightly shady position – though *V. phu* 'Aurea' needs a sunny spot. Propagate by division or seed.

Valeriana phu 'Aurea'

VERATRUM
False hellebore

The veratrums are good value in that not only are they superlative when in flower, but also make excellent foliage plants. The only two disadvantages are that it can take up to seven years to get a flowering plant from seed and that slugs can reduce the leaves to tatters. The leaves are very heavily pleated and, when forming a rosette, they resemble a pale-green turban. From this eventually rises a tall – 1.8m (6ft) – flowering stem with many small hanging flowers, clustered along horizontal arms. In some species the flowers are white or light green, but in the most popular species, *V. nigrum* (below), they are dark red and appear to glow when the sun is behind them. The stems are equally attractive when the plant is in seed.

Veratrums like a moist, humus-rich soil. While some grow in the open, the majority, including *V. nigrum*, prefer a slightly shaded position out of the hot sun. Propagation is from seed or offsets.

Veratrum nigrum

VERBASCUM
Mullein

Mulleins are among the most stately plants in the garden. They rise from large hairy leaves to 2.5m (8ft) or more, forming tall spikes that are usually covered in saucer-shaped yellow flowers. Most of these forms are biennial and must be sown each year, but fortunately some species are more permanent and can be grown in the perennial garden. It is a pity that they are not as tall as the biennial forms, but they are nonetheless very impressive.

Mulleins can be grown in any garden soil, including quite dry ones, but they nearly all require a sunny position. The taller species need to be staked if in an exposed position. Increase is by sowing seed or relying on self-sown seedlings. Propagate coloured forms by root cuttings.

V. chaixii

This grows to 90cm (3ft) or so. The flowers are yellow with red stamens; there is also a white form. The foliage is dark green.

V. phoenicum hybrids (below)

This species is not frequently grown in its own right but is one of the parents of a number of very popular hybrids. The best known are the 'Cotswold Hybrids', with a wide range of colours beyond the normal yellow of most mulleins. Among them are 'Cotswold Queen' (deep burnt yellow), 'Gainsborough' (pale yellow), 'Helen Johnson' (pink), 'Mont Blanc' (white) and 'Pink Domino' (rose-pink).

Verbascum 'Pink Domino'

VERBENA
Vervain

Most verbenas are too tender for growing in the perennial garden and are treated as annuals. However, a few are tough enough, and these usually produce, late in the season, small domed or flat heads of purple or pink flowers, much loved by bees and butterflies. There seems to be a vervain suitable in height for every part of the border from the front to the back.

Verbenas grow in any reasonable garden soil, although they do best and last longest in well-drained ones. A sunny position is required. Propagation is by seed, division or basal cuttings taken in spring.

V. bonariensis (below)

This is one of the more popular species. It is a tall, spindly plant reaching 1.8m (6ft) or more, with wiry branches topped with clusters of reddish-purple flowers. Although it is tall, its wiry nature makes it 'see-through', so it can be grown very effectively in the middle or even at the front of the border. Although hardy it is short-lived.

Verbena bonariensis

VERONICA
Speedwell

Speedwells are one of the mainstays of the high-summer border. They provide a series of blue-flowered plants that come in a range of heights up to 1.2m (4ft) or more. *Veronica* is a very large genus, and has a considerable number of species and cultivars in cultivation. As well as blues, there are white varieties and an increasing number of pink forms. The majority carry flowers in elegant spikes which are held well above the foliage, but in a few of the lower-growing forms the flowers are in loose sprays.

Speedwells can be grown in any garden soil, but soon look distressed if the soil becomes too dry. Taller forms need some support. Deadhead to prevent self-sowing. Propagation is by division or, in some cases, from seed.

White varieties

A low, white variety for the front of the border is *V. spicata* 'Icicle'. The flowers show up well against the dark foliage. It grows up to 45cm (1½ft).

Veronica spicata 'Rotfuchs'

Pink varieties (above)

A low-growing, pale pink form that grows no more than 25cm (10in) tall is *V. prostrata* 'Mrs Holt'. The varieties *V. spicata* subsp. *incana* 'Minuet' and *V. s.* 'Heidekind' both have rose-pink flowers, while *V. s.* 'Rotfuchs' ('Red Fox') has rose-red flowers.

Pale blue varieties

Some of the best pale blues are those of *V. gentianoides*, with its shiny leaves and thin spires of relatively large flowers. Its form 'Variegata' has creamy variegations to the leaves and pale blue flowers. *V. spicata* 'Blaufuchs' ('Blue Fox') has lavender flowers.

Dark blue varieties

V. austriaca subsp. *teucrium* 'Crater Lake Blue' is one of the best dark blues. In *V. peduncularis* 'Georgia Blue' the dark blue flowers are carried in much looser spikes over a low-growing, purple-tinged foliage. The brilliant-flowered 'Shirley Blue' is halfway in height between the two.

VERONICASTRUM
Veronicastrum

Veronicastrum virginicum (below) is so close to Veronica, especially *V. longifolia*, that it can be very difficult to distinguish the two species. Both grow to about 90cm (3ft) with stiffly erect stems and whorls of leaves. The pale blue flowers are carried in attractive spikes. If anything the *Veronicastrum* is more elegant, with its longer flower spikes, and it has more leaves in each whorl. *V. v.* 'Album' is a beautiful white form that is well set off against the dark green leaves.

Veronicastrums grow in any garden soil and are best in full sun, though they tolerate some light shade. In exposed positions they may need staking; elsewhere the stems are rigid enough without support. Propagation is by division.

Veronicastrum virginicum

VIOLA
Viola

No garden should be without violas of one sort or another. These cheerful flowers can be either planted as a clump or used to fill in between other plants. They are easy to grow and there is a very wide range of colours. The majority are low-growing plants that form loose or tight hummocks. A few are scramblers and love to pull themselves up through shrubs and other plants. Violas come in a number of forms. Pansies are the largest-flowered, and are usually treated as annuals, although if trimmed with shears after flowering they will grow a second and even a third year. Violets are the smallest and are usually grown as one of the various species. Violas and violettas are intermediate between the two, the former being distinguished from the latter by the presence of whiskers radiating from the centre of the flowers.

Violas grow in most soils, as long as they are moist. They prefer a lightly shaded spot out of the hottest sun. With the exception of violets, most benefit from being trimmed after flowering and will often produce a second flush of blooms. Propagate by taking basal cuttings.

Viola 'Jackanapes'

Violas (above)
In the perennial border it is the viola that reigns supreme in this genus. A large selection of different colours is available. 'Ardross Gem' is dark yellow and blue. 'Bowles Black' has small black flowers. 'Molly Sanderson' has large black flowers. 'Chantreyland' has apricot-orange petals, darkening towards the centre, and can be bought as a seed strain. 'Irish Molly' is a strange mixture of greenish-yellow and bluish-brown. 'Jersey

Gem' is deep purple. The top petals of 'Jackanapes' are maroon and the lower ones bright yellow. 'Maggie Mott' is a mixture of blues and creamy yellow.

Viola cornuta

V. cornuta (above)
One of the best of the species. It behaves more like a viola, with moderately large flowers, and benefits from being sheared after blooming. The species has pale lilac flowers but there are a large number of variations on this. 'Alba' is pure white and is wonderful for enlivening a dark corner. 'Belmont Blue' is a soft blue. 'Rosea' has rosy purple flowers.

V. labradorica
This plant has purple-violet flowers and wonderful purple coloured leaves, especially in spring. It makes an excellent foliage plant. It has recently been renamed *V. riviniana* 'Purpurea'.

V. sororia
This violet is not particularly distinguished but has become very popular in its form 'Freckles'. This is white and strongly spotted with purple-blue.

WALDSTEINIA
Barren strawberry
This is a small genus of five species, of which just two are in cultivation. They are all low-growing and used as a ground

cover, usually in rock gardens, although they could be put at the front of a shady border. The main species in cultivation is *W. ternata* (below). This has evergreen leaves and small, strawberry-like yellow flowers that appear in late spring. The whole plant grows no more than 10cm (4in) high, but spreads vigorously by short rhizomes to form a dense carpet of foliage.

This plant will grow in most soils but is best in shade. Propagation, by dividing the creeping plants, is simple.

Waldsteinia ternata

ZAUSCHNERIA
California fuchsia
Having for a time been relegated to *Epilobium*, this small group of species is once again recognised as a genus in its own right. These plants are valuable for their late flowering. The most frequently grown and hardiest is *Z. californica*. Its fuchsia-like flowers are bright scarlet. 'Glasnevin' has very bright flowers and dark green leaves, while 'Solidarity Pink' has pink flowers but is more shy to flower. They will grow up to 45cm (1½ft) high. They can be put at the front of a border, but look particularly fine when grown over the top of a wall or bank.

Zauschnerias must have a free-draining soil and a warm, sunny position. They can be increased by cuttings or by division. Some will run underground, and their spread will need to be checked.

HARDINESS ZONES

One of the most critical factors governing the range of plants which it is possible to grow in a garden is the climate. Perennials grow naturally in a range of climatic conditions and in gardens they grow best in conditions which resemble those in which they grow in the wild. So we plant woodland plants in the shade and meadow plants in the open.

But temperature is a crucial factor. Some plants simply will not grow where winter temperatures are too cold for them. Plants from the southern United States or much of southern Africa will rarely survive winters in northern Europe or much of Canada out of doors.

Plants that survive most winters outside, unprotected, are termed hardy; those that will grow happily outside in summer but that are often killed in winter are termed half-hardy; those which never survive the winter outside are termed tender.

Catalogues and reference books are often vague about hardiness, so as a guide to the hardiness of every plant in the Plant Directory, each is given a hardiness zone rating that relates to the maps shown here (p. 228–229). You may find this information helpful when looking at other books and magazines.

There are eleven hardiness zones, defined according to lowest winter temperatures. Zone 1 represents the coldest conditions with winter temperatures below -46°C (-50°F); zone 11 is the warmest with a minimum winter temperature of above 4°C (above 40°F). The classification of a plant into a particular hardiness zone means that the plant will normally thrive in that zone and in any zone marked with a higher number.

The dividing line between one zone and the next is not rigid because weather varies from one year to the next, the landscape can be an influence, and towns are warmer than country areas. Also, by utilizing the shelter of walls and evergreen shrubs, plants can be encouraged to survive in zones in which they would normally be killed. Remember, some plants will not survive in very hot climates.

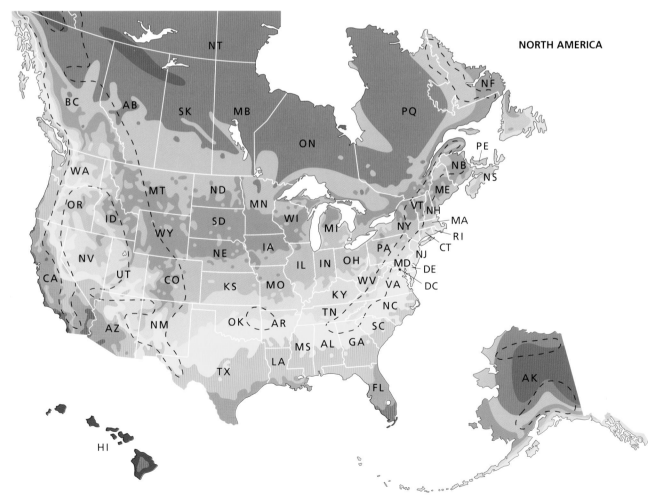

NORTH AMERICA

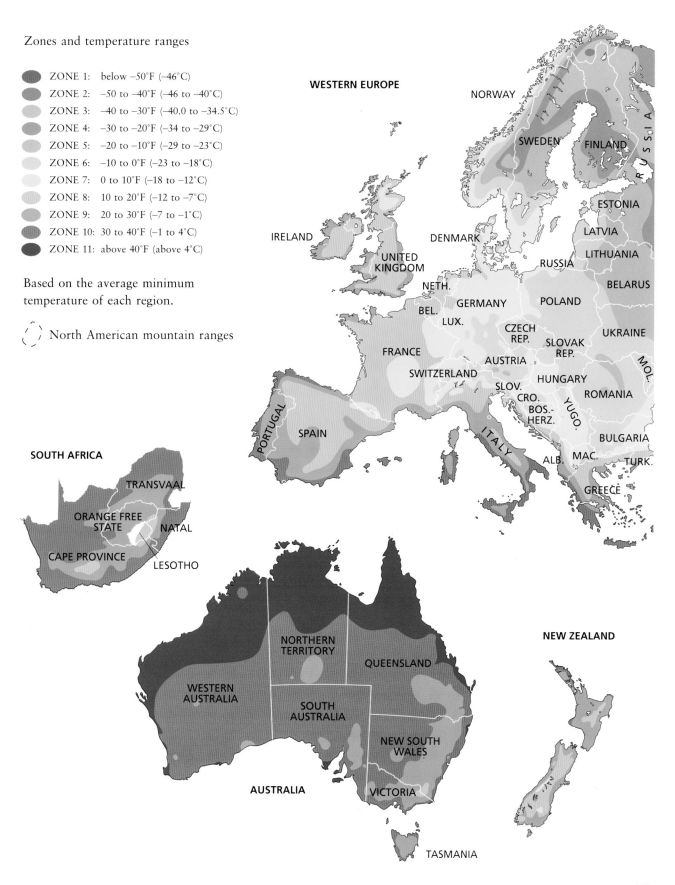

Zones and temperature ranges

- ZONE 1: below −50°F (−46°C)
- ZONE 2: −50 to −40°F (−46 to −40°C)
- ZONE 3: −40 to −30°F (−40.0 to −34.5°C)
- ZONE 4: −30 to −20°F (−34 to −29°C)
- ZONE 5: −20 to −10°F (−29 to −23°C)
- ZONE 6: −10 to 0°F (−23 to −18°C)
- ZONE 7: 0 to 10°F (−18 to −12°C)
- ZONE 8: 10 to 20°F (−12 to −7°C)
- ZONE 9: 20 to 30°F (−7 to −1°C)
- ZONE 10: 30 to 40°F (−1 to 4°C)
- ZONE 11: above 40°F (above 4°C)

Based on the average minimum temperature of each region.

North American mountain ranges

WESTERN EUROPE

NORWAY

SWEDEN FINLAND

RUSSIA

ESTONIA

LATVIA

LITHUANIA

IRELAND DENMARK RUSSIA

BELARUS

UNITED KINGDOM

NETH. POLAND

GERMANY

BEL. UKRAINE

LUX.

CZECH REP. SLOVAK REP.

FRANCE MOL.

AUSTRIA

SWITZERLAND HUNGARY ROMANIA

SLOV.

CRO. YUGO.

BOS.-HERZ. BULGARIA

PORTUGAL ITALY ALB. MAC.

SPAIN TURK.

GREECE

SOUTH AFRICA

TRANSVAAL

ORANGE FREE STATE

NATAL

CAPE PROVINCE

LESOTHO

NEW ZEALAND

NORTHERN TERRITORY

QUEENSLAND

WESTERN AUSTRALIA

SOUTH AUSTRALIA

NEW SOUTH WALES

AUSTRALIA

VICTORIA

TASMANIA

A

Acanthus *Bear's breeches* 6–10
Achillea *Yarrow* 3–10
Aconitum *Monkshood* 2–9
Acorus *Sweet flag* 5–9
Actea *Baneberry* 2–9
Adiantum *Maidenhair fern* 3–8
Aegopodium *Goutweed* 4
Agapanthus *African lily* 8–10
Agastache *Mexican bergamot,
    Giant hyssop* 5–9
Ajuga *Bugle* 2–10
Alcea *Hollyhock* 2–10
Alchemilla *Lady's mantle* 3–9
Alstroemeria *Peruvian lily* 7–10
Amsonia *Blue star* 3–9
Anaphalis *Pearl everlasting* 3–9
Anchusa *Anchusa* 3–10
Anemone *Anemone* 6–10
Anthemis *Anthemis* 3–10
Aquilegia *Columbine* 3–10
Arabis *Rockcress* 4–10
Artemisia *Mugwort* 4–10
Aruncus *Goat's beard* 3–9
Asarum *Wild ginger* 2–9
Asclepias *Milkweed* 3–10
Asperula *Woodruff* 5–9
Asphodeline *Jacob's rod* 6–8
Asphodelus *Asphodel* 5–9
Asplenium *Spleenwort* 5–6
Aster *Aster* 3–10
Astilbe *Astilbe* 4–8
Astrantia *Masterwort* 4–9
Athyrium *Athyrium* 4–8
Aubrieta *Aubrieta* 4–9

B

Baptisia *False indigo* 3–10
Begonia *Begonia* 6–8
Bellis *Daisy* 3–11
Bergenia *Elephant ears* 3–10
Blechnum *Blechnum* 5–8
Boltonia *Boltonia* 3–10
Borago *Borage* 7–10
Brunnera *Brunnera* 3–8
Buphthalmum *Buphthalmum* 4–8

C

Calamintha *Calamint* 5–10
Caltha *Marsh marigold* 3–10
Campanula *Bellflower* 3–10
Carex *Sedge* 4–8
Centaurea *Knapweed* 3–9
Centranthus *Red valerian* 3–10
Cephalaria *Cephalaria* 3–10
Ceratostigma *Plumbago* 5–10
Chelone *Turtlehead* 3–9
Cimicifuga *Bugbane* 3–10
Cirsium *Thistle* 4–10
Clematis *Clematis* 3–9
Codonopsis *Bonnet bellflower* 5–9
Convallaria *Lily of the valley* 3–9
Convolvulus *Convolvulus* 7–10
Coreopsis *Tickseed* 4–10
Cortaderia *Pampas grass* 4–9
Cortusa *Cortusa* 4–8
Corydalis *Corydalis* 7–11
Cosmos *Cosmos* 7–10
Crambe *Crambe* 6–9
Cynara *Cynara* 6–10
Cynoglossum *Hound's tongue* 4–9

D

Darmera *Umbrella plant* 6–9
Delosperma *Delosperma* 8–10
Delphinium *Delphinium* 3–10
Dendranthema *Chrysanthemum*
    4–10
Dennstaedtia *Cup fern* 4–8
Deschampsia *Hair grass* 5–9
Dianthus *Pinks* 4–10
Diascia *Twinspur* 6–8
Dicentra *Bleeding heart* 3–10
Dictamnus *Burning bush* 2–9
Digitalis *Foxglove* 3–10
Doronicum *Leopard's bane* 4–9
Dracocephalum *Dragon's head*
    2–8
Dryopteris *Shield fern* 2–8

E

Echinacea *Coneflower* 3–8
Echinops *Globe thistle* 3–11

Elymus *Elymus* 2–9
Epimedium *Barrenwort* 5–8
Eremurus *Foxtail lily* 5–9
Erigeron *Fleabane* 4–9
Eryngium *Sea holly* 3–10
Eupatorium *Boneset* 3–10
Euphorbia *Spurge* 3–10

F

Festuca *Fescue* 3–9
Filipendula *Meadow sweet* 3–9
Foeniculum *Fennel* 4–10
Fragaria *Strawberry* 5–8

G

Gaillardia *Blanket flower* 3–10
Galega *Goat's rue* 3–9
Gaura *Gaura* 6–10
Gentiana *Gentian* 3–9
Geranium *Geranium, Hardy
    cranesbill* 3–10
Geum *Avens* 5–10
Gillenia *Indian physic* 4–8
Glyceria *Glyceria* 5–9
Gunnera *Gunnera* 7–10
Gypsophila *Baby's breath* 3–10

H

Hakonechloa *Hakonechloa* 4–8
Helenium *Sneezeweed* 3–10
Helianthus *Sunflower* 3–10
Helictotrichon *Helictotrichon*
    4–10
Heliopsis *False sunflower* 4–9
Helleborus *Hellebore* 3–10
Hemerocallis *Day lily* 3–10
Heuchera *Alumroot* 3–10
x Heucherella *Heucherella* 3–10
Hosta *Hosta* 3–9
Houttuynia *Houttuynia* 6–10

I

Imperata *Imperata* 5–10
Incarvillea *Incarvillea* 4–10
Inula *Inula* 3–9
Iris *Iris* 3–10

J

Jasione *Jasione* 6–9

K

Kalimeris *Kalimeris* 3–8
Kirengeshoma *Kirengeshoma* 5–9
Knautia *Knautia* 5–10
Kniphofia *Red hot poker, Torch lily* 6–10

L

Lamium *Dead nettle* 3–10
Lathyrus *Pea* 3–9
Leucanthemella *Leucanthemella* 4–9
Leucanthemum *Shasta daisy* 5–10
Liatris *Blazing star* 3–10
Ligularia *Ligularia* 4–10
Limonium *Statice, Sea lavender* 3–10
Linaria *Toadflax* 3–10
Linum *Flax* 5–10
Liriope *Lilyturf* 5–10
Lobelia *Lobelia* 2–9
Lupinus *Lupin* 4–9
Luzula *Luzula* 3–9
Lychnis *Campion* 3–10
Lysichiton *Skunk cabbage* 4–9
Lysimachia *Loosestrife* 3–10
Lythrum *Purple loosestrife* 3–10

M

Macleaya *Plume poppy* 4–10
Malva *Mallow* 4–9
Matteuccia *Ostrich fern* 3–8
Meconopsis *Blue poppy* 6–9
Melissa *Lemon balm* 5–9
Mentha *Mint* 5–10
Mertensia *Mertensia* 3–10
Milium *Millet grass* 3–9
Mimulus *Monkey flower* 7–10
Miscanthus *Miscanthus* 5–9
Molinia *Moor grass* 5–9
Monarda *Bergamot* 4–10
Morina *Morina* 6–9

N

Nepeta *Catmint* 3–10

O

Oenothera *Evening primrose* 4–10
Omphalodes *Navelwort* 5–9
Origanum *Marjoram* 3–10
Osmunda *Royal fern* 3–8

P

Paeonia *Peony* 3–10
Papaver *Poppy* 3–9
Patrinia *Patrinia* 5–9
Pennisetum *Fountain grass* 6–10
Penstemon *Penstemon* 3–10
Perovskia *Russian sage* 5–10
Persicaria *Knotweed* 3–9
Phalaris *Ribbon grass* 4–9
Phlox *Phlox* 3–9
Phygelius *Cape figwort* 6–10
Physalis *Chinese lantern* 3–10
Physostegia *Obedient plant* 5–9
Phytolacca *Pokeweed* 3–9
Platycodon *Balloon flower* 3–10
Pleioblastus *Bush bamboo* 3–9
Polemonium *Jacob's ladder* 3–9
Polygonatum *Solomon's seal* 4–9
Polystichum *Shield fern* 4–8
Potentilla *Potentilla* 3–10
Primula *Primula* 3–9
Prunella *Self-heal* 4–9
Pulmonaria *Lungwort* 3–10
Pulsatilla *Pasque flower* 5–9

R

Ranunculus *Buttercup* 4–9
Rhazya *Rhazya* 6–9
Rheum *Rhubarb* 5–9
Rodgersia *Rodgersia* 4–9
Rudbeckia *Coneflower* 3–10

S

Salvia *Sage* 4–10
Sanguisorba *Burnet* 3–9
Saponaria *Soapwort* 2–10
Sasa *Sasa* 2–9

Saxifraga *Saxifrage* 5–9
Scabiosa *Scabious* 3–11
Scrophularia *Figwort* 6–9
Sedum *Stonecrop* 4–10
Senecio *Senecio* 8–10
Sidalcea *Prairie mallow* 5–11
Silene *Campion* 4–10
Sisyrinchium *Sisyrinchium* 3–10
Smilacina *False Solomon's seal* 3–9
Solidago *Golden rod* 3–10
Stachys *Betony* 4–10
Stipa *Stipa* 3–11
Stokesia *Stoke's aster* 5–10
Symphyandra *Symphyandra* 6–9
Symphytum *Comfrey* 3–9

T

Tanacetum *Tansy* 3–9
Tellima *Fringe cup* 4–9
Thalictrum *Meadow rue* 3–10
Thermopsis *False lupin* 3–10
Tiarella *Foam flower* 3–9
Trachystemon *Trachystemon* 3–8
Tradescantia *Spiderwort* 5–10
Tricyrtis *Toad lily* 5–9
Trollius *Globe flower* 3–10

U

Uncinia *Uncinia* 5–10
Uvularia *Uvularia* 3–9

V

Valeriana *Valerian* 5–10
Veratrum *False hellebore* 3–9
Verbascum *Mullein* 5–10
Verbena *Vervain* 3–10
Veronica *Speedwell* 3–10
Veronicastrum *Veronicastrum* 3–10
Viola *Viola* 3–10

W

Waldsteinia *Barren strawberry* 3–10

Z

Zauschneria *California fuchsia* 8–10

GLOSSARY

Acid (of soil) Relatively lime-free; having a pH level of less than 7; the opposite of alkaline.

Alkaline (of soil) Limy; having a pH level of more than 7; the opposite of acid.

Alpine 1. A plant growing naturally in mountainous regions, usually above the tree line. **2.** Any small plant grown in rock gardens. **3.** Also sometimes used rather too loosely to describe any small perennial plant.

Alternate leaves Leaves staggered singly on opposite sides of the stem.

Annual A plant that completes its life-cycle from germination to shedding seed in a single growing season.

Anther The male organ of a flower, the part producing pollen.

Apex The tip of a petal or leaf or the growing point of a shoot.

Basal leaves Leaves arising directly from the crown rather than the stem.

Biennial A plant that completes its life-cycle in in two seasons. It grows and builds up reserves of nutrients in its first season, then flowers, sheds seed and dies in its second season.

Biological control The use of one organism, such as a parasitic insect, to control another organism that is harmful to plants.

Bract A small leaf-like organ positioned alongside a flower.

Bulb A storage organ made up of a number of tightly packed fleshy scales. Often used more generally for any underground storage organ.

Cluster A group of flowers held together.

Coir A fine, peat-like material made from coconut fibre.

Cold frame A low structure consisting of a timber, brick or concrete frame with the top and sometimes the sides glazed with glass or clear plastic. Used to protect plants from cold weather and to harden off developing plants.

Compost 1. A special mixture, usually of loam, peat, grit and fertilizer, used for raising seed or potting plants; hence seed compost and potting compost. **2.** Rotted vegetable matter, often called garden compost.

Cross 1. To raise a new plant through combining the characteristics of two different plants by fertilizing one with the pollen of the other. **2.** The plant which results from this.

Crown The part of a plant at or immediately below the soil surface from which leaves and shoots develop.

Cultivar A named selection – usually one that originated in cultivation – of a particular species. For example, the full name *Phlox paniculata* 'Fujiyama' indicates that 'Fujiyama' is a cultivar of *Phlox paniculata*, of which there are many other cultivars.

Cutting A piece of stem detached from the parent plant that produces roots and develops into a new plant usually identical to its parent.

Deadhead To remove flowers as they die and before they shed seed; this promotes continuous flowering and prevents the seed being shed.

Deciduous Losing leaves completely in the autumn or early winter.

Division The splitting of a plant into a number of small plants.

Dormancy 1. A resting period in which a plant does not grow. **2.** A period during which a seed does not germinate owing to the absence of appropriate conditions.

Drainage The percolation of water through the soil. Well drained soils allow water to percolate through them quickly; badly drained or waterlogged soils hold water and remain wet for much longer.

Drill A long, narrow, shallow trench in the soil in which seeds are sown.

Evergreen A plant which retains leaves throughout the year.

F₁ hybrid A strain of seed-raised plants created by crossing two parent plants themselves the result of repeated selection for special characteristics.

Family A collection of broadly similar genera. For example, *Iris* and *Crocosmia* are both genera in the Iridaceae family.

Frond The leaf of a fern.

Fungicide A natural or synthetic chemical that kills fungal infections.

Genus (plural: genera) A group of related species having certain characteristics in common. For example, *Iris sibirica* and *Iris pseudacorus* are two species that belong to the genus *Iris*.

Germination The development of a seed into a seedling.

Ground-cover plant A dense, usually low-growing plant which has a tendency to cover the ground and smother weeds.

Half-hardy A plant that grows well outside in summer but requires protection from the weather in winter.

Hardening off The gradual acclimatization to the open garden of plants raised in the protected environment of a cold frame or greenhouse.

Hardy A plant that will survive outside all year round without the need for special protection.

Heavy soil Soil with a high clay content. Heavy soil is usually sticky, holds a great deal of water and tends to dry out slowly.

Herbaceous plant A plant whose leaves and stems die away every year, usually in late autumn or winter (*but see p. 10*).

Humus Well rotted vegetable matter.

Hybrid A plant resulting from the crossing of two other plants.

Interplant To plant a number of individuals of two different plants among each other.

Leaching The draining of liquid through soil; notably, a solution of nutrients.

Leaf cutting A leaf detached from the parent plant which produces roots and develops into a new plant, usually identical to its parent.

Leaf mould Humus derived exclusively from rotted leaves of deciduous trees and shrubs and used to improve soil.

Light soil Soil containing a high proportion of sand or gravel. Light soil is usually very crumbly, holds little water and dries out quickly.

Lime Material containing mainly calcium. Lime is used to reduce the acidity of the soil.

Liquid feed Fertilizer applied as a liquid.

Marginal 1. Describing plants that grow in moist soil, such as along the margins of ponds. **2.** Describing the edges of leaves, usually in relation to variegation. **3.** Describing plants that may not survive the winter.

Mulch Layer of organic matter or gravel spread over the soil to suppress weeds, prevent evaporation of moisture and improve the soil.

Native plant A plant which grows naturally in a particular area.

Naturalize To allow plants to develop with the minimum of interference; for example, to permit their seedlings to mature where they spring up, or to let plants spread into one another.

Neutral (of soil) Neither acid nor alkaline; having a pH of 7.

Offset A new plant that develops at the base of a larger, established plant.

Opposite leaves Leaves held in opposite pairs at single points up the stem.

Peat 1. Humus comprising partially rotted moss or sedge. **2.** Any of several commercial products, more correctly called peat substitutes, used as soil-improvers (*see p.26–27*).

Perennial Correctly, a plant that lives for more than two years (*but see p.9*).

Pesticide A natural or synthetic chemical that kills insects or other creatures harmful to plants.

pH A measure of alkalinity and acidity. A pH of 7 is neutral; above 7 is alkaline; below 7 is acid.

Pinching out The removal of the tip of a stem to encourage the development of side shoots.

Pricking out The removal of a seedling from the pot or seed tray in which it germinated to an individual pot or a large tray where it will have more space to develop.

Propagation The process of producing one or more new plants from an existing one.

Raceme An unbranched flowering stalk on which the flowers are carried individually on short side shoots.

Rhizome A stem which creeps horizontally at or just below the surface.

Root cutting A piece of root which, detached from the parent plant, then produces roots and develops into a new plant which is usually identical to its parent.

Rosette A cluster of leaves radiating from the crown of a plant and with the new, smallest leaves held in the centre.

Run To spread rapidly, especially through the growth of roots.

Runner A stem which creeps across the surface of the soil, often rooting into the soil below.

Seed head A flower which is developing or has developed seeds.

Seedling A young plant resulting from the germination of a seed.

Selection A plant chosen as being noticeably distinct from others of its type. For example, a plant which has larger flowers.

Self-sowing Describing the tendency of some plants to shed seed which then germinates and develops into new plants nearby.

Slow-release fertilizer A plant food specially formulated to be released into the soil over a long period.

Species A naturally occurring group of almost identical plants. A number of botanically related species, sharing generally similar features (although these may not always be immediately obvious), is grouped into a genus. For example, *Iris sibirica* and *Iris pseudacorus* are both species of the genus *Iris*.

Specimen A plant grown for its striking or distinctive growth habit or general appearance.

Spike An unbranched flowering stalk on which the flowers are carried without individual stems.

Stake To support tall or floppy plants with canes, brushwood or steel rods.

Stolon A shoot that grows across the soil or arches above the soil and produces a new plant with roots at its tip.

Succulent Having swollen or fleshy leaves providing a store of moisture.

Tender Describes plants susceptible to damage caused by frost.

Top-dress To apply fertilizer to the surface of the soil so that it is incorporated shallowly.

Tuber An underground storage organ developed by the swelling of a root or stem.

Umbel A domed or flat-topped flower head, each flower being carried on a slim stem attached to the top of the main stem.

Underplant To plant short plants around or underneath taller ones.

Variegated (of leaves) With edging, streaks, spots, splashes or stripes of another colour, usually yellow, cream or white.

Variety A naturally occurring wild variant of a species. The term is often used loosely as an alternative for 'cultivar' (*q.v.*).

Waterlogged soil Soil which remains very wet and which rarely dries out.

Weed Any plant that is a nuisance.

SUPPLIERS

At the time of writing, all the nurseries listed below operated a mail-order service. It may be useful to telephone to find out catalogue prices and opening hours before ordering and visiting.

Allwood Brothers
Mill Nursery, Hassocks, West Sussex BN6 9NB
Tel (01273 84) 4229
Pinks

Apple Court
Hordle Lane, Hordle, Lymington, Hampshire SO41 0HU
Tel (01590) 642130
Ferns, grasses, hemerocallis and hostas

Axeltree Nursery
Starvecrow Lane, Peasmarsh, Rye, East Sussex TN31 6XL
Tel (01797) 230470
Good general range, especially hardy geraniums

Steven Bailey Ltd
Silver Street, Sway, Lymington, Hampshire SO41 6ZA
Tel (01590) 682227
Pinks and alstroemerias

Blackthorn Nursery
Kilmeston, Alresford, Hampshire SO24 0NL
Tel (01962) 771796
General range including hellebores and epimediums

Blackmore and Langdon Ltd
Pensford, Bristol, Avon BS18 4JL
Tel (0117) 9332300
Delphiniums and phlox

Bosvigo Plants
Bosvigo House, Bosvigo Lane, Truro, Cornwall TR31 3NH
Tel (01872) 75774
New and unusual perennials

The Botanic Nursery
Rookery Nurseries, Cottles lane, Atworth, Melksham, Wiltshire SN12 8NU
Tel (01225) 706597 or 706631
Lime-tolerant perennials

Ann and Roger Bowden
Cleave House, Sticklepath, Okehampton, Devon EX20 2NN
Tel (01837) 840481
Hostas only

Bregover Plants
Hillbrooke, Middlewood, North Hill, Launceston, Cornwall PL15 7NN
Tel (01566) 782661
Good general range

Bressingham Gardens
Bressingham, Diss, Norfolk IP22 2AB
Tel (01379) 888289
Very good general range

Mrs P.J. Brown
Westlees Farm, Logmore Lane, Westcott, Dorking, Surrey RH4 3JN
Tel (01306) 889827
Iris only

Cally Gardens
Gatehouse of Fleet, Castle Douglas, Dumfries and Galloway DG7 2DJ
No telephone
Unusual perennials

R.G.M. Cawthorne
Lower Daltons Nursery, Swanley Village, Swanley, Kent BR8 7NU
No telephone
Violas and violettas only

Charter House Nursery
2 Nunwod, Dumfries, Dumfries and Galloway DG2 0HX
Tel (01387) 720363
Unusual perennials, especially geraniums and erodiums

Coombland Gardens
Coombland, Coneyhurst, Billingshurst, West Sussex RH14 9DG
Tel (01403) 741549
General range, especially geraniums

Croftway Nursery
Yapton Road, Barnham, Bognor Regis, West Sussex PO22 0BH
Tel (01243) 552121
Good general range, especially iris

Foliage and Unusual Plants
The Dingle Nursery, Pilsgate, Cambridgeshire, PE9 3HW
Tel (01780) 740775
Foliage plants

Four Seasons Nursery
Forncett St Mary, Norwich, Norfolk NR16 1JT
Tel (01508) 488344
Excellent general range ; mail- order only

Glebe Cottage Plants
Pixie Lane, Warkleigh, Umberleigh, North Devon EX37 9DH
Tel (01769) 540554
Good general range, especially primroses

Goldbrook Plants
Foxne, Eye, Suffolk IP21 5AN
Tel (01379) 668770
Good general range, especially hostas

Hoecroft Plants
Severals Grange, Wood Norton, Dereham, Norfolk NR20 5BL
Tel (01362) 844206 or 860179
Foliage plants, and grasses

Home Meadows Nursery
Martlesham, Woodbridge, Suffolk IP12 4RD
Tel (01394) 382419
Garden chrysanthemums

Hopleys Plants
High Street, Much Hadham, Hertfordshire SG10 6BU
Tel (01279) 842509
General range

Margey Fish Plant Centre
East Lambrook Manor, East Lamnbrook, South Petherton, Somerset TQ13 5HL
Tel (01460) 40328
Good general range, especially geraniums

Monksilver Nursery
Oakington Road, Cottenham, Cambridge CB4 4TW
Tel (01954) 251555
Good general range, especially new varieties

Old Court Nurseries
Colwall, Malvern, Worcestershire WR13 6QE
Tel (01684) 40416
General range, especially Michaelmas daisies

Padlock Croft
19 Padlock Road, West Wratting, Cambridge CB1 5LS
Tel (01223) 290383
Mainly campanulas

Rougham Hall Nurseries
Ipswich Road, Rougham, Bury St Edmunds, Suffolk IP30 9LZ
Tel (01359) 70577
Good general range, especially delphiniums and phlox

Rushfields of Ledbury
Ross Road, Ledbury, Herefordshire HR8 2LP
Tel (01531) 632004
Good general range

Peter J. Smith
Chanctonbury Nurseries, Rectory Lane, Ashington, Pulborough, Sussex RH20 3AS
Tel (01903) 892870
Modern alstroemerias

Stillingfleet Lodge Nurseries
Stillingfleet, Yorkshire YO4 6HW
Tel (01904) 728506
Good general range, especially pulmonarias

Three Counties Nurseries
Marshwood, Bridport, Dorset DT6 5QJ
Tel (01297) 678257
Pinks and other dianthus

Unusual Plants
Beth Chatto Gardens, Elmstead Market, Colchester CO7 7DB
Tel (01206) 822007
Excellent general range

Washfield Nursery
Horns Road, Hawkhurst, Kent TN18 4QU
Tel (01580) 752522
Select general range

Woodfield Brothers
Wood End, Clifford Chambers, Stratford-on-Avon, Warwickshire CV37 8HR
Tel (01789) 205618
Lupins and delphiniums

INDEX

Page numbers in *italic* refer to the illustrations

PHOTOGRAPHIC ACKNOWLEDGEMENTS

A-Z Botanical Collection 177 centre, /Lance Beacham 170 left, /Anthony Cooper 133, /Terence Exley 132

Eric Crichton 139, 148 top, 148 below, 149 right, 149 below, 150 right, 152 right, 153 left, 153 right, 155 right, 156 left, 156 right, 157 top, 158 top, 158 left, 159 left, 161 centre, 162 right, 162 centre, 163 centre, 163 right, 166 left, 167 below, 169 centre, 169 right, 171 centre, 174 left, 175 centre, 178 left, 179 centre, 180 centre, 181 centre, 182 left, 186 right, 188 right, 188 centre, 189 right, 190 centre, 192 right, 193 centre, 194 right, 196 centre, 198 left, 198 right, 200 centre, 202 left, 202 centre, 204 right, 204 centre, 207 centre, 209 right, 210 right, 210 left, 211 right, 214 right, 214 centre, 215 right, 217 left, 220 left, 222 left, 222 right, 224 centre

Elizabeth Whiting Associates 76 top right, 122

John Fielding 3 right, 3 left, 97 top, 145 below, 146 below, 147 right, 158 below, 159 right, 162 left, 168 right, 168 centre, 173 left, 197 left, 207 right, 208 left, 211 left, 212 centre, 213 centre, 217 centre, 219 right, 223 left, 224 left, 226 right

Garden Picture Library /Brian Carter 19, /Erika Craddock 13 centre, /Elizabeth Crowe 17, /Ron Evans 100, /John Glover 16, 89, /Neil Holmes 13 top, 127 top, /Michelle Lamontagne 47, /Jane Legate 97 below, /John Miller 96, /Clay Perry 81, /Gary Rodgers 52, /Brigitte Thomas 101, /Steven Wooster 128

Garden Matters /J. Feltwell 42

John Glover 43 bottom left, 91, 107, 120, 124, 130 top, 131, 134, 135, 147 left, 151 centre, 155 left, 173 centre, 177 left, 180 left, 182 centre, 182 right, 184 right, 186 top, 193 left, 193 right, 194 centre, 195

left, 200 left, 201 right, 201 left, 205 left, 213 right, 215 centre, 215 left, 216 left

Jerry Harpur 2, 4, 8, 9 right, 15 right, 28, 41, 45, 46, 64, 76 left, 82, 83, 88, 92, 103, 105, 113, 117 below, 130 below

Marijke Heuff 115

Andrew Lawson 3 centre, 18, 21 left, 38 top, 43 bottom right, 55, 57, 70, 86, 111 top, 112, 127 below, 129 left, 136, 144 left, 144 top, 144 right, 145 right, 146 right, 148 right, 149 left, 150 centre, 150 top, 151 right, 151 left, 154 left, 154 right, 156 top, 157 left, 160 centre, 160 right, 164 top, 165 left, 165 right, 168 left, 169 left, 172 right, 173 right, 174 right, 176 centre, 176 left, 178 right, 179 left, 180 right, 181 left, 181 right, 183 right, 184 left, 185 centre, 186 below, 187 right, 187 centre, 189 centre, 189 left, 190 left, 192 centre, 194 left, 195 centre, 199 right, 200 right, 207 left, 208 right, 211 centre, 213 left, 217 right, 218 centre, 220 centre, 221 right, 221 left, 222 centre, 224 right, 225 left, 226 left, 227 right, 227 left

Tony Lord 94, 99 right, 106, 110 below, 118 left, 119 top, 129 right, /Arley Hall 98 below, 104, /Broughton Castle 117 top, /Chatsworth 98 top, /Great Dixter 123, /Heslington Manor 75 centre, /The Manor House, Heslington 119 below, /Kemerton Priory 121, /Aster Collection, Picton Memorial Garden 93

Clive Nichols 58, 227 centre, /Designer: Sue Barker 142, /Brook Cottage, Oxfordshire 95 top, /Chenies Manor House Garden, Buckinghamshire 116, /Dartington Hall, Devon 90, /Eastgrove Cottage Garden and Nursery, Sankyns Green, Worcestershire 108, /Hadspen House Garden and Nursery, Somerset / Designers: Sandra and Nori Pope 125, /Longacre, Kent 95 below, /The Manor House, Upton Grey, Hampshire 30, /The Old Rectory, Burghfield. Berkshire 111

below, /The Picton Garden, Colwall, Worcestershire 20, 65, /The Picton Garden, Carnwall 143 centre, /The Priory, Kemerton, Worcestershire 74, /Red Gables, Worcestershire 0 back jacket, 14, /Sticky Wicket, Dorset / Designer Pam Lewis 102, /Turn End, Buckinghamshire 126, /Waterperry Gardens, Oxfordshire 6, /Designer, Anne Waring 109

Hugh Palmer 21 right

Jerry Pavia 13 bottom

Perdereau 1, 2, 12, 22, 50, 77 below, 85, 114

Photos Horticultural 31, 110 top, 137, 145 top, 145 left, 146 left, 147 centre, 152 centre, 153 centre, 160 left, 161 left, 164 left, 164 right, 165 centre, 166 below, 167 left, 167 right, 170 centre, 171 right, 172 below, 172 left, 175 right, 176 right, 178 centre, 179 right, 183 left, 183 centre, 184 centre, 185 right, 185 left, 187 left, 188 left, 190 right, 191 right, 191 centre, 195 right, 196 right, 196 left, 199 centre, 201 centre, 203 right, 204 left, 205 centre, 205 right, 206 left, 206 right, 209 left, 209 centre, 212 left, 214 left, 216 centre, 216 right, 218 right, 218 left, 219 centre, 219 left, 220 right, 223 right, 225 centre, 225 right, 226 centre

Reed International Books Ltd. Picture Library /Jerry Harpur 154 centre, 155 centre, 166 right, 170 right, 174 centre, /WF Davidson 161 right, /Jerry Harpur 177 right, 197 right, 198 centre, 199 left, /Jerry Hapur 202 right, /Jerry Harpur 203 centre, 212 right, /Mark Williams 26 bottom left, 26 top right, /George Wright 191 left, 192 left

Graham Rice 186 left

Harry Smith Collection 157 right, 175 left

Mark Williams 26 top left, 26 bottom right

Macmillan Publishers Ltd 229 supplying information for the European zone map

Reader's Digest Association 229 supplying information for the N American zone map